Ernest Chester Thomas, Frederick Albert Lange

The history of materialism and criticism of its present importance

Vol. 3

Ernest Chester Thomas, Frederick Albert Lange

The history of materialism and criticism of its present importance
Vol. 3

ISBN/EAN: 9783743355774

Manufactured in Europe, USA, Canada, Australia, Japa

Cover: Foto ©Thomas Meinert / pixelio.de

Manufactured and distributed by brebook publishing software (www.brebook.com)

Ernest Chester Thomas, Frederick Albert Lange

The history of materialism and criticism of its present importance

THE
ENGLISH AND FOREIGN
PHILOSOPHICAL LIBRARY.

VOLUME III.

IN THREE VOLUMES.

———

Vol. I.

MATERIALISM IN ANTIQUITY.
THE PERIOD OF TRANSITION.
THE SEVENTEENTH CENTURY

Vol. II.

THE EIGHTEENTH CENTURY.
MODERN PHILOSOPHY.
THE NATURAL SCIENCES.

Vol. III.

THE NATURAL SCIENCES—*Continued*.
MAN AND THE SOUL.
MORALITY AND RELIGION.

HISTORY OF MATERIALISM

AND

CRITICISM OF ITS PRESENT IMPORTANCE.

BY

FREDERICK ALBERT LANGE,

LATE PROFESSOR OF PHILOSOPHY IN THE UNIVERSITIES OF ZÜRICH AND MARBURG.

Authorized Translation

BY

ERNEST CHESTER THOMAS,

LATE SCHOLAR OF TRINITY COLLEGE, OXFORD.

IN THREE VOLUMES.

VOL. III.

BOSTON:
HOUGHTON, MIFFLIN, & CO.
1881.

TABLE OF CONTENTS.

Second Book—(*continued*).

HISTORY OF MATERIALISM SINCE KANT.

Second Section continued.—The Natural Sciences.

CHAPTER III.

THE SCIENTIFIC COSMOGONY, ... Pp. 3-25

Modern Cosmogony connects itself with Newton; the condensation-theory, 3-5. The geological stability-theory, 5-6. Long periods of time, 6. Conclusions as to the necessary destruction of the solar system, and of all life in the universe, 7-13. The origin of organisms, 13 ff. The hypothesis of spontaneous generation, 14-21. The transmission-theory according to Thomson and Helmholtz; Zöllner's opposition, 21-24. Fechner's views, 24-25.

CHAPTER IV.

DARWINISM AND TELEOLOGY, ... Pp. 26-80

Interest in Darwinism has greatly increased; the questions have been specialized, but the main features have remained unaltered, 26-27. The superstition of species, 27. Necessity of experiment, 28. Teleology, 32-36. Individual, 36-41. The network of classification of the animal world is inapplicable to the lower forms, 42. Stability of organic forms as necessary consequence of the struggle for existence; the equilibrium of forms, 43-47. Mimicry, 48-51. Correlation of growth; morphological kinds; the law of development, 51-59. Differences between apparently like primitive forms, 59-62. Monophyletic and Polyphyletic descent, 62-66. False and true Teleology, 66-70. Von Hartmann's Teleology as a model of false Teleology based upon a gross misunderstanding of the calculus of probabilities, 71-79. The value of the 'Philosophy of the Unconscious' does not depend upon this, 79-80.

THIRD SECTION.—THE NATURAL SCIENCES CONTINUED. MAN AND THE SOUL.

CHAPTER I.

THE RELATION OF MAN TO THE ANIMAL WORLD, . Pp. 83-110

Growing interest in Anthropological as compared with Cosmical questions; progress of the Anthropological Sciences, 83-85. The application of the theory of descent to man obvious, 85. Cuvier's dicta, 87-88. Discovery of diluvial human remains; their age, 89-93. Traces of ancient civilizations, 94-101. Influence of the sense of beauty, 101. The upright position; origin of speech, 102. The course of the development of civilization at first slow, then more and more rapid, 104. The question of unity of species, 105-107. Relation of Man to the Ape, 107-110.

CHAPTER II.

BRAIN AND SOUL, ... Pp. 111-161

The difficulties of the subject have become more obvious with the progress of the sciences. Injurious reaction of scholastic psychology, 111-112. Phrenology, 113-125. Reflex movements as the basis of psychical activity. Pflüger's experiments, 125-127. Various misunderstandings and erroneous interpretations of physiological experiments, 127-133. The brain does not produce any psychological abstractum, 133. Erroneous theories of Carus and Huschke, 134-137. Scholastic ideas must be discarded, 137-138. Stubbornness of the prejudice as to the localizations of mental functions, 138. Meynert's brain researches, 139-142. Psychological importance of the motor paths, 142-144. Identity of the excitation in all nerves, 144. Experiments of Hitzig, Nothnagel, and Ferrier; their meaning, 145-153. Wundt's remarks on the elementary phenomena of the psychical functions, 153. Carrying out of the laws of the conservation of energy by the cerebral functions, 154-159. Intellectual value of the content of sensation, 159.

CHAPTER III.

SCIENTIFIC PSYCHOLOGY, ... Pp. 162-201

Errors in the attempts at a Scientific and Mathematical Psychology: Herbart and his School, 162-167. Necessity of a criticism of Psychology, 167. Hypotheses as to the 'Nature of the Soul;' a psychology without a Soul, 168-169. Criticism of self-observation and of observation by means of the 'internal sense,' 169-174. Scientific Method and Speculation, 175-178. Animal psychology, 178, 179. Ethnopsychology; ethnographical accounts of travel, 180-183. Darwin's influence, 183-184. Somatic method; application of experiment, 184-186. Empirical psychology in England: Mill, Spencer, Bain, 186-193. Moral statistics, 194-201.

CHAPTER IV.

THE PHYSIOLOGY OF THE SENSE-ORGANS AND THE WORLD AS
REPRESENTATION, ... Pp. 202–230

The physiology of the sense-organs shows that we do not perceive external objects but produce the appearance of such objects, 202–205. The projection of objects outward and erect vision according to Müller and Ueberweg, 206–209. Further exposition and criticism of Ueberweg's theory, 209–215. Helmholtz on the nature of the sense-perceptions, 215–216. The sense-organs as an abstraction-apparatus, 217–218. Analogy with abstraction in thinking, 218. Psychological explanation of phenomena does not exclude the existence of mechanical cause, 218–219. The sense-world a product of our organization, 219. Unconscious inferences, 220–222. The assumption of a mechanism for all psychical functions not necessarily Materialism, because the mechanism itself is only representation, 223–224. Ueberweg's attempt to demonstrate the transcendental reality of space, 224–225; results, 225–229. Rokitansky's contention that the atomistic theory supports an idealistic view of things, 229–230.

FOURTH SECTION.—ETHICAL MATERIALISM AND RELIGION.

CHAPTER I.

POLITICAL ECONOMY AND DOGMATIC EGOISM, . Pp. 233–268

Origin of the theoretical assumption of a purely egoistic society, 233–235. Right and limits of abstraction; confusion of abstraction and reality, 235–237. The accumulation of capital and the law of the increase of wants, 237–241. Supposed utility of Egoism, 242–244. Origin of Egoism and Sympathy, 244–246. Moral progress wrongly denied by Buckle, 246–247. Egoism as a moral principle and the harmony of interests, 247–253. Examination of the doctrine of the harmony of interests, 253–259. Causes of inequality and rise of the proletariat, 259–268.

CHAPTER II.

CHRISTIANITY AND ENLIGHTENMENT, . . . Pp. 269–291

The ideas of Christianity as remedies for social evils: their apparent inefficacy according to Mill, 269–270. Mediate and gradual influence; connexion of Christianity and social reform, 270–273. Moral influences of belief partly favourable, partly unfavourable, 273–276. Importance of form in Morality and Religion, 276–280. Pretension of Religion to truth, 280–282. Impossibility of a Religion of Reason without Imagination, 282–287. Pastor Lang and his argument against this view, 287–291.

CHAPTER III.

THEORETICAL MATERIALISM IN ITS RELATION TO ETHICAL MATERIALISM AND TO RELIGION, . . . Pp. 292–334

Character of the usual attacks upon Religion, 292–293. Predominance of the rational principle, 294–295. Plans for a new religion: Comte's new hierarchy, 295–297. Scientific knowledge cannot be handled ecclesiastically but only secularly, 297–298. It is not moral teaching that makes religion but the tragical stirring of the soul, 299. Our cultus of humanity does not require religious forms, 300. Materialism would be most consistent in rejecting Religion altogether, 301. Examination of the connexion between Ethical and Theoretical Materialism, 302–305. Development of Materialism with Ueberweg, 305. His earlier standpoint, 306. Materialistic basis of his Psychology, 306–309. His Teleology, 310. Consciousness of its weakness, 311. The existence of God, 312. Transition to Materialism: vouchers for it from his letters to Czolbe and to the Author, 313–316. Doubt as to Ueberweg's asserted Atheism, 316. Ethical consequences of his philosophy: relation to Christianity, 316–323. David Friedrich Strauss: his last and definitive philosophy Materialistic, 323–325. His Materialism correct and thought out, 325–327. Superficial treatment of social and political questions; Conservative tendency, 327–328. Rejection of the specific features of Christian ethics; Optimism; condemnation of the worship of the Free Congregations, 328–330. Neglect of the people and its needs, 331. Leaning of the propertied classes to Materialism; the Socialists and the danger of the ruin of our civilization, 332–334.

CHAPTER IV.

THE STANDPOINT OF THE IDEAL, ... Pp. 335–362

Materialism as the philosophy of reality; nature of reality, 335–337. The functions of Synthesis in speculation and in religion; origin of Optimism and Pessimism, 337–338. Value and import of reality, 339–340. Its limits: the step to the Ideal. Pessimism of reflexion and optimism of the Ideal, 341–342. Reality needs to be supplemented by an ideal world; Schiller's philosophical poems; the future of religion and its inner essence, 342–348. The philosophy of religion, especially Fichte; grouping of men by the form of their inner life, 349–352. Fortunes of religion in critical times; possibility of new forms of religion; conditions of its existence, 353–356. Conditions of peace between opposed standpoints, 356–359. The Materialistic controversy as a serious sign of the time; the social question and the impending conflicts; possibility of their mitigation, 359–362.

PREFACE TO THE SECOND BOOK [AS POSTSCRIPT], . Pp. 363–365

INDEX . . . . Pp. 367–376

Second Book
Continued.

HISTORY OF MATERIALISM SINCE KANT.

SECOND SECTION

Continued.

THE NATURAL SCIENCES.

CHAPTER III.

THE SCIENTIFIC COSMOGONY.

ONE of the most important questions in ancient Materialism was the question of the natural cosmogony. The much-ridiculed doctrine of the endless parallel motion of the atoms through infinite space, of the gradual entwinings and combinations of the atoms into solid and fluid, living and lifeless bodies, for all its singularity, had still a great work to accomplish. And beyond doubt these ideas have had a mighty influence upon modern times, though the connexion of our natural cosmogony with that of Epikuros is not so clear as the history of Atomism. It is rather the very point which subjects the ancient ideas to the first decisive modification, from which that idea of the origin of the universe was developed, which, despite its hypothetical character, even yet has the utmost importance. Let us hear Helmholtz on this point.

"It was Kant who, feeling great interest in the physical description of the earth and the planetary system, had undertaken the laborious study of the works of Newton; and, as an evidence of the depth to which he had penetrated into the fundamental ideas of Newton, seized the masterly idea that the same attractive force of all ponderable matter which now supports the motion of the planets must also aforetime have been able to form the planetary system from matter loosely scattered in space. Afterwards, and independently of Kant, Laplace, the great author of the 'Mécanique Céleste,' laid hold of the same thought, and introduced it among astronomers." [42]

The theory of gradual condensation possesses the advantage that it admits a calculation, which through the discovery of the mechanical equivalent of heat has reached a high degree of theoretical perfection. It has been calculated that in the transition from an infinitely slight density to that of the present heavenly bodies as much heat must be produced from the mechanical force of attraction of the particles of matter, as if the whole mass of the planetary system were expressed 3500 times in pure coal and this mass were then burned. It has been inferred that the greatest part of this heat must have lost itself in space before the present form of our planetary system could arise. It has been found that of that enormous store of mechanical force of the original attraction only about the 454th part is maintained as mechanical force in the motions of the heavenly bodies. It has been calculated that a shock which should suddenly stay our earth in its course would produce as much heat as the combustion of fourteen earths of pure coal, and that in this heat the mass of the earth would be completely fused, and at least the greatest part of it would evaporate.

Helmholtz observes that in these assumptions nothing is hypothetical but the presupposition that the masses of our system were in the beginning distributed in space as vapour. This is so far right, that from such a distribution, in co-operation with gravitation, the total sum of heat and mechanical motion may be approximately reckoned. But

---

[42] Helmholtz, On the Interaction of Natural Forces, Königsberg, 1854, S. 27; reprinted in his Popular Lectures, Braunschw. 1871, E.T. 1873, p. 174. The following remarks on the relation of heat and mechanical force in the universe are from the same lecture.

in order to produce our solar system as it actually is, we need further certain presuppositions as to the mode of distribution of the nebular masses in space. The rotation of the whole mass, once given, must of necessity become ever greater with the increasing contraction and condensation; its original existence may be deduced in many ways, but also belongs to the more special assumptions in which considerable play is still left to hypothesis. It is most simply explained by not making the nebular masses concentrate immediately and equably into a single great ball, but by making several such masses collect around their own centres of gravity and then fall together with a noncentral impact. We will here, in passing, with reference to Ueberweg's theory, to be mentioned later, interject that the whole process can be built also upon the collision of solid bodies, which, in consequence of the collision, first dissolve into a mass of vapour, and then, in the course of immeasurable time, are again organised into a new system.

The condensation hypothesis has gained an important support of late through spectrum analysis, which shows us that we find the same materials of which our earth consists in the whole solar system, and partly also in the stellar world. To the same method of inquiry we are indebted for the view that the nebulæ which appear scattered through the heavens by no means all consist, as might have been supposed earlier, of distant clusters of stars, but that a considerable number of them are really nebular masses, which may therefore present to us a picture of the earlier condition of our solar system.

In view of these confirmations, it is, on the other hand, of slight importance that recent geology has given up the revolutionary theory, and, so far as is at all possible, explains the formation of the surface of our planet from the same forces which we now see everywhere at work. The stability theory, which is supported on this geological tendency, can at most claim importance in a relative sense. We can regard the condition of the earth's crust and the progress of the changes taking place in it as *comparatively* stable, as opposed to the theory of catastrophes, with which is frequently enough combined the shrinking from large figures referred to in the previous chapter. If, on the contrary, we assume sufficiently long periods, then a change, a becoming and perishing, is not only probable in itself, but it may be demonstrated on the strongest scientific grounds.

We may therefore well ask how it comes that we do not willingly deal with long periods of time; that, on the contrary, the idea of absolute stability lies comparatively so close to us; that in particular it has so little that is strange to our feelings? We descry the reason of this curious phenomenon only in the dulling habituation to the notion of eternity. This notion is familar to us from childhood, and, as a rule, we do not examine it carefully. Such, indeed, is the constitution of our mind, which is so closely connected with sensibility, that it seems necessary to lessen, as it were, absolute eternity in our conception, and to make it relative, in order in some degree to realise its meaning; much as we try to make the tangent of 90° in some degree picturable by making it *become*—*i.e.*, by making before the eye of fancy a very great and ever greater tangent—although for the absolute there can no longer be any becoming. Thus the popular images of the theologians deal with eternity, which heap one period of time upon another in thought, and then make the very utmost that the imagination can reach, as it were, 'a second of eternity.' Although the notion of an absolute eternity includes so much, that all that the soaring imagination can possibly think compared with it is no more than the most trivial space of time, yet this notion is so familiar to us that the man who speaks of an eternal existence of the earth and of mankind seems comparatively modest beside the man who would merely multiply, say, the period of transition from the diluvial man to the man of to-day a millionfold, in order to go back to the origin of man from the simplest organic cell. Here sensibility is everywhere opposed to logic. What we can only in some degree picture to ourselves easily appears to us exaggerated and improbable, while we play with the most enormous conceptions when we have once brought them into the shape of an entirely abstract notion. Six thousand years on the one hand, eternity on the other—to this we are accustomed. What lies between them seems first remarkable, then bold, then magnificent, then fantastical; and yet all such predicates belong only to the sphere of feeling—cold logic has nothing to do with them.

It was formerly supposed, on a calculation of Laplace, that the period of the earth's revolution, from the days of Hipparchos to the present, had not altered by the three-hundredth part of a second; and Czolbe has employed this calculation to support his stability theory. But it is quite clear that nothing more could follow from such a fact than that the retarding of the speed of revolution, which must be assumed as necessary from the physical theory, never goes more quickly than about ·1 second in 600,000 years. But let us suppose that it reached a single second only in 100,000,000 years; still, after a few billions of years, the relations of day and night upon the earth must have been so totally changed that all the existing life of the surface must disappear, and the entire cessation of the axial revolution could not be far distant. We have, however, a thoroughgoing physical principle of this retardation in the effect of ebb and flood tides. Here all the conclusive keenness of mathematical conclusions finds its application. Only on the supposition of an absolute rigidity of the earth must the effects of the attraction which hinder the rotation completely cancel those which accelerate it. Since now there are some portions which may be delayed, the earth must of necessity receive an ellipsoid swelling, the delaying of which produces on the surface a friction, however slight it may be. The force of this inference cannot be in the least shaken by the fact that, according to recent observations, the phenomena of ebb and flood which we perceive on our coasts are not so much produced by a progressive swelling, but rather by one considerable elevation, which takes place when the middle of the largest expanses of sea is exactly opposite the moon or sun. Though the circular waves propagated from this elevation, as they proceed equally in every direction, have no retarding influence on the speed of rotation, yet the retarding influence of the flood must be equally present, though less perceptible. The process cannot possibly be the same as if the earth were to turn backwards, and in the position in which the flood-wave is formed were each time to remain motionless for some seconds. There must be a progressive flood-wave, unless all physics are deceptive. The actual flood-tide we may regard as composed of the effects of a standing and a progressive flood-wave. Even if the effect of the latter may apparently disappear in the infinitely complicated phenomena of ebb and flood, yet its retarding effect can never be lost. And however small a constantly acting cause may be, we have only to take sufficiently long periods of time and the result is inevitable. A portion of the living force of the planetary movement is absolutely destroyed by ebb and flood. "We come thereby," says Helmholtz, "to the unavoidable conclusion that every tide, although with infinite slowness, still with certainty, diminishes the store of mechanical force in the system; and as a consequence of this, the rotation of the planets in question round their axes must become more slow, and they must approach nearer to the sun or their satellites to them."

There is but one means of avoiding the conclusion that at last the revolution of the earth must cease, namely, if we can discover an opposite effect, which again accelerates the speed retarded by ebb and flood. Such an effect Mayer, the well-known discoverer of the equivalent of heat, formerly believed he had found, by supposing that the cooling of the earth is not yet finished. The earth—

and with this he connected an explanation of earthquakes —is still constantly contracting, and therefore lessening its circumference, and with this must necessarily be involved an acceleration of the axial revolution. Mayer saw, however, very well that even in this assumption there lies no guarantee of eternal stability, since the two opposing influences cannot possibly maintain constantly an even pace. He assumed, therefore, three periods: one in which the acceleration in consequence of the contraction prevails; a second in which acceleration and retardation balance each other; and a third in which the retardation by ebb and flood prevails. Mayer believed at first that we are in the middle period, that of equilibrium; but he has abandoned this view. "It is ten years since the English astronomer Adams, in London, led by the discovery of the retarding influence of ebb and flood, proved that Laplace's calculation as to the constant duration of the sidereal day is not absolutely exact, since the speed of the earth's rotation is lessened, and the sidereal day, therefore, is already augmenting. This makes, indeed, in the course of thousands of years, only a small fraction of a second, for a whole thousand years namely only $\frac{1}{100}$ second! So that we must marvel at the human sagacity which has succeeded in ascertaining such an infinitesimal quantity."[43]

An equally indispensable condition of an eternally unchanging planetary motion, as the absolute rigidity of the heavenly bodies, is the absolute emptiness of the space in which they move, or at least the entire absence of resistance in the æther, with which we suppose space to be filled. It appears that this condition too is not ful-

---

[43] Naturwissenschaftl. Vorträge, Stuttg. 1871, S. 28. The passage belongs to a lecture 'On Earthquakes,' delivered in June 1870. We need not discuss the improbability of the theory on earthquakes there set forth. Some further details on Adams's calculation are in Zöllner, D. Natur d. Kometen, S. 469 ff. Zöllner shows, l. c. 472 ff., that Kant, as early as 1754, had demonstrated that ebb and flood must retard the rotation of the earth.

filled. Enke's comet describes, as it were, before our eyes an ever closer ellipse about the sun, and the most obvious way of explaining this is to suppose a resisting medium. Here indeed there is not the compulsion of a necessary deduction; but we have an observation which compels us to assume, as at least probable, the existence of a resisting medium. But with the mere fact of a resistance, however slight, of the æther nothing more need be said." [44]

Absolutely convincing, again, is the conclusion that the heat of the sun cannot last for ever. It is impossible to avoid this conclusion by denying the fiery condition of the sun and supposing a source of heat in an eternal friction between the body of the sun and its covering, or the æther, or anything of the kind. Notions of this kind have, in fact, for the most part, been rendered impossible by the recent keenly prosecuted studies of the sun. More rational is the hypothesis of the conservation of the sun's heat by the continual falling in of meteorites and smaller bodies; but even this theory leads to no stability. And this is still less so with the view of Helmholtz, which we may well regard as the truest, viz., that the main source of the conservation of the sun's heat is to be sought in gravitation.[45] The sun contracts, lessens its circumference,

---

[44] The explanation here assumed for the changes in the orbit of Enke's comet has, however, recently become very doubtful, as we have on the most exact examination not found a similar change in several other comets. On the other hand, it has been shown by Zöllner that all space must be filled with traces of atmospheric gases of the various heavenly bodies, as without such an assumption atmosphere could not exist in equilibrium in empty space. Should then the æther too be given up, as many scientific men seem inclined to do, yet the existence of very thin masses of gas must be assumed, which must produce an effect, however small, in the sense indicated.

[45] "If, however, we adopt the very probable view that the remarkably small density of so large a body is caused by its high temperature, and may become greater in time, it may be calculated that if the diameter of the sun were diminished only the ten-thousandth part of its present length, by this act a sufficient quantity of heat would be generated to cover the total emission for 2100 years. So small a change it would be difficult to detect even by the finest astronomical observations." Helmholtz, Pop. Lect., E.T. 190. On the 'Meteor Theory,' first proposed by Mayer and afterward by some English physicists, see Tyndall, Heat Considered as a Mode of Motion, 1863.

and thus mechanical force is converted into heat. That this process must, however, ultimately cease is matter of course. No motion can be conceived by which heat is produced without the consumption of other forces. We may suppose, therefore, any theory we choose as to the sun's heat: it will always come to this, that the source of this heat is finite, while its consumption is infinite. We must always come to the conclusion that in the course of infinite time the to us so interminable duration of the sun's heat and light will not only fall off, but will completely disappear.

Finally, there seems to result also, as a simple consequence of the mechanical theory of heat, the destruction of all life in the whole universe. As regards the earth, this destruction of course is involved in that caused by the extinction of the sun. Mechanical force can always be converted into heat, but heat can only be converted into work when it flows from a warmer to a colder body. With the equalisation of temperature in any system whatever ends the possibility of further changes, and accordingly of any kind of life. The sum of possible changes, or the 'Entropy,' as Clausius calls it, has reached its maximum.[46] Whether, however, this conclusion, though it rests upon conclusive mathematical reasoning, can actually be applied to the universe in the strictest sense of the term, depends essentially upon the ideas which we form of its infinity; and here we again find ourselves in a transcendental sphere. There is nothing, that is to say, to prevent us from multiplying such frozen systems at pleasure, and supposing them to attract each other from infinite distances, and then producing afresh from their collision the play of cosmogony as it were upon a larger

---

[46] Clausius, Abh. über d. mechan. Wärmetheorie, ii. 44, proposes the two following principles: (1) The energy of the world is constant; (2) The entropy of the world tends to a maximum. On the notion of 'Entropy,' comp. *l. c.* S. 34 f. The whole deduction, however, presupposes the finiteness of the material world in infinite space. Helmholtz treats this inference popularly in his 'Vortr. über die Wechselw.'der Naturkr.,' S. 24 f.

scale. Nothing prevents us from making such an assumption except the question whether we are entitled, merely because we cannot conceive any limit to creation, to suppose a material infinity of worlds as actually existing.

Materialism taught even in ancient days the origin and destruction of our universe, while by the doctrine of the infinity of worlds it secured that satisfaction of the mind which lies in the simple belief in the permanence of things. Amongst our modern Materialists Czolbe especially has not been content with this, and postulates an eternal persistence of terrestrial life from the standpoint of our spiritual needs. Feuerbach's categorical imperative, 'Content thyself with the given world!' seems to Czolbe impracticable until at least the persistence of this 'given world' is secured against the destruction threatened by the conclusions of the mathematicians. But it is very doubtful whether, from the standpoint of our peace of mind, it seems better completely to carry out one's system while its very foundation remains exposed to the most violent concussions, or once for all to acquiesce in a limit to knowledge and opinion beyond which all questions are left open. In fact, in view of the convincing proofs which we have adduced, it must be seen that Czolbe's satisfaction-theory is built upon sand, and therefore, in the long-run, can no more attain its end than the popular dogmatism which, on the contrary, will not give up a beginning and an end of things—the Creation and the Day of Judgment. If we once rise above this standpoint—if we seek the peace of the soul in what is given, we shall easily learn to find it not in the eternal duration of material conditions, but in the eternity of natural laws, and in such a duration of existing things as removes the idea of their destruction to a proper distance from us. The architectonic inclination of the reason will content itself, if we reveal to it the charm of a view of things which has no sensible support, but which also needs none, because the absolute is wholly set aside. It will remember that this whole world of relations is conditioned by the nature of our knowing faculty. And even though we always come back to this, that our knowledge does not disclose to us things in themselves, but only their relation to our senses, yet this relation is always more perfect, the freer it is; nay, it is, in fact, the more intimately related to the justified imagination of the absolute, the more free it holds itself of arbitary admixtures.

Almost more even than the origin of the universe has the origin of organisms for a considerable time occupied the thoughtful mind. This question is of importance for the history of Materialism, if only because it forms the transition to those anthropological questions about which the Materialistic controversy has been wont to turn. The Materialist demands an explicable world: it is enough for him if the phenomena can be so conceived that the compound proceeds from the simple, the great from the small, manifold motion from simple mechanics. The rest affords him no anxiety, or rather he overlooks the difficulties which only come to view when the explicable world has been so far established in theory that the law of causality has no further sacrifice to demand. Even in this sphere Materialism has drawn nourishment from things which must be recognised from any rational standpoint; yet, until quite recent times, the origin of organisms was a point of which the opponents of Materialism made emphatic use. In particular, it was believed that the origin of organisms necessarily led us to a transcendental creative act, while in the arrangement and preservation of the organic world fresh supports for teleology were supposed to be constantly found. In fact, a certain opposition to Materialistic views was frequently connected with the very terms 'organic,' 'living,' inasmuch as here was found, as it were, the embodied antithesis of a higher, spiritually working force, as opposed to the mechanism of dead nature.

In mediæval, and still more at the outset of modern

times, especially so far as the influence of men like Paracelsus and Van Helmont extended, no such chasm was found between the organic and inorganic worlds as in the last centuries. It was a widespread notion that all nature was animated. If even Aristotle made frogs and snakes originate from mud, such ideas were only too natural under the dominion of alchemy. Those who descried spirits even in metals, and a process of fermentation in their combination, could hardly find any special difficulty in the origin of life. There was, indeed, in general a belief in the invariability of species—a dogma which comes direct from Noah's ark—but it was, at the same time, not taken too literally, and especially the lower creatures were made to the fullest extent to develop from inorganic matter. Both articles of faith have lasted till to-day — the one more amongst professors, the other amongst peasants and carters. The former believe in the invariability of species, and search twenty years perhaps in the bite of snails for proof of their belief; the latter are continually finding confirmation in their experience that fleas originate from sawdust and other materials. Science has only succeeded here later than elsewhere in bringing articles of faith down to hypotheses, and in stemming the broad current of opinions by experiment and observation.

The very question which first confronts us is even yet the object of a bitter controversy—the question of spontaneous generation (*generatio aequivoca*). Carl Vogt has given us a humorous account of how in Paris the scientific battle between l'asteur and his allied opponents, Pouchet, Joly, and Musset, is carried on with the bitterness of theologians, and with a dramatic effect which reminds us of the magistral theses of the fifteenth century. On Pasteur's side are the Academy and the Ultramontanes. To controvert the possibility of spontaneous generation is a mark of conservatism. The old authorities of science were unanimous that no organic being can ever be produced without egg or seed. *Omne vivum ex ovo* is a scientific article of faith. But why do the orthodox take this side? Perhaps only to establish a something inexplicable, to spite the reason and the senses by holding fast to a purely mystical creation. The older orthodoxy, in the lead of S. Augustine, took quite another standpoint—to some extent a half-way one. There was no disdain of the notion of making things as intelligible as possible. Augustine taught that from the beginning of the world there had existed two kinds of seeds of living things: visible ones, which the Creator had placed in animals and plants, that each might bring forth after its kind; and invisible ones, which are concealed in all elements, and become active only under certain conditions of combination and temperature. It is these invisible seeds, latent in the elements from the first, which produce plants and animals in great numbers, without any co-operation of existing organisms.

This standpoint would be quite favourable to orthodoxy; it might even, without much trouble, be so far modified that, in the present state of the sciences, it might be maintained just as well as either of the two conflicting dogmas. But as in the heat of a contest the champion is often half compelled, half involuntarily changes his position, so too it happens in the whole course of scientific controversies. The Materialism of the last century here plays its part. In endeavouring to explain life from the inanimate, the soul from matter, the supposed origin of insects from decaying matter was ranged together with the resuscitation of dead flies by salt, with the voluntary movements of beheaded birds and other instances, for the Materialistic view. Friends of teleology and natural theology, supporters of the dualism of mind and nature, adopted as their tactics to controvert utterly the origination of insects and infusoria without generation; and the conflict of ideas led, as so often in the history of science, to fruitful and ingenious experiments, in which the Materialists were behindhand. After the much-read and admired Bonnet, in his 'Contemplations de la Nature,' had refuted *generatio aequivoca*, it was counted as spiritualism to maintain the *omne vivum ex ovo*, and in this point orthodoxy harmonised literally with the results of exact research. Indeed, it seemed almost to our own times as though that principle would be the more inexpugnably established the more exactly and carefully investigation went to work.

Metaphysic went mad over the new discovery. It was concluded that in natural propagation all future generations must be already contained in the egg or spermatozoon; and Professor Meier of Halle exhibited this 'preformation theory' so naïvely and vividly, that it would be unfair to our readers not to give them a sample. "Thus," says the Professor, "Adam must have carried all men in his loins; for instance, the very spermatozoon from which Abraham was. And in this spermatozoon all the Jews lay as spermatozoa. When, then, Abraham begat Isaac, Isaac went out from his father's body and took with him, as part of himself, the whole race of his descendants." [47] The remaining unused spermatozoa, which it was natural to regard as possessing some share of soul, gave rise, as we may understand, to much wilder fantasies, which do not concern us here.

In recent times it was Schwann in particular who partly demonstrated the true element of all organic formations in the cell, partly showed by a series of experiments that in the apparent origin of organisms by *generatio aequivoca* the presence of eggs or germ cells must always be presupposed. His methods of proof were generally regarded as excellent, but it was one of our own Materialists, Carl Vogt, who definitely expressed his doubts of their sufficiency, long before the old controversy burst again into such violent flame in France. We gather the tenour of his keen and thorough criticism from the *Bilder aus dem Thierleben*, 1852.

---

[47] Meier's Metaphysik, 3 Th. § d. Seelen d. Menschen u. Thiere: 785; cit. in Hennings, Gesch. von Halle, 1774, S. 504 n.

The infusoria originate from the combination of air, water, and organic matter. Schwann found means to destroy all organic germs in these constituents. If now they are isolated and yet infusoria originate, then *generatio aequivoca* is proved. Hay was boiled with water in a retort until not only all the fluid, but even the air in the neck of the retort, was heated to the boiling-point. It was known that in closed retorts no infusoria would originate. If now ordinary air was admitted to the retort, then infusoria always appeared despite the previous boiling; if, on the contrary, only air was admitted which had been passed through a red-hot tube, through sulphuric acid, or through caustic potash, no infusoria ever appeared. Now it is supposed that the composition of the air is not altered by the means employed. This is, however, only approximately true. The atmosphere contains not only oxygen and nitrogen. "It contains a certain quantity of carbonic acid, of aqueous vapour, of ammonia, perhaps infinitesimal quantities of many other matters. These are by the means adopted more or less decomposed and absorbed, the carbonic acid by the potash, the ammonia by the sulphuric acid. The heating of the air must produce a partial influence upon the arrangement of its molecules. . . . We have cases enough in chemistry where apparently very inconsiderable circumstances are needed to produce a combination or decomposition. . . . It is possible that just the precise quantity of ammonia, of carbonic acid, that a certain disposition or tension of the atmospheric molecules is necessary in order to set up and complete the process of the fresh formation of an organism. The conditions in which the two retorts are placed are therefore not perfectly alike, and therefore also the experiment does not appear quite conclusive." In fact, this argumentation shows the inadequacy of Schwann's experiment, and the question may therefore be treated as an open one, especially as a series of weighty considerations is opposed to the assumption that all the germs of the countless infusoria which appear in these experiments circulate in the air in a condition capable of life. Ehrenberg supposed a division of the infusoria, which proceeding in geometrical ratio would in a few hours people the water; Vogt, on the contrary, has shown the improbability of this hypothesis.[48] Recently the practice has arisen of systematically collecting the dust particles which may be floating in the air before the experiment is begun. Pasteur throws his collection of supposed germs and eggs into the fluids intended to be experimented with, and believes that he thus sows infusoria and funguses; Pouchet previously examines the collection. "He lets hundreds of cubic metres of air stream through water, and examines the water; he invents an instrument which blows the air against glass plates, to which the seminal dust remains attached; he analyses dust which has been deposited, and he makes these experiments on the glaciers of Maladetta in the Pyrenees, as well as in the Catacombs of Thebes, on the continent as well as on the sea, on the Pyramids of Egypt as well as at the summit of Rouen Cathedral. Thus he brings together a mass of air-inventories, in which, indeed, everything conceivable figures, but only very seldom a germ-spore of a fungus plant, and much seldomer still the dead body of an infusorium."

For all this, the state of things remained that spontaneous generation had not been demonstrated despite the pains spent upon it. Schwann's experiments were varied and modified in the most manifold ways, but as often as spontaneous generation seemed to be reached, more exact experiments showed that the possibility of a communication of germs was not excluded. The greatest impression was produced in the last few years by the experiments of Bastian and of Huizinga. The latter in particular were very seductive, since in a hermetically fused glass retort, after ten minutes' boiling of the liquid, there appeared Bacteria, and only Bacteria; so that it seemed safe to assume spon-

---

[48] According to recent researches, such a mode of propagation must be assumed for certain organisms of the lowest kind—*e.g.*, for Bacteria.

taneous generation at least for these simplest of organisms. But in Pflüger's laboratory the same liquid, fastened up in the same way, was kept boiling for hours, and even after it had cooled no Bacteria were produced. There remained, therefore, the possibility that there were germs in the liquid which were not destroyed by ten minutes' boiling, though they could not resist a longer application of heat.[49]

At the same time it must be admitted that continuous boiling might possibly destroy other and as yet unknown conditions of Bacterial existence. So that the proof is by no means convincing that there were actually germs present in the liquid which were in the first case developed, and in the second destroyed. The result, therefore, of all these experiments remains, that spontaneous generation is not established, and just as little shown to be impossible.

A fresh possibility for the origin of organisms seemed to be opened by the discovery of Monera, those formless, and, so far as our means of examination reach, structureless lumps of protoplasm, which maintain, nourish, and propagate themselves without possessing any distinct organs. Haeckel, who regards spontaneous generation as an indispensable, if as yet unconfirmed hypothesis, promises himself much in this regard from a slime-creature living in the still depths of the sea of the following kind:—"Even among the Monera at present known there is a species which probably even now always comes into existence by spontaneous generation. This is the wonderful *Bathybius Haeckelii*, discovered and described by Huxley." This Moneron is found "in the greatest depths of the sea, at a depth of between 12,000 and 24,000 feet, where it covers the ground partly as retiform threads and

---

[49] A review of these experiments, according to Pflüger's Archiv für d. ges. Physiol., vii. S. 549, viii. 227, appears in Dr. Sklarek's Naturforscher, vi. Jahrg. (1873), Nos. 33 and 49. On the refutation of Bastian's experiments, see *inter alia* Naturf. vi. No. 26 (S. 209 f.) and No. 48 (S. 453 f.).

plaits of plasma, partly in the form of larger or smaller irregular lumps of the same material." [50]

"If we do not accept the hypothesis of spontaneous generation," he says further on, "then at this one point of the history of development we must have recourse to the miracle of a *supernatural creation*. The Creator must have created the first organism, or a few first organisms, from which all others are derived, and as such He must have created the simplest Monera or primitive Cytods, and given them the capability of developing further in a mechanical way." Haeckel rightly finds the latter idea "just as unsatisfactory to a believing mind as to a scientific intellect." We may, however, go further, and assert that such an alternative is logically quite inadmissible. To scientific research the intelligibleness of this world must be an axiom; and if, therefore, we hold spontaneous generation to be improbable, the origin of organisms remains simply as a yet unsolved problem. Natural science has not the slightest occasion now or ever to suppose a "supernatural" act of creation. To fall a victim to such explanations is accordingly always an abandonment of scientific ground, which in a scientific inquiry can never be mentioned as admissible, or even as matter for consi-

---

[50] Haeckel, Natürl. Schöpfungsg., 4 Aufl., Berl. 1873, S. 306, 309 ff., E. T. i. 344. Comp. the same writer's 'Beiträge z. Plastidentheorie' in the Jenaische Zeitschr., Bd. v. Hft. 4. In this essay, which has for its subject the modification of the cell-theory necessitated by recent discoveries, and the consequences of the new conception, is the following passage (S. 500):—"The most important fact which results from Huxley's very careful investigation of Bathybius is that the bottom of the ocean in its greater depths (beyond 5000 feet) is covered with enormous masses of fine living protoplasm, and this protoplasm persists there in the simplest and most primitive shape—*i.e.*, it has as yet no definite form at all, and is hardly yet individualised. We cannot ponder this highly remarkable fact without the deepest astonishment, and cannot help thinking of Oken's 'primitive slime.' This universal slime of the older philosophy of nature, which was supposed to have originated in the sea, and to be the primitive source of all life, the productive material of all organisms, —this famous and notorious primitive slime, whose all-embracing importance was indeed already implicitly established by Max Schultze's protoplasm theory, seems by Huxley's discovery of Bathybius to have become completely true."

deration. To those, however, who regard a creative act as a spiritual necessity, it must be left to consider whether they prefer to take refuge with it in that dark corner which the light of science has not yet reached, or whether they rather declare against all science, and, untouched by the rules of the understanding, believe what seems good to them; or whether, lastly, they know how to take up their stand on the ground of the ideal, and revere what science calls a natural event as an outcome of Divine power and wisdom. That only the last standpoint is suited to an advanced state of culture, while the first is indeed the commonest, but also in every way the weakest, we need here only indicate.

Finally, it by no means follows that to give up terrestrial spontaneous generation involves the giving up of any possibility of asserting a consistent causal connexion in nature.

Here we have first to consider a recently proposed hypothesis of the English physicist Thomson,[51] which derives the origin of the organisms upon our earth from space, and makes use of meteorites to carry them. "When a volcanic island springs up from the sea, and after a few years is found clothed with vegetation, we do not hesitate to assume that seed has been wafted to it through the air or floated to it on rafts. Is it not possible, and, if possible, is it not probable, that the beginning of vegetable life on the earth is to be similarly explained?"

Thomson regards the meteorites as fragments of ruined worlds which were once covered with life. Such ruins may in a collision partly remain tolerably uninjured, though a great portion of them is melted. If, then, we suppose "that there are at present, and have been from time immemorial, many worlds of life beside our own, we must regard it as probable in the highest degree that

---

[51] Thomson has developed this hypothesis in a very pregnant address at the opening of the British Association in 1871 on the latest discoveries in natural science. The passages here in question are also printed in Zöllner, Die Natur d. Komet., S. xxiv. f.

there are countless seed-bearing meteoric stones moving about through space. If at the present instant no life existed upon this earth, one such stone falling upon it might, by what we blindly call natural causes, lead to its becoming covered with vegetation."

Zöllner tries to show that this hypothesis is unscientific; first of all formally, because it only postpones the problem, and so makes it more complicated. We must then ask, Why was this ruined world covered with vegetation and our own not? But he would also call it materially unscientific to make meteorites the bearers of the seed, because the friction with our atmosphere must make them red-hot.

Helmholtz, who defends Thomson's hypothesis against the reproach of being unscientific, reminds us that the large meteorites are heated only externally and remain cold internally, where such seeds might very well be sheltered in crevices. And even the seeds situated at the outside, upon entering the outer strata of the atmosphere, would be blown inwards before the heat could reach a destructive degree. Helmholtz, who had even before Thomson mentioned, in a scientific lecture, the same hypothesis as admissible, is ready to leave it to every one whether to regard it as so extremely improbable. "But," he remarks, "it seems to me a thoroughly correct scientific procedure, when all efforts to produce organisms from lifeless matter have failed, to ask whether life ever has originated, whether it is not as old as matter, and whether its germs may not have been carried about from one world to another, and have been developed wherever they found a favourable soil." [52]

It is, in fact, very easy to answer to Zöllner's "formal" objection, that we must suppose our earth to have been originally devoid of vegetation simply because it had to pass from a fiery-fluid condition into a condition capable

---

[52] Comp. Zöllner, D. Natur. d. Komet., Vorr. S. xxv. f., and Helmholtz's reply in the preface to the second part of the first volume of the translation of Thomson and Tait's 'Handbook of Theoretical Physics,' S. xi. ff.

of vegetation. If we suppose that the other world has gone through just the same process, only at an earlier period, it must of course have derived its life from a third world, and so on. This indeed is to push the question further back, but by no means makes it more complicated. In any case, that great shoal is avoided which the explanation of organisms finds in Kant's hypothesis of condensation. We find ourselves in a process *ad infinitum*, and this kind of 'postponement' has at least the advantage that it brings the unsolved difficulty into good company. The origin of life thus becomes as explicable and as inexplicable as the origin of the world generally; it comes into the sphere of transcendental problems, and to transfer it into this sphere is by no means logically improper, as soon as natural science has good grounds within its sphere of knowledge to regard such a theory of transmission as relatively the most probable.

Zöllner agrees with Haeckel that *generatio aequivoca* can only be denied on *a priori* grounds by doing violence to the law of cause. Instead, however, of admitting at the same time the possibility of a supernatural creative act, he regards the question, deductively considered, as decided, and even regards it as a lack of philosophical culture that the men of science still attach so much value to the inductive proof of *generatio aequivoca*. With formal correctness he observes, that by no perfection of experiment could we escape the germ-theory, since we could not prevent any one from maintaining that "the primitive organic germs belonged in point of size to the order of æther-atoms, and forced their way with the latter through the intervals between the material molecules which form the boundaries of our apparatus." At the same time this remark can at most only be sometimes applied satirically to the certainty with which Pasteur and similar dogmatists hold that their experiments have definitely refuted *generatio aequivoca*. No one will seriously propose such an hypothesis, as long as we see that in certain cases a fluid sealed up for a very long period remains without any trace of life.

Inductive inquiry, therefore, is here by no means so indefensible, as long as it reaches various results by various methods and can compare these. Even the principle laid down by Zöllner of acquiescence in the axiom of the intelligibility of the world is by no means free from serious doubts. If Zöllner is more right than Haeckel in regarding the supposition of an *unintelligible* origin as not worth mentioning, Haeckel is right on the other hand when he tries to form to himself, even on the basis of a bold hypothesis, a picturable conception of the way in which the thing may have happened. Helmholtz quite correctly points out that Zöllner is here in the path of metaphysic—so dangerous to the man of science—and he shows that the correct alternative must be: " Organic life has either begun to be at some particular time or it exists from eternity."

Leaving aside the critical objections to the notion of an absolute eternity, the question is correctly stated; but even then it will still ever remain a desirable maxim of research not to relax the effort to demonstrate the terrestrial origin of organisms, in order that the more convenient removal of the problem into the universe may not hinder the progress of empirical knowledge by a metaphysical construction.

Let us finally mention again here the view of Fechner, who, in a treatise rich in thought but also in hypothesis, attempts to carry out the view that the organic molecules are *older* than the inorganic molecules, and that on the " principle of increasing stability " the latter might well be developed from the former, but not conversely. This whole assumption rests, however, upon a presupposition as to the mobility of the atoms in the molecules which still greatly needs confirmation, if it is indeed capable of confirmation.[53]

---

[53] Fechner, Einige Ideen zur Schöpfungs- u. Entwicklungsgeschichte der Organismen, Leipz. 1873. In this valuable book—especially as regards the questions raised by Darwin—Fechner proposes the hypothesis,

In all this sphere scientific research can on the whole pursue but one single course, and if this be called Materialistic, we must not forget the limits of the Materialistic view of things demonstrated in the previous chapters. Here it is only a single point which reminds us of these limits and of the critical standpoint of the theory of knowledge—the notion of infinity in its application not only to the co-existent worlds and world-materials, but also to the course of time in the problem of beginning or no beginning, and how the one hypothesis or the other is to be represented in thought. We do not intend, however, to go here into the subjective origin of these notions, and to show how they can only find an adequate explanation in a 'world as representation.' We shall find better opportunities to oppose the Idealistic to the Materialistic standpoint; it is enough to establish that genuine Idealism in the whole sphere of the explanation of nature, so far as the relations between phenomena are concerned, goes at least as entirely hand in hand with natural science as Materialism by any possibility ever can.

that the particles in organic and inorganic molecules are in a different state of mobility. In the latter the particles vibrate about fixed positions of equilibrium without the displacement of a point b, with regard to a point a, ever reaching more than 180° (measured on the motion of the radius vector to b from a as centre). There then occurs no change in the initial sign of their relative position. On the other hand, Fechner supposes that the particles of organic molecules move with regard to each other in such a way that the initial sign of the relative position constantly changes, "as may happen through circular and other complicated movements of the particles with regard to each other." This state of motion is supposed to be kept up, however, by the "inner" forces of the molecule. Fechner then supposes further, that this state of matter is the original one; the inorganic state, on the contrary, a later arising one. Organic and inorganic molecules can enter into the closest union with each other, and this mixture brings it about that the distinction between organic and inorganic states is a relative one, and an absolutely fast limit between the two cannot be assigned.

CHAPTER IV.

DARWINISM AND TELEOLOGY.

WHEN the first edition of the 'History of Materialism' appeared, Darwinism was still new; the parties were just taking up their positions, or, more strictly, the rapidly growing party of 'German Darwinians' was still in process of forming, and the reaction, which at present sees here the most threatened point in the old theory of things, was not yet properly in harness, because it had not yet properly appreciated the range of the great problem and the inward power of the new doctrine.

Since then, the interest of friends and foes has been so much concentrated on this point, that not only an extensive literature has sprung up on Darwin and Darwinism, but that we may say that the Darwinian controversy is to-day what the general Materialistic controversy was formerly. Büchner is still ever finding new readers for 'Kraft und Stoff,' but we no longer hear a literary outcry of indignation when a new edition appears. Moleschott, the true author of the Materialistic movement, is almost forgotten by the great public, and even Karl Vogt is now seldom mentioned except in reference to some special question in anthropology or some isolated and immortal utterance of his drastic humour. Instead of this, every periodical takes sides for or against Darwin; there appear almost daily larger or smaller treatises on the theory of descent, natural selection, and especially, as we may expect, on the descent of man, since there are many members of this particular species who lose their wits, if any doubt is raised of the genuineness of their ancestral tree.

Despite this great movement, we may still maintain unchanged nearly everything that we wrote on Darwinism eight years ago, though we can no longer leave the matter where it was then. The material has grown, even if the *scientific* material has not grown quite in proportion to the printed paper: the questions have been specialised. Formerly Darwin was the only influential champion, not only of the theory of descent, but we may almost say of the natural explanation of organic forms in general. At present it happens that bitter attacks are directed against Darwin and Darwinism by people who confine themselves to the theory of natural selection, as though everything else would have existed even without Darwin. The manifold adumbrations of views, which then existed only in germ, have now become definite and prominent, and have brought with them new supports and new doubts. What we then said on the subject, therefore, can only now serve, as it were, as a general introduction to a more thorough discussion; but as many of our previous utterances have been made the subjects of approving or dissenting comments, we print them here quite unchanged, and make the necessary modifications in the notes and in the subsequent additions.   There is in the whole of modern science, perhaps, no such instance of so empty and at the same time so crass a superstition as that of Species, and there are probably few points in which men have gone on rocking themselves with such baseless argumentations into dogmatic slumber.[54] It almost passes understanding how a scientific inquirer who has specially interested himself for

---

[54] The absolute idea of species here attacked has its double root in the metaphysical import of the Platonico-Aristotelian εἶδος and in the traditions of Noah's Ark. The classification of organic forms according to species may, it is obvious, not only serve the practical purpose of mastering detail, but may even assume a certain material importance, without any dogma as to the invariableness and transcendental basis of kinds. From Darwinism itself, by the help of the principle of increasing stability,

twenty years in the establishing of the notion of species, who undertakes to set up in the capacity of propagation a new criterion of species, during all this time institutes no single experiment on the matter, but confines himself as a genuine natural historian to sifting critically the casual traditional narratives. It is true that even in the sphere of scientific inquiry the division of labour between experiments and the critical comparison of experiments is perfectly safe, and that to a wider extent than is usually recognised. But when a field is still so completely unbroken as that of the formation of species, it is assuredly the first critical utterance to which sound reason and scientific method must lead, that in this sphere, as in every other, only experiment can teach us anything. Yet Andreas Wagner erred so widely from the path of scientific research as to suppose himself to be doing a great service when he demands a juristic proof for the supposed bastard forms, and regards his dogmas as established until this is produced.[55] This may indeed be the most suitable course if we regard a darling prejudice as a personal possession, and answer him who would rob us of it with a title by prescription; but this whole standpoint has not the most distant similarity with scientific inquiry. A single trait may serve to characterise a method with the results of which it would be a frivolous waste of time to busy ourselves further.

We are acquainted with a series of obviously bastard

we may deduce that organisms within very long periods must adopt a tendency to group themselves into species and to define themselves from each other. But this is something quite different from the absolute idea of species which, during the reaction against the Materialism of Vogt and others, made its appearance in a shape which violated all the principles of natural science.

[55] Andreas Wagner, Naturwissenschaft u. Bibel, im Gegensatze zu dem Köhlerglauben des Herrn Carl Vogt, als des wiedererstandenen u. aus dem Französischen in's Deutsche übersetzten Bory. Stuttg. 1855. Cf. e.g., S. 29. Such stories (of fertile hybrids) . . . "gründen sich auf Aussagen von Landwirthen und Reisenden, denen jedoch der stringente Nachweis, wie ihn der Untersuchungsrichter zur rigorösen Constatirung des Thatbestandes verlangt, abgeht." S. 31: "Entweder sind solche Angaben geradezu falsch, oder sie ermangeln der juridischen Beweiskraft," &c.

forms which have resulted from the trifling of fanciers or from chance, and which, more or less accredited, pass from mouth to mouth. From such materials, then, the question is decided what is the fertility of the bastards (*a*) with each other (*b*) with the parent race. We see at the first glance, if we sample the excellent material, that as to *a* there are no, or very few, examples, because there was only one bastard, which, therefore, could not be coupled with another of the same kind, or because the bastards of different sexes were separated and given away, as no one thought of experimenting on the production of new kinds. As to *b* there results the great truth that the bastard races gradually return again to the original races, because from generation to generation they have been paired with one of the same race. From this, then, the final conclusion is drawn that bastards are either infertile, or can only reproduce themselves by pairing with the parent races, since the opposite assertions " lack legal proof." The opponent must lose the case: the inventory of prejudices is saved.

Everybody knows how we ought to set to work here, if our object is not to save a prejudice but to find the truth, which can hardly be considered an unsuitable object for a man who busies himself for twenty years with the question of species. Obviously he should, with all the care exhibited by modern science in other departments, and to which it owes its great successes, first have produced a long series of hybrid forms, *e.g.*, between canaries and linnets. A long series is necessary, not only to eliminate accident and secure a true average, but it is demanded by the very nature of a problem which turns upon a question of more or less. Let us take an equal number of pairs of the same hybrids, and, moreover, of hybrids with the father's and the mother's race respectively. Let these pairs be brought into as nearly as possible the same circumstances of relative and absolute age, of nurture and environment, or let these circumstances be varied methodically, and we shall have a result on the strength of which we may express certain probable conclusions; which would be of more value than Wagner's twenty years' testing of the legal value of gamekeepers' stories.

Darwin has taken a mighty stride towards the completion of a philosophical theory of the universe which can satisfy equally the understanding and the soul, since it bases itself upon the firm foundation of facts and portrays in magnificent outlines the unity of the world without any inconsistency with details. His account of the origin of species, however, as a scientific hypothesis demands the confirmation of experiment, and Darwin will have done great service if he succeeds in calling the spirit of methodical research into a sphere which promises the richest reward, while it demands also, it is true, the utmost sacrifice and perseverance. Many of the experiments thus required may surpass the powers or even the duration of the individual inquirer's activity, and only future generations will reap the fruits of the work which the present must begin. But in this very circumstance will be announced a fresh advance towards a noble conception of the task of science, and the right appreciation of this task must strengthen the feeling of the solidarity of mankind and the community of his daring aims.

What renders Darwin's theory capable of such an effect upon inquiry, is not only the clear simplicity and satisfactory rounding of the fundamental idea which lay ready in the experience and methodical needs of our days, and must easily have resulted from the casual combination of the various ideas of the age. An incomparably higher merit undoubtedly lies in the persevering prosecution of an object which as early as 1837 took firm hold of the naturalist on his return from a scientific voyage, and to which he dedicated his future life. The abundant material which Darwin has collected is for the most part still delayed; more exact proofs for his assertions are still lacking, and a greater work still to come will, it may be hoped, exhibit in its full extent the gigantic labours of this distinguished man.[56] Many wish to postpone their judgment on Darwin's theory until this material has appeared, and this caution cannot be objected to, since criticism will have much to say even to this work of human industry and acuteness, until the permanent is separated from the temporary and subjective elements. But we must quite understand that a satisfactory verification of this great hypothesis by no means depends upon this material only, but that the independent activity of many, and, perhaps, the experimental labours of generations, are required in order to confirm the theory of *natural* selection by *artificial* selection, which may repeat in a comparatively short period the work for which nature requires thousands of years. On the other hand, Darwin's theory possesses even in its present form an importance stretching far beyond the reach of a casually suggested problem. His collection of observations exhibits not the least similarity to Wagner's clumsy protocols on the legitimacy of isolated hunters' tales. Darwin understands how, by the subtle and ingenious combination of verified observations, to bring the whole natural history of plants and animals into connexion with his theory. Every ray is gathered into one focus, and the rich development of theory guides the apparently most remote phenomena of organic life into the stream of proof. But if we would indicate the most admirable aspect of his work, we must point out that this very articulation of the fundamental idea, its support by numerous doctrines and auxiliary hypotheses, has scarcely ever anything arbitrary or forced about it; nay, that many of these are not only more self-evident than the main idea, but at least as high also, if not higher, in scientific importance. We are thinking

---

[56] Instead of a single great work, a series of special treatises has appeared, amongst which that on 'The Variation of Animals and Plants under Domestication,' 2 vols., 1868, is especially rich in material.

here in particular of the doctrine of the struggle of species for existence, and the far-reaching relations of this doctrine to teleology.

The theory of the origin of species carries us back to a primeval period, which bears a character of mystery from the fact that the fancies of mythology are here opposed only by a series of possibilities whose great number extraordinarily weakens the credibility of each single one. The struggle for existence, on the other hand, goes on before our eyes, and yet for centuries it escaped the observation of an age watching for the truth. A reviewer of Radenhausen's 'Isis,' a recent excellent, if not quite thoroughgoing, naturalistic system,[57] feels called upon to make a remark which shows us with what difficulty a totally unprejudiced observer surveys the position of these questions at a moment when any one who can appreciate it must come to a perfectly unequivocal result. Radenhausen employs Darwin's doctrine in order to draw conclusions which lead us back to the primitive radical opposition of Empedokles to teleology, though he admits that the perfect demonstration of Darwin's doctrine is yet to come. Two sentences from his reviewer in the 'Literarisches Centralblatt' may here serve us as the text of a discussion which would in any case be unavoidable, and for which we can only here find a suitable connexion. "People prefer," says the anonymous writer, "for an extramundane causality, operating designedly but mysteriously, to substitute the *possibility* of happy accidents, and find in the progressive development of what a happy accident has begun a compensation for the fact that all

---

[57] My judgment on Radenhausen's 'Isis' would, however, hardly be so favourable now, especially as to the historical and historico-psychological developments, which are often hazardous and inaccurate. This, however, little affects the argumentation in regard to teleology. Let me add, moreover, that the reviewer in the Liter. Centralblatt (1863, S. 486) writes of it:— "The book is throughout written with an impassive calm and self-confidence which remind us of Spinoza." The polemic mentioned in the text of what we may describe as the Empedoklean standpoint, is in the Lit. Centralb., 1864, S. 843 f.

phenomena are at bottom senseless and purposeless, and that the beautiful and the good lie not at the beginning, but only come to view at the end, or at least only in the course of events. . . . So long as these discoveries are not yet really made, we may be allowed to ask ourselves the question whether the hypotheses which this naturalism holds to be justified are less bold and hazardous than the presuppositions of the teleological view of the world."

The reviewer is a type; most of those who, in spite of modern science, feel themselves justified in holding fast to teleology, cling to the gaps in scientific knowledge, overlooking the fact that at all events the form of teleology which has existed until now, that is, the anthropomorphic, is utterly disposed of by the facts, and that whether the naturalistic view has been sufficiently established or not. All teleology has its root in the view that the builder of the universe acts in such a way that man must, on the analogy of human reason, call his action purposeful. This is essentially even Aristotle's view, and even the Pantheistic doctrine of an 'immanent' purpose holds to the idea of a purposefulness corresponding to human ideals, even though it gives up the extramundane person who in human fashion first conceives and then carries out this purpose. It can now, however, be no longer doubted that nature proceeds in a way which has no similarity with human purposefulness; nay, that her most essential means is such that, measured by the standard of human understanding, it can only be compared with the blindest chance. On this point we need wait for no future proof; the facts speak so plainly and in the most various provinces of nature so unanimously, that no view of things is henceforth admissible which contradicts these facts and their necessary meaning.

If a man, in order to shoot a hare, were to discharge thousands of guns on a great moor in all possible directions; if, in order to get into a locked-up room, he were to buy ten thousand casual keys, and try them all; if, in order to have a house, he were to build a town, and leave all the other houses to wind and weather,—assuredly no one would call such proceedings purposeful, and still less would any one conjecture behind these proceedings a higher wisdom, unrevealed reasons, and superior prudence.[58] But whoever will study the modern scientific laws of the conservation and propagation of species, even of those species the purpose of which we cannot see, as, *e.g.*, the intestinal worms, will everywhere find an enormous waste of vital germs. From the pollen of the plant to the fertilised seed, from the seed to the germinating plant, from this to the full-grown plant bearing seed in its turn, we constantly see repeated the mechanism which, through thousandfold production for immediate destruction, and through the casual coincidence of favourable conditions, maintains life, so far as we see it maintained in the existing state of things. The perishing of vital germs, the abortion of the process begun, is the rule; the 'natural' development is a special case among thousands; it is the exception, and this exception is the result of that Nature whose purposeful self-conservation the teleologist short-

---

[58] Wigand, D. Darwinismus u. d. Naturforschung Newtons u. Cuviers, Braunschw. 1874, i. 421, has completely misunderstood this passage if he supposes that "the greatest purposelessness and fortuitousness are represented as the character of Nature;" whereas I am chiefly concerned to exhibit sharply the contrast between the way in which Nature and that in which man pursues a purpose. The procedure of a man who should act on the analogy of Nature must be described as extremely unpractical and purposeless; and this proves that the procedure of Nature (using this figurative expression for brevity) is in any case actively distinct in principle from that of man, and that accordingly the anthropomorphic form of teleology, of which only we are speaking in this connexion, is utterly untenable. That on my view the "utmost parcimony" is the purpose of Nature is in nowise suggested. What is done is simply to compare the action of Nature with that of man in following up a purpose. That Nature does in fact attain her purpose, as Wigand observes, as it were against my view, is the obvious presupposition of the whole inquiry. But when Wigand adds, "and that, too, without hindrance to other purposes," this is, like the whole of his subsequent remarks, nothing but optimistic metaphysic, to which, on the basis of the facts, a pessimistic might with at least equal justification be opposed. Comp. moreover, in the text the last paragraph on this subject, 'And yet there is another side to the matter,' &c. (p. 36).

sightedly admires. "We behold the face of nature," says Darwin,* " bright with gladness; we often see superabundance of food; we do not see, or we forget, that the birds which are idly singing round us mostly live on insects or seeds, and are thus constantly destroying life; or we forget how largely these songsters, or their eggs, or their nestlings, are destroyed by birds and beasts of prey; we do not always bear in mind that although food may be now superabundant, it is not so at all seasons of each recurring year." The struggle for a spot of earth, success or non-success in the persecution and extermination of other life, determines the propagation of plants and animals. Millions of spermatozoa, eggs, young creatures, hover between life and death that single individuals may develop themselves. Human reason knows no other ideal than the presence and perfection, as far as may be, of the life that has begun, combined with the limitation of births and deaths. To Nature luxuriant propagation and painful destruction are only two oppositely working forces which seek an equilibrium. Even for the 'civilised' world political economy has revealed the sad law that misery and famine are the great regulators of the increase of population. Nay, even in the intellectual sphere it seems to be the method of Nature that she flings a thousand equally gifted and aspiring spirits into wretchedness and despair in order to form a single genius, which owes its development to the favour of circumstances. Sympathy, the fairest flower of earthly organisms, breaks forth only at isolated points, and is even in the life of humanity more an ideal than one of its ordinary motives.

What we call Chance in the development of species is, of course, no chance in the sense of the universal laws of Nature, whose mighty activity calls forth all these effects; but it is, in the strictest sense of the word, chance, if we regard this expression in opposition to the results of a humanly calculating intelligence. Where, however, we find

* Origin of Species, 6th ed., p. 49.

adaptation in the organs of animals or plants, there we may assume that in the eternal slaughter of the weak countless less adapted forms were destroyed, so that here too that which maintains itself is only the favourable special case in the ocean of birth and death. This, then, would be, in fact, a fragment of the much-reviled philosophy of Empedokles, confirmed by the endless materials which only the last decades of exact research have brought to light.

And yet there is another side to the matter. Is it quite true, as the reviewer of Radenhausen thinks, that in place of mysteriously working causality we have only the "possibility" of happy accidents? What we see is not possibility but actuality. The single case seems to us only 'possible,' seems to us 'fortuitous,' because it is regulated by the activity of natural laws, which in our human apprehension have nothing to do with this special result of their reciprocal action. In the great whole, however, we can see the necessity. Amongst the countless cases the favourable ones too *must* happen; for they are actually there, and everything actual is produced by the eternal laws of the universe. In fact, this does not so much refute all teleology as afford an insight into the objective nature of the adaptiveness of the phenomenal world. We see clearly that this adaptiveness in the individual case has nothing human about it; nay, that, so far as we have yet observed, it is not brought about by higher wisdom, but by means which, in their logical value, are clearly and distinctly the lowest that we know. This estimate, however, is again only based on human nature, and so there remains for the metaphysical, the religious conception of things, which overpasses these limits in its imaginations, room for the setting up of a teleology which must be simply and definitively rejected from physical research and the critical philosophy of nature.

The study of the lower animals, which has made great strides in the last few decades, especially since Steenstrup's discoveries on alternation of generation, not only discards the old idea of species, but it also throws remarkable light on a very different question, which is of the highest interest in the history of Materialism,—the question of the nature of the organic individual.[59] In connexion with the cell-theory, modern discoveries are beginning here also to exert so profound an influence on our scientific and philosophical views, that it looks as though the ancient questions of existence were now for the first time in a clear shape being submitted to the inquirer and thinker. We have seen how ancient Materialism fell into absolute contradiction by regarding the atoms as the only existent, though they cannot be the bearers of a higher unity, because without pressure and collision no contact takes place between them. But we also saw that precisely this contradiction of manifoldness and unity is peculiar to all human thought, and that it only becomes most obvious in Atomism. The only salvation here, too, consists in regarding the opposition of manifoldness and unity as a consequence of our organisation, in supposing that in the world of things in themselves it is resolved in some way unknown to us, or rather does not exist there. In this way we escape the inmost ground of the contradiction, which lies in the assumption of absolute unities, which are nowhere given to us. If we conceive all unity as relative, if we see in unity only the combination of our thought, we have indeed not embraced the inmost nature of things, but we have certainly made possible the consistency of the scientific view. It fares ill indeed with the absolute unity of self-consciousness, but it is not a misfortune to get rid of a favourite idea for some thousand

---

[59] We have allowed this passage of the first edition to follow here unaltered, although it has no longer a direct reference to Darwinism. 'Individual' and 'kind' belong together, at least in connexion with the theory of knowledge. It is the same synthetic process which brings the manifold in the phenomenon under the one as under the other of these notions, and the question as to the priority of the whole or the parts is at bottom only another form of the question as to the Platonic pre-existence of the idea compared with the individual existence.

years. In this section let us keep close to the more general phenomena of organic nature.

Goethe, whose Morphology may be regarded as one of the soundest and most fertile pieces of work done during the troubled age of our Philosophy of Nature, through his thoughtful study of the manifold forms and variations of the vegetable and animal world, had already attained the standpoint to which all our recent discoveries are forcibly carrying us. "Every living thing," he teaches, "is not a single thing, but a plurality; even in so far as it appears to us as an individual, it still remains a collection of living independent beings, which in idea and disposition are the same, but phenomenally may become the same or similar, other or dissimilar. Those beings are partly connected from their origin, partly find each other and combine. They divorce themselves and seek each other again, and so effect an endless production in all ways and in all directions. The more imperfect the creature is, the more are these parts the same or similar, and the more they resemble the whole. In the one case the whole is more or less like the parts, in the other the whole is unlike the parts. The more like the parts are to each other, the less are they subordinated to each other. The subordination of parts points to a more perfect creature."

Virchow, who has made use of this utterance of Goethe in an excellent essay on Atoms and Individuals,[60] is to be reckoned amongst those who by means of positive research and acute theory have contributed to throw light upon the relation of the beings whose inner community forms the 'individual.'

Pathology, hitherto a region of wild and superstitious preconceptions, was explained by him from the same cell-life, which in its normal phenomena produces the common life of the healthy individual. The individual, according to his explanation, is a "unitary community, in which all the parts co-operate towards a like object, or, as it may be otherwise expressed, are active on a definite

[60] Vier Reden über Leben u. Kranksein: Berlin, 1862, S. 37-76, esp. 58, 59.

plan." This object Virchow further declares to be an inner, immanent one. "The inner object is at the same time an external standard, beyond which the development of the living thing does not reach." The individual which bears its object and its standard within itself is, therefore, an *actual* unity in opposition to the merely conceptional unity of the atom.

Here, then, in the recognition of an immanent object, we have again the primitive formal element, with which our conception of Nature can so little dispense that we find it recognised even by Vogt. With a clearness of conception to which he has not otherwise accustomed us, he declares in his 'Pictures of Animal Life,' after he has explained how the first recognisable forms of the embryo proceed from the cell-masses of the yelk: "So that here again the organism as an individual is given only on the appearance of the form, while before there was only the shapeless material."[61] This utterance comes close to Aristotle. The form makes the essence of the individual; if this be so, we may also designate it *substance*, even though by a natural necessity it proceeds from the properties of the *matter*. These properties, when clearly seen, are in their turn only forms combining themselves into higher forms. The form, too, is the true logical core of force, when we once clear this idea of the false bye-idea of a compelling anthropomorphic violence. We only *see* form as we only *feel* force. If we regard the form of a thing, it is unity; if we disregard the form, it is multeity or matter, as we have explained in the chapter on Scholasticism.

Vogt, theoretically stricter, emphasises the metaphysical idea of unity; Virchow holds to the physiological idea, to

[61] Bilder aus d. Thierleben, Frankf. 1852, S. 233. As to the matter, the recently discovered monera, especially the Bathybius, seem to contradict it. But it is a difficult question how much individuality is to be assigned to such a living lump of slime. The structurelessness of the protoplasm creatures can certainly not be concluded from the failure of our means of examination to recognise a structure. On this light can only be shed if ever the mechanism of these simplest vital phenomena is explained up; but as yet we are far from this.

the community of the life-purpose, and this idea makes very clear to us the relativity of the antithesis of unity and multeity. In the vegetable world many regard as a unit not only the cell and the whole plant, but also the branch, the shoot, the leaf, the bud. For practical reasons we may choose the single shoot which can lead an independent existence as an individual; then the single cell is only a part of this, and the plant is a colony. The difference, however, is relative. If the single cell of a higher plant cannot lead an independent existence, but must remain surrounded by other cells, neither can the offshoot without being rooted either in the plant or in the ground. All life is possible only in connexion with the natural environment; and the idea of an independent life in the whole oak-tree is just as much an abstraction as in the smallest fragment of a fallen leaf. Our modern Aristotelians lay great stress upon this, that the organic part can only arise and only exist in the organism. But there is not much to be done with the mystical dominion of the whole over the part. The separated plant-cell carries on its cell-life in fact longer than the separated heart of the frog beats. If no fresh sap comes to the cell it dies, as in the like case the whole tree dies; the shorter or longer duration depends upon the circumstances, not upon the nature of the thing. Rather should we lay stress upon this, that plants do not collect together externally from cells, that the single cells do not form themselves directly from the nutritive element and so accede to the whole, but that they always arise in other cells by means of their division. In fact, the Aristotelian principle that the whole is before the part applies for the most part, as far as we can see, to the organic world; but the circumstance that Nature so proceeds as a rule by no means entitles us to attribute an absolute universality to this principle. The mere fact even of inoculation is enough to confine it to the narrow limits of ordinary empirical principles. In the last century experiments were very popular in the transfusion of blood from one animal to another, and at least partially they succeeded.[62] In more recent times organic parts have been actually transferred from one body to another and brought to live, and yet our experimentation on this aspect of vital conditions has scarcely begun. Nay, in the lower plants we find, in fact, the fusion of two cells as well as the division, and in the lower animals the fusion of two individuals has been ascertained. The Radiopods, the descendants of the Vorticella, frequently approach each other, embrace each other, and there arises at the point of contact first flattening and then perfect fusion. A similar process of copulation occurs with the Gregarines, and even in the case of a worm, the Diplozoon, Siebold found that it arises through the fusion of two Diporpæ.[63]

Relative unity occurs amongst the lower animals very remarkably in those polyps which possess a common stem, on which there appears by gemmation a mass of creatures, which in a certain sense are to be regarded as independent, but in another sense only as organs of the entire stem. We are led to the supposition that in these beings even the voluntary movements are partly general, partly special in their nature; that the sensations of all these semi-independent stems stand related to each other, and yet have their separate operation too. Vogt is quite right when he calls the controversy as to the individuality of these beings a controversy as to the Kaiser's beard. "There occur gradual transitions. The individualisation step by step increases."[64]

[62] As is well known, these experiments have very recently been taken up again, and have repeatedly produced favourable results.

[63] Comp. Vogt, Bilder aus d. Thierl., S. 124-142. The recent discoveries on this head are briefly put together in Gegenbaur, Grundz. d. vergl. Anatomie, Leipz. 1870, S. 110 ff. Here we only call attention to the fact that (S. 112) in Actinosphaerium *three* individuals can unite in this manner. Comp. moreover, for the whole question, Haeckel's theory of individuality in the 'Generelle Morphologie,' i. 265 ff.

[64] One of the most remarkable facts in this subject is the *colonial* nervous system in the Bryozoa: cf. Gegenbaur, *l.c.*, S. 19 f.

So far in our first edition. We come back now to the notion of Species, and must first make some remarks which rest not so much on modern discoveries and observations, as on a more exact survey of the whole field, and of the principles of the struggle for existence. The first remark is this, that the notion of species, on more accurate inspection, reveals itself as a product of those times in which the attention of mankind was chiefly directed to the large or more highly organised creatures, and in which the microscope and all the infinite fulness of the lower animal and vegetable worlds were yet unknown. This becomes still plainer if we take into account, besides species, the genera, orders, and classes, which even in Linné's time appeared to embrace so admirably the entire animal world. Nowadays the whole network covers only the upper part of the animal series, and the lower we descend the more is the inquirer puzzled. A crowd of fresh marks appears, now agreeing, now crossing each other, to require even in the narrowest field a multiplicity of divisions and subdivisions, with which at the higher end of the series it was possible comfortably to embrace, *e.g.*, the whole 'typus' of the vertebrates. While, however, on the one side downwards the wealth of forms becomes so great that no logical network of ideas suffices to embrace it, on the other side the old-fashioned criterion of common descent here becomes utterly inconceivable. When, therefore, Haeckel, in his 'Philosophy of the Sponges,'[65] develops twelve different, partly natural, partly artificial systems merely from the narrower and wider view of the notion of species, we must descry in this neither an untrustworthy playing with marks nor an isolated anomaly. If man had commenced his study of natural beings with the lower animals, the idea of species, by many held so sacred, would probably never have arisen. The view which we must now form

---

[65] Die Kalkschwämme, eine Monographie in 2 Bdn., Berl. 1872, 1 Bd., 4 Abschn.; Philosophie der Kalkschwämme, S. 476 ff.

of the whole series of organisms is no longer that of a ladder in regular and intelligible succession from the lowest to the highest, but we have an enormous substructure to the whole system, which is still in continuous movement, and from this arise upwards the ever more firmly marked and clearly sundered forms of the higher plants and animals.

With this connects itself a second remark, which mainly applies to the higher organic forms. If, namely, we presuppose that these forms have in the course of long spaces of time so formed and marked themselves off from one another as we now see them before us, it necessarily follows from this that they must in general possess a high degree of stability, and that varieties and intermediate forms can no longer easily arise in free nature so long as the relative life-conditions of the species do not change with climate, cultivation, and other circumstances. For if we start from a condition of variability, and have the struggle for existence at work for long spaces of time, the best adapted forms must necessarily keep the ground; and, in fact, not only those which are best adapted in themselves, but also the best adapted combination of those species which, in the competition with each other, enable, as it were, the maximum of life to be maintained. Amongst the animals, for example, the hunger and the strength of the lion will bring themselves into a kind of equilibrium with the rapidity of the gazelle, with a simultaneous adaptation of both species to all other competitors for existence. This relation agrees with Fechner's 'principle of decreasing variability,' but is, as we conceive it, a simple consequence of the principles of the theory of evolution and the struggle for existence, while Fechner tries to develop *a priori* an entirely universal cosmical principle of this kind.[66]

---

[66] Fechner's principle of the tendency to stability has a certain similarity with the way in which Zöllner, by the aid of Schopenhauer's philosophy and the mechanical principle of the least compulsion, tries to de-

The consequences of this pretty obvious remark have not always been sufficiently kept in view. Otherwise, for example, the transitional forms which evolution postulates would not have caused so much difficulty. We may regard the influence of man as a variation of the natural conditions which make existence possible for certain forms, that in a state of nature would probably soon disappear again before the older forms which had maintained themselves in the struggle for existence. As it is, however, we see how man, in the case, for instance, of pigeons and dogs, in the course of a few generations reaches new forms, which, so long as they are kept under the same protecting conditions, very speedily attain the purity and exclusiveness of a separate species, and are only in deference to theory to be called 'varieties.'[67] And this by no means happens only in the case of 'artificial' selection, which strives after a definite model, but also in the case of 'unconscious' selection,[68] *i.e.*, in the case of a procedure which brings a variety to the ever greater perfection and persistence of a new type, through the simple effort to keep the race pure and to develop a peculiarity, so that for the rest Nature here strives freely, as it were, after a definite model, where a halt is made. If this is once attained, it may then maintain itself unaltered for any length of time.

duce that every system of atomic vibrations in a given space has the tendency to let the number of collisions (and thus of sensation and pain) fall to a minimum. In the principle of tendency to stability Fechner finds at the same time the reconciliation of causation and of teleology, since on this principle the earth must necessarily approximate to a condition in which "everything harmonises as well as possible" (Einige Ideen, &c., S. 88 ff.).

Fechner's idea, as well as Zöllner's, are at present but boldly hazarded metaphysical notions, which as yet entirely lack proof and demonstration. If we limit ourselves, on the contrary, to the relative adaptation of organisms to the conditions of existence in a given extended period, then the tendency to stability follows immediately from the principle of the struggle for existence.

[67] Comp. Darwin, The Variation of Animals and Plants under Domestication, i. 32. Here it is shown that the domesticated pigeons, although they all descend from a single wild species, number more than a hundred and fifty kinds, and must be divided into at least five new classes if they are to be dealt with on the same principles as the wild classes.

[68] Darwin, *loc. cit.*, i. 214.

Similarly, then, we may also assume that the changes in organisms which have been left to themselves have not been completed with quite such imperceptible slowness as Darwin's own view seems to require, but that after every important change in the conditions of existence there has resulted, as it were by starts, a rapid development of some forms and a retrogression of others. We may very well assume also that every such disturbance of the natural equilibrium produces a tendency to variation, and thus gives opportunity for the origin of new forms, which rapidly establish and perfect themselves when the conditions are favourable to them. All the various principles which modern inquirers have introduced into the doctrine of descent in order to complement the principle of natural selection, as, *e.g.*, migration, the isolation of species, &c., are only more or less happily apprehended special aspects of the decisive main principle of the *disturbance of equilibrium*, which must necessarily produce the stability of species where the conditions long remain identical.

It is easy to see how by this view of the doctrine of transmutation a great many objections which have been raised against it are at once disposed of, while, on the other hand, Darwin's theory is modified in a very essential point.

Darwin's view so far runs quite parallel with Lyell's geology, in that chief importance is laid upon the silent and continuous, though to ordinary observation imperceptible, changes which are continually going on, but the result of which only becomes apparent in long periods of time. Agreeably with this view, Darwin supposed that modifications of species originally arise quite fortuitously, and that the majority of them again disappear, like ordinary malformations, without leaving any sign, while some few of them, which bring some advantage to their possessors in the struggle for existence, maintain and establish themselves through natural selection and heredity.

We must, of course, admit, even on our view, that very

slow modifications of form may occur, especially where they are produced by very slow modifications of the conditions of existence, as, *e.g.*, in the gradual elevation or depression of whole countries. But even in this case it will appear to us more probable that the organic forms oppose a certain resistance to the change in their life-conditions, which maintains their state unaltered until, when the disturbing influences reach a certain height, a disturbing crisis breaks in. This does not exclude, however, a gradual modification, and we do not wish our view of the attainment of a condition of equilibrium to be so taken as though it were a condition of absolute immutability. On the other hand, the development of new kinds from the purely fortuitous development of new qualities must indeed be doubted, so far at least as the main lever of the change is supposed to be found here.

Let us again remember that we have to deal with long periods of time, and that the general tendency to variation must have been greatest at the beginning of these periods. Then we can easily see that at a given moment of time the whole series of variations has, as it were, been tried, and that what at the beginning of the period has not led to a new kind will be ever less likely to do so, because the forms are ever slowly becoming more definite and disparate. But if we choose to consider the period which we here regard as the period of adaptation for the relations indicated as at least in itself exclusively governed by the law of the persistence of useful accidents, there arise further objections of different kinds.

First let us suppose that the period of adaptation follows upon a disturbance of equilibrium, and for that very reason involves an increased tendency to variation. Why now are we to exclude all immediate causal connexion between the change of the conditions of existence and the change of forms? Why, we are even now rightly restoring Lamarck to honour, who derived from immediately efficient causes combined with heredity all modifications of forms, and therefore, *e.g.*, the increase, strengthening, and development of any organ from its increased use. But here many still unknown forces may be in operation, without our being therefore obliged to take refuge in a mystical intervention of the teleological principle. Fechner even brings in psychical influences too, and that without leaving the circle of the mechanical conception of nature, since psychical phenomena are at the same time physical.

"The cock," he says, "has spurs, a crest of feathers, a high red comb. The two first are explained on the principle of the struggle for existence. Cocks on which these had been fortuitously formed conquered their adversaries in fight by means of the spurs, and by the crest were better protected against bites, so that they remained masters of the field. But undoubtedly they must have waited long for these fortuitous arrangements to occur; and when we think that such accidents must be supposed in the case of all other animals, in order to explain the existence of all these adaptations, our brain will grow dizzy. I am more inclined to think that when the organisation was more easily variable than it is now, the psychical effort to be a vigorous match for the foe, to protect oneself against his attack, and the fury against him which still sets the spur in activity, ruffles the crest, and swells the comb, was able, if not to produce these parts by a suitable modification of the nutritive processes in existing cocks, yet to implant the disposition thereto in the germs, and so in their descendants; and here I regard, of course, the psychical efforts and conditions only as the inner side of the physical organisation on which these modifications depended, while I hold the whole play of psychical impulses as connected with their physical basis by the general principle of tendency to stability, without attempting a more precise explanation." [69]

We leave the value of this idea undetermined, only observing that there is just as little reason for rejecting

[69] Fechner, Einige Ideen, &c., S. 71 f.

it unexamined as for accepting it without proofs. Amongst other phenomena, however, which are difficult to explain from mere selection, there is one in particular which is very widely spread that seems to demand a direct and positive causal connexion between the form and the conditions of life. This is 'mimicry,' an adaptation extremely common, especially in insects, and leading to the most remarkable illusions, of the form and colour of animals to their environment, or even to other organisms.[70]

On the general principle this illusive imitation of strange forms seems to agree admirably with natural selection, for it is always a protection to the particular animal against its enemies. We may, therefore, easily suppose that individuals which have fortuitously undergone a modification of this protective kind must have lived longer and exercised a greater influence in the propagation of their kind than others. If this be once admitted, the protective adaptation of form and colour must necessarily have gone further. But here comes the great difficulty of explaining the first variation of a protective kind. An opponent of Darwin, Mr. Bennet,[71] has pointed out that the resemblance of many insects to the ground on which they live, to the colour of dry bark or fallen leaves, or to the bright colours of the flowers on which they commonly settle, comes about through so long a series of illusive traits and markings, that it is the less possible to admit the sudden appearance of such a variation, as the nearest related species often possess an entirely different aspect. Then Mr. Bennet goes on to argue that a fortuitous occurrence of *one portion* of this new marking would be of no advantage, because the creature would certainly not have deceived its enemies. But until by mere fortuitous variation, which may just as easily occur

---

[70] Comp. Wallace, Contributions to the Theory of Natural Selection.

[71] We follow an address of Mr. Bennet to the British Association at Liverpool, given in the Naturforscher, iv. No. 15, 1871, S. 118 ff, which is said to have "been approved by very competent inquirers."

in one direction as in another, the whole of the colour-marks and changes of form happen to meet so that the illusion is perfect, requires such a combination of coincidences that the probability against it is enormous. We must also assume enormous periods of time in order that a single such coincidence of all these modifications may be expected. In dealing with the questions of cosmogony, indeed, we have deliberately impugned the blind dread of great numbers; but here the case is very different. Mimicry can only be developed during a period of much the same climatic conditions, in the face of the same enemies and the same vegetation; and these periods must, generally speaking, not be made too long.

Darwin explains protective imitation by supposing the creature to have had originally a certain rough similarity with some element of its environment, so that natural selection would only have to develop further this important beginning, partly by more distinctly marking the protective similarity, partly too by adapting the habits of life to the employment of this protection. In fact this explanation seems the only one which is compatible with the exclusive application of the principle of selection. Instead of the fortuitous concourse of a quantity of delicate lines and combinations of colour, we should thus have a rough primitive whole, which at least in some cases could already deceive enemies, and thus give an impulse to the known process of natural selection. But now it must be observed that there are cases to which this kind of explanation cannot possibly be applied. These are all those cases in which the protective form, and especially the colour, deviates very strongly and strikingly from the forms and colours of the nearest related species. But such cases are uncommonly numerous. Bennet mentions a case where a kind of butterfly deviates very far from all its relatives, which are almost pure white, and imitates the brilliant colours of a butterfly of quite a different class. The latter is poisonous to birds, and is therefore avoided by them; but the imitating butterfly, which would agree very well with the birds, protects itself by its likeness to the poisonous butterfly.

These, and like cases, must necessarily lead us to assume other, though it may be yet unknown, factors, which produce the phenomena of mimicry. That rational science will not, despite the difficulty of these cases, take refuge in a mystically interfering teleological force, but here too will apply the axiom of the intelligibleness of the world, is of course obvious. Here comes to our aid the fact that an influence of the environment on the colouring of animals, in all probability produced through the eyes and nervous system, is otherwise not unknown. We refer here particularly to Pouchet's experiments on colour-changes in turbot and perch.[72] That fish very frequently have the colouring of the ground at the bottom of the water had long been known, and it need not be doubted that in this very simple 'mimicry' natural selection has often been the chief cause. But in Pouchet's experiments these fish change their colour within a few hours, according to the colour of the bottom on which they are placed. Even though there exists in the variable pigment cells of the fish a mechanism which we shall hardly find in the wings of insects, and which makes the phenomena of this rapid change of colour intelligible, yet the main point in the two cases is quite analogous, viz., that the colours of external objects through the mediation of the nervous system produce analogous colours in the animal. Whether the nerve-changes in question are connected with an internal excitation of desire and will may be regarded as quite indifferent. The solution of the problem, or rather the core of the problem to be resolved, lies in the still undiscovered mechanism which brings about the effect, and which may very well be ranked with the 'ordered reflexes,' as soon as we familiarise ourselves with the idea that, besides the instantaneously acting reflex processes, there

[72] Naturforscher, iv. No. 38, 1871, S. 310 f.

may also be very slowly acting ones, of which the result, it may be, only appears in the course of generations. That these reflex actions, like the well-known regular reflex actions in the spinal marrow of vertebrates, are at the same time purposeful, may then again be very simply referred to the old Empedoklean principle that only the purposeful can maintain and develop itself, while misformations, which in themselves may be equally possible and frequent, perish and disappear without any trace.

The view here put forward as the most natural and probable must by no means be supposed to set aside natural selection and the struggle for existence. On the contrary, we regard these powerful levers of all development as equally proved both empirically and rationally, and they seem to us to co-operate under all circumstances with the more positive influences on the origination of forms, in such a way that the true completion and elaboration of all forms, the elimination of imperfect intermediate forms, and the entire maintenance of the equilibrium amongst organisms, essentially rest on this great factor introduced by Darwin into natural science.

We must not, indeed, overlook the fact that even in the completion and elaboration of organic forms other, and those more positive factors, may co-operate, with which natural selection and the struggle for existence are connected only as a great regulator, promoting what is perfect and destroying what is imperfect. Let us mention, to begin with, the principle so often pointed out by Darwin himself of the 'correlation of growth.'[73] According to this principle, modifications of form, which have in themselves nothing to do with the struggle for existence, arise as necessary consequences of a prior modification determined by natural selection; and, in fact, the connexion of the secondary modifications thus arising with the primary ones is sometimes easy to see, but sometimes

[73] Origin of Species, 6th ed., 114-118; Variation of Plants and Animals.

utterly obscure. That, *e.g.*, the heavy pendulous ears of some kinds of rabbits must exert a modifying pressure on the skull is easy to understand on mechanical principles; that where the fore-limbs are strongly developed the hind-limbs have a tendency to become slighter, seems equally intelligible; but why, *e.g.*, white cats with blue eyes are generally deaf, why scarlet-coloured dahlias have their coronal leaves indented, is for the present utterly incomprehensible to us. As, however, such connexions exist in very great number, we see that there obtain in the structure of organisms laws of formation which are still unknown to us, not only in the extent, but even as to the very character of their operation. But it is, of course, not necessary to think of forces as yet unknown to us; a peculiar combination of well-known natural forces is enough to explain these striking consequences, which may be summed up with Darwin: that there never occurs a modification of any single part with a maintenance of all the other peculiarities of the form.

The generally operating laws of formation which are here manifested are, however, probably the same which in some circumstances form purely 'morphological kinds,' without any demonstrable advantage in the struggle for existence. The origin of such forms was first emphatically maintained by Nägeli, who combined with this the view that there is in organisms an innate tendency to progressive development. Darwin in the later editions of his work has recognised the existence of morphological characters, without, however, adopting the doctrine of the natural tendency to progressive development, which, in fact, at first sight seems to conflict sharply with the whole of Darwinism.[74] So, too, Kölliker conceives the law of the development of organisms, which he assumes, to be in-

---

[74] Origin of Species, 6th ed., 170. Comp. Nägeli, Entstehung u. Begriff der naturhist. Art, Münch. 1865; and also Oscar Schmidt, Theory of Descent and Darwinism, p. 156.

compatible with Darwin's hypothesis.[75] The main defect of this hypothesis he finds in the laying down of the principle of utility as the basis of the whole, and a basis which 'is meaningless.' We are so far entirely agreed with Kölliker that positive causes of development must be assumed which have their explanation not in the principle of utility, but in the internal disposition of organisms; but besides all these positive causes, the principle of utility has a meaning in combination with the law of the struggle for existence, which in a negative way controls the blind stress of origin and growth, and separates the actual forms from those which are possible according to the 'law of development.'

Kölliker observes that Darwin, as well as his followers, in explaining variation had also thought of internal causes; "but in doing this they abandon the ground of their hypothesis and take the side of those who assume a law of development, and lay down as the causes of their modification internal causes lying in the organisms themselves."

It is true that Darwin, with that splendid and so often successful one-sidedness which we find with especial frequency amongst Englishmen, has carried out his principle as though he must deduce everything from it exclusively; and as the principle, as we presuppose, has everywhere a decisive action in the production of the actual, this proceeding can naturally be carried very far. The everywhere *co-operating* cause was treated as though it was the only cause, but a dogmatic assertion that it is the only one is not a necessary part of the system. Wherever Darwin sees himself led to the co-operation of internal causes, he adopts it into his explanation of natural forms so unhesitatingly, that we are rather led to suppose that he regards it as self-intelligible. That he draws as little as possible from this source, and, on the contrary, as much as

[75] Kölliker, Morphologie u. Ent- stammes, &c.: Frankf. 1872; esp. wickelungsgesch. des Peunatuliden- S. 26 ff.

possible from natural selection, is again for him, as the advocate of a new scientific principle, an entirely correct method; for the effect of selection, that is natural, explained by artificial selection, is entirely intelligible—at least on its negative and regulative side, which we have repeatedly pointed out as the important point. The struggle for existence is completely clear to us, and any reduction of a phenomenon to this great factor of creation is therefore a real explanation, while recourse to the laws of development is for the present only to refer us to the future, when some day, perhaps, we may gain an insight into the nature of these laws of development.

Nevertheless, the services of Nägeli and Kölliker in pointing out the positive and inner causes of formation are to be very highly estimated, and a philosophical and critical examination of the whole problem of development will do justice to both points, and must bring into the true connexion their contributions to the understanding of phenomena.

A specially striking example of the action of a law of development is rightly found in the transformation of some examples of the branchial axolotl into a gill-less newt-form. Of some hundreds of these creatures brought from Mexico to Paris, the great majority remained at the lower stage; some few crept to land and became lunged and air-breathing animals. They attained a form to which their earlier form is related as a larva-form or as an earlier stage of development, so that the whole phenomenon immediately connected itself with a series of already known phenomena. As a rule, indeed, an animal which passes through several stadia of development must reach the highest stage before it can propagate itself; but there are now many known exceptions to this rule; nay, we can actually prevent the tritons from reaching their last stage of development. If they are kept in a closed water-basin, they do not lose their branchiæ, but remain at the stage of the water-newt, and become at the same time sexually mature and reproduce themselves. In like manner peculiar conditions of existence not unfrequently produce similar changes without the co-operation of man; *e.g.*, that one kind of frog passes through the tadpole state in the egg and jumps from the egg as a ready-made frog. In all these cases the co-operation of inner formative causes with the conditions of existence is obvious, and it cannot be denied that natural selection plays the decisive part in some of them, though in the transformation of the axolotl, which suddenly changes from a water-creature into an air-creature, there can be no question of natural selection or the struggle for existence. From the standpoint of one-sided Darwinism the thing can only be explained by bringing the whole transformation under the notion of variation, and perhaps making the removal into another climate the occasion of the variation. In wild nature the new form would now have to undergo the struggle for existence, and to fix itself by breeding in before the process of forming a species would be completed. But it is very easily seen that such an extension of the notion of variation really includes everything that the champions of the law of development can require; for nobody will believe that this change is an accidental one, compared with which any other conceivable change might just as well have occurred; but we see that here a movement was made in, as it were, a predescribed course.[76]

The whole difficulty of understanding lies in rightly apprehending the notion of the law of development. The word sounds somewhat suspicious to many men of science, much as if we spoke of a 'plan of creation,' implying a succession of repeated interferences of supernatural forces. There is, however, not the least reason in the 'inner causes,' of which we are here speaking, to presuppose any mystical assistance to the wonted course of natural forces. So that the 'law of development' also, according to which organisms rise in a definite gradation,

[76] Haeckel, N. Schöpfungsgesch., 4 Aufl., S. 315 f., E.T. 354.

can be nothing else than the co-operation, conceived as a unity, of the universal laws of Nature in order to produce the phenomenon of development. Kölliker's 'law of development,' just as well as the numerous laws of formation which Haeckel propounds, is, logically considered, primarily only a so-called 'empirical law,' *i.e.*, a collection, drawn from experience, of certain rules in natural phenomena, whose ultimate causes we do not yet know. We may, however, attempt to form a picture to ourselves of the true natural causes which underlie the law of development, even were it only to show that there is not the slightest occasion to take refuge in a mystical conception.

Haeckel has expressed the idea that his plastid theory is to be reduced to a carbon theory, *i.e.*, that we are to seek in carbon—of course in some way as yet completely obscure to us—for the cause of the peculiar movements which we observe in protoplasm, and which we regard as the elements of all vital phenomena. This idea does not carry us very far, but we may here employ it as a point of connexion in order to explain our idea of the nature of the law of development.

If we look somewhat closely into the chemistry of carbon compounds, we find that there already exists a complete theory for the formation of organic acids, which we may very well compare with a law of development. The 'plan' of this whole development lies prescribed in the doctrine of the 'quantivalence' of atoms; and as by a fixed principle of substitution any given organic acid can, as it were, be developed onward into another, we have a possibility, running, as it seems, to infinity, of ever more complicated and ever more manifold formations before us, which, despite their enormous multitude, follow only a narrow and predescribed course. What can or can not arise is determined in advance by certain hypothetical properties of the molecules.[77]

---

[77] Weihrich, Ansichten d. neueren Chemie: Mainz, 1872, S. 43 f., refers to Kolbe's theory, on which an atom of hydrogen can be replaced by me-

DARWINISM AND TELEOLOGY.

We might here break off, and simply compare the plan, known in its main features, of all possible organic substances, as an illustration, with the as yet unknown plan of all possible animal forms. We will go, however, a step farther, and refer to the connexion between the form of crystals and the mode of composition of the crystallised matter. That a similar connexion exists between matter and form even in organisms is no new idea. The analogy is obvious, and has often been employed for many purposes. That this brings us back finally to peculiarities of the molecules is very natural. For our purpose it is quite indifferent whether the form is brought into combination with a definite animal material, which has a definite position in the genealogical tree of materials, or whether it is regarded as the result of a co-operation of all the materials present in an animal body; and both may at bottom come to the same thing. It is enough to admit any kind of connexion between form and matter, and we have before us the law of development of organisms in the most palpable shape as the law of substitution of carbon compounds.

Whether this be so or not, in any case this illustration will suffice to show that we need not conceive the law of development as anything supernatural or mystical, and thus the chief obstacle to the recognition of its importance will be removed. The law of development gives the *possible* forms; natural selection from their enormous multitude chooses the *actual* forms; but it can summon forth nothing that is not contained in the plan of organisms, and the mere principle of utility becomes impotent if a modification of the animal is required of it which is

---

thyl, C_2H_3. The methyl itself contains hydrogen, for each atom of which an atom of methyl may be substituted. By such substitutions formic acid is turned into acetic acid, acetic acid into propionic acid, this into butyric acid, and so on. Of course the general idea developed in the text is independent of this special theory; but this latter shows very well what may be conceived as a law of development, so far as the more complex formations are imagined as successively arising out of the more simple.

against the law of development. But this does not touch Darwin, since he chooses only what is useful amongst the spontaneously occurring variations. His doctrine is only completed in so far as we must assume that the circle of possible variations is determined by a universal law of development.

We might now suppose that the assumption of such a law of development renders the theory of natural selection superfluous, since the multitude of forms must be produced in course of time without any selection. Such a view overlooks, in the first place, the enormous importance of the competition for existence, which is not a theory, but a demonstrated fact. At the same time we must maintain that the law of development, no matter what we imagine to lie behind it, is at all events not a dæmonically working power producing unconditionally the pure forms answering its requirements. If even in crystallisation, where the conditions are so much simpler, we discover the most manifold irregularities, so that the crystal of theory is strictly only an ideal, we shall easily understand in the case of organisms, that the law of development cannot prevent perturbations and malformations of all kinds, mixed forms by the side of pure ones, imperfections beside the type, although it exercises its influence upon all the forms that occur. But if even the pure forms, according to the law of development, run into infinity, the possible number becomes very much greater through the modified forms, and yet it remains always a mere fraction of what is conceivable. Everything cannot come from everything, as even the ancient Materialists understood. Amongst this luxuriant multitude of forms comes now the struggle for existence, ordering and sifting, and establishes the equilibrium described above, which we recognised as the maximum of simultaneously possible life. Whether those forms to which natural selection finally leads, and which it renders stable, are finally at the same time the purest types according to the law of development, may remain undetermined; but at all events, we shall assume that the stability of species is the greater the more often this coincidence is attained.

A more serious question which here presents itself is whether, on the assumption of a mechanically working law of development, the apparently like primitive forms of organisms, from which we deduce all living forms, are to be considered as really constituted alike or not? In putting this question, we do not wish to shake that law which the most influential representatives of the doctrine of descent declare so extremely important—the law of the agreement of 'ontogeny' and 'phylogeny,' as Haeckel says, or the doctrine that in each creature the stadia of its prehistory are summarily repeated in the history of its own development, especially in fœtal life. We will, in the first place, only remark that this law is indeed of great heuristic importance to the theorists of the doctrine of descent, but that its necessity is precisely from the standpoint of pure Darwinism difficult to understand. Of advantage in the struggle for existence from traversing these stadia there can be no question, and the principle of heredity is not so unconditionally valid that it could explain this correspondence. It can hardly be, then, but that there are chemical and physical causes present which render it necessary to traverse these stadia, and in this there is already involved the recognition of the law of development as we conceive it.

If now it is asked whether the forms which look the same or like in the first stadia of development are also really constituted alike, we may infer the contrary simply from the fact that they produce a different result. If, *e.g.*, the embryo of the dog has a striking likeness to that of man in the fourth week, yet from the one is produced a dog and from the other a human being. It might be supposed that this not unimportant difference was only gradually developed through the one of the two like embryos being constantly nourished by the juices of a dog, and the other by those of a human being; but this somewhat crude way of looking at the matter will not answer, *e.g.*, in the case of the eggs of a bird. If we think of the principle, so well demonstrated by Darwin, of the transmission of acquired qualities, we shall soon see how much more subtly we must here represent to ourselves the true state of the case. Let us take, *e.g.*, two pigeon's eggs, one of which contains an individual possessing the hereditary disposition to tumble in the air, the other as like an individual as possible, but without this disposition. Where now lies the difference? It can no longer come from without; it must lurk in the egg; but how we do not know. All that we now know is that this likeness of external appearance is infinitely removed from essential likeness. Haeckel, who lays very great weight on the identity of the first stadia, because he descries in it a speaking testimony for the original essential unity of all organisms, recognises at the same time the necessity of assuming internal differences. "The differences," he says, "which really exist between the eggs of different mammals and that of man do not exist in the form, but in the chemical mixture, in the molecular composition of the albuminous combination of carbon, of which the egg essentially consists. These minute individual differences of eggs, which depend upon indirect or potential adaptation (and especially upon the law of individual adaptation), are, indeed, not directly perceptible to the exceedingly imperfect senses of man, but are cognisable through indirect means as the primary causes of the difference of all individuals." [78]

[78] Haeckel, Hist. of Creation, E.T. i. 296. Again he says very rightly at p. 334: "All the vital phenomena, and, above all, the two fundamental phenomena of nutrition and propagation, are purely physico-chemical processes, and directly dependent on the material nature of the organism, just as all physical and chemical qualities of every crystal are determined solely by its material composition." In the 'Generelle Morphologie,' i. S. 198, Haeckel says: "We know that these very simple beginnings of all organic individuals are unlike in kind, and that extremely slight differences in their material composition, in the constitution of

Chemical differences are, however, essential differences; and accordingly we have before us in the similar eggs things which are essentially very different, though obviously by a general but as yet unknown law they are brought into externally similar forms. Whether differences of *structure* do not also co-operate, we do not know. For what do we mean when we speak of the absence of structure in protoplasm? Surely nothing more than that we, with our coarse methods of observation, cannot recognise any structure. So long as the movements of protoplasm are not mechanically explained, the question of its structure must remain an open one.[79] And ultimately even the chemical constitution of the molecule is structure!

their albuminous compound, suffice to effect the resulting differences of their embryonic development. For it is certainly only such extremely slight differences which produce, e.g., the hereditary transmission of individual ancestral qualities to the offspring through the minimum quantity of albumen in the spermatozoon."

But should we not draw further consequences from this correct view, in which the importance of "internal causes" for development appear in the clearest light? Must not, in particular, the exaggerated importance which is attributed to merely morphological likeness' disappear before the fact that we find the most important differences in creatures already established in the germ, while, with our means of observation, we cannot as yet even contemplate the possibility of directly exhibiting the differences? Assuredly no one will find unimportant the first basis of the difference between Mozart and an utterly unmusical man, or even the first difference between Goethe and a fowl, merely because it is connected with an infinitesimally small material quantity. The fact, however, that this quantity is something to us as yet quite inappreciable, justifies the man of science in not specially concerning himself with it, and so engaging in fruitless inquiries. And, moreover, in a professedly purely morphological inquiry this inappreciable quantity may be disregarded; only that then as soon as we wish to form an idea of the nature of development, where the morphological aspect of the matter is not sufficient, to neglect this quantity would be to commit as bad a blunder as it would be to omit one of the most important factors in a calculation because it is unknown to us; for here, of course, we are no longer concerned with the material quantity in itself, but with the importance of the consequences of its presence.

[79] Comp. Preyer, Ueber die Erforschung des Lebens, Jena, 1873, S. 22: "Through the movements of the protoplasm in the tiny germ of a seed of corn, the environing earth, air, and water are transformed under the influence of heat into a giant tree; and through the movement of the protoplasm in the warmed egg, its contents are transformed into a living creature. What gives the impulse? What makes the materials so arrange themselves that life results from them? In vain does chemistry grope for an answer."

Let us imagine the ready-hewn stones for a Gothic and a Byzantine cathedral so piled up, on two sites of like form and most limited dimensions, as to use every inch of space, and that the two heaps attain the same external shape. Then it is very easily conceivable that these masses of material at some distance appear like two exactly similar structures. But if the stones are separated and properly put together, from the one of these piles there can only result the Gothic, and from the other the Byzantine cathedral.

If this is once recognised, we must also draw the consequences, partly by recognising that chemical relations have their rule, and, as it were, their plan of development, but partly, too, by appreciating the whole attitude of morphology to the genesis of organisms. We must, that is, admit the principle that unknown peculiarities of matter, probably chemical, may exercise a decisive influence on the development of beings, on their future form and their modes of life, although these very peculiarities are already present in the first elementary forms without producing any difference cognisable by us.

What is true for the individual must, however, be true also for the whole sum of organisms in their historical development: the simple primitive forms, which all beings must pass through, are not necessarily essentially the same. They may, in a subtler and to us incognisable structure, or in their chemical composition, be as different as they are morphologically alike. However important, therefore, Haeckel's gastrula theory may be for the completion of morphology, and as the hypothetical complement of the whole doctrine of descent, we can never find in it a proof of 'monophyletic' descent, *i.e.*, of the origin of all organisms from one and the same species of primitive creatures.[80]

[80] In the Gen. Morph., i. 198, Haeckel observes: "It is, in our view, for the essential principles of organic development pretty indifferent whether in the primeval sea, when the first autogony took place,

A priori, it is, of course, very much more probable that from the beginning of life there was a greater number of germs not completely alike and not equally capable of development, whether these germs came from the meteoric dust of cosmical space, or whether life developed itself from the monera of the ocean depths. But if special weight is laid upon the 'polyphyletic' origin of organisms, because it seems to offer a means of sundering man from the rest of the animal world, we shall in the next chapter have an opportunity of showing that no deeper philosophical interest depends upon this possibility. The strife of opinions may, therefore, have free course here in the apprehension and appreciation of facts. Principles are only concerned so far as the question of the law of development is concerned, which, however, does not receive its decision here. If an extreme Darwinism would so understand monophyletic descent as to deny all differences in the internal constitution of the primitive organic forms, and refer all the differences that have resulted, to natural selection without any co-operation whatever of internal causes of development, this would be, indeed, a very consistent metaphysic, but a very improbable scientific theory. On the other hand, the moderate and cautious way in which Haeckel declares monophyletic descent to be more probable, at least for the animal world, and especially for the higher forms

---

there arose in different localities numerous originally different monera, or whether many monera of the same kind arose, which only afterwards became differentiated (through slight changes in the atomistic composition of the albumen)." That Haeckel since then has gone over more and more to the one-sided assertion of monophyletic descent—for he regards as especially important the proof of the gastrula form in the calcareous sponges—we may explain as a too great predominance of the purely mor- phological point of view. Haeckel has, when speaking of the theory of individuality (Gen. Morph., i. 265 ff.), luminously distinguished between morphological and physiological individuality. If we would apply the same distinction to the doctrine of descent, there would, in our opinion, be no serious objection to make against a merely morphological monophyletism, yet we regard the question of the internal constitution and its relation to the necessary future development as still more important.

of it, is thoroughly admissible.[81] For this purpose we rest chiefly upon the doctrine of the 'centre of creation' of each single species and each genus, and this doctrine is in turn empirically supported by the observation that the often curiously marked sphere of extension of species may, as a rule, be very well explained by assuming a particular point of origin, and by examining the possibilities of migration from this point with regard to the probable earlier condition of the earth.

That in this whole doctrine there is very much that is hypothetical and doubtful does not affect its value, since we are dealing with the first foundation of a history of organisms. An exacter examination, a stricter weighing of probabilities, will here, as everywhere, come with the progress of science. On the other hand, we must remember that the whole doctrine of the unitary centre of creation, if it is not to become metaphysical and even mystical, can only be a maxim of research and a generally valid empirical observation. To a generalisation by induction it by no means lends itself, as no natural cause is conceivable which should prevent one and the same new species from proceeding from a widely spread parent form at two different points at the same time. For the same reason we must not over-estimate the support given to the monophyletic theory by the doctrine of centres of creation. The latter theory might be shown to be correct in nine cases out of ten, without its therefore following that the

---

[81] Nat. Hist. of Creat., E.T., ii. 45. The proposition there expressed, that in general monophyletic hypotheses have greater integral probability than polyphyletic, is not the simple conversion of our proposition in the text. The latter relates exclusively to the first origin of life, so far as we can judge of its conditions and conclude from these to the course of events. Haeckel, on the contrary, has in view the descent of any given existing species or hypothetical primitive form with regard to the question whether this form was originally formed in different places and with corresponding variations, or only in one place and in like form, so that, e.g., a widely dispersed occurrence of a species would have to be referred to migration, not to simultaneous origin in different places. Comp. the preceding note.

DARWINISM AND TELEOLOGY.

first origin of the simplest organisms must have proceeded from such a unitary centre.

The whole question receives, of course, another aspect if we confine ourselves strictly to the morphological point of view; for here at least causes are conceivable which might compel all organisms to run through a certain gradation of forms, all the same whether their inner nature —by which we mean primarily their chemical composition—were identical or not. Yet the difference would even then show itself in this, that the one kind of these organisms must remain constantly in the lowest stages, while the other under the influence of natural selection and of the immanent law of development would rise into higher forms.

We cannot undertake to discuss here all the numerous formally and materially interesting questions which have been raised by Darwinism and its opponents. The essential thing for us is to show how all the improvements and limitations which have been and yet may be introduced into Darwin's doctrine, must at bottom be made always on the same ground of a rational study of nature, admitting only intelligible causes. The strict application of the principle of causality, with the rejection of all vague hypotheses of forces which are drawn from mere notions, must remain the guiding principle for the whole field of natural science, and what there may be in this consistent elaboration of the mechanical cosmology unsatisfying and repulsive to our feelings will, as we shall sufficiently show, find its compensation in another sphere.

If, therefore, the opposition to Darwin proceeds in part openly, in part half unconsciously, from predilection for the old teleological view of the world, sound criticism can only in answer draw the line, that no opposition is scientifically justified which does not just as much as Darwinism itself start from the principle of the intelligibleness of the world, joined with the thorough application of the principle of causality. Wherever, therefore, in calling in the aid of a 'plan of creation' and similar notions, the idea lurks that from such source a foreign factor may be introduced into the regular course of natural forces, then we are no longer in the sphere of science, but of a confused mixture of scientific and metaphysical, or rather as a rule theological views. Every interference of a mystical power, that turns a number of molecules from the path in which they move according to the universal laws of Nature, in order to dispose and order them, as it were, upon a plan—every such interference would, in a scientific view, produce an effect which may be measured by equivalents, while it yet disturbs the series of equivalents, just like a slip of the pen in a correct equation, which spoils the whole result. The whole 'plan of creation' which we recognise, the whole result of previous scientific discoveries, this beautiful harmony of an all-embracing equal and unitary law, would be broken down like a fragile toy. And wherefore? In place of an as yet imperfect but real understanding to patch on a fragment from a view of the world on which only a feeble analogue of an explanation, only a classification of phenomena by empty notions and gross anthropomorphic phantasies, is possible.

All these inadmissible violations of the causal series may be ultimately referred to the nature of the false teleology on which we shall still have a few words to say. Meanwhile there is also a teleology which is not only compatible with Darwinism, but is almost identical with it, and there are ideal developments and speculative extensions of this correct teleology which lie in a transcendental sphere, but for this very reason can never come into conflict with the natural sciences.

If Darwinism, as compared with the gross anthropomorphic teleology, appears as a theory of chance, this is only its thoroughly justified negative side. Adaptations proceed from the conservation of relatively fortuitous formations, but these formations can only be called fortuitous so far as we can assign no reason why this particular form appears at this moment. In the great whole everything, and therefore even the appearance of those formations which by adaptation and transmission become the basis of new creations, is necessary and determined by eternal laws. These laws indeed do not immediately produce what is adapted, but they produce a multitude of variations, a multitude of germs, in which the special case of what is adapted, of the persistent, is perhaps relatively very rare. We have shown that this mode of forming adaptations, judged by *human* views of adaptation, is very low; but man is just the most complicated of all the innumerable organisms that we know, and is furnished with an infinitely complex apparatus, in order to meet special needs in the most special and peculiar way. The mechanism which accomplishes this remains hidden from his own consciousness, and human or quasi-human activity seems therefore to rough and unscientific observation as an immediate effect of force exerted by mere thought upon its object, while it is, in fact, only that which is most subtly effected. If we get rid of the errors arising from this source, the mechanism by which nature attains its ends is through its *universality* at least as high, as human purposefulness through its *rank* as the most perfect special case. It might be easily demonstrated that even in the highest actions of man this principle of the conservation of what is relatively best adapted still plays its part, everywhere co-operating with the most subtle apparatus of a specific reaction. Even the great discoveries and inventions, which form the basis of higher civilisation and intellectual progress, are still subordinate to that universal law of the conservation of the strongest, while they are at the same time tested by the most delicate methods of science and art.

The whole question of correct teleology may be reduced to this, that we inquire how far something may be found in this arrangement of nature, combined with the mechanically operating law of development, that can be compared to a 'cosmical plan.' If we carefully discard anything pointing to a humanly scheming 'architect of the universe,' the logical core of the question remains: Is this world a special case among innumerable equally conceivable worlds, which would remain eternally chaotic or eternally inert, or must we assert that whatever might be the constitution of the beginning of things on the Darwinian principle, there must finally result order, beauty, perfection, in the same manner in which we see them? We may also extend this question, and doubt whether an ordered and self-developing world would necessarily be intelligible to the human mind, which needs definite classes and species of things for its guidance, or whether such a multiplicity of forms and phenomena might not be conceivable, that it must necessarily remain unintelligible to a being organised after the manner of man.

It will doubtless be admitted that our world may be called a special case in this sense, for however possible it may be to deduce all existence mathematically from simple assumptions, yet positive assumptions must be made, and such assumptions as make the development of our world possible, while without this consideration they might be quite different. In this respect even Empedokles is not without teleological elements, for however consistently he makes the adaptation of the individual arise from the mere trial of all possible combinations, yet the play of combination and separation on the whole necessarily results from the properties of the four elements and the two moving forces. Let us only suppose the latter omitted, and we have eternal inertia or eternal chaos. It is just the same with the system of the Atomists. Here we may indeed use the doctrine of the infinity of worlds, in order to make the special case of our world relatively accidental, yet the necessary bases of an intelligible world are found in the fundamental assumptions as to the properties of the atoms and their mode of motion. Let us suppose, *e.g.*, a world with only round and smooth atoms, and no part of that fixed order of things which we see around us can be formed. Here, in fact, conscious application has been made of the principle of the intelligibleness of the world, in order to make the world a special case, in the very subtle and profoundly conceived theory of the limits to the variety in the forms of atoms.

In the Kantian philosophy, therefore, which has sounded these questions deeper than any other, the first stage of teleology is directly identified with the principle which we have repeatedly spoken of as the axiom of the intelligibleness of the world, and Darwinism in the wider sense of the word, *i.e.*, the doctrine of a scientifically intelligible theory of descent, not only does not stand in contradiction with this teleology, but, on the contrary, is its necessary presupposition. The 'formal' finality of the world is nothing else than its adaptation to our understanding, and this adaptation just as necessarily demands the unconditional dominion of the law of causality without mystical interferences of any kind, as, on the other hand, it presupposes the comprehensibility of things by their ordering into definite forms.[82]

Kant, indeed, goes on to lay down a second stage of teleology, the 'objective;' and here Kant himself, as in the doctrine of free will, has not everywhere strictly drawn the line of what is critically admissible; but even this doctrine does not come into conflict with the scientific taste of natural research. On this view we regard organisms as beings in which every part is throughout deter-

[82] The interpretation of the Kantian teleology here put forward is indeed not the usual one. We follow partly our own studies, but partly the recently published luminous investigation of August Stadler, Kant's Teleologie u. ihre erkenntniss-theoretische Bedeutung: Berlin, 1874. If Stadler, perhaps, here and there goes too far in establishing an entire agreement between Kant and the principles of natural science and under-estimates real weaknesses in Kant, on the other hand, the proof that only this interpretation answers to the principles of the transcendental philosophy and reduces the contradictions in Kant to a minimum is completely established by Stadler. As we cannot here go further into detail, we simply refer to this treatise.

mined by every other part, and we shall thus be brought, by means of the rational idea of an absolute reciprocal determination of the parts of the universe, to regard them as if they were the product of an intelligence. Kant regards this conception as indemonstrable and as demonstrating nothing, but he wrongly regards it as at the same time a necessary consequence of the organisation of our reason. For the natural sciences, however, this 'objective' teleology, too, can never be anything but a heuristic principle; by it nothing is explained, and natural science only extends as far as the mechanical and causal explanation of things. If Kant believes that in the case of organisms this explanation will never be sufficient, this view—which is, moreover, not a necessary part of the system—is by no means to be understood as if the mechanical explanation of nature can ever strike upon a fixed limit, on the other side of which the teleological explanation would begin; rather Kant conceives the mechanical explanation of organisms as a process running on to infinity, in which there will always be an insoluble residuum, just as in the mechanical explanation of the universe. This view, however, does not conflict with the principle of scientific research, even though men of science may be for the most part inclined to form other ideas on this point, which lies beyond our experience.

For similar reasons Fechner's teleology also is scientifically not open to attack. He makes the principle of 'tendency to stability' mediate between causality and teleology, since he supposes that the universal laws of nature themselves of necessity gradually produce greater perfection, and in this he finds a teleological disposition of the universe which he further brings also into connexion with a creative intelligence. The principle of tendency to stability itself is at once a scientific hypothesis and a metaphysical idea, and it must submit to criticism from both sides; the rest consists of articles of faith which have their basis beyond the sphere of experience.

All the grosser and more palpable, on the contrary, does the false teleology appear in Hartmann's 'Philosophie des Unbewussten,'—that teleology which creates mechanical work out of nothing, and thereby destroys the causal connexion of nature. Hartmann protests, indeed, against the view that his 'finality' is "something existing in addition to or even despite causality," but his application of 'finality,' and especially his remarkable establishing of it by a supposed calculus of probability, show at once that this very interruption of the strict causal connexion of nature forms the basis of his whole philosophy, which is a complete return to the standpoint of the 'charcoal-burner' and of savage peoples.[83]

This apparent contradiction is easily explained by the way in which Hartmann distinguishes between mind and matter, mental and material causes. "Very far," says he of his teleology, "from denying the absolute validity of the law of causality, it rather presupposes it, and that not only for matter and matter, but also between mind and matter, and mind and mind." Immediately afterwards he very calmly develops the hypothesis that the efficient cause of any event, called M, is *not entirely* based in the concurrently operating material circumstances; that we must "further" look for the sufficient cause of M in the intellectual sphere.

The difficulty of a complete analysis of the concurrent material causes gives Hartmann no trouble. The cases are very rare "where the essential conditions of the phenomenon lie beyond a narrow circuit, and all the unessential circumstances need not be regarded." We look, therefore, in the "narrow circuit" with as much intelligence and science as we happen to possess; use, perhaps, a microscope, a thermometer, or something of the kind, and what we have not thus discovered does not exist or is unessential. If, after this, we have not found the

[83] Comp. Phil. des Unbewussten: zur Annahme von Zwecken in der Einleitendes. ii. Wie kommen wir Natur?

complete explanation of M, then "devil-devil" is at work.[84]

That even in the "narrow circuit" an infinity of forces and arrangements of a material kind is at work we must not assume; otherwise there would be no 'Philosophy of the Unconscious.' To the man of science it seems the proper thing in such cases simply to say that the physical cause of M is not yet discovered, and in the whole history of his never-resting science he will find the impulse to new researches, which ever lead him a step nearer to the goal. The Australian savage, however, and the Philosopher of the Unconscious halt where their power of natural explanation ceases, and attribute all the rest to a new principle, by which a single word very satisfactorily explains everything. The limit at which the physical explanation ceases and supernatural apparitions replace it is different in the two cases; but the scientific method is the same. To the Australian black, *e.g.*, the spark of the Leyden jar is probably devil-devil, while Hartmann can explain it naturally; but the method of transition from the one principle to the other is entirely the same. The leaf that turns to the sun is for Hartmann what the Leyden jar is for the Australian black. While the indefatigableness of inquirers in this very department is daily making new discoveries, all pointing to mechanical causes of these phenomena, the Philosopher of the Unconscious has here stopped his botanical studies at a point, as it happens, which leaves the whole mystery untouched,

[84] Waitz, Anthropol. der Naturvölker, fortges. v. Gerland, vi. Th., Leipz. 1872, S. 797; comp. Oscar Schmidt, Doctrine of Descent and Darwinism, 1873, E.T. 1875, p. 301. —The aborigines of Australia refer everything which they cannot explain to the devil-devil; "manifestly only a name, derived from the English devil, for a deity of whom they have not preserved any distinct conception." With justice Schmidt condemns the shallowness of this evidence for the hypothesis of earlier better developed, but now forgotten, religious ideas. The reference of all that is inexplicable to devil-devil is obviously rather the rudiment of a philosophy which has no need of individual deities. Devil-devil is to the Australian black probably omniscient, omnipotent, and so on, without therefore being a person; exactly like the "Unconscious."

and here too, of course, is the limit where the fantastic reflex of one's own ignorance, the "intellectual cause," comes in and explains without further trouble what is still inexplicable.[85]

That Hartmann's intellectual causes are identical with the devil-devil of the Australian black scarcely needs proof. Science knows only one kind of mind, that is, human; and where we speak of 'intellectual causes' in a scientific sense, it is always understood that these manifest themselves through human bodies. Any other kind of 'mind' we may assume is transcendental and belongs to the sphere of ideas. If we have forced our way through Materialism to Idealism, we are entitled to declare everything existing to be intellectual in its nature so far as it is primarily our conception; but so long as we still distinguish between mind and matter, we have not the right to invent minds and intellectual causes which are not given to us.

[85] It is not uninteresting to compare the wholly unscientific way in which Hartmann discusses 'Instinct' in the vegetable kingdom with the latest scientific inquiries into the phenomena here in question of the growth of plants, heliotropism, opening and shutting of flowers, curling of tendrils, &c. The uncommonly instructive discoveries of Sachs, Hofmeister, Pfeffer, Frank, Batalin, Famintzin, Prillieux, and others, have, without exception, been reached through the presupposition of a strictly mechanical basis of these facts in the vegetable life, and this presupposition has in many cases been already brilliantly confirmed. We mention only briefly that heliotropism has been referred to retardation of growth by light, and consequent concave curvature; that the embracing of objects by tendrils rests upon an also experimentally demonstrable irritability of the more weakly growing side; that the day and night position of the leaves of Oxalis rests upon an effect of light on particular points of inclination, and that the plant (despite the omniscience of the Unconscious) allows itself to be deceived if we allow a special light to fall exclusively on these points of inclination, &c. Compare with this the observation of Knight, who grew plants on the radial side of a rapidly revolving wheel, and found that the chief roots grew in the direction of the centrifugal force; further, the experiments of Sachs on the influence of moisture in the soil on the direction of the roots. (Comp. Sachs, Grundz. d. Pflanzenphysiol., Leipz. 1873; Hofmeister, Allg. Morphol. d. Gewächse, Leipz. 1868; Pfeffer, Physiol. Unters., Leipz. 1873; Naturf. 1871, No. 49; Botan. Z. 1871, No. 11 and 12; Naturf. 1872, No. 4, &c.) What would have become of all these valuable investigations if the respective inquirers had referred the phenomena to the teleological interference of the 'unconscious' or of any other phantom?

As concerns the human mind, we will for the time assume that the view may be defended which makes mechanical work disappear in the brain and transform itself into 'mind,' as well as conversely makes a definite amount of work arise from the mind. That we do not share this view, but rather adopt an uninterrupted causal series of material phenomena, has already been sufficiently shown; yet let us here assume the contrary, that we may at least reach an example of 'intellectual causes' producing material phenomena. It can now be the less admissible to generalise this hypothetical cause, as all analogy is wanting between the phenomena in nature and those in man. We may well recall here Du Bois-Reymond's challenge—that if he is to accept a world-soul, its brain should first be shown him somewhere in the universe. Why does this challenge seem so strange? Simply because with regard to those things in nature in which an anthropomorphic conception most easily suggests itself, we are not at all accustomed to think of the brain, or of the molecular movements within it. It is rather human hands that we make the hands of God; it is the vital manifestations of imaginary beings which interfere with the course of things on the analogy of human actions, not of human brain-movements. The believer sees in the series of events "the hand of God," not a molecular movement in the brain of the world-soul. Savage peoples imagine ghostly beings of superhuman-human kind everywhere present. From these ideas, and not from the theory of the brain, have proceeded all the notions of immaterial causes; and the whole hypothesis of an "intellectual sphere" of the effects which we observe is nothing but a notion borrowed from these varied creations of faith and superstition. Science knows no such "intellectual sphere," and can therefore borrow no causes from it. What she cannot explain naturally on the principles of the mechanical cosmology she simply does not explain at all. It remains for the present an unsolved problem.

But the charcoal-burner's creed and false philosophy have at all times agreed in explaining the inexplicable by means of words, behind which there is nothing but the more crudely or more subtly conceived sphere of phantoms, which is but the fantastic reflex of our ignorance.

Upon these principles rests now the possibility of a very interesting calculus of probabilities. To establish it we need a complete disjunction. If under "intellectual causes" we were to imagine something definite, such as actions of a human or anthropomorphically conceived divine being, the disjunction would not be safe. There might very well be causes of a third kind as, *e.g.*, enchantment, planetary influences, spiritualism, &c., all of which from this standpoint would deserve serious consideration. But so soon as we understand by "intellectual" simply everything that at present cannot be shown to be material, the disjunction is complete. Any as yet undiscovered material causes fall away, and all that remains is devil-devil.

Now it can be shown that the probability that devil-devil is in play is in all natural phenomena equal to certainty. Hartmann does not apply it to all natural phenomena, but only to that portion of them which belongs to the philosophy of the unconscious. The method, however, is just as simple as its universal applicability is evident. We call the probability that M has a material cause $\frac{1}{x}$, then the probability of an "intellectual" cause is $1 - \frac{1}{x}$. If, now, we cannot find the material causes, $\frac{1}{x}$ becomes infinitely small, and the converse becomes a certainty which is expressed by 1.

The thing takes a still more beautiful shape if we consider one particular natural phenomenon. Here, namely, we have the advantage that we can resolve every such phenomenon into a series of various partial phenomena, which all, as is fitting, admit a doubt whether they too have a purely physical foundation. Then, relying upon a well-known elementary principle in the calculus of probabilities, we may be bold without danger. We may place the probability that the partial phenomena, taken singly, come about from material causes pretty high; since the probability of their coincidence will still be very slight, as it is the product of the separate probabilities. If, for instance, we have 15 partial phenomena, let us put the probability of a physical cause $= 0.9$. The man of science will indeed be inclined to put it at once $= 1$; but that is only because he takes into account also the as yet unobserved natural causes, and because he has drawn from the previous course of natural research the inductive conclusion that when inquiry has been carried far enough everything will finally be explained from the ordinary laws of nature. With such a presupposition the artifice of the philosophy of the unconscious is no longer possible. But if we stick to the probability 0.9, the probability for the continued phenomenon on the above assumption will be the fifteenth power of this, and that is a very small fraction against which the contradictory opposite, the 'intellectual cause,' stands in the *éclat* of a very considerable probability.

In like manner it may be shown that a man cannot win at dice ten times in succession without the help of Fortuna or of a *spiritus familiaris*. Il n'y a que le premier pas qui coûte. Let us assert with simple confidence the disjunction that in each stroke of luck Fortuna either co-operates or does not. Let us put the probability of winning without the aid of Fortuna in the individual case $= \frac{1}{2}$, and we immediately have the tenth power of this fraction for the probability of a tenfold repetition of the success. The co-operation of Fortuna now comes close to certainty.

Any one who knows the calculus of probabilities somewhat more thoroughly knows that the probability of any particular series of equally possible events is in itself equally great; that, therefore, the case, *e.g.*, in which our player wins in the 1st cast, loses in the 2nd, 3rd, and 4th, wins again in the 5th and 6th, loses in the 7th, wins in the 8th and 9th, loses again in the 10th, is every whit as improbable as the case of his winning ten times in succession.[86] The reality itself, where it depends upon many individual circumstances, or where it is a particular case among many possibilities, appears always, regarded *a priori*, as extremely improbable, which, however, does not affect its reality. The simple explanation is, that the entire doctrine of probability is an abstraction from the efficient causes which we happen not to know, while cer-

[86] Comp. on this the lucid discussions of Laplace, Essai Philosophique sur les Probabilités, 6ᵉ Principe.

When the editor of the German translation (Langsdorf, Heidelberg, 1819) makes an objection at this very point and (S. 20 *n.*) blames the division of possible cases into ordinary and extraordinary, because the latter are identical with the less probable, he has simply failed to understand the force of this very subtle psychological observation. The object is to show that amongst certain equally improbable (and, quite abstractly considered, also equally 'extraordinary') cases we immediately recognise and appreciate some in their entire 'extraordinariness,' *e.g.*, as a case which only occurs once in millions of times, while others lose themselves psychologically in a long series of similar cases, and, therefore, produce the impression of ordinariness, although their probability is just as little as that of the former cases. Thus it is with the example given in the text of a player who wins on one occasion ten times in succession, on another wins and loses by turn in a definitely determined order.

Laplace, moreover, brings this distinction into connexion with the inference backwards from a phenomenon to its causes, and this is, be it said in passing, the point in the calculus of probability from which Hartmann should have started in his investigation, instead of keeping in a clumsy and obviously perverse way to Laplace's third principle, from which here no result whatever can follow but that complicated cases are in fact complicated cases. In the cases under the sixth principle, however, the remarkable or extraordinary cases are always those which in a measure have the type of human purposefulness about them, even though it is only in a certain purely external symmetry; as, *e.g.*, if amongst a million numbers the figures 666666 should appear. Here, that is, we overlook at a glance the entire relation of numerator and denominator in the fraction of probability, and are at the same time reminded of the possibility that some one has put these figures together *intentionally*. And this latter impression is specially overpowering when the particular result has a peculiar significance. Thus, *e.g.*, if the letters EUROPA appear exactly in this order,

tain general conditions are known to us on which we base our calculation. When the dice has received its impulse and is hovering in the air, it is already determined by the laws of mechanics which side will ultimately remain uppermost, while for our judgment *a priori* the probability in favour of this side as for every other is $\frac{1}{6}$.

If there are a million balls in an urn and I put my hand in to withdraw one, the probability for any particular ball is only a millionth, and yet one, and that a particular one, must of necessity be drawn. The fraction of probability here means nothing more than the degree of our subjective ignorance as to what will happen, and which is at the same time not in the least more improbable than any other meaningless combination. But the numerator of the fraction of probability here is $=1$, and the denominator $=$ the number of the possible combinations of these six letters, and incomparably greater, if we suppose that they were drawn blindly from a compositor's case. Here again we must first of all observe that the reality of such chances, and, therefore, also their general possibility, can by no means be affected by the calculus of probabilities. This is the point which Diderot had already remarked in the 21st chapter of the 'Pensées Philosophiques,' when he shows that the origin of the 'Iliad,' or of the 'Henriade,' by a mere fortuitous combination of letters, is not only not impossible, but is, in fact, very probable, so soon as we can increase the number of experiments to infinity. In reality, however, we compare in these cases the extraordinarily small probability of fortuitous formation with the incomparably greater probability of voluntary formation. Here, now, in fact, the temptation is very great to assume with Hartmann a phantom for all those who believe in phantoms. Nay, even the acute mathematician Poisson says, in treating this point in sect. 41 of his 'Théorie du Calcul des Probabilités :' "If we have observed a fact, which in and for itself had very slight probability, and it presents something symmetrical or remarkable, we are quite naturally led to the idea that it is not the effect of chance, or, more generally, of a cause which would give it this slight probability, but that it arises from a mightier cause, as, *e.g.*, the will of a being which had a definite purpose therein." Here the thing is treated with such mathematical generality that the very natural fallacy of the savage who believes in a phantom and the correct conclusion of the scientifically trained mind are embraced by the same expression. The latter, however, despite all allurements, will not, on analogy, bring into calculation any such 'beings' as are not given him, and given him are only man and the higher animals as acting towards ends. He may indeed carry his reflections beyond this as to a purposeful disposition of the universe, but no single case of a combination, however *a priori* wonderful, will induce him to assume the mystic interferences of a 'being' of which he has no conception.

it is just the same in the instances which Hartmann borrows from organic nature. That, *e.g.*, among the natural causes of sight certain nerve-cords, which are sensitive to light, proceed from the brain and spread over the retina, is a fact, the conditions of which again are so complicated and still so unknown to us, that it would be ludicrous to speak here of a 'probability' $= 0.9$, or even 0.25. The probability that this happens accidentally is rather equal to nil, and yet the fact is real, and, as every thinking student of nature will assume, also necessary by the universal laws of nature. Here because of the 'improbability,' which is, after all, only the mathematical expression of our subjective ignorance, to embrace a principle which lies beyond natural research is simply to abandon science and to sacrifice sound method to a phantom.

A closer examination of the 'Philosophy of the Unconscious' is no part of our plan. The way from the point where we leave it to false teleology through the interference of the 'unconscious' is obvious, and we have only to do with the foundations of the new metaphysical edifice. That in our view the value of metaphysical systems does not depend upon their demonstrative foundation, which rests entirely upon illusion, we have already sufficiently shown. If the 'Philosophy of the Unconscious' should ever gain so much influence upon the art and literature of our time and thus become the expression of the predominant intellectual tendency, as was once the case with Schelling and Hegel, it would, despite its mischievous foundation, be legitimatised as a national philosophy of the first rank. The period which should be marked by it would be a period of intellectual decay; but even decay has its great philosophers, as Plotinos at the close of the Greek philosophy. In any case, however, it remains a remarkable fact that so soon after the campaign of our Materialists against the whole of philosophy, a system could find so much acceptance, which opposes itself more decidedly to the positive sciences than any of the earlier systems,[87] and which in this respect repeats all the errors of Schelling and Hegel in a much coarser and more palpable shape.

[87] It will hardly be necessary for our readers once more to disturb the illusion that the 'Philosophie des Unbewussten' contains "speculative results on the inductive scientific method." There can hardly be another modern book in which the scientific material swept together stands in such flagrant contrast to all the essential principles of scientific method.

THIRD SECTION.

THE NATURAL SCIENCES
Continued.

MAN AND THE SOUL.

THIRD SECTION.

THE NATURAL SCIENCES
Continued.

MAN AND THE SOUL.

CHAPTER I.

THE RELATION OF MAN TO THE ANIMAL WORLD.

THROUGH the whole History of Materialism runs this marked feature that cosmical questions gradually lose in interest, while anthropological questions excite an increasing eagerness of controversy. It may, indeed, appear that this anthropological aspect of Materialism reached its highest point in the last century; for the magnificent discoveries of modern times in the fields of chemistry, physics, geology, and astronomy have brought forward a series of questions upon which Materialism had to take up a distinct attitude. This might, however, happen without any need for essentially new principles or startling and strife-provoking views. On the other hand, anthropology, too, has made the most astonishing progress; partly, it is true, in departments which have little to do with the problem of Materialism. We have got rid of the phantoms of disease, have begun to shake a little medical ecclesiasticism, and by means of comparative and experimental physiology have reached surprising results as to the functions of the most important internal organs. In those departments, however, which stand most closely related to the questions of Materialism, recent discoveries have shown the inadequacy of earlier conceptions, without substituting a new theory upon which Materialism might securely rest itself. The nervous system in its activity is no longer such a mystery to us as it was—or, indeed, must have been—for the Materialists of last century. The brain was in some respects better understood than before; it was with gigantic industry anatomised, measured, weighed, analysed, microscopically examined, studied in morbid conditions, compared with the brain of animals, and in animals submitted to experiment; but as to the physiological connexion and the mode of action of its parts, we have never succeeded in propounding a comprehensive hypothesis; there is all the more idle talk, and in this, of course, the Materialists are not behindhand. A department which offered them a better opportunity is that of molecular change, as indeed generally the application of physics and chemistry to the functions of the living organism. Here, indeed, many of the results of professedly exact research still call for a severely winnowing criticism: yet, on the whole, we may consider successful the attempt to exhibit the living man, as he is externally given us, like all organic and inorganic bodies, as a product of the forces operating throughout nature. An extremely important department, the physiology of the sense-organs, has, on the other hand, produced decisive grounds for the refutation of Materialism; but it has, as yet, been little drawn into the debate, because the opponents of Materialism partly cannot employ this kind of refutation for their purposes, but partly because they do not possess the requisite knowledge. Meanwhile the attempt has also been made to submit psychology to a scientific, and even a mathematical and mechanical mode of treatment. In psycho-physics and moral statistics sciences have been established which appear to lend support to this effort. Since the Materialistic controversy has recently been often described precisely as a battle for the soul, we shall have in the course of this section to consider all these departments.

First of all, however, we must deal with the question of the origin and age of mankind, and the relation of man to the animal world, a question which at the time of the controversy excited by Büchner and Vogt was most eagerly discussed, but which since then, through the remarkable energy of research in all those concerned, has been in some measure rescued from the caprice of subjective opinions and hazardous hypotheses. This question is generally treated in intimate connexion with Darwin's theory of the origin of organisms, almost, in fact, as its most interesting point, and, strictly speaking, as its highest result. So much now is clear, that the strictly scientific interest of the theory of descent coincides with the carrying out of the general principle for the origin of organisms. That man is part of the great chain of this origin is, from a scientific standpoint, quite obvious; but so far as the rise of human civilisation and intellectual life requires a special explanation, it is quite natural that investigations on this point are completed even in special sciences in the closest connexion with the entire sphere of anthropological questions. And so even the history of the world is treated meanwhile as no part of natural history, however clearly we may trace that the principles of the struggle for existence here too play their part.

The dualism of mind and nature may be critically resolved or speculatively "surmounted;" we may, from the standpoint of natural science, assert as an axiom that ultimately the intellectual life also must be capable of being understood as a product of the general laws of nature; but we cannot prevent a distinction being made between nature and mind so long as we have different starting-points for the knowledge of the two spheres and different standards for the appreciation of their phenomena. That man only raised himself from an animal pre-existence by internal development, and so first became man, was treated by Kant as obvious; but he regarded the appearance of the idea of the 'ego' as the true moment of the creation of man.[1] So that even now the main problem will always remain that of the primitive history of the mind and of civilisation, since the proceeding of man from the animal world is scientifically obvious, while, on the contrary, his intellectual life still remains a problem, even though all the consequences of the theory of descent are conceded. At the same time, to make the true philosophical view intelligible to wider circles, it will be necessary to explain and clear the way by some preliminary discussion, especially in the sphere of geology and palæontology.

---

[1] Comp., *inter alia*, the following passages:—Anthropol., § 1: "That man can conceive the Ego, raises him infinitely above all other creatures living on the earth. Through this he is a *person*, and by virtue of the unity of consciousness in all the changes which may affect him, one and the same person, *i.e.*, a being entirely distinct in rank and dignity from *things*, such as are the irrational animals which we can dispose of as we will." Further, the 'note' to the essay Muthmasslicher Anfang d. Menschengesch. (1786), Hart. iv. 321: "From this account of early human history, it results that man's departure from the paradise which reason represents as the first abode of his kind was nothing else but the transition from the savagery of a merely animal creature to humanity, from the go-cart of instinct to the guidance of reason; in a word, from the guardianship of nature into the condition of freedom." In the review of Moscati's treatise (1771), Hart. ii. 429 ff., Kant admits the grounds assigned by the Italian anatomist for the original four-footed state of man. The concluding words are: "We see from this that the first care of nature was that man, as an animal, should be preserved for himself and his kind, and for this end the attitude which is most suitable for his internal structure, the position of the embryo, and its preservation in danger, was the four-footed; but that a germ of reason was implanted in him, by which, when it is developed, he is intended for the social state, and by means of which he adopts for good the attitude most adapted to this, viz., the two-footed, through which he gains, on the one hand, an infinite advantage over the animals, but must also put up with the inconveniences arising from his thus so proudly raising his head above his old comrades." Not quite so decided as to the four-footed gait is the passage in the Anthropol. II. E., Hart. vii. 647, where Kant discusses the "technische Anlage" of man derived from the animal state, and finally raises the question again: "Whether he is by nature a social or a solitary and neighbour-shunning animal, of which the latter is the most probable alternative."

The dogmas of the terrestrial revolutions, of the successive appearance of the creatures, of the late appearance of man, were from the first opposed to Materialism and still more to Pantheism. While Buffon, De la Mettrie, and later the German Philosophers of Nature, with Goethe at their head, eagerly embraced the idea of the unity of creation, and attempted to develop throughout the higher from the lower forms, it was notably Cuvier, who, as the most profound master of details, came forward to oppose these unitary tendencies. He was afraid of Pantheism. Goethe most completely represented this very Pantheistic and unitary philosophy; still earlier he had had differences with Camper and Blumenbach as to the Wormian bones, which were supposed to distinguish the ape from man, and until his death he followed the controversies as to the unity of all organisms with the greatest attention. Thus he informs us of a malicious utterance of Cuvier's: "I know well that for certain minds behind this theory of analogies there may lurk, at least confusedly, another very old theory, which, long ago refuted, has been sought out again by some Germans in order to favour the Pantheistic theory which they call the Philosophy of Nature."[2]

This pride of positive knowledge, as compared with a comprehensive survey of the whole, the zeal of the observer who distinguishes as compared with the comprehensive thinkers, made Cuvier blind to the great logical difference between the absence of proof and the proof of absence of a phenomenon. No fossil men were known, and he delivered the axiom that there cannot be any.

Such an expression must strike us the more, as a negative proposition in natural history generally has only a subordinate value. Considering the extremely small portion of the earth's surface which had then been examined, it would have been very puzzling to explain how so

---

[2] Goethe in his 'Zur Natur-Wissenschaft im Allgemeinen;' Principes de Philosophie-Zoologique, par Geoffroy de St. Hilaire, towards the end of the first section.

general a statement could be justified, if its connexion with the favourite theory of successive creation did not afford an explanation. But successive creation was a sort of modification of the biblical doctrine of the creative days, which even now, when the facts render it quite untenable, finds many followers. Vogt, in his lively polemic, contrasts the theory of those days and the discoveries of the present so pregnantly and comprehensively, that we cannot refrain from introducing his picture, despite some superfluous pleasantries:—

"It is scarcely thirty years since Cuvier said, There is no fossil ape and cannot be any; and to-day we speak of fossil apes as of old acquaintances, and bring fossil man not only amongst diluvial forms, but even into the latest tertiary formations, though some obstinate people may maintain that Cuvier's assertion is an utterance of genius and cannot be overturned. It is hardly twenty years since I learned from Agassiz: transitional strata, palæozoic formations—kingdom of fishes; there are no reptiles in this period, and cannot be any, because it would be contrary to the plan of creation; secondary formations (Trias, Jura, chalk)—kingdom of reptiles; there are no mammals, and cannot be any, for the same reason; tertiary strata —kingdom of mammals; there are no men, and cannot be any; present creation — kingdom of man. What is become of this plan of creation with its exclusivenesses? Reptiles in the Devonian strata, reptiles in the coal, reptiles in the Dyas—farewell, kingdom of fish! Mammals in the Jura, mammals in Purbeck chalk, which some reckon as the lowest chalk formation—goodbye, kingdom of reptiles! Men in the highest tertiary strata, men in the diluvial forms—*au revoir*, kingdom of mammals!"[3]

It is remarkable that in the very next year after Cuvier's and Goethe's death a discovery was made known which would have alone sufficed to upset the theory of the former, if the plague of authority and blind prejudice were

[3] Vorlesungen über den Menschen: Giessen, 1863, ii. 269.

not much commoner than simple receptivity of facts. This was the discovery of Dr. Schmerling in the bone-caves of Engis and Engihoul, near Liège. Some years later Boucher de Perthes began his restless researches for human remains in the diluvial formations, which were only rewarded after long pursuit by the discoveries in the valley of the Somme. These results were only recognised at last after a long controversy, and from that time the opinion of science gradually changed. A new series of extremely interesting discoveries at Aurignac, Lherm, and in Neanderthal on the Düssel, coincided in time with the gradual victory of Lyell's view of the formation of the earth's crust, and with Darwin's new doctrine of the origin of species. With the changed views of specialists many earlier notices were brought forward and combined with the recent discoveries. The joint result was, that, in fact, human remains were extant, the structure and position of which proved that our race existed together with those earlier species of the bear, the hyena, and other mammals, which are named after the caves where their remains are generally found.

As to the age, however, to be assigned to these remains, such varying and discrepant suppositions have been made, that we can gather nothing from them but the great uncertainty of all modes of calculation yet tried. Ten years ago the general tendency was to the assumption of periods running to hundreds of thousands of years; but at present a strong reaction has set in, although not only has the material for diluvial man considerably increased, but traces have been obtained of the existence of our race in the tertiary period.[4]

[4] Vierteljahrs-Rev. d. Fortschr. d. Naturw. hg. von d. Red. der Gäa (Dr. H. Klein), I. Bd. 1873, S. 77 f. "Even though the bones of the Elephas meridionalis, found by Desnoyers in the tertiary sand of the Somme valley, with obvious marks, can claim only a doubtful importance, since Lyell has shown conclusively that similar marks, due to rodent animals, are produced in the deposits of that district, yet the marks demonstrated by Delaunay on two ribs of the Halitherium, an extinct sea-cow of the later tertiary formation, cannot be referred to a

In the cave of Cro-Magnon [5] were found (in 1868) human remains of five different individuals, together with the bones of a great bear, of the reindeer, and other animals of the diluvial epoch. The peculiarities of these human skeletons pointed to a race of athletic force, savage wildness, but at the same time of highly developed brain. In some deeper strata of the same cave were found stone implements and other traces of human activity, which must partly have belonged to a considerably older race. At Hohlenfels, not far from Blaubergen,[6] Professor Fraas discovered (in 1870) an ancient abode of men who hunted and devoured three different kinds of bears, amongst them the cave-bear. In the same cave are found numerous remains of the reindeer, whose horns were manufactured by flint knives into tools. Even a lion, which in size must have greatly surpassed our present African lion, had fallen before the rude weapons of these cave-dwellers. Rhinoceroses and elephants were amongst their contemporaries.

The very discoverer, however, of these memorials of the past is one of the chief advocates of short periods of time. With great sagacity Fraas is still seeking everywhere in ancient and medieval traditions for a shadowy recollection of the social condition of this cave-epoch and the relations with the then existing animals. In fact, the notion of separate periods of thousands of years for the mammoth, the cavê-bear, the reindeer, appears untenable.

later period, but obviously date from a time when the bones were not yet petrified. Abbé Bourgeois found near Pont-Leroy beneath the marly chalk of Beauce a layer of pebbles which had been undoubtedly worked by human hands (cit. Mort. Materiaux, 2 Ser. v. 297). It is well known how difficult it sometimes is to decide whether we are dealing with natural or artificial products. In the case before us, however, Lartet, Mortillet, Worsae, and other experienced inquirers, are unanimously of opinion that the flint-stones of Thenay, near Pont-Leroy, have been worked by human hands, and that they come from an undisturbed position belonging to the middle tertiary period."

Comp. l. c., S. 81, on Tardy's remarkable find, "who discovered near Aurillac, together with fossil remains of the Dinotherium, a rudely hewn stone knife, which must have been made in the meiocene period."

[5] Vierteljahrs-Rev., i. 99 ff.
[6] L. c., i. 102 ff.

All these creatures have lived together in Central Europe, though one race may have disappeared earlier than another. The preservation or destruction of their bones seems to be almost solely determined by the degree of moisture of their situs, and their state affords no indication of their age. If Fraas, through his peculiar combination of geological criticism and mythological or etymological tradition, comes down to periods which are within the limits of the 6000 years of the biblical cosmogony, nothing is to be said against it so far as his arguments are good. The entire independence of natural science from this tradition must show itself not merely in admitting in astronomical and geological theories whatever periods of time we may require, but also in our contenting ourselves, without regard to the smile of triumph in the enemies of free science, with periods of a few thousand years, if the facts point to them. Free inquiry no more suffers a real injury in this way than Christian faith on its inner side receives a support which is indispensable for its continuance. At the same time, we must here again recall to mind that it is logically quite inadmissible to treat large numbers as in themselves improbable, while in doubtful cases, as a rule, the greater number has the greater probability on its side. The proof must be alleged for the minimum, and from any such proof the considertions which Fraas has adduced from tradition in language and story are still far removed.

The decisive word in this question must in all probability be spoken by astronomy. Already the traces of the glacial epoch are brought in two different ways into connexion with astronomical facts: first, with the periodical variation in the obliquity of the ecliptic, and, next, with the changes in the eccentricity of the earth's orbit. While the latter explanation removes the ice-age, at least 200,000, if not 800,000 years, from the present, the former brings us to a period of only 21,000 years, within which now the northern and then the southern hemisphere of the earth would have its ice-age.[7] Here, then, the different views must in time be brought to an inexpugnable decision whether these changes could or could not exercise so profound an influence upon the climatic conditions of the earth. Should the result be a negative one, there would then remain only the terrestrial changes in the height of the continents and of the sea, the course of cold and warm sea-currents, &c., to serve as explanation, when, of course, our expectation of an exact chronology of these changes would become very faint. Moreover, we must observe that not only might the two astronomical causes of an ice-age exist together, but also that a co-operation of these with terrestrial changes is to be seriously considered. Let us assume, *e.g.*, that the northern hemisphere had a maximum of cold some 11,000 years ago, then in the period of transition from that state of things to the present age, especially during the period from about 8000 to about 4000 years ago, under the influence of terrestrial causes the ice-age may have disappeared several times and returned again, until at length the increasing heat drew firmer limits for the glaciers.

On this view, even the traces of the presence of man, which reach back to the tertiary age, would be no proof for an existence of our race to be reckoned by hundreds of thousands of years.

What, then, regarded in the light of science, is the meaning of the 'antiquity of the human race?' Since man, like all other organisms, draws his physical origin from the first development of organic life upon the earth,

---

[7] Comp. Lubbock, Pre-historic Times. See p. 413 ff. for the theory of Adhémar, according to which the northern and southern hemispheres *receive* indeed the same amount of heat from the sun, but do not *retain* the same amount, because of the greater number of night (and therefore radiating) hours in the southern hemisphere. This difference once conceded, the change in the condition of both hemispheres results in the known period of some 21,000 years.

On the climatic effects of the changes in the eccentricity of the earth's orbit, see *l. c.* p. 420 a table which goes back a million years, and in which two periods of maximum cold appear, of which the one (preferred by Lyell) must have occurred some 800,000 years, the other, on the contrary, only some 200,000 years ago.

the question can only be this: at what period are creatures first found which are like us in their organisation, so that from that period no essential development of the external form and organisation has taken place? With this question connects itself, on the one hand, that of the transitional forms and early stages of humanity, on the other, the question of the beginnings of human civilisation.

The transitional forms we have to seek in all probability not on the soil of modern Europe, which man seems to have trodden only as an immigrant after attaining his complete organisation. "The great break in the organic chain between man and his nearest allies, which cannot be bridged over by any extinct or living species, has often been advanced as a grave objection to the belief that man is descended from some lower form; but this objection will not appear of much weight to those who, from general reasons, believe in the general principle of evolution. Breaks often occur in all parts of the series, some being wide, sharp, and defined, others less so in various degrees; as between the ourang and its nearest allies—between the Tarsius and the other Lemuridæ—between the elephant, and, in a more striking manner, between the Ornithorhynchus or Echidna, and all other mammals. But these breaks depend merely on the number of related forms which have become extinct. At some future period, not very distant as measured by centuries, the civilised races of man will almost certainly exterminate and replace the savage races throughout the world. At the same time the anthropomorphous apes, as Professor Schaaffhausen has remarked, will no doubt be exterminated. The break between man and his nearest allies will then be wider, for it will intervene between man in a more civilised state, as we may hope, even than the Caucasian, and some ape as low as a baboon, instead of, as now, between the negro or Australian and the gorilla."[8]

[8] Darwin, Descent of Man, 2d. ed., p. 156.

All the more light have we very recently obtained with regard to the social condition of these primitive inhabitants of Europe; indeed, it appears that we have found a pretty certain clew reaching from diluvial man down to the historical period. It is principally the tools, the products, and means of his art-industry which afford testimony as to the mode of life of man in the different periods of the progress of civilisation. In the cave of Lherm were found human remains mingled with bones and teeth of the cave-bear and the cave-hyena beneath a thick layer of stalagmites. "Besides man's remains were found evidences of his industry, a triangular flint stone knife, a cylindrical bone of the cave-bear which has been converted into a cutting instrument, three under-jaws of the cave-bear, the ascending branch of which was bored with a hole to hang it by, and the eye-troching of a stag's horn, which was cut and pointed at its base. But the most notable weapons consist of twenty half-jaws of the cave-bear, on which the ascending branch was broken away, and the body of the under-jaw so far cut as to form a convenient handle. The markedly projecting canine tooth formed in this way a spike, which might serve equally as a weapon or as a hoe to turn up the soil. Had we found only one of these remarkable instruments," say the authors (of a report published at Toulouse, MM. Rames, Garrigou, and Filhol), "it might be objected that it owed its origin to chance, but when we find twenty jaws, all of which were worked in the same manner, is it any longer possible to talk of chance? Moreover, we can follow the work by means of which the primitive man gave this form to the jawbone. We can count on each of these twenty jaw-bones the blows and saw-marks which were made by the edge of a badly sharpened flint-knife."[9] The stone in-

[9] Quite a similar tool Professor Fraas found at Hohlenfels "from the under-jaw" (of a bear); "its condylus and its processus coronoideus were struck off in order to make the thing handy, and so a tool was produced which, with the sharp canine tooth at its extremity, had to perform the function of a butcher's hatchet. The finding of a single

struments have also been found in great quantities in the valley of the Somme, and Boucher de Perthes has not a little hindered the recognition of his discoveries by his attempt to give a too artificial significance to many specimens. The chalk of that district is rich in flint nodules, which need only be struck one against another till one breaks, in order to obtain pieces amongst the fragments which, after a little further treatment, give us the hatchets and knives of diluvial man. As now the ape sometimes makes use of a stone as a hammer, it might appear that we were here surprising man at a stage still bordering quite closely on the development of the animal. Yet the distinction is enormous, for the mere perseverance which is bestowed on the preparation of an instrument that is but a slight advance on the performances of a natural stone or fragment of stone, shows a capacity of abstraction from the immediate necessities and enjoyments of life, and of turning the attention entirely upon the means to the attainment of an end, which we shall not easily find among the mammals and even among the apes. Animals sometimes build themselves highly artificial homes, but we have not yet seen that they use artificial tools also in their construction. Political economy, it is well known, tries to trace the nature of the accumulation of capital to the construction of the first tool. Well, this beginning of human development was at least present in the diluvial man. Our present ourang or chimpanzee would, economically considered, be a clod compared with him, a mere vagabond. If we assume a development of mankind

---

lower jaw thus prepared would, of course, be unimportant; but so soon as a large number of specimens treated in exactly the same way was found, the intentional working into this form was recognised." "After most careful examination of all the blows visible on the bones of the bears, I was completely convinced that it was usual with this people to hew out the bones of their prey from the flesh with the jaw of the bear." "I have tried striking fresh bones with the thousand-year-old bear's jaw, and have, c.g., in fresh, hard deer-bones, with great care produced just the same holes that we observe on the bear-bones" (Arch. f. Anthrop., v. 2, S. 184, cit. Viertelj.-Rev., i. S. 104 ff.).

through endless stages from the most invisible organic forms to the present epoch, then certainly not the smallest period elapsed from the time when man with a vigorous organisation exercised well-formed hands and strong arms to the moment when he assisted these organs by painfully elaborated flint-knives and the jawbones of bears.

Beside these rude instruments we find, however, also unequivocal traces of fire. Even in the earliest times the primitive dwellers in Europe seem to have known and used this most important of all human auxiliaries.[10] "The animal," says Vogt, "rejoices in the fire that has accidentally arisen and warms itself at it; man tries to keep it in, to produce it, and to make it serve various purposes." In fact, a Knight of the Absolute Distinction between Man and Animal could find no prettier principle in order to defend his standpoint in face of the latest discoveries. It is just this forethought, the care for later necessities, that has led man step by step to higher civilisation, and which accordingly we find characteristic of him in his so distant early history. Nevertheless, it is, on a calm consideration, obvious that we know nothing of any such absolute distinction, and do not find in the sphere of science the slightest occasion to assume it. We have neither any knowledge of the further capacity of development in the animal world,[11] nor of the stages

[10] Whether *all* the races of whose existence in very ancient times we find traces were acquainted with fire is indeed doubtful, as races have been found even in modern times that knew nothing of fire (cp. Lubbock, *l. c.* 453). In Europe, however, we find traces of fire not only in the oldest pile-dwellings and in the Danish shell-mounds known as 'Kjökkenmöddings,' but also in some caves, as *e.g.*, at Aurignac (cp. Lyell, Antiquity of Man, p. 181), where were found, besides coals and ashes, sandstones reddened by heat, which must have formed a hearth. At Pasly, Colland examined a diluvial stratum of very great antiquity, in which, besides remains of coal and ashes, very many traces of the mammoth, the cave-bear, the giant-stag, &c., occurred (Vierteljahrs-Rev., i. 94; cp. *l. c.* 99 f., on remains of coal in the cave of Cro-Magnon).

[11] Kant makes the remark in the Anthropolog. II. E., Hart. vii. 652, that no creature except modern man has the habit of entering upon life at birth with a cry. He believes that even in man this betraying and enemy-attracting cry cannot originally have occurred,—that it belongs

through which man had to pass until he came to keep up fire and make it serve his purposes.

With extreme sagacity the results of several discoveries of remains have been combined in order to draw conclusions here as to the remnants of a cannibal feast, there as to the ceremonies of interment. We pass by these interesting attempts in order to recall again briefly the conclusions as to the organisation of diluvial man which have been based upon the constitution of the bones discovered. Here it must unfortunately be reported that the material is sadly deficient. The find of Aurignac, perhaps the most interesting of all, has become a monument of the ignorance of a physician, who had seventeen diluvial skeletons of different ages and sizes interred in a churchyard, where afterwards, probably from fanaticism, no one could tell where they were buried. After eight years, all the persons concerned, together with the spectators, had forgotten the spot! Perhaps later it may be better recollected. As it is, we are only told that all the skeletons were of very low stature.[12] The skeleton of the Neanderthal may be inferred to be that of a man of middle stature and of extraordinarily powerful muscular development. The skull is the most ape-like of all that we know, and hence it might be inferred that the condition of this diluvial race was one of great barbarism. Besides this, we have, however, a skull from the cave of Engis near Liége, which is thoroughly well formed, and bears with it no indication of a lower stage of development. In the skeletons of Cro-Magnon, finally, there is a highly developed skull structure, combined with an unfavourable formation of the face, and

to the period of domestic life, without our knowing through what co-operating causes such a development has taken place. "This remark," continues Kant, "leads us far; e.g., to the idea whether upon this same second period, by a great revolution of nature, there might not follow a third, when an ourang-outang or a chimpanzee might form the organs which serve for going, for handling objects, and for speaking, into the structure of a man, the innermost part of which should contain an organ for the use of the understanding, and should gradually develop itself by social culture."

[12] Lyell, Antiquity of Man, p. 183.

a development of the jaw which points to brutality, while the constitution of the skeleton testifies not only to a powerful development of muscular force, but also exhibits several ape-like features.[13]

We see from this, first, that there cannot be supposed to have been a single race of diluvial man, and then, further, that a very considerable brain development not only reaches back to the earliest times of which we have any knowledge, but that it is also compatible with a state of great rudeness and savage force. Whether in that case we must regard the Neanderthal skull as a pathological malformation or as the type of a specially low race, may here remain undetermined. We shall, at all events, have to suppose that even in that primitive age Europe was inhabited not by one but by several different races of man. None of these races, even in the earliest times of which we have traces, was in a condition standing very essentially behind that of the most uncultured savage of our time. Even though we regard the Neanderthal skull as the type of a race, we are not even then justified in removing this race to a stage which leads from the ape to man. Science may easily be overhasty in the case of such new and surprising phenomena, especially if they appear to be a brilliant confirmation of dominant ideas. With impatient haste we eagerly seize upon each new find, that we may employ it to complete that chain of development which the causality of our understanding demands. But this very haste is a remnant of mistrust in the understanding; just as though the game might suddenly be lost again in favour of dogmatism, unless positive proofs were at once got together for the agreement of Nature with a rational conception of things. The more completely we are freed from all dogmatic mists of every kind, the more thoroughly will this distrust disappear. For Epikuros it was still the most important point merely to show that all things might have arisen in some intelligible manner.

---

[13] Lubbock, Prehistoric Times, p. 346 ff. Viertelj.-Rev., i. S. 101 ff.

This principle of the intelligibility of all that is is sufficiently established for us; all the same whether it is derived from a sufficient experience or deduced *a priori.* Why then this haste? The same stamp of men that once swore most eagerly by Cuvier's dogma that there are no fossil men, now swear by the absence of the transitional stages: the everlasting effort to save by negative propositions the prejudice that cannot be established by positive propositions! Let us rest thereupon content with this, that even the diluvial age does not as yet lead us to a state of man essentially distinct from that of the Australian negro.[14]

[14] The question may be raised, What can have been the use of a fully developed human brain in so low a state of civilisation, or what can its use at present be to the Australian or the native of Tierra del Fuego? Wallace has used this idea to show that special conditions are probably required for the development of man as distinguished from the whole animal series. He maintains expressly that the large brain of the savage is much beyond the actual requirements of his condition; from which it would be quite unintelligible how such a brain could have been formed through the struggle for existence and by means of natural selection. (Cp. 'Contributions to the Theory of Natural Selection,' 1871, p. 339 ff.) But Wallace, on the one hand, puts the savage much too low compared with the beast, and, on the other, starts from an incorrect view of the nature of the brain. The large brain does not serve, as might have been once supposed, exclusively for the higher mental functions, but it is a co-ordinating apparatus for the most manifold movements. Let us only think what a number of centres of co-ordination and ways of connexion are required only by speech and the association of spoken sounds with the most diverse kinds of feeling! This complicated apparatus once given, the distinction between the highest rational functions of the philosopher or poet and the thought of the savage may rest upon very subtle distinctions, which partly can never be demonstrated in the brain, because they lie rather in function than in substance. (Cp. the chapter "Brain and Soul".) How otherwise —not to speak at all of savages and primitive man—could we explain the likeness in the most general features of the brain structure of a poor and uneducated countryman and of his talented and scientifically educated son? Moreover, it is very doubtful whether the great mass of men in our day exercise so much more complicated mental functions than the savages. Those who invent nothing, improve nothing, and, confined to their trade, swim with the great stream of imitators, understand only a small part of the manifold machinery of modern civilisation. The locomotive and the telegraph, the prediction of eclipses in the almanac, and the existence of great libraries with hundreds of thousands of books, are taken for granted by them, and do not trouble them any farther. Whether now, with the rigid division of labour, running ever into higher social positions, the functions of such a passive member of modern society are much higher than those of the

It is more satisfactory with regard to the transitional steps between diluvial man and historical times. Here a field has been gained in the last few years which, when zealously worked, promises us a complete early history of humanity. To it belong the much talked of 'Kjodden-möddings,' primeval accumulations of emptied oyster and mussel shells, which have been found on the coasts of Denmark, accompanied by undoubted traces of human activity. To it belong especially, too, the pile-buildings of the Swiss and other European lakes; originally, no doubt, places of refuge and storehouses, later perhaps even marts for the commerce of the dwellers on the shores. These extremely remarkable structures were discovered in great numbers, and in rapid succession, after Dr. Keller made the first discovery in the winter of 1853–54, near Meilen, on the Lake of Zürich, and had recognised its importance. At present we distinguish in the objects, which are found in great numbers, especially where the pile-buildings bear traces of fire, three different ages, the

native of Australia may be very much doubted, especially as the latter are undervalued not only by Wallace, but generally in Europe. The 'Australische deutsche Zeitung' of Tamunda (reproduced in the 'Kölnische Zeit.') remarks, in noticing Petermann's last map of South-Eastern Australia, "The extraordinarily favourable climate of Australia spares what is perhaps the happiest of all wild races the labour of raising solid dwellings for shelter and protection; and the geographical conformations and the great variety and change in the scenery of the country do not permit him to establish fixed dwelling-places. The nature of the country compels him to a constant wandering life. Everywhere he is at home, and everywhere he finds his table spread, which, however, he has to fill with the most strenuous exertion and the utmost sagacity. He knows most exactly when and where these or those berries, fruits, or roots ripen in this neighbourhood, when the duck or the tortoise lays there, when this or that migratory bird settles here or there, when and where this or that caterpillar or chrysalis invites to a dainty feast, when and where the opossum is fattest, when this or that fish is here or there, where are the drinking springs of the kangaroo and emu, and so on. And just this life, thus forced upon him, becomes dear to him and a second nature, and makes him in a certain sense more intelligent than any other savage people. The children of these savages, when sent to school and well taught, are hardly inferior to European children, and in some branches even outstrip them. It is quite incorrect to conceive the Australian negroes as standing in the lowest grade of races. In a certain sense there is no more sagacious people than they are."

latest of which, the *iron*, reaches to the present time. The earlier ages are not, however, as in the ancient myth, the silvern and the golden, but carry us back to a time when the respective races possessed only implements of *bronze*, and finally to the *stone* age, the dawning of which we have already seen in the case of diluvial man.

But these periods also, as the progress of research has shown, have only a relative significance. Here there may have been peoples living in the state of the stone age, while at the same time elsewhere a high civilisation may have been developed. Stone tools, which had become familiar, and when good material and skilful workmanship enabled them for many purposes to do good service, may have long been retained in use, while side by side with them metals were employed; just as even to-day we find amongst savage tribes various implements of stone and shell, and that side by side with imported metal implements of European manufacture. We may therefore congratulate ourselves upon the plentiful results which the pile-buildings in particular afford us for the history of the earliest handicrafts, of the mode of life, and the gradually growing civilisation of prehistoric races. As to what it was that at first more rigidly distinguished man from the animals, and therefore as to the true beginnings of specifically human existence, we find here no result.

One fact, however, deserves to be pointed out, which seems, indeed, to be essentially connected with the first beginnings of what is specifically human—that is, the appearance of the sense of beauty and certain beginnings of art in times when man was obviously still living in savage conflict with the great beasts of prey, and was painfully maintaining an existence full of terror and vicissitudes of the most exciting kind. In this regard we must especially mention the outlines of animal figures on stones and bones, which were first discovered in the caves of Southern France, and recently also not far from Schaffhausen, near Thaingen. It may be added, that even in the oldest and rudest remains of pottery we may almost always observe a certain regard to pleasantness of form, and that the elements of ornament appear to be nearly as old as any facility in the production of arms and utensils.[15] We have here a remarkable confirmation of the ideas which Schiller set forth in his 'Künstler;' for if we conceive the savage passions of the primeval man, we have hardly any source of educating and elevating ideas to oppose to them but society and the sense of beauty. We are thus involuntarily reminded of the well-known question whether man first sang or spoke. Here palæontology is silent, but instead we have anatomical and physiological considerations. According to Jäger's acute remark, the delicate management of the movements of the breath, especially the easy and free control of expiration, is a condition precedent of language, and this condition can only be completely fulfilled by the erect posture. This is true also of song, and therefore birds, which possess this freedom of the chest, are born singers, and at the same time learn to speak with comparative ease. Darwin is inclined to yield priority to song: "When we treat of sexual selection, we shall see that primeval man, or rather some early progenitor of man, probably first used his voice in producing true musical cadences, that is, in singing, as do some of the gibbon-apes at the present day; and we may conclude, from a widely spread analogy, that this power would have been especially exerted during the courtship of the sexes,—would have expressed various emotions, such as love, jealousy, triumph,

[15] A good compilation of the facts on this subject is to be found in Baer, Der vorgeschichtl. Mensch, S. 133 ff.; cp. also Naturf., 1874, No. 17, on the find of Thaingen (on the Schaffhausen-Constanz line), which contains on a reindeer's antler the drawing of a reindeer, that is said, "in delicacy and character of form and in detail of execution," to greatly surpass all yet known drawings from the caves of Southern France. The reporter (A. Heim, in the Mittheil. d. antiquar. Ges. in Zürich, xviii. 125) points out that these drawings of animals are always found in connexion only with unfinished flint implements; he supposes them to be considerably older than the oldest pile-dwellings of Switzerland, in which nothing of the kind is found. Here, therefore, an older race, in a much lower stage of civilisation, had attained to a proficiency in art which was afterwards lost again.

and would have served as a challenge to rivals. It is, therefore, probable that the imitation of musical cries by articulate sounds may have given rise to words expressive of various complex emotions."[16]

That in the origin of language the imitation of animal sounds, as Darwin supposes, has played a part is very probable, since a sound produced by the mere impulse of imitation must very easily have acquired significance. The raven, e.g., that imitates out of its own head the barking of the dog and the cackling cries of hens, certainly connects with these sounds the idea of the kinds of animal in question, since it knows to what animals these cries belong, and to what not. It has, therefore, in its invention a foundation for the formation of ideas, the beginnings of which are by no means unknown to the animals. The reflex natural sounds of surprise, fright, &c., must without this have been intelligible to all similarly organised beings, since even in the animals they form an unmistakable means of intelligence. Here we have a subjective, there an objective element of the formation of speech. The combination of the two must give to the subjective element stricter form, to the objective element greater content.[17]

If we regard the history of human civilisation in the light of the latest researches, we are reminded by the

---

[16] Descent of Man, 2d ed., 87.

[17] It would lead us too far to enter here upon a discussion of the so warmly controverted question of the origin of language. Let it only be observed, that the attempt to find in any factor of speech, e.g., in the formation of significant roots, an 'absolute' distinction between man and animal, must break down as completely as any other proof of such supposed absolute distinctions. All the separate factors of human life and civilisation are of a general kind; but so far as every genuinely imprinted peculiarity has in its persistence something absolute, we may say that an absolute distinction of man from the animals lies in the peculiar way in which here all relative distinctions co-operate in order to produce a particular form. The like absolute peculiarity of form belongs in this sense, of course, also to the animal species, and by no means involves any immutability. In man, however, it attains a higher significance, not from the standpoint of natural history, but of ethics; and here it is quite adequate to establish, e.g., the distinction between the intellectual and the 'animal.'

course of the results of the lines of a hyperbola, whose coordinates, representing the development of civilisation, at first rise with infinite slowness over immense tracts of time, then quicker and quicker, until finally there follows an immense progress in a moderate space of time. We use this figure in order to make perfectly clear an idea which seems to us of importance. It is very different with the development of the physical and even of the psychical qualities of nations. Here the progress in the aptitude of individuals and nations appears only a very slow and gradual one. This is doubtless due to the fact that man, with the same capacities, attains a much higher goal if he is in a very advanced environment, then if he grows up amidst the rudest traditions. It seems almost as if a very moderate aptitude is sufficient to enable him in the course of some twenty years of childhood and youth so far to familiarise himself with the most developed civilisation as to take an active and independent part in it. But if we reflect that in earlier ages, for the most part, mere *facts* and isolated experiences or contrivances were handed down, while modern times hand down also *methods*, by means of which whole series of discoveries and inventions are attained, we easily see the reason of the rapid progress of contemporary civilisation, without, therefore, being obliged to descry in the present a sudden advance of humanity to a higher intellectual and physical existence. Nay, as the individual often attains to his most important intellectual productions only at an age when the powers of his brain are already in decline, so, too, it is not in itself inconceivable that there by no means underlie our present advance that elastic youthfulness and energy of humanity which we are so ready to suppose. We are far from laying down in this respect any positive view, for which no one has the necessary evidence. But we cannot leave the subject of the development of the human race without at least pointing out how little objective foundation there is for the dogma of the continual progress of humanity. The short span of history, which, of course, does not afford us sufficient material to admit of even a probable empirical law, to say nothing of a 'law' properly speaking, has shown us already more than once how external development and internal mortality may go in a nation hand in hand, and the inclination of the masses as well as of the 'cultured' to care only for their material welfare and to submit to despotism, has been in antiquity, and perhaps, too, in several Oriental peoples, a symptom of such internal mortality. We have thus indicated the theoretical position of a question which we propose in the last Section to consider from a very different point of view.

As the question of the Age of the Human Race concerns Materialism at bottom only as the most obvious and palpable opponent against vague theological ideas, while it has little to do with the innermost basis of specific Materialism, so is it also with the question of the Unity of the Human Race. This question is merely another form of the question of Descent from a Single Pair, as Cuvier's theory of the Revolutions of the Earth was another form of the tradition of the Creative Days, and as the doctrine of the Immutability of the Species may be referred to Noah's Ark. But for our very gradual deliverance from these traditions, science, which professes to be so unprejudiced, would never have treated these questions so passionately, and the conflict of the greater error with the less has here too been a source of much profitable knowledge. In order to determine a matter of which no one has a clear conception, namely, whether mankind is a unity, skulls have been measured, skeletons studied, proportions compared ; and at all events ethnography has been enriched, the sphere of physiology widened, and innumerable facts of history and anthropology gathered and saved from oblivion. But as to the main point all this industry has decided nothing, except perhaps this, that the innermost spring of these discussions lies not in a purely scientific interest, but in great party questions. The matter was the more complicated in that, besides the supposed religious interest, the North American slave question has occupied a great share in this controversy. In such cases men easily content themselves with the cheapest and most threadbare arguments, to which emphasis is then lent by pomp of erudition and the varnish of scientific form. Thus the work of Nott and Gliddon in particular ('Types of Mankind,' 1854), is completely saturated with the American tendency to represent the negroes as creatures of the lowest possible kind and of almost brutish organisation; but as previously the opposite tendency had dominated the treatment of these questions, this very book contributed greatly to a sharper appreciation of the characteristic features of races. The in many respects excellent 'Anthropologie der Naturvölker' of Waitz (too early lost to science) suffers, on the contrary, from a constant exaggeration of the arguments for the 'unity' of mankind. This goes so far that Waitz frequently appeals to the utterly untrustworthy and unscientific Prichard; that he still regards Blumenbach (1795!) as the first authority on questions of the differences between species and races; that he honours Wagner's collection of cases of hybridism (in Prichard) with the epithet "careful," and finally commits himself to this sentence: "What importance, in fact, could be attributed even to specific differences in nature, and how fortuitous would their fixity appear, if their effacement were possible by continuous hybrid productions!" That from such a standpoint nothing can be accomplished for the main point, even if its solution were in itself possible, needs no proof. What may happen in fact when people attempt by painful periphrases to prove things that may any minute be refuted by experience, may appear from the single illustration that Waitz quite calmly adduces hares and rabbits as different species, while M. Roux in Angoulême for eight years had been attaining excellent results with his three-eighth hares—a new species of animal, or race, if it is preferred, invented by him.[18]

The idea of the unity of mankind no longer needs the support which it may once have found in the doctrine of a common descent; although we may doubt whether the myth of Adam and Eve exercised any softening influence on the relations of the Spaniards with the Indians, or the Creoles with their Negro slaves. The essential points —the extension of the claim to humanity to men of every race, the maintenance of equality before the law in the national commonwealth, the application of international law in neighbourly intercourse—may very well be established and maintained, without therefore bargaining for absolute equality in the capacities of different races. But the descent from a common primitive stock by no means guarantees equal capacities, since to lag behind in development for thousands of years might finally lead to any given degree of inferiority. Only so much seems to be guaranteed by the concurrent descent, that a backward race, or even one that has become hardened and perverted in its lower qualities, might yet, by circumstances which we cannot calculate, be led to a higher development. But this, on the principles of the doctrine of descent, must always be conceded as a possibility not only for backward human races but even for the animals.

The 'descent from the ape,' which is most bitterly denied by those who are least raised by inner dignity of

---

[18] It has been attempted to make this very case of successful crossing a witness for this immutability of species, by asserting that M. Roux's three-eighth hares, by continued breeding in, return entirely to the maternal rabbit-type (Rev. des Deux Mondes, 15 Mar. 1869, p. 413 ff.). But this is by no means to refute the persistence of the crossed race, and as little can it be said that the new 'rabbits' do not differ very essentially and permanently from the primitive maternal stock, for otherwise there would be no object in breeding them. It is not necessary to waste a single word on this main point, since these creatures, as well as similar productions, form a notable article of commerce. But as to the tendency of the middle form to return to one of the two types maintained and consolidated for thousands of years, this is entirely in harmony with what has been said above, p. 43 ff.

mind above the sensual basis of our existence, is of course in the strict sense not a consequence of Darwin's theory. This goes rather to indicate in the earlier history of man a common stock,[19] from which on one side, tending upwards, man branched off, and on the other, persisting in the animal form, the ape. Thus the ancestors of man must be conceived as being indeed formed like the ape, but already endowed with the disposition to a higher development, and something like this appears to have been Kant's idea. Things look still more favourable for the traditional pedigree of man on the hypothesis of polyphyletic descent. Here we may carry back man's advantage in the capacity for development to the first beginnings of organic life. It is, nevertheless, obvious that this advantage, which is at bottom merely a convenience in the arranging of our thoughts and feelings, cannot throw the least weight into the scale in favour of the polyphyletic theory; for otherwise the scientific grounds would be corrupted by the admixture of subjective and ethical motives. And, in fact, much is not

[19] The 'descent from the ape' derives its hatefulness in the popular objection to Darwinism, of course, only from the comparison with the *now existing apes*, on which alone the popular idea of the nature of an ape is formed. It may here, therefore, be quite indifferent whether or not this obsolete ancestral form is in the zoological sense described as an 'ape,' as it had at all events very different qualities from the present apes. Oscar Schmidt (Doctrine of Descent, &c., E.T. p. 292 f.) says on this: "The development of the anthropoid apes has taken a lateral course from the nearest human progenitors, and man can as little be transformed into a gorilla as a squirrel can be exchanged into a rat. . . . The bony skull of these apes has reached an extreme comparable to that of our domestic cattle. But this extreme appears only gradually in the course of growth, and the calf knows little of it, but possesses the cranial form of its antelope-like ancestors. . . . Now as the youthful skull of the anthropoid apes exhibits, with undeniable distinctness, a descent from progenitors with a better-formed, still plastic cranium, and a dentition approaching that of man, the transformation of these parts, together with the brain—the latter by reason of its persistently smaller volume—has, as it were, struck out a fatal path, while, in the human branch, selection has effected a greater conservation of these cranial qualities." Comp. the same writer's lecture, Die Anwendung d. Descendenzl. auf den Menschen: Leipz. 1873, S. 16-18. Haeckel, Natürl. Schöpfungsg., 4 Aufl., S. 577, E.T. ii. 268.

gained for the pride of man, on a closer examination, by this merely superficial removal from the animal stock; and much need not be gained for this pride, since it is but an unjustifiable rebellion against the idea of the unity of nature and of the uniformity of the formative principle in the great whole of organic life, of which we form only a part. Let us give up this unphilosophical rebellion, and it will be found that to proceed from an already highly organised animal, in which the light of thought manifests itself creatively, is fitter and more agreeable than to proceed from an inorganic clod of earth.

However far we may, on scientific grounds, remove man from the existing apes, we shall not be able to refrain from carrying back into his earlier history a number of characteristics of the ape which are now most repulsive to us. Snell, who in his clever treatise on the 'Schöpfung des Menschen' (Jena, 1863), has very nearly attained his object of combining the most rigorous requirements of science with the conservation of our moral and religious ideas, is at all events wrong in believing that humanity must have announced itself, even in the earlier animal forms from which it arose, by something salient and presentient in look and gesture. We must by no means confound the conditions of perfectibility with an early appearance of their results. What now appears to us most noble and sublime may very well only unfold itself as the last blossom of a calmly and safely passing life, richly saturated with familiar impressions, while the possibility of such a life must be attained by very different qualities.

The first step towards the possibility of the civilisation of man was presumably the attaining of superiority over all other animals, and it is not probable that he employed for this end essentially different means from those which he now employs with the object of lording it over his kind. Cunning and cruelty, savage violence and lurking knavery, must have played an important part in those struggles; nay, the fact that even now, when he might succeed so much better with a little exercise of reason, he is continually relapsing into those freaks of the robber and oppressor, may perhaps be derived from the reaction of his struggle for thousands of years with lions and bears, and earlier still perhaps with anthropoid apes. This by no means excludes the simultaneous development of genuine virtues side by side with intelligence in the circle of the tribal and family community. Let us only think for a moment of the enormous gulf which even in ancient civilisation still prevails between the internal life of the individual states and towns and their often infinitely barbarous behaviour towards defeated foes!

We cannot, therefore, even on psychological grounds, reject the relationship of man with the ape, even though it were on this score, that at least the ourang and the chimpanzee are much too gentle and peaceable for those cave-dwellers to have proceeded from them, who conquered the gigantic lions of primeval times and greedily devoured the smoking brains from their shattered skulls.

CHAPTER II.

BRAIN AND SOUL.

WE take up the old and favourite theme of Materialism, which it is indeed no longer so easy to dispose of as in the last century. The first intoxication of great physical and mathematical discoveries is over; and as the world, with each fresh deciphering of a secret, offered yet new riddles, and as it were visibly grew great and wider, so there revealed themselves, too, in organic life abysses of unexplored connexions which as yet had been hardly thought of. An age that could quite seriously believe that in the mechanical masterpieces of Droz and Vaucanson [20] it had come upon the traces of the secrets of life, was hardly capable of measuring the difficulties which have accumulated in the mechanical explanation of psychical phenomena only the higher as we have gone on. Then the childishly naïve conception could still be put forward with the pretension of a scientific hypothesis, that every idea has its particular fibre in the brain, and that the vibration of these fibres constitutes consciousness.

The opponents of Materialism of course easily showed that between consciousness and external motion there is an impassable gulf; but natural feeling made no great matter of this gulf, because we easily see that it is inevitable. In some form or other the opposition of subject and object always recurs, only that in other systems it may be more easily bridged by a phrase.

If in the last century, instead of this metaphysical

[20] *Vide* vol. ii. p. 75.

objection, all the physical experiments had been made which are now at our service, Materialism would perhaps have been defeated with its own weapons. Perhaps, too, not; for the same facts which dispose of the then views of the nature of the cerebral activity, strike no less heavily perhaps at all the favourite ideas of metaphysics. There could hardly be propounded, in fact, a single proposition as to brain and soul which is not refuted by the facts. There are, of course, excepted partly vague generalities, as, *e.g.*, that the brain is the most important organ for the activities of the soul; partly propositions relating to the connexion of particular parts of the brain with the activity of particular nerves. The unfruitfulness of brain investigations is due, however, only partially to the difficulty of the matter. The main cause seems to be the entire absence of any workable hypothesis, or even of any approximate idea, as to the nature of the cerebral activity. So that even educated men constantly fall back again, as it were from despair, upon the theories, long since refuted by the facts, of a localisation of the cerebral activity according to the various functions of the intellect and the emotions. We have, it is true, repeatedly expressed ourselves against the view that the mere continuance of obsolete opinions is so great a hindrance to science as is commonly supposed; but here it does in fact appear as though the phantom of the soul showing itself on the ruins of Scholasticism continually confuses the whole question. We could easily show that this ghost, if we may so designate the reaction of the obsolete doctrines of the school-psychology, plays a great part amongst the men who consider themselves entirely free from it, amongst our Materialistic leaders; nay, that their whole conception of the way in which we must conceive the cerebral activity is essentially dominated by the popular conceptions which were formerly held as to the mythical faculties of the soul. Yet we believe that these conceptions, if only a rational positive idea appears as to what is

BRAIN AND SOUL.

properly to be expected of the functions of the brain, will disappear just as easily as they now stubbornly maintain their ground.

Here we cannot but think above all of the crudest form of this theory of localisation, viz., of Phrenology. It is not only a necessary point for our historical treatment, but at the same time, because of its intelligible working out, a suitable subject for the development of those critical principles which will farther on find an extended application.

When Gall propounded his theory of the composition of the brain from a series of special organs for special mental activities, he started from the entirely correct view that the commonly accepted primary faculties of the soul, such as Attention, Judgment, Will, Memory, &c., are mere abstractions; that they classify the various modes of cerebral activity, without however possessing that elementary significance which is ascribed to them. He was led by observations of the most various kinds to assume a series of primary organs in the brain, whose prominent development was supposed to lend the individual certain permanent qualities, and whose joint action to determine the individual's whole character. The mode in which Gall made his discoveries and ranged his proofs was that he sought for some very striking examples of particular peculiarities, such as may easily be found amongst criminals, lunatics, and men of genius or eccentricity. He looked now on the skull of the individual in question for a particularly prominent spot. If it was found, the organ was provisionally treated as discovered, and next 'experience,' comparative anatomy, animal psychology, and other sources had to lend their aid to confirm it. Many organs were established merely on observations in the animal world, and then carried farther in the case of man. Of more exact scientific method there is in Gall's procedure not the faintest trace discoverable, a circumstance that was not unfavourable to the spread of his theory. For this kind of inquiry every one has talent and aptitude; its results are almost always interesting, and 'experience' regularly confirms the doctrines which are built upon such theories. It is the same kind of experience which confirmed Astrology too, which still confirms the healing power of most medicines (not merely the homœopathic ones), and which daily renders manifest the visible aid of saints and deities in such surprising instances. Phrenology is, therefore, not in bad company; it is not a relapse into some fabulous degree of fantasy, but only a fruit of the common soil of the sham sciences, which even yet form the great mass of the learning on which jurists, doctors, theologians, and philosophers pride themselves. Its position is indeed hazardous, in that it falls within a sphere which very well admits of all the cautions of the exact sciences, and that it is nevertheless carried out without any kind of regard to the requirements of scientific method; yet even this it has at least in common with homœopathy.

Our present phrenologists defend their opinions, as a rule, by violent tirades against those objections which are often levelled against sham science without much reflection, because no one cares to trouble himself seriously with the matter. Any attempt, on the other hand, at a positive foundation will be sought in vain in the modern treatises on phrenology. While Gall and Spurzheim worked at a time when the methods of investigating such subjects were still quite undeveloped, our modern phrenologists engage in sterile polemics instead of doing even slight justice to the enormous progress of science. It still holds, as Johannes Müller said in his 'Physiology': "With regard to the principle, its possibility cannot *a priori* be denied; but experience shows that the system of organs proposed by Gall has absolutely no foundation in facts, and the histories of injuries to the head are directly opposed to the existence of special regions of the brain destined for particular mental activities." [21] Some examples may make this

[21] Handbuch d. Phys. d. Menschen, 3 Aufl., 1837, i. 855.

clear. Castle, in his 'Phrenology,' adduces after Spurzheim several cases of loss of considerable portions of the brain, in which the intellectual faculties, it is said, suffered no interruption. He complains that in all these cases the locality of the injury is not properly given. Had the injury in question been in the cerebellum, "even a phrenologist can admit, without the slightest difficulty, that the thinking faculty might remain uninjured." [22] The apologetic standpoint here is unmistakable. One would think, since the opposite possibility was equally justified, that the phrenologist must try to get hold of such cases; above all, one would expect that in a case which came under his own observation he would endeavour to ascertain quite accurately the injured organs and the degree of injury, and that he would then observe and ascertain the mental activity of the individual in question as a true *instantia praerogativa* with the utmost carefulness and keenness. Instead of this, Castle actually offers us with unsuspecting calmness the following narrative:—

"I myself had the opportunity of observing a similar case. An American had received a quantity of shot in the occiput, which resulted in his losing a part of the skull, and besides, as he himself expressed it, 'several spoons-full of brain.' It was said that his intellectual faculties were unaffected. According to his own account, the sufferings he felt arose from the nerves. His position obliged him to speak very often in public; he had, however, lost the energy and firmness which previously distinguished him. This fact was employed as a proof against the phrenologists—a proof as credible as all similar ones—though it is easy to see that it is entirely consonant with the principles of this science. The injured spot of the brain was not the seat of the intellectual faculties, but was that of the animal energy, which accordingly was the only thing affected."

This, in fact, is enough. No information as to the

[22] Die Phrenologie, 1845, S. 27 f.

injured organs, as to the extent of the wound or scar! Considering the great part which the 'duplicity' of the brain-organs plays in the apology for untenable theories, we should at least have been told whether the injury to the 'occiput,' which carried away 'a part of the skull' and 'several spoons-full of brain,' was in such a spot that the organs of the one half might be supposed to have been uninjured. If the shot struck the middle of the occiput to a moderate extent, it might easily have totally destroyed the organ of 'Philoprogenitiveness.' How was it with this organ? How was it with 'Concentrativeness' and 'Habitativeness'? How with 'Cohesion'? Nothing of all this! and yet all these organs lie in the occiput, and a case of their partial destruction would have been for a man of scientific zeal—always supposing that such a man could be a phrenologist—quite invaluable. The 'animal energy' had suffered. This, at any rate, might point to 'Combativeness,' which lies at one side of the occiput; but we must unfortunately conjecture that, if the shot had struck this organ, Castle would hardly have omitted to let us know it. The man had 'lost the energy and firmness which previously distinguished him!'

Thus, then, we must not be surprised if the phrenologists still quite cheerfully regard the cerebellum as the organ of the sexual impulse, although Combette in 1831 observed a case of strong sexual impulse with an entirely absent cerebellum, and although Flourens in a cock from which he had excised a great part of the cerebellum, and which he kept alive for eight months, found the sexual impulse still persisting.[23]

The frontal lobes of the cerebrum have to carry a mass of such important organs, that the destruction of a part of them in serious injuries of this region must always become noticeable, especially as intelligence, talent, &c., are here concerned, the disappearance of which is easier to

[23] Comp. Longet, Anat. et Physiol. du Système Nerveux, i. p. 765; and p. 768.

establish than the change of a moral quality. Yet in the large number of brain injuries in the frontal part of the head, which have been under exact scientific observation, nothing has ever yet been found that can be made without extreme violence to point in this direction. Recourse is had, of course, to the duplicity of the organs; but how does it come to pass that the reduction of an organ to one-half does not perceptibly change the character, while a moderate prominence or depression in the skull is enough to explain the most striking contrasts of the whole mental nature? But let us not weaken our criticism by an exposition against which at least a hypothesis can be invented! There are even cases in which quite unequivocally *both* frontal lobes of the cerebrum have been seriously affected and destroyed, and in which not the least disturbance of intelligence was observed. Longet reports two such cases which had been thoroughly observed. One such instance, however, is enough to overturn the whole system of phrenology.[24]

And not only the system of phrenology; for the doctrine of the seat of intelligence in the frontal lobes of the cerebrum has been shared by many anatomists who by no means stood on so narrow a basis; and yet there is absolutely nothing either in the more general localisation by larger groups of mental qualities. Series of very arbitrarily chosen skulls of great men have been taken, and as a rule, though not always, the forehead has been high and broad. But it has been forgotten that even if a large frontal development coincides as a rule with great intelligence, there is as yet not the slightest proof of a localised activity in these parts of the brain. For while all the facts hitherto observed lead to the conclusion that the various portions of the cerebrum have essentially the same destination, it may yet very well be that a particularly favourable organisation of the whole is also connected with a particular form of it.

[24] Longet, *loc. cit.* i. 671 ff..

To the objections against which a part of our modern phrenologists bitterly turn their weapons, belongs also the observation that phrenology necessarily leads to Materialism. This is about as correct as such general propositions generally are; that is, it is obviously false. Phrenology, if it were scientifically justified, might not only be excellently supported on Kant's system, but it may, in fact, be harmonised with those obsolete ideas according to which the brain is related to the 'soul,' much as a more or less perfect instrument is to the person playing it. It is always noteworthy, however, that our Materialists, and amongst them men of whom it would certainly not be expected, have expressed themselves surprisingly in favour of phrenology. So B. Cotta; so too especially Vogt, who in his 'Bilder aus dem Thierleben' wrote the characteristically hasty words: " Is phrenology, therefore, true to its minutest application ? Must every change of function have been preceded, or rather simultaneously accompanied, by a material change of the organ ? I cannot but say, Truly it is so."

The reason of this inclination is easily perceived. The general principle, that is to say, that thinking is an activity of the brain, may in this generality be made very probable, without therefore being made very effective. Only when we succeed in following up this activity, in resolving it somehow into elements, and in demonstrating in these elements still the correspondence of the physical and the mental, only then will this mode of regarding things be generally adopted, and great weight attributed to it in the formation of our collective theory of things. If we can, moreover, construct the character of man from such knowledge, as astronomy predicts the position of the heavenly bodies from the laws of their motion, then the human mind can no longer resist the theory which produces such fruits. Our Materialists are of course not such phantasts as to credit phrenology in its present state with these performances. Vogt has in other works repeatedly expressed himself quite unequivocally as to the unscientific character of this theory; Büchner treats phrenology indeed with conspicuous tenderness, but admits that "the most important scientific considerations are opposed to it." The unhappy 'innate ideas,' however, are followed up even into the hiding-place of a barely possible phrenology. In order to dispose of a sort of innate ideas, which is entirely strange to modern philosophy, and only exists in popular and homiletic writings and speeches, he thinks he must also controvert the conclusions which have been drawn in favour of innate ideas from phrenology. He overlooks in the heat of the fight that innate ideas, which necessarily result from the structure and composition of the soul, entirely harmonise with the most consistent Materialism; nay, that such a supposition goes farther, and would more entirely agree with the rest of his principles than the standpoint of Locke's *tabula rasa*, where he himself stands. But as no important modern philosopher believes in ideas which unfold themselves without any influence of the external world, or lie already conscious in the foetus, so too no phrenologist could suppose that the sense of sound could develop and become active without sounds, or the sense of colour without colours. The controversy is only between the one-sided view of Locke, which dominated the last century in a degree difficult to understand, that the whole intellectual content comes through the senses, and between the other view, on which the brain or the soul brings with it certain forms, by which the shaping of sense-impressions into concepts and ideas is predetermined. Perhaps these forms have sometimes been conceived too much as matrixes, into which the type-metal is poured, or as earthen pots, which are filled with the sense-impressions as with water from a spring. However much these sherds may be shattered, it still remains true that there are material conditions present which exert the most essential influence on the formation of all ideas. In order to controvert such an influence in reference to a merely possible phrenology, Büchner propounds the hypothesis that the relation of phrenological organs and external impressions may also be inverted, inasmuch as "at the time when the brain is growing and forming, by means of continued and repeated external impressions and psychical activity in a particular direction, the phrenological organ in question is also materially more strongly developed—exactly as a muscle is strengthened by exercise."

"Good!" the phrenologist will say; "but still the muscles are innate; they are different even from birth, and it can hardly be denied that in like circumstances a strong-muscled child will exert its muscles more than a weak-muscled child can. Deny the innate brain, and you will also have denied the innate tendencies of the mental activity!" But Büchner does not go so far as that. He exclaims: "Nature knows neither purposes nor aims, nor any mental or material conditions forced upon her from outside and above her!" Well, if nothing more is meant, if the conditions of our ideation coming from within outwards and springing from Nature herself are conceded, why all this fuss?

Here, again, we are brought sharply to the main point of the whole materialistic controversy. *Why* all this fuss? Well, perhaps in order to meet the hypocritical affectation of modern science. Never was the gulf between the thought of this privileged society and the masses greater than now, and never had this privileged society so completely made its egoistic and separate terms of peace with the unreason of existing things. Only the times before the fall of ancient civilisation offer a similar phenomenon; but they had nothing of that democracy of Materialism which to-day half-consciously, half-unconsciously, revolts against this aristocratical philosophy. It is easy from the standpoint of this philosophy theoretically to refute Materialism, but difficult to destroy it. In practical debate Materialism playfully breaks up all those esoteric subtleties, in shattering the crude exoteric ideas with which they have formed so delusive an alliance. 'We never meant anything of the kind!' cries terrified Science; but she receives as answer: 'Speak plainly and for every one or die!' Thus there towers up behind the logical criticism of Materialism its historical importance, and therefore too it can only be adequately appreciated in an historical inquiry.

We will then, like Büchner, assume for a moment that there is a phrenology, in order to submit the whole idea of the localisation of the mental functions to a criticism in which for the present we leave out of view the opposing facts of pathological anatomy. For convenience we will take the theory as it was developed by Spurzheim, Combe, and others, and as it is pretty widely spread in Germany. We have, then, somewhat such a picture as this of the processes of concrete thinking.

Each organ has its own special activity, and yet the activity of all co-operates towards a joint effect. Each organ thinks, feels, and wills for itself; the man's thinking, feeling, and willing is the result of the sum of these activities. In each organ there are manifold degrees of mental activity. The sensation rises to conception and finally to imagination, as the thinking excitability of the organ is weaker or stronger: emotion may become enthusiasm, impulse may become desire, and finally passion. These activities have reference only to the matters which are natural to each organ. "Each mental organ," says one of our cleverest phrenologists, "speaks its own language and understands the language which it speaks itself; conscience speaks in matters of right and wrong; benevolence only in matters of sympathy, and so on." Through their union into a whole there then result the more general phenomena, such as 'Understanding,' as an activity of the whole six-and-thirty faculties of thought; they co-operate, however, in the particular individual activities of man, partly in antagonism, partly in support, in modification, and so on, like a group of muscles in the movement of a limb.

We see at the first glance that this whole way of regarding things moves in the most shadowy abstractions. Gall wished to put in the place of the conventional mental faculties natural and concrete bases of psychology. In this he apparently succeeded by means of the hypothesis of his supposed organs; but so soon as we come to the activity of these organs the old shadow-play begins again. Gall himself, it is true, concerned himself little with such developments, and even yet it is hardly clear to the majority of his disciples that we must be able to form some notion of the mode of activity of these organs. Phrenology might, indeed, be actually correct so far as regards the correspondence of cranial formation with intellectual qualities, without our therefore having the slightest information as to the manner of the cerebral activity. If the brain, and consequently the skull, forms a prominence at the top of the head and towards the front, it by no means follows that the convolutions lying at this spot are exclusively occupied with emotional sympathy, and so on.

What, then, is the meaning of 'sympathy'? When I hear a child crying piteously in the street, I feel besides the waves of sound a series of sensations, especially in the muscles of the respiratory apparatus (and hence the ancients placed the feelings in the breast). Moreover, one person may have a quickened beating of the heart, another a peculiar feeling in the epigastric region, and a third a feeling as though he must cry too. Simultaneously there comes up the idea of succour. A slight innervation of certain locomotor muscles is set up, as though I must turn towards the child and ask what is the matter. The association of ideas pictures to me my own children in helplessness; there arises an image of the parents of the crying child, who might comfort it, and are not there. I think of various causes—perhaps the little one is lost, perhaps half-starved or cold, and so on. At last I run, with or without a special resolve, to the aid of the little screamer. I was *sympathetic;* have perhaps made myself ridiculous by needless sympathy; perhaps, too, intervened at the right time. At all events, I was so organised that the symptoms above described occur more easily and quickly with me than with others, just as one man must sneeze sooner under the stimulus of snuff than another. The moral judgment calls the first quality good, the latter indifferent; but physically the phenomenon is related somewhat as a line from a symphony of Beethoven and the piece of some musician at a fair, both of which consist of sequences of sound. What now is sympathy? Was the sound of the child's cry carried to the organ of benevolence, which alone understood this language? Did there arise in this organ first sensation, excitation, impulse, then at last will and reflection? Was the will to help then carried back ready-made from this organ to the central focus of motion, to the medulla oblongata, which put itself on this occasion at the disposal of the organ of benevolence? This way of representing things only pushes the difficulty farther back. We conceive the activity of the organ as that of an entire man; we have the most reckless anthropomorphism applied to individual parts of man. In the organ of benevolence everything must concur; not only thinking, feeling, and willing, but also hearing and seeing. If I renounce this anthropomorphism, which only postpones the matter to be explained, nothing can appear to me more probable than that in the phenomenon under consideration my whole brain was engaged, although in very various degrees of activity.

Here the phrenologist falls upon me, and flings at me all the ignorance of his science. He too assumes an activity of the whole brain, or at least of great groups of organs, only that Benevolence takes the lead in this case. What was the object of sympathy? A child? Then 'Philoprogenitiveness' is also at work! How is the boy to be helped? Shall I show him the way? There is 'Locality' engaged; 'Hope' and 'Conscientiousness' appear; 'Judgment' has its share in the proceedings. But these organs think, feel, will, each for itself. Each hears the cry, each sees the child, each imagines causes and consequences, for each of these organs has its own imagination; the difference is only that Benevolence gives the ruling tone with the idea: 'Here is some one suffering, and help must be given!' 'Certainly,' says Conscientiousness; 'to help our fellow-men is a duty, and duties must be observed.' 'It will be easy to comfort the little thing,' thinks Hope. Then there arises opposition in the cerebellum. 'Don't make oneself absurd,' cries 'Love of approbation;' and 'Cautiousness' points out that her neighbour, 'Love of approbation,' is quite right, and that the thing must be well considered. The predominant feeling asserts meanwhile some egoistic reasons in favour of help, and finally the 'Impulse of activity' leads to the closing of the debate and to a decision. We have a parliament of little men together, of whom, as also happens in real parliaments, each possesses only one single idea, which he is ceaselessly trying to assert.

Instead of *one* soul, phrenology gives us nearly forty, each in itself as mysterious as the life of the soul is generally. Instead of resolving it into real elements, it resolves it into personal beings of various character. Men and animals, the most complicated of machines, are the most familiar to us. We forget that there is something to be explained in them, or we only find the matter 'clear' when we can imagine everywhere little men over again, who are the bearers of the entire activity. "Indeed, sir, and there is a horse inside!" cried the peasants at X——, when their spiritual shepherd had spent some hours in explaining the nature of the locomotive. With a horse inside everything becomes clear, even though it must be a rather wonderful horse. The horse itself needs no farther explanation.

Phrenology takes a run in order to get beyond the standpoint of the spectral soul, but it ends by peopling the whole skull with spectres. It falls back to the naïf standpoint, which will not be content without putting a machinist to sit in the ingenious machine of our body to guide the whole, a virtuoso to play the instrument. A man who has marvelled all his life at a steam-engine and never understood it, might perhaps think also that there must be in the cylinder again a little steam-engine, which produces the to-and-fro action of the piston.

Was it, however, worth while to deal at such length with wholly unscientific phrenology to gain nothing but a new example of the long-known "irresistible tendency to personification," which has created this flock of active intellectual faculties? Though it may be that some representatives of Materialism have come nearer this view than they should have done, it has, nevertheless, had but little influence on the development of modern nerve-physiology.

Well, but the great reason why there has hitherto been no progress in our explanations of the relation of the brain to the psychical functions seems to us to lie simply in the same ground which doomed phrenology to failure—in the personification of abstract ideas instead of the simple apprehension of the actual, so far as it is possible. What is the way that leads us to the brain? The nerves. In them we have before us a part of that complicated mass as it were unfolded before us. We can experiment on the nerves, since we have before us what is assuredly a single thing. In them we find conduction, electric currents, effects on the contraction of the muscles, on the secretion of the glands; we find reactions on the central organs. We find the peculiar phenomenon of reflex movements, which have already with a very promising tendency towards better things been repeatedly regarded as the primary element of all psychical activity.[25] How

---

[25] Comp. Piderit, Gehirn u. Geist; 1863. Here, of course, the idea of a Entwurf einer physiol. Psychologie, resolution of mental activity into re-

seriously personification stands in the way, or rather how hardly from habitual conceptions emerges the true idea, viz., to derive the personal from the impersonal, is shown in a most notable example by the history of Pflüger's experiments on the psychical importance of the spinal centres. Pflüger showed with great ingenuity and experimental skill that decapitated frogs and other creatures, even amputated tails of lizards, for a considerable time make movements to which we cannot refuse the character of adaptation. The most interesting case is this:—A frog, decapitated, is smeared on the back with acid; it wipes the drop away with the most convenient foot. Now this thigh is cut off; it tries with the stump, and as several efforts are unsuccessful, it at last takes the opposite foot, and completes the movement with this. This was no mere reflex action;—the frog seems to consider. It forms the conclusion that it can no longer attain its object with the one foot, and so it makes the attempt with the other. It seems demonstrated: there are spinal souls, actually tail-souls. Only a soul can think! Whether it is a materialistic soul, too—that is not the matter in dispute; but the entire frog is represented in its spinal marrow. There it thinks and decides after the manner of frogs. A scientific opponent now takes an unhappy frog, beheads it, and boils it slowly. To make the experiment quite perfect, it is proper that a frog which still enjoys its head should be boiled with it, and that another decapitated specimen should be placed alongside the pot for exact comparison. Now the result is that the beheaded frog quietly lets itself be cooked without struggling against its fate like its more perfect companion in misfortune. Conclusion: There are no spinal souls; for

flex activity is still combined with the untenable distinction of an "organ of ideation" and "organ of will." Wundt, who has not only sketched but also carried out most admirably a 'physiological psychology,' shows at S. 328 f. quite clearly the complete analogy between the "compound brain-reflexes" and the spinal reflexes. Comp., too, Horwicz, Psychol. Analysen, 1872, S. 202.

if there were, it would have noticed the danger from the rising heat, and must have thought of flight.[26]

Both conclusions are equally forcible. Pflüger's experiment, however, is more valuable, more fundamental. Let us drop personification; let us cease to seek everywhere in the parts of the frog thinking, feeling, acting frogs, and try instead to explain the phenomenon out of simpler phenomena, *i.e.*, from reflex movements, not from the whole, the unexplained soul. Then we shall easily discover, too, that in these already so complicated sequences of sensation and movement there is afforded the beginning of an explanation of the most complicated psychological activities. This would be a path to follow up.

And what is there to prevent it? Lack of invention or ingenuity for the most difficult experiments? Assuredly not. It is the lack of perception that the explanation of psychical life requires us to carry it back to individual processes which form a necessary part of the activity, but which are utterly and entirely distinct from the mode of action of a complete organism.

But the reflex movement happens unconsciously; and therefore the most composite activity of this kind cannot explain consciousness!

Another objection of the crudest prejudice. Moleschott, as a proof that the consciousness is only in the brain, alleges the well-known observation of Jobert de Lamballes, according to which a girl injured at the top of the spine remained conscious for half an hour, although the whole body, with the exception of the head, was completely paralysed. "Thus the whole spine may become inactive without the consciousness being affected." Good! But when it is concluded from this case that decapitated crea-

---

[26] Comp. Pflüger, Die sensorischen Functionen des Rückenmarks der Wirbelthiere, Berl. 1853; and, on the counter-experiment, Goltz, Die Functionen der Nervencentren des Frosches, in the Königsberg. Med. Jahrb. ii. (1860). For a detailed account, especially of the latter experiment, see Wundt, Vorles. über d. Menschen-u.-Thierseele, Leipz. 1863, ii. 427 ff. Comp. besides, Wundt, Physiol. Psych., 824-827.

tures have no sensation and no consciousness, Moleschott overlooks that the head separated from the spine might show its consciousness in a way we can understand, but not the trunk. What sensation and what consciousness there may or may not be in the spinal centres when separated from the head, we cannot possibly know. This only we may certainly assume, that this consciousness can do nothing that is not based in the mechanical conditions of the centripetal and centrifugal nerve-conduction and the constitution of the centre.

We may not therefore conclude, either, that the spinal centres feel, and *therefore* can do more than a mere mechanism. On the contrary, that the thing takes place quite mechanically is not only certain *a priori*, but, by way of supererogation, is established also by the counter-experiment of gradual heating. For the one class of stimuli there exists in the spine of the frog mechanism producing adapted reflex actions, but for the other class not. Whether in the latter case sensation too is wanting, or only the capacity to react upon the sensation by manifold movements, we do not know. It is, however, not improbable, although we have nothing here to support us but analogy, that everywhere where sensation arises there is also an apparatus to react upon the sensation; conversely we may assume that every reflex apparatus carries with it at least the possibility of a sensation, however weak, while it remains, of course, very doubtful whether, in a whole and sound creature, any part of this sensation of the subordinate centres comes clearly into consciousness.[27]

[27] We are not, therefore, by any means inclined to regard the reflex act itself as that which objectively corresponds to the (subjective) sensation: this would rather be the opposition which the reflex act has to overcome in the central organ, so that sensation must be the less assumed the more uninhibited is the reflex act. Where the reflex act is inhibited from a superior centre, we shall have to suppose that the place where the sensation arises is also transferred to the superior centre; and in the case of a full-grown animal with a developed brain, perhaps definite and distinct sensation occurs only in the brain, while the sensory phenomena of the subordinate centres only contribute to the tuning of the

We see that we are here on the way to make Materialism for the first time consistent, and this, in fact, will be the common feeling. This involves the uncommonly difficult question of consciousness, for obviously we cannot indicate any definite degree of a physical condition of excitation in any part of the central organs which would in itself and necessarily be connected with consciousness. Rather the passing of a condition of excitation into consciousness seems always to depend on a relation between the strength of all simultaneously present excitations in the seats of sensation. Precisely the same physical phenomenon might therefore occur with equal reflexive effect, at one time consciously, at another unconsciously. This is to be borne in mind for the doctrine of 'latent' or 'unconscious' ideas, as to which so much uncertainty has prevailed down to quite recent times. Here we have to do, of course, not with an "unconscious consciousness," but quite simply with an unconscious play of the same mechanism, which in another state of the collective condition is connected with the subjective effect of a particular idea. That there are latent ideas in this sense is the A B C of every empirical psychology, and it cannot escape on a careful examination that not only purposeful but conscious actions, but also phenomena of association of the most various kind result from this play of the same mechanism, which in another collective condition of the brain is connected with ideation.

Because of this unmistakable influence of the collective condition in the organically connected whole, we are also at one with Wundt that in the question of consciousness it is by no means indifferent whether a spinal centre is in connexion with the brain or is separated from it. (Comp. Physiol. Psychol., S. 714 f.) And we should be inclined also to argue that we must suppose a clearer consciousness in the spinal marrow of an animal which, in consequence of its organisation, possesses no cerebrum at all, than in the separated spine of an animal of higher organisation. Moreover, there is no doubt that the assumption of a consciousness in the separated centres of the second and third rank contributes nothing to the explanation of movements (Wundt, *loc. cit.* 829). On the other hand, we cannot agree with Wundt that the absence of any recollection and of anything resulting in spontaneous movement (S. 825 f.) in the decapitated frog is an argument against the real existence of consciousness. To all consciousness there appears, indeed, to belong, as Wundt too supposes, a synthesis; but this need not necessarily reach over a long period, and embrace different sensations in a unity. Even in the mere connexion of the newly arising state with the previous one, there lies a synthesis which makes consciousness logically intelligible. Sensation must refer to a change; that is sufficient. For the rest, let us repeat here that the question can never be to explain movements out of merely hypothetical partial consciousness, but the converse: from the peculiar combination of a more simple and intelligible mechanism with partial consciousness to explain how, in a much more complicated fashion, the whole can follow a strictly physiological mechanism and yet be at the same time the substratum of a manifold content of ideas. We must explain the engine out of its separate wheels, and attribute to the separate wheel, in addition to its other properties, a mysterious potency which belongs to it as part of the engine.

necessary condition of successful investigation into the relation of brain and soul, without Materialism being thereby justified in a metaphysical sense. If the brain can produce the whole spiritual life of man, we may well venture to credit a spinal centre with simple sensation. As to decapitated animals, let us remember how it used to be maintained against Descartes that the animals are not mere machines! Their sensations as such we cannot see; we only *infer* them from the signs of pain, pleasure, fright, anger, &c., which agree with the corresponding gestures in man. But in decapitated animals we find partly the same signs. We should conclude that they are equally connected with sensation. Animals from which the cerebrum has been removed scream or quiver if they are pinched. Flourens found fowls deprived of the brain reduced to a state of coma, and hence concluded that they do not feel. The same animals, however, could walk and stand. They wake if they are pushed, and rise if they are placed on their backs. Johannes Müller therefore rightly draws quite different conclusions: "Flourens concluded from his experiments that the cerebral hemispheres are alone the central organ of sensations. But this is not a legitimate inference from his highly interesting observations, which, in fact, as Cuvier has remarked, prove directly the contrary. An animal in which the cerebral hemispheres have been removed is in a state of stupor, but presents, nevertheless, manifest signs of sensibility, and not merely of the reflexion of impressions (reflex activity)."[28]

Müller himself fails only in holding apparently that the sensation of the animal deprived of its brain is much the same as the sensation of the uninjured animal. This is the result of Müller's complete entanglement in the theory of localisation. He regards the medulla oblongata as the centre of volitional influence; the cerebrum is the seat of ideas, and accordingly of thought. Thus he says, when speaking of the insensibility of the cerebral hemispheres: "That

[28] Handb. d. Phys., i. 845, E.T. i. 826.

part of the brain in which the sensations are converted into ideas and the ideas hoarded up, to appear again as it were as shadows of sensation, is itself devoid of sensibility." Of these remarkable processes, however, we know simply nothing. It is, moreover, very doubtful whether our so-called 'ideas' are anything else but complexes of very subtle sensations. Müller makes the medulla oblongata take care of will and sensation, requires the organs at the base of the brain specially for sensations of sense, and makes thinking take place in the cerebrum. There are accordingly again abstractions to which different provinces are assigned. The personification of the abstract is here not so striking as in phrenology, but it is there. If the reflexion of the inquirer were entirely directed to the phenomena of thinking, feeling, willing, his first thought would be to observe the overflowing of the excitation from one part of the brain to another, the progressive disengagement of tensive forces as the objective element of the psychical act, and not to seek after seats of the different forces, but after the paths of these currents, their relations and combinations.

Müller appeals to comparative anatomy to support his view of the cerebrum, that is, to the department which is still the most important, and almost the sole basis of this conception, since pathological anatomy has shown itself so refractory. It must, in fact, be admitted that the gradual development of the cerebral hemispheres in the animal world leads us to conclude with extreme probability that in this important organ must be sought the essential ground of the mental superiority of man. But it does not follow from this that it is also necessarily the seat of the higher intellectual activity. It is clear that here we have to make a considerable leap. But we will try to make the matter plain. A mill with a very large pool can work more regularly the whole summer through with the same and on the whole a moderate flow of water, than a mill with a very small pool or none at all. It can also, in case of need, make a special effort without immediately exhausting itself; it is altogether more favourably placed and works to greater advantage. The pool is the reason of this advantage; yet the labour is not in the pool, but in the result of the outflow from it and its setting in motion an elaborate mechanism. As we wish here only to indicate the logical chasm, and not ourselves to set up a hypothesis, we add another illustration. Gutenberg's simple printing-press did little compared with our most complicated steam-presses. The superiority of the latter lies not in their form, but in their elaborate machinery; shall we thereupon assume that the printing is done in this machinery? We may, in fact, take our senses as an example. The more perfectly constructed eye determines better seeing, but the seeing takes place not in the eye, but in the brain. Thus, then, the question of the seat of the higher mental functions is at least open, if not altogether misstated; but that the cerebral hemispheres have a decisive import with regard to these functions may be at once admitted.

Müller believes too, it is true, that Flourens with his knife has given direct proof of the seat of the higher mental functions in the cerebrum. Büchner's phrase is well known, that Flourens has cut away 'the soul' from his fowl bit by bit. But even conceding that the higher mental functions of the fowl—functions so difficult to define—had really fallen away in these vivisections, even then the supposition does not follow, since the cerebrum need still be only a necessary factor in the production of these activities, but by no means their seat. But we must further observe that in the organic body the removal of an organ like the cerebrum cannot be effected without the animal's becoming unwell, and especially without the neighbouring parts being seriously disturbed in their functions. This is shown, *e.g.*, by an experiment of Hertwig's (in Müller), where a pigeon from which the upper portion of the hemispheres was removed could not hear for fifteen days, but at length recovered its hearing and so lived for ten weeks. In Flourens' experiments the animals usually lost their sight as well as hearing, a circumstance which led this inquirer to believe that they no longer retained consciousness. Longet has proved, on the other hand, by a very remarkable experiment, that if the optic thalami and the other parts of the brain except the hemispheres are carefully spared, the sight of the pigeons partially remains. Suppose now we took and blinded the most brilliant writer, deprived him of hearing, disabled his tongue, and besides gave him a slight fever or a permanent intoxication. He must retain the cerebrum, and we are convinced that he will not exhibit many traces of his higher mental functions. How, then, can we expect it from the mutilated fowl?

The latest cerebral researches, of which we shall speak presently, secure the cerebrum its preponderant importance in quite another way. It appears here not as 'soul' or as an organ which in some unintelligible way produces 'intelligence' and 'will,' but as that organ which brings about the most complicated combinations of sensation and motion. Not 'will' as such is here produced, but an effect entirely analogous to reflex acts, only more manifoldly compounded and determined by more manifold impulses from other parts of the brain. The brain does not produce a psychological abstraction which would still have to transform itself into the concrete action; but there is concrete action, as in a reflex action, as the immediate consequence of the cerebral conditions and the conditions of excitation existing in the various paths. We do not, therefore, cut away the 'soul' of the fowl bit by bit, but the knife destroys a combining apparatus consisting merely of individual parts of the most various and decided import. The individual character of the creature, its animal peculiarity continues until the last trace of life disappears. But whether consciousness is exclusively attached to the functions of this apparatus is still very doubtful.*

* Comp. Note 27.

As an example of a one-sided and arbitrary philosophy of the brain, we may mention farther the views of Carus and Huschke, which in slight modifications have been widely spread, although they rest entirely on the principle of the personification of traditional abstractions. They carry us back indeed into the sphere of the Philosophy of Nature, without, however, too widely deviating from the present standpoint of science; for in the treatment of the brain we have hardly, even in the most recent period, passed beyond the Philosophy of Nature.

Huschke taught in a dissertation of 1821 that to the three vertebræ of the skull there correspond three main divisions of the brain, and that, therefore, we must also assume three main intellectual faculties—a curious causal connexion, but one quite in the modes of thought of the time. To the medulla oblongata and the cerebrum is assigned *willing*, to the parietal lobes *feeling*, and to the frontal lobes *thinking*. Of course 'polarity' plays a part in all this. The cerebellum is opposed in a polar way to the cerebrum; the former serves for motion, the latter for sensation and thinking; the former has active, the latter receptive activity. In this respect the parts of the bases of the brain are completely attached to the cerebrum; but then, again, within this mass there arises polar opposition. As assisting us to understand the mode of origin of scientific ideas, it will always be interesting to observe that Huschke regarded the famous experiments of Flourens, which were published some years later, as an experimental demonstration of his theory.[29]

Carus lately proposed a very similar trichotomy, but found the original seat of the soul in the corpora quadrigemina, while Huschke claims also the optic thalami, the posterior lobes of the cerebrum, and other portions. Huschke thinks the corpora quadrigemina too insignificant for so important a function as that of the life of the soul,

[29] Huschke, Schädel, Hirn u. Seele, Jena, 1854, S. 177 ff.

especially as they visibly lose in importance in the development of man, as well as in the ascending animal series. This circumstance does not disturb Carus, since he starts from the *original disposition*, and thinks it an absurdity to regard emotion, intelligence, and will as so localised in the developed mass that they would be, so to speak, "imprisoned each in one of the three divisions of the brain." But it must be very different "if we speak of the primary disposition of these structures, when as yet the conducting fibres are not developed, or only imperfectly so, and when, therefore, there can as yet be no question of the finer shades of intellectual life." Only, then, in this mere disposition to a later developed intellectual activity are its three main tendencies to be considered as localised. In so far as Carus conceives this whole localisation as at bottom only the symbol of the peculiar development of mind, his standpoint evades refutation by losing itself in metaphysical vagueness.

If we examine the proofs of the two physiologists whose views are so nearly related, we are met at once by that extended use of comparative anatomy in which from the outset the standpoint of the Philosophy of Nature is so remarkably fused with that of positive science. Because comparative anatomy rests upon the most precise apprehension of particulars, because it requires for its foundation the most exact operations, especially in the anatomy of the nervous system, inquirers only too easily transfer the feeling of their exactness to the conclusions which they think themselves bound to draw from the comparison of corresponding forms. Now, in all conclusions as to the relation of brain formations to mental activities, the procedure is by no means simple. We compare visible human organisms with those of animals. Good! This comparison admits of exact methods. We can weigh the corpora quadrigemina of a fish; we can reckon the proportion of the cerebellum in birds to the whole of the brain. We can compare this proportion with that which we find in man. So far the way is smooth. But now in the same way I must know the mental functions of animals, compare these with each other and with the functions of man. Here begins the most difficult of tasks. For I must now, as it were, adapt striking similarities and differences of the one field to those of the other, compare the degree and regularity of the phenomena observed, gradually find a network of such correspondences, and thus become more certain of the individual facts. In this process I must avoid the illusions which our fertile imagination is ready to suggest to us in such numbers.

Yet, instead of accumulating difficulties, we will rather pointedly indicate the impossibility of the procedure. This lies in the want of a comparative psychology. In psychology we can undertake no dissections, can weigh and measure nothing, can exhibit no preparations. Names like thinking, feeling, willing are mere names. Who will point out exactly what corresponds to them? Shall we make definitions? A treacherous element! They are of no use, at least for any exact comparisons. And with what are we to connect our observations? With what measure shall we measure? In this groping in the dark it is only childish prejudice or the clairvoyant impulse of the metaphysician that is sure of finding anything. The understanding has only one way: it can only compare the positive, attested, observed actions of the animal world with their organs. It must resolve the question into the question of modes and causes of motion. This is a way yet to be trodden; for men like Scheitlin, Brehm, and other friends of the animal world, for all their services, can hardly be regarded as even pioneers in those things that we must possess before we can move with even moderate confidence among such comparisons.

What shall we say, then, if the larger size of the cerebellum in birds and mammals is attributed to their *motor* character as opposed to the more *receptive* nature of man?

It is clear that nothing at all can be learnt in this way.

An anatomist observes that in the sheep the anterior pair of the corpora quadrigemina is large, the posterior pair small; conversely in the dog. This leads him to the notion that the anterior pair is sensible, the posterior pair motor. Can such an idea do more than at the most serve as a direction-post for farther researches? These researches, however, must not consist in the accumulation of similar observations with the like arbitrary interpretation, but they must pass into a defined sphere which can be worked by means of experiment. Above all things, we must get rid of the general ideas of scholastic psychology! If any one shows me that a slight injury to some portion of the brain makes an otherwise healthy cat give up mousing, I will believe that we are in the right path of psychological discoveries. But even then I will not assume that the point has been found in which the ideas of mouse-hunting have their exclusive seat. If a clock strikes the hours wrongly because a wheel is injured, it does not follow from this that it was this wheel that struck the hours.

Above all, we must be clear that in all the paragraphs of the old scholastic psychology there is nowhere mention of things that we may ever expect to find again in the elements of the cerebral functions. It is with them much as if one tries to find the various activities of a locomotive, so far as they can be externally observed, localised in the individual steam-pipes or in particular parts of the machine. Here the faculty of expelling smoke, there a similar faculty for puffs of steam, here the turning power, there the faculty of running quickly or slowly, and elsewhere again the capacity for drawing burdens. In our whole traditional psychology the actions of men are classified, without any regard to the elements of their origin, according to certain relations to life and its aims, and indeed in such a way that the mere psychological analysis often shows clearly how little what is denoted by a single word forms a true unity. What is, for instance, the 'courage' of the sailor in the storm, and then on the other hand in regard to supposed ghostly apparitions? What is 'memory,' what is 'ratiocination,' having regard to the various forms and spheres of their effects? Almost all these psychological notions give us a word by means of which a portion of the phenomena of human life is very imperfectly classified. With this classification is combined the metaphysical delusion of a common substantial basis of these phenomena, and this delusion must be destroyed.

How deeply the prejudice as to the localisation of the mental faculties may be rooted is shown by a still almost pathetic example from the life and activity of one of the earliest inquirers in this whole department. Flourens, who in the beginning of the 'twenties' gained a European reputation by his famous experiments in vivisection, returned forty years afterwards to the investigation of the functions of the brain, and applied a method which deserves admiration for its novelty and ingenuity. He applied small metal balls to the surface of the brain of animals and let them slowly sink through. The balls in every case forced their way in course of time right through to the base of the brain, without *any disturbance of function whatever resulting.* Only where the balls stood directly over the vital centre, death followed when they had sunk completely through. Flourens recounts these experiments in a dissertation on the curability of brain wounds (Compte Rendu, 62), which shows, moreover, that there are numerous cases of such lesions in which the individual sustained no hurt, and that, in fact, brain-wounds heal with surprising ease. And yet in the same dissertation Flourens still declares the division of the mental faculties in accordance with the organs of the brain to be the aim of science!

Only of late have we entered upon better paths, and small as the positive results may still be, there appears at once firm ground and a sure starting-point of investigation. We must especially mention here the anatomical inquiries and theories of Meynert on the structure of the brain.[30] Meynert has undertaken the first thoroughgoing attempt, leaving aside all psychological views, to gain a collective view of the structure of the brain and the arrangement of its parts, and thus to determine the general course of all the cerebral functions, especially in regard to the possible modes of physiological phenomena. As a fixed starting-point in the latter regard he employs merely the well-known partly sensory, partly motory nature of the nerve-cords of the spinal marrow penetrating into the brain. These he follows up along their paths until he comes to the cerebral cortex, whose different regions there obtain one fixed character, and conversely backwards from the cerebral cortex through definite anatomically given steps to the spinal cord and the peripheral nerves.

The general picture resulting from this mode of consideration is, so far as we are here concerned, briefly as follows. The nerve-paths multiply as they mount towards the cortex of the cerebrum, and simplify in their descending course. The sites of this multiplication are organs of the grey substance, that is, meeting-points of ganglion cells, which are traversed by the white substance of the conducting fibres. In the same organs takes place an extremely manifold combination of conducting paths. The grey substance, which undoubtedly effects these junctions and ramifications, separates from the standpoint of this classification as it were into three categories: the first forms the cerebral cortex, the grey substance of the first degree; then follow the great ganglia at the base of the brain as grey substance of the second degree; and, finally, the central grey substance of the cavities as third stage. Besides this, there is of course too the grey substance of the cerebellum, which is an organ of a specially rich and manifold complication of sensory and motory paths.

[30] Comp. chiefly Meynert, Vom Gehirne d. Säugeth. in Stricker's Hdb. d. Lehre v. d. Geweben, Leipz. 1871, S. 694 ff., E. T. ii. 367 ff.

Meynert makes this, for simplicity's sake, into a fourth class of grey substance, which does not, however, belong to this procession of classes, but has a separate position most akin to the organs of the second order.

The conducting fibres (white substance) Meynert classes summarily into the system of association and of projection. The fibres of the former serve to connect the different portions of the cortex; those of the latter maintain intercourse between the cortex of the cerebrum and the external world, which projects itself, as it were, by means of the nerves in the hemisphere of the cortex. This conception of the projection of the external world in the cortex might indeed be regarded as a disturbing psychological addition, but it is so generally held, that it may, in fact, be separated from the apparently necessary consequence that consciousness is a function of the cortex. At bottom, we may say that the outer world projects itself in every nerve-centre; in the rudest, simplest form in the grey matter of the spine and brain-cavities; more perfectly in the great ganglia, and finally, in the most perfect and peculiarly human way in the cerebral cortex. In all this there is to be observed a certain succession of classes. The grey matter of the third class brings about reflex acts. These may be inhibited from certain points of the second class; the impression received does not act again immediately outwards, but it is taken up in a more complicated psychical image, or it is sometimes as it were stored up for the production of a state of excitation. But the organs of the second rank are at least partially themselves again of a reflex nature. They are the more compound reflex acts, directed towards a vital end, that are here formed. A stimulus arriving here, according to its nature and to the state of the centre, sometimes causes no movement at all, sometimes causes, perhaps, a whole series of simultaneous or even successive movements.

But these reflex acts of the second class may again be inhibited and modified by the intervention of the third and highest kind, the cerebral cortex. Here, it is said, it is conscious will that interferes, and yet the apparatus, the results of the function, are of the same kind as in the second class, only again much more manifold and developed. Conscious will itself seems, therefore, to exhibit itself physiologically only as the highest kind of reflex action, which, be it said in passing, does not affect either its consciousness or its ethical dignity as 'will.' Our psychical functions remain what they are, even though we have before us in their physiological manifestation nothing but an extremely perfect mechanism, which in its complexity far surpasses our power of mathematical apprehension.

We have wandered a little from the exposition of Meynert's theory. He confines himself strictly to exhibiting the morphological organisation of the brain; but it is just the greatest advantage of a really luminous and orderly morphology that it immediately gives to us also an insight into functions. This becomes still more evident when we follow somewhat more particularly the course of the nervous processes.

The projection system has, that is to say, a double path. The one leads from the cerebral cortex through the crusta of the cerebral peduncle to the spinal cord, the other through the tegmentum of the peduncle. In the former path the second class is chiefly represented by the nucleus caudatus and the nucleus lenticularis; in the latter by the optic thalami, the corpora quadrigemina, and the inner corpus geniculatum; the former is purely motor, the latter mixed. The path of the crusta of the peduncle grows together with the nuclei enclosed in it, as we mount in the animal series, proportionally with the development of the hemispheres of the cerebrum. In man the crusta of the peduncle and nucleus lenticularis are very strongly developed; the height of the crusta of the peduncle equals the height of the tegmentum, while, *e.g.*, in the roe its proportion is one to five. We must conclude from this that the forms of movement and sense impressions which are most indispensable for animal life are conducted and collected on the path of the tegmentum. The great nuclei imbedded here are also pre-eminently the seats where compound reflex actions are formed, which, as it seems, are only inhibited, strengthened and generally regulated from the cortex. In the path of the crusta of the peduncle, on the contrary, such movements appear to be especially conducted, the combination of which takes place in the cerebral cortex itself.

It might surprise us that it is just a motor path whose higher development runs parallel with the increase of the hemispheres and attains its maximum in man. Are not many animals superior to man in the grace and quickness of their movements? Does not, *e.g.*, the gibbon sporting in the boughs laugh to scorn all the gymnastic feats of which man is capable? Are we not, on the other hand, superior to the animals in the strength and variety of our sensations? Do not our scientific perceptions demand an exercise of the senses which is unknown to the animals? Nay, since all consciousness is ultimately based upon sensations, should we not expect that a relatively higher development of the sensory paths must go hand in hand with the development of intellectual life?

In answer, we must take into consideration speech and the skilful hand of man in their import for the intellectual life. As to speech, we already know in fact the part of the cerebral cortex in which sounds are combined into significant words; and of all the phenomena of mental disturbance none is at present nearer to being understood than aphasia. But speech as well as manual skill show us that the most important points are not the strength and swiftness of movements, but complexity and nicely calculated purpose. But for this there is required an extensive co-ordinating apparatus with connexions which run from any point of a given system into a multiplicity of points in other systems. In speech it is not only necessary to measure nicely the pressure of the lips which produces a *b* or a *p*, or to make the movements of the organs which form a word of difficult pronunciation follow each other fluently. Speech must also mean something; and therefore from the place where the word is combined, there must run again manifold connexions to the places where sense-impressions are combined. These connexions can in part hardly be otherwise conceived than that each definite sensation or definite impulse towards muscular movement finds itself represented in a whole series of cells in the cerebral cortex, each of which again has its special connexions. As in the apparatus of Corti in the snail a whole series of nerves lie ready to receive impressions, very few of which, however, are required for the conducting of a particular sound; so we must conceive that in the nerve-centres also, and especially in those of the higher kinds, a stimulus arriving is received by many cells, in only a few of which the phenomenon of excitation receives an immediate psychical import; just in the same way that a motor impulse, calculated to set a group of muscles in motion, may proceed from many brain-cells, while their connexions with other parts of the brain determine whether the impulse is really given or not. It is true that we shall seek in vain for an apparatus in the brain that regulates this choice of activity so simply as the vibrations of the membrana basilaris regulate the activity of the auditory nerves in the snail. But as soon as we suppose that the conducting or non-conducting of the nerve-processes is determined by nothing so much as by the state of excitation in the fibres and cells which already exists, and is also determined by the accessory conductions, we need seek no further mechanism as a sort of switching-place on the lines of conduction. The regulating principle is given.

As to the control of the human hand, we must not only, because of its great mobility and adaptability for the most ingenious uses, assume for the motory portions of the brain a rich development of the combining apparatus, but we must also take into account writing, for example, which stands in very intimate relation with speech. If we then think farther of the achievements of a pianist, a painter, a surgeon, &c., in which the nicest adjustment of motor impulses co-operates with the most manifold combinations, the need of a great extension of the motor apparatus of the brain for human activities will become clear. To this we must add the mobility of the features and the extraordinary significance of the movements of the eyes, which play a very essential part in the formation of visual images and in the apprehension of delicate relations. The training of the senses for scientific perceptions also makes demands upon the motory apparatus. Sight is most closely connected with the activity of the muscles of the eye, touch with the muscular sense of the hand. But even in general bodily movement, man, despite all the gymnastic performances of the apes, is far superior to the animals in variety and nicety of attitudes and movements. Nor need we point here to the performances of dancers, of Japanese jugglers, or of pantomimists. Walking, the upright position, the free movement of the arms, lead to a quantity of movements which we regard immediately as the expression of mind, and in which even the awkwardest man announces his character by a strictly adapted conformation. But even amongst sensations, those of the muscular sense (let us only recall speech, the features, ocular movements) are perhaps just the most important, whether they have their seat directly in the motor apparatus or depend upon its activity.

Meantime physiology, too, has not been idle, and has taught us that the processes in all nerves in the condition of excitation are essentially the same.[31] There is not a special nervous process of sensation and another of motion, but the physical process is in all cases of the

---

[31] Comp. Hermann, Grundr. der Physiol., 4 Aufl., S. 316 f.; Wundt, Physiol. Psych., S. 104, *et saep.*

excitation of a nerve essentially the same, and differs only in strength or weakness, quickness or slowness, &c. Moreover, each fibre irritated in any part of its course conducts centrifugally as well as centripetally; only that in the sensory fibres the former, in the motory fibres the latter, conduction passes off without effect. We have here, therefore, a perfectly certain case of the principle that a conduction propagating itself in more ways than one nevertheless attains a result in only one of its paths, and there is nothing to prevent us from applying this principle in the widest extent to the functions of the brain.[32]

Finally, direct experiment also has done its part. The experiments of Hitzig and Nothnagel in Germany and of Ferrier in England have shown that the cortex of the anterior cerebral lobes influences particular movements. A rabbit, e.g., whose forefoot is affected by the destruction of a particular small portion of the cortex, is not exactly paralysed; it may still continue to carry out even combined movements, as they are probably formed in the nerve-centres; but it is uncertain, it sets its foot down awry, allows the affected part to be placed in another position without resistance, and seems to have no distinct consciousness of the position of this limb; and even though the animal finally succumbs to the cerebral injury, yet a period of six to ten days, if the creature lives so long, suffices to remove again the perturbation of movement. How is this to be explained? One of the projectors of these experiments, Nothnagel, believes that we have, as it were, a 'partial paralysis of the muscular sense,' but that it is not the ultimate centre, the real 'terminus' which is injured, but only a station on the line, and therefore other paths may open themselves again for

---

[32] Here then exists the very important principle that a weak state of irritation already existing in a nerve at the same time increases the irritability of the nerve by a fresh stimulus. Comp. Hermann, Physiol., 4 Aufl., S. 323. This connexion especially throws a clear light upon the association of ideas.

the same function.[33] On injuring a neighbouring spot, the 'muscular sense' did not show itself affected, but there appeared a certain deflexion in the placing of the foot; this perturbation also gradually disappears again. Here Nothnagel assumes a station for the exciting will-impulse, but again supposes it not to be the terminus. "The *restitutio in integrum* compels us to the conclusion that here only a path is interrupted; that the part of the brain cannot be eliminated where alone the will-impulse passes to the nerve-fibres; that is where alone the will-impulse is formed. If a restoration is possible, then other paths must act vicariously, or at least the capacity to produce the will-impulse must inhere in other places." The experiments when the corresponding places in both hemispheres were destroyed did not succeed. It remained, therefore, doubtful whether the gradual restoration of the functions is effected by the intervention of the other hemisphere, or by the arising of new paths in the same hemisphere. In any case, the reporter believes himself authorised to conclude, "even if it were at all possible that a circumscribed spot, in which psychical functions would arise, should after its elimination be replaced by another, we must yet come to the conclusion that there is no rigid localisation of the mental functions in particular centres of the cerebral cortex."[34]

Let us next occupy ourselves a moment with the premiss, that is, with the recurring axiom—only a mediating, transmitting region can be replaced after its destruction; if the original organ of a psychical function is destroyed, a substitute for it is inconceivable.

Why? Is it because with the destruction of the psychical faculty its impulse to express itself also disappears, and therefore the occasion for a new formation? That would end in a dualism which it were impossible to reconcile with the principle of the conservation of energy. Or is it because the psychical function is something absolutely

[33] In Virchow's Archiv, Bd. lvii., S. 196 f. [34] Loc. cit., 201, 205.

original, which cannot be reproduced by the organic connexion with corresponding, perhaps subordinate, functions of the neighbouring parts? That would be a quite new principle, which attributes to the intellectual rank of phenomena a physiological influence which nowhere shows itself, and which, in fact, contradicts every principle of physiological inquiry. We see, therefore, in the scruples of the reporter merely an effect of the old theory of mental faculties which so long rendered the study of the brain fruitless. If the 'muscular sense' or the 'will-impulse' is hypostasized in the sense of this old psychology as a 'faculty,' which is served by a greater or lesser portion of the brain, then on the materialistic view the 'faculty of the soul' is destroyed together with the corresponding part of the brain; on the dualistic view its indispensable instrument is destroyed, and then, indeed, we cannot see where the impulse is to come from that is to take its place. If, on the contrary, we keep strictly in view that from the standpoint of physiology, even in the production of a conscious impulse of will, we have to do with an organic process like every other, that the 'faculty' of psychology is only a name, with which the possibility of the process is apparently elevated to a special thing, that finally the inquiry into the intellectual classification of the functions has nothing at all to do with physiology; then we cannot at all see why even the 'terminus' of a psychical line or the place of origin of a 'faculty,' like any other part of the brain, may not be replaced in its activity by new lines.

Here on the ground of the old psychology yet another consideration might arise, that is strange enough, but yet deserves mention, because prejudices of this kind must be followed to their last retreat. We might, that is to say, demur that the will-impulse to move a particular part of the body is destroyed, while the mastery of the will over the other parts continues. The will itself, which is a whole, seems thus to be merely a sum of partial functions.

But why not? we must ask again: for, to begin with, we know nothing but that certain actions of the creature disappear and again appear, when a certain portion of the brain is injured. These actions are of the kind in which the causal connexion is most complicated, and which we attribute to a 'will.' But what do we know of this will? Apart from the inventions of the psychologists absolutely nothing but what is contained in the facts, in the manifestations of life. If in a certain sense we speak rightly of a unity in the will, this is merely general unity of character, of mode and manner. But this general unity also belongs to the sum of the particular manifestations of life, and at bottom only to this. When we speak in this of 'will,' we only add a comprehensive word for a group of vital phenomena. Every supposition of a thing for a name is to exceed the facts given us, and is, therefore, scientifically worthless.

Now we shall be able to see too whether we are to expect or not a "rigid localisation of the mental functions in particular centres of the cerebral cortex." Nothnagel is here quite right; his experiments are opposed to such a rigid localisation, even if the restoration of the functions could be explained by the intervention of the other hemisphere. For even the will-impulse proceeds after this process of restoration from another point than before. But the will-impulse, and even the will-impulse to move a particular member, is again merely a name for a sum of functions, which has a definite external result. The elementary functions of the single cells and threads may withal be very strictly localised, and yet it is conceivable that the same result under special circumstances may be attained by another road. But so soon as we see again the same result, we say, in accordance with ordinary psychological notions, "The will-impulse is restored." What was destroyed, however, is by no means restored, but merely the same product by means of quite different factors.

To be clear as to this is of the utmost importance; for it is very probable that the most manifold substitutions of this kind only occur when we come to the highest mental functions of man. He who, for instance, is accustomed to think more in notions than in sensible images will probably have his thinking at first very much hindered by an attack of aphasia, until he succeeds in completing the transition from the premiss to the conclusion in mere intuition, and so reaching the same goal which he formerly reached only through "dumb speech." It is very probable that the participation of different regions of the brain in thinking is very different, even in healthy individuals, while the result, the thought, remains the same.

While Nothnagel concluded from his experiments that the psychical functions in the brain are *not* localised, Hitzig, on the contrary, concludes "that certain particular psychical functions, probably all, at their entrance into matter or at their origin, are assigned to circumscribed centres of the cerebral cortex."[35] The opposition between the views of the two inquirers is not so great as it appears, for Hitzig is free from the old psychological conceptions, and by "psychical functions" understands not hypostasized words, but—since we have to do with the functions of the simplest possible parts of the brain—really simple psychical phenomena, and simplicity is here to be gained only by most strictly keeping to the corresponding physical fact. The will to bend or stretch this particular member is quite simply and naturally transferred to that point of the cerebral cortex, through the electrical stimulation of which the movement in question is excited. In this respect the pioneering experiments of Hitzig are made with such delicacy, that he succeeds in resolving the physical phenomenon into finer elements than in a certain sense exist for the psychical phenomenon. When, *e.g.*, from a particular point of the cortex, one ear, and only this, is set into violent movement, it is fair to ask

[35] Untersuchungen über d. Gehirn, Berl. 1874, S. 31, 56.

whether the will can ever produce so definite a partial effect. It need not do so, since it serves no object involving life. The delicacy of the psychical functions consists again in other points in which of course no physiological experiment can approach even afar off; above all, in the incredibly sharply defined intensity of every excitation and the exact measure of the corresponding movement; then also in the combination of different muscular activities into a collective movement of adaptation. Here again let us only recall the performances of the human hand, of the tongue, of the facial muscles in mimic expression, and we shall easily see where the intellectual element lies. We find it everywhere in measure, in form, in the relation of the co-operation of the physical functions, where the smallest feature, especially in artistic treatment, attains the highest importance. From the purely physical side of the process, however, the elements of these most delicate mixtures of various impulses can be shown to us isolated in a way which is impossible for the will.

It is not uninteresting that Ferrier,[36] in his crude and unmethodical repetitions of Hitzig's experiments, came much oftener than the latter upon the origin of complete purposeful movements, whose origin he attributed to the stimulation of a particular portion of the brain. By the use of too strong currents he had irritated also neighbouring parts, and as, *e.g.*, the centres for bending, stretching, the adduction and rotation of a limb, all lie near to one another, it is very natural that a simultaneous irritation of several centres may produce in their collective action, *e.g.*, a running movement, or in a cat the movement of scratching. Hitzig's experiments with their exacter isolation are physiologically incomparably more valuable; but for psychology it would be of special interest to see how the adapted

---

[63] Ferrier describes his investigations in the West Riding Lunatic Asylum Reports for 1873; there is a short notice in the 'Academy,' Nov. 1, 1873. Comp. the criticism of Hitzig, *loc. cit.*, S. 63–113.

movements might be made to arise artificially and with exacter calculation of the individual impulses. It is, moreover, not improbable that in the deeper lying layers of the cerebral cortex there are cells, by exciting which a whole series of points lying on the surface may be secondarily excited at the same time, and in a definitely regulated manner. But in whatever the co-ordinative mechanism may consist that unites a group of elementary effects into one purposeful activity, in any case we have good ground to assign to the idea of this purposeful activity and to the will to call it forth no other seat than that part of the cerebral cortex in which this activity itself has its origin.

This must be quite otherwise if we had an immediate consciousness—a consciousness to be ranked with sensation in the widest sense of the word—of our own muscular activity. We should then have to suppose that somewhere in a sensory centre the idea of the action in question was formed, and that from here a transmission was propagated into the mechanism of the motory system; but in all probability both kinds of 'idea' must be assumed side by side in order to satisfy the requirements of a rational psychology. The idea of an action, *e.g.*, of running, as it might be formed in a sensory centre, can, it is probable, from its originating from pictures of objects, never be quite the same as the idea which is produced from its own activity. At the same time both may perform the same service in a train of thought. Thus, *e.g.*, in following a narrative, we may develop the images excited in us calmly and objectively; but if we are more affected by it, we put ourselves into the place of the person engaged, and then every one may observe in himself how the idea of a blow is often connected with a twitching sensation in the arm, the idea of a leap with an inclination to spring. In man speech appears furthermore as the most important focus of ideas, and here it can hardly be doubted that the idea of the word has its seat where the word is produced. Our thinking, it has often been observed, is a gentle, and, as it were, internal speaking. But careful observation shows us very easily that there are very frequently, and in case of great emotion always, actual impulses in the vocal organs connected with this 'internal' speaking.

All this might also be the effect of 'association,' but association itself can hardly be brought into harmony with the facts of physiology, except by referring it, on the one hand, to the existence of the most manifold conductions, but, on the other hand, to the partial identity of the sphere of excitation.

The facts of mnemonics show that from the idea of 'castle' the transition is very easy to 'wall' or 'tower,' but just as easy to 'mountain,' 'nobility,' 'middle ages,' 'estate,' 'Rhine,' &c. Especially easy, too, is the transition to mere homonyms, as, *e.g.*, from the habitable castle (Schloss) to the 'lock' (Schloss) of the door, the 'key' (Schlüssel), 'locksmith' (Schlosser), and so on.

On the association theory of last century all the individual fibres, which were conceived as the bearers of such ideas, must lie in close connexion with each other, in order that the vibration might pass from one to the other. Yet here we come upon the most obvious impossibility, especially if we think of the simple and easily repeated feat of the teachers of mnemonics, which consists in linking together the most heterogeneous ideas that can be suggested to them by the interposition of one, or at most two connecting words. Everything must lie close together. If, however, we assume extended spheres of excitation for an idea, and besides the proper connexions from the purely objective image of the idea to the motory foci of excitation connected with it, and again to the speech-centre of the corresponding word, we shall be easily led to assume for related ideas a partial identity of the sphere of excitation.

It will always be of service, in order to avoid a relapse into the old psychological ideas and to assist the right view to come to the front, if it is shown how even the complex psychical images can be explained from those simple beginnings with which exact research is now concerning itself. For the rest, we must entirely approve the reserve with which Hitzig thinks himself bound to refrain from all ulterior speculations on the activity of the brain and mind. The inquirer who has once trodden the right path is more surely led by the narrowly defined, but at the same time significant results of his labour, than by prematurely developed theories, and at the same time he must surely and strongly influence his colleagues by the mere example of his labour. Hitzig quotes a saying of Fechner to the effect that the safety, fruitfulness, and depth of a general conception depend not upon the general, but the elementary in it.[37] Everything depends only upon our certainly apprehending what is the elementary, and it is then an enormous stride in investigations into the brain and the psychical functions if it is once generally recognised that the elementary in psychical functions can be nothing else than the physiologically elementary. In this way, too, Materialism in this sphere has become a good deal more consistent, and accordingly brought near its end also; for its consistency is its destruction.

We possess now, too, at length, in Wundt's admirable 'Principles of Physiological Psychology' a work which has already made the new and only fruitful views the basis of a comprehensive treatment of the psychological sphere. Let us hear how Wundt deals with the decisive point.

"We can conceive that a particular nerve-fibre or a particular ganglion-cell operates only in the form of the sensation of light or of a motor impulse, but not how it is that certain central elements are supposed to serve the imagination and others the understanding. Apparently the contradiction here lies in this, that we conceive complex functions attached to simple forms. But we must necessarily assume that elementary forms are also capable of elementary performances only; and such elementary

[37] Hitzig, loc. cit., S. 52; comp. Fechner, Elemente d. Psychophysik, i. S. 7.

performances, in the sphere of the central functions, are sensations, impulses of movement, but not imagination, memory, &c." "Everything," observes Wundt farther on, "that we call will and intelligence resolves itself, as soon as it is traced back to its physiological elements, into nothing but sentient impressions transforming themselves into movements."[38]

What will become, then, of the 'unity of thought,' if the individual idea is something so uncommonly complex? Just what becomes of the unity of an artistically constructed building when we consider its composition from individual stones. It is a *formal* unity, which may very well exist along with the composite nature of the material in which it is realised. But as to this material and its elements—sensation and the consciousness of motor impulses—we must carry out, in the strictest sense of the word, the law of the conservation of energy. This is the road to that consistent Materialism which leads us immediately to the 'limits of natural knowledge.'

Let us try to apply consistent Materialism in a particular example.[39]

---

[38] Op. cit., Leipz. 1873, S. 226, 228.
[39] The example here given might perhaps have been dropped in the second edition, if a highly characteristic misunderstanding had not shown me that such illustrations are not only necessary for many readers, but that, where it is possible, a commentary should be added to them, and that for those in whom we would expect a better understanding. Professor R. Seydel, in a lecture entitled 'Widerlegung des Materialismus u. der Mechanischen Weltanschauung,' Berl., 1873, has dealt at length with our example, and with an astonishing naïveté has treated the main point, for the sake of which alone the example was taken, as an obvious "oversight"! He says (S. 17): "Here now Lange is guilty of an oversight, which we must not attribute to the mechanical theory as such. It is, of course, obvious enough that the telegram, as a physical object—*i.e.*, paper, pencil, and light waves—could not be taken up into this causal series. What has been the causal element in the merchant's springing up is obviously only the *content* of the message, that is, not what the telegram was, but what it imported. This is so obvious," &c. Here I really cannot help expressing the wish that even among the 'philosophers' it may at last become usual to learn something reasonable about things before venturing to talk of them. Any one who has the most superficial notion of the consecution of a physical causal series, to say nothing of the law of the conservation of energy, must know that here 'paper, pencil, and lightwaves' do, in fact, belong to the

A merchant sits comfortably in his easy-chair and does not know himself whether the greater part of his ego is occupied with smoking, dozing, reading the paper, or digestion. The servant enters, bringing a telegram, "Antwerp! Jonas & Co. failed."—"Let Jacob put the horses to!" The servant flies. The master jumps up, completely sobered: some dozen steps through the room—down into his counting-house—gives instructions—dictates letters—despatches telegrams—then enters his carriage. The horses pant; he is at the bank, on the Exchange, amongst his business friends: before an hour is over he is at home, throwing himself again into his chair with a sigh. "Thank heaven, I have provided against the worst! Now I must think further!"

A splendid chance for a psychological picture! Alarm, hope, feeling, calculation, ruin and victory crowded into

causal series; and whoever carefully follows the course of my exposition must see very well also that I have chosen this example at all only for the sake of its paradoxical appearance. I wanted to force the thinking reader for once to realise the mechanical theory in its full consequences, and this must also be the case with all those who have at least so much physical knowledge as to know that 'content' and 'meaning' are not forces which pass over from the message into me, but that they only originate within me. Nothing comes into me but these light-waves, and now the question is simply whether we will draw the consequences of the mechanical theory or not. We must know whether we say yes or no to the question which Hermann (Physiol., 4 Aufl., S. 459) has formulated with exemplary clearness, "whether precisely the same concatenation of centripetal impressions in the same organism would not always have precisely the same effect (the same apparently voluntary movement)." We must know whether, with Helmholtz (Pop. Vortr., 2 Heft, S. 200), we consider the law of the conservation of force to be valid for living creatures also, or not.

Of course there are plenty of easy-going Materialists who have never fully realised these logical consequences, and who are by no means disinclined, in the case of such an example as ours, also to take refuge in phrases about 'content' and 'meaning,' but then they are just the people who have never learned anything properly. But there are again thorough inquirers and keen minds who shrink from this extreme, and become confused over the validity of the law of the conservation of force in the case of man. A popular 'refutation of Materialism' might therefore plausibly rest itself upon an example somewhat as follows: 'If the mechanical theory is true, the whole of the effect here resulting must have proceeded from the light-waves penetrating to the eye, combined with the elastic forces already present in the brain. But this is incredible, therefore, &c. In fact, an instant, and all excited by a single idea. What does not human consciousness embrace?

Gently! Let us consider the man as an object of the corporeal world. He jumps up. Why does he jump up? His muscles contracted accordingly. But why was this? They were struck by an impulse of nervous activity, which released the stored-up supply of tensive forces. Whence came this impulse? From the centre of the nervous system. How did it originate there? Through the—'soul.' The curtain falls: the *salto mortale* from science to mythology is accomplished.

But we wanted a logical Materialism. The soul is the brain! From the brain then. If now we stop here, the thing is precisely as mythical as before. It all avails nothing. We must follow back the physical causal series, without any regard to what we call consciousness, right through the brain till we come to the first occasion of the whole sudden movement. Or shall we take the opposite however, the incredibility is by no means so great if we take into account also the principles of physiological psychology. We have before us not merely 'light-waves' in general, but particular forms and combinations of letters. The series of these impressions in reading acts partly through the optic nerves, but partly through the motor centre of the ocular muscles by means of the fibres of the association system primarily upon the centre of speech. Here, now, are released words of much 'meaning.' What does that mean, physiologically speaking? Nothing but that a group of cells and nerves is excited, which possesses unusually numerous and powerful conductions to other parts of the cerebral cortex. A very lively process of 'association' of ideas spreads itself and sets the whole brain in a state of lively excitement, while 'unimportant' words, *i.e.*, such as have slight or no old and powerfully conducting communications to other parts of the brain, cannot do this. The effect of the jumping up, &c., results then through the well-known 'teleological' mechanism, which we see at work even in the decapitated frog.

We do not give here, of course, an 'explanation' of the physical process, but merely the suggestion of the possibility of an explanation for those readers who, with Seydel, may think it "obvious" that the thing is otherwise. The true foundation of the principle of the conservation of force is, according to an everywhere consistently applied view, its axiomatic nature as the principle of the interconnection of the phenomenal world. The 'réfutation of Materialism,' however, is partly to be drawn from the deeper sources of the theory of knowlege, and partly is found with regard to our illustrations in the remarks which we have made above upon Du Bois-Reymond's 'Limits of the Knowledge of Nature;' comp. especially vol. ii. p. 314 ff.

direction—what entered into the man? The image of a few lines in blue on a white ground. Certain light-rays struck the retina, which do not develop more living force in their vibrations than any other light-rays. The living force for the transmitting process is ready prepared in the nerve, as that of muscular contraction in the muscles; it can only be set free by the infinitely feeble impulse of the light-wave, as the elastic forces of a barrel of powder by the glimmering spark. But how comes it now that precisely these lines in this man produce precisely this effect? Every answer which appeals to 'ideas' and so on is simply no answer at all. I wish to see the transmission, the paths of the living force, their extent, the mode of propagation and the sources of the physical and chemical processes from which the nerve-impulses proceed, which bring into activity, first, the *musculus psoas*, then the *rectus femoris*, the *vasti* and the whole co-operative society, to effect the act of jumping up. I wish to see the incomparably more important nerve-currents which propagate themselves into the organs of speech, the respiratory muscles, produce command, word, and cry, which by the way of sound-waves and the auditory nerves of other individuals repeat the same play tenfold. I will, in a word, give up for the present the so-called psychical action to scholastic pedantry, and will have the physical action which I see explained by *physical causes*.

The reader will not suppose that I am summoning up impossibilities only in order to invoke at last a *Deus ex machina*. I proceed from the principle that man is throughout thoroughly intelligible, and I am content though we cannot at once explain the whole. As to the palæontologist the solitary maxilla from the Somme valley represents an entire race of primeval men with all its generations, so I will be content if the connexion between the first impression of the light-wave and the motory impulses connected with the more exact reading of the letters is only made to me as clear as is the reflex movement in the twitching of a frog's thigh. Instead of that, people grope in the brain for 'thinking,' 'feeling,' and 'willing,' as though they would discover in the muscles of the under-arm of a pianist sharp, flat, allegro, adagio, and fortissimo, each in its own particular corner!

It will be long, of course, before the only just dawning rational treatment of cerebral physiology can answer these questions: nay, in a certain sense we are only just beginning to see the endlessness of the problems that here pile themselves together. Ancient Materialism and the Idealism of ancient metaphysic solve these riddles with equal facility by mere phrases; for whether I suppose an immaterial soul, and simply attribute to it as many 'faculties' as I need to explain the phenomena, or whether I make the same 'faculties' a function of matter, is quite indifferent as regards the question whether we have a phrase or real insight. The word which veils the phenomenon instead of explaining it in both places takes the place of the physical problem. We may, therefore, shortsightedly abuse the mechanical theory of things as we will; it has nevertheless the grand merit that at the same moment it lets us look into an infinity of problems, while it affords us a first small victory as a pledge that we are on the right path.

I am told, 'But fear, hope, zeal in your merchant are surely something too; the man *feels* something. Has this no cause?' In fact, we had almost forgotten the *nervus sympathicus*, the influence of the *nervus vagus* on the heart's movements, and all the numerous effects radiating through the whole body of the revolution going on in the brain, when so slight an impulse from the outer world throws the man into the liveliest agitation. We must learn these currents, too, before we announce ourselves content. We must know as exactly as possible how the numerous sensations, now strong now vanishing, which one feels in the tongue, another in the epigastric region, one in the calf, another in the back, arise; whether merely in the central part or through a circuit of centrifugal and centripetal conductions. That this circuit plays a great part in all sensations is certainly shown by innumerable phenomena.

Czolbe was especially criticised by his opponents because he required for the development of self-consciousness a movement of the nervous fluid returning upon itself, which he made to proceed in the individual ganglion-cells. The fact has always struck me that the really occurring circuit of nervous activity which has so great a share in all sensations has hitherto been almost entirely neglected. On every lively excitation of cerebral activity there runs a stream of positive or negative effects by means of the vegetative and motory nerves through the whole body, and only when, by means of the sensible nerves, we receive the reactions from the changes thus produced in our organism do we 'feel' our own emotion. Whether now the subjective condition which we name sensation is connected with this whole circuit, or with the conditions of tension which arise after its completion in the central organ, or with other simultaneously arising movements and tensive conditions within the central organs, we leave undetermined; if only we might have these tensive conditions demonstrated to us and the rules of this circuit with all its million-fold various combinations revealed.

It is objected that in the consideration of mere symptoms we lose the thing itself. Yes, if any one could show us that after the elimination of all the symptoms that we could consider there is anything at all left! Let us make it clear to ourselves what there is besides to look for behind the nerve currents and tensive conditions of the act of sensation. This is either the subjective state of the sentient person, or the intellectual value of the content of the sensation. With the former, of course, no one will ever make acquaintance except in himself; and in the numerous discussions of Vogt's famous urine illustration it has become clear enough that we cannot regard the 'thought' as a separate product in addition to the material phenomena, but that the subjective state of the sentient individual is at the same time to external observation an objective one, a molecular movement. This objective state must, on the law of the conservation of energy, fit into the unbroken causal series. Let this series be fully exhibited to us! This must be possible, without any regard to the subjective state, as this is not a special link in the chain of organic phenomena, but as it were merely the aspect of some of these phenomena from another side. We stumble here, indeed, upon a limit to Materialism, but only in carrying it out with the most rigid consistency. We are, in fact, of opinion that there is hardly anything to look for in sensation over and above the nerve processes above spoken of; only these processes have themselves a quite different mode of appearing, namely, that which the individual calls sensation. It is quite conceivable that some time we shall succeed in determining more precisely that portion of the physical processes which coincides in point of time with the origin of a sensation in the individual. This would be extremely interesting, and we certainly could offer no objection if this particular portion of the circuit of nerve processes were then described absolutely as 'the sensation.' A more exact definition of the relation of the subjective phenomenon of sensation to the objectively observed nervous phenomenon would, on the contrary, be impossible.

But now, as to the intellectual value of the content of sensation, this, too, can hardly be completely separated from the physical phenomenon. A masterpiece of sculpture and a rough copy of it present to the retina of the observer a similar crowd of light-stimuli; but so soon as the eye follows the lines, there arise in the muscles of the eye quite different sensations of movement. That these continue to act not according to the absolute mass of the movement, but according to the most delicate numerical relations between the individual motory impulses cannot appear unnatural if we reflect what a part is played by numerical relations even in the first forming of sensations. It is true, indeed, that this very point will be one of the last and most difficult riddles of nature, but we have not the slightest occasion, therefore, to seek for that which is intellectually significant, the artistically moulded sensation or the ingenious thought, outside the ordinary processes of sensation. Only, of course, let us not proceed like a man who should try to discover the melodies that an organ can play in the individual pipes.

The co-operation of very many, and, individually considered, extraordinarily feeble nerve impulses, must give us the key to the physiological understanding of thinking, and the form of this co-operation is the characteristic feature of each individual function. What in this remains unexplained—the manner, the external, natural phenomenon—is at the same time an internal one for the thinking subject: that is the point which altogether overpasses the limits of the knowledge of nature.

CHAPTER III.

SCIENTIFIC PSYCHOLOGY.

BUT what, then, will psychology say if we for the present remove quite into the background the inner subjective side of human nature ? And yet we have had given us in this century not only a scientific, but even a mathematical psychology too, and there are a number of sensible and excellent people who quite seriously believe that Herbart with his differential equations has as thoroughly mastered the world of ideas, as Kopernikus and Kepler the world of the planets. This is indeed as thorough a delusion as phrenology, and as to psychology as a natural science, so much mischief has been worked by this pretty name, that we might easily run the risk of pouring away bath and child together. We shall, however, be able to give their full value to the beginnings of a really scientific and, in parts, even mathematical treatment of psychological questions, without abandoning the standpoint we have already taken up.

First of all, we must point out that the notion of psychology can only be a rigidly determined and completely clear one to the scholastic or the ignorant pedant. It is true that even able and sagacious men have begun their supposed scientific investigations with a section 'Of the Nature of the Soul ;' but it was merely a reaction of the hollow scholastic metaphysic when they imagined that they could thus gain a firm basis for their investigations. Those cases, of course, must be excepted where the notion of the soul is only historically or critically treated.

But the man who begins with positive principles as to the soul, as, *e.g.*, of its simplicity, extensionlessness, and so on, or who feels bound to carefully hedge in the field of his inquiry into the soul before he begins to build, can hardly be expected to give us a scientific treatment of the subject. What should we say of a physicist who began by explaining the nature of Nature, and who would only consider his inquiries as likely to be of service when he had first made it quite clear what Nature is? It is still more obvious if we think of special departments. Had Gilbert not rubbed his bits of amber until he was clear as to the nature of electricity, he would probably never have taken a great step towards the knowledge of its nature. What inquirer could to-day exactly define magnetism? The idea becomes transformed in the hands of inquirers. From the power of the magnet to attract iron there comes a more general power. The earth is perceived to be a magnet. The connexion with electricity is discovered. Diamagnetism is traced through a mass of the most surprising phenomena. Where would have remained the brilliant discoveries of Oersted, Faraday, Plücker, if they had first sounded metaphysically the notion of magnetism and then proposed to begin their scientific investigations?

It is a remarkable monument of the philosophical fermentation in Germany that so subtle a thinker as Herbart, a man of admirable critical acuteness and great mathematical skill, could have come upon so adventurous an idea as that of finding by speculation the principle of the statics and mechanics of ideas. It is still more striking that so enlightened a mind, with a genuinely philosophical tendency to practical life, could lose himself in the laborious and thankless task of working out a whole system of mental statics and mechanics from his principle, without having any voucher whatever in experience for its truth. We see here how peculiar are the relations between a man's gifts and achievements. That Gall should not be protected by his great experience, his extensive and special knowledge, from the invention of phrenology is, with his imaginative and ardently creative character, easily intelligible; but that Herbart could invent a mathematical psychology, while he was pre-eminent in the very qualities which are calculated to protect men against such courses, must always be regarded as a highly remarkable testimony to the violence of the metaphysical whirlpool, which in our country at that time mastered even him who struggled against it, and hurled him out into the intellectual comet-orbit of visionary discoveries.

Nevertheless, Herbart's powerful effort deserves a better refutation than that of mere disregard. But the previous attempts at a worthy critical disproof of mathematical psychology have the defect of losing themselves in miscellaneous discussions, and partly do not at all indicate, partly do not indicate precisely enough, the elementary logical fallacy in the deduction of the fundamental formula. We have attempted in a separate essay [40] to fill this gap in our philosophical literature, because our rejection of mathematical psychology shall not go into the world without proofs: but here the troublesome task of demonstration would disturb the connexion and confuse the clearness of our criticism, so far as it concerns Materialism. If there were a mathematical psychology, we should have to take it into account even on this ground—that it would be the surest proof for that regularity of all psychical processes which Materialism rightly maintains, and at the same time the most complete refutation of the reduction

---

[40] Die Grundlegung d. mathemat. Psychol., Duisb. 1865. Cornelius has attempted a refutation in the Zeits. f. ex. Phil., Bd. vii., H. 3, which, despite its dogmatic tone, seems to demand no answer. A calm comparison of the grounds and countergrounds would be enough to show the untenableness of mathematical psychology. Wittstein has attempted a new foundation of mathematical psychology, which avoids the errors pointed out by me in Herbart's foundation, but at the same time leads also to quite other results than those of Herbart. It is, however, easy to see that if once the pretension to rigid metaphysical deduction of the principle is given up, in point of method there is as yet no occasion for propounding such a theory at all.

of all that exists to matter. We should have at the same time seriously to modify our account of the relation between brain and soul, since Herbart's mathematical psychology can hardly be separated from his metaphysic. As it is, however, there is for us no mathematical psychology, and only in its existence could we find any reason for another detailed discussion of a metaphysical basis for psychology after Kant. If later it becomes generally conceded that we can know nothing of the ultimate ground of all things; if it has been agreed to reckon the constructive instinct of speculation amongst the artistic impulses; if we become unanimous—in this point passing beyond Kant—that the instinct of unity in our reason always leads to poesy, which only indirectly advances science; then we may again bring forth Herbart's metaphysic also without danger of confusing our ideas, and a point will be discovered in it which exhibits a remarkable analogy with the metaphysical principles of the natural science of our present mathematical physicists. The really existent is, according to Herbart, a multeity of simple beings, which differ, however, very essentially from Leibniz's Monads. These produce the whole world as representation from themselves. Herbart's 'real things,' on the contrary, are in themselves quite devoid of representation; but they act upon each other and struggle to avert from themselves this action. The soul is such a simple being, a 'real' thing, which comes into conflict with other simple beings. Its acts of self-preservation are ideas. As without pressure there is no resistance, so without disturbance there would be no ideation. New is it here, at all events—and worthy of noting for future metaphysical home-use — that the essence of the activity of the soul consists in a reaction against our external influences. We are obliged to compare with this the view of recent molecular theorists that the notion of a force by no means belongs to the single atom, and exists only in the reciprocal relations of several atoms. Herbart has, it is true, never quite seen that in consistency he must have said that all ideas lie not in the 'soul,' the simple being, but that they are reciprocal relations between the separate realities, like the physical forces between the atoms. By this consistency in his fundamental theory Herbart would have escaped innumerable contradictions which resulted from the fact that the soul had to be simple and unchangeable without any internal statics, and yet had to carry the ideas within itself. He thus maintains a sort of immortality of the soul, which is much like an everlasting death, if there are no other simple beings to be found to enter into so close an interaction with it, as the constituent parts of the body. This is to pay dearly for an empty notion!

As it is from Herbart's school that the efforts have mostly proceeded to found a scientific psychology, it is often of interest to exhibit the latent contradictions necessarily involved in the assumption of a soul absolutely simple and yet having ideas. The absolutely simple is also incapable of any internal change, because we can only conceive this in the form of a changing arrangement of parts. Therefore, too, Herbart does not say that the 'realities' act upon each other, but that they would if they did not offer resistance to this action by an act of self-preservation. As if this could possibly mean anything else than the assumption of a simple reciprocal action! Waitz in his 'Psychology' (p. 81) attributes much value to the distinction between dispositions to a state and actual states. So it goes in metaphysic. States the soul must not have —not on any account, otherwise its absolute unity would be gone! But dispositions, that is something quite different; 'efforts,' why not? The metaphysician with an enormous show of acuteness refutes all other possible views, and, when he unfolds his own opinion, he throws a logical somerset of the usual kind. Every one else sees that a disposition to a state is also a state, that self-preservation against a threatening influence is not conceivable without an actual, however slight, influence. The metaphysician does not see this. His dialectic has carried him to the edge of the gulf; he has turned about, dragged out, flung away every notion a hundred times over, and at last it is absolutely necessary to know something. So then he shuts his eyes and boldly makes the *salto mortale* from the heights of the keenest criticism into the most vulgar confusion of word and notion! If this succeeds, he cheerfully goes on. The greater are the contradictions that are taken up into the first basis, the more freely may we draw conclusions, just as we can often deduce, as everybody knows, the most remarkable things from mathematical propositions that have the latent factor zero.

Herbart has himself said in one place that instead of a 'History of Psychology,' such as F. A. Carus has written, we need much more a criticism of psychology.[41] We are afraid that if this were to be written now, there would not remain very much of the whole supposed science.

Yet we have a scientific psychology in its first beginnings, and in fact Herbart's school forms for Germany an important link in the epoch of transition, although here science is only beginning painfully to struggle free of metaphysic. Waitz, an acute thinker, who obviously, however, in common with lecturers and assistant-professors, began to write much too early, and so as it were froze in the midst of his development, so far freed himself from Herbart that he rejected mathematical psychology and transformed the whole metaphysical basis of Herbart's psychology into what is supposed to be a hypothesis on the nature of the soul. This is, indeed, but a trifling gain. To have clear hypotheses instead of obscure and absurd dogmas would be a great step forward. But what is the good of a hypothesis on the nature of the soul, or even a hypothesis merely on the existence of a soul, so long as we still have so little accurate knowledge of the particular phenomena which are the first things to be consi-

[41] Psychol. als Wissenschaft, i. S. 44 (§ 17).

dered by any exact investigator? In the few phenomena which so far have been made accessible to more precise observation, there is not the smallest occasion to assume a soul in any very definite sense at all, and the secret reason for the assumption lies ever only in tradition, or in the mute effort of the heart to resist pernicious Materialism. This involves a double misfortune. Scientific psychology is spoiled and corrupted, while the saving and strengthening of the ideal, which is believed to be threatened by Materialism, are not secured, because it is supposed that something wonderful has been accomplished when a new glimmer of demonstration is brought for the old myth of the soul.

"But does not psychology then mean the doctrine of the soul? How, then, is a science conceivable which leaves it doubtful whether it has any object at all?" Well, here we have again a charming example of the confusion of name and thing. We have a traditional name for a considerable but by no means accurately defined group of phenomena. This name has come down from a time when the present requirements of strict science were unknown. Shall we reject the name because the object of science has been changed? That were unpractical pedantry. Calmly assume, then, a psychology without a soul! And yet the name will still be useful, so long as we have something to study that is not completely covered by any other science. It is true that its boundaries on the side of physiology are not easy to draw. But that is no harm either. If the same discoveries are made in two different ways, their value is all the greater. Yet we can only clearly understand this relation when we come to consider the question of the procedure of psychology, which will involve a criticism of the notorious notion of self-observation.[42]

Of 'observing oneself' Kant says that it is a methodical collection of the observations made upon ourselves, which

[42] Comp. Brentano, Psychol. vom empir. Standpunkte, Leipz. 1874, i. S. 13.

affords the material for a diary of the self-observer, "and easily leads to enthusiasm and hallucination." He warns us against "occupying ourselves at all with the examination, and, as it were, studied redaction of an inner history of the involuntary course of our thoughts and feelings;" and that "because it is the straight road in mental confusion from supposed higher inspirations and powers— who knows from where?—influencing us without our will to be landed in illuminatism or terrorism." "For, without perceiving it, we make supposed discoveries out of those things we have ourselves introduced into our minds, like Bourignon or Pascal, and even an otherwise admirable intellect, Albrecht Haller, who through the long-continued though often interrupted diary of his spiritual condition at last reached the point of asking a famous theologian, his former academic colleague, Dr. Less, whether in his extensive treasures of divine learning he could not find consolation for his troubled soul." And further, "that the knowledge of man through internal experience, because to a great extent he judges others also by it, is of great importance, but yet, at the same time, is perhaps of greater difficulty than the right judging of others, since the inquirer, instead of merely observing, introduces much into his self-consciousness which makes it advisable, and even necessary, to start from the phenomena observed in oneself and then only to pass on to the affirmation of certain principles concerning the nature of man, *i.e.*, to internal experience."

Kant based his own empirical psychology, therefore, not on self-observation, but essentially on the observation of others. He had, however, in his 'Critick' assigned a special department to the "internal sense," and the abuse of this arena of metaphysical caprice was the necessary result.[43] Enthusiasm and hallucination indeed were left

---

[43] The doctrine of the 'internal sense' has its roots in the reflexions of Aristotle (De An. iii. 2) on the perceiving of perceptions. It is developed in Galen, who distinguishes three internal senses: the φανταστικόν,

to the previous century, the excited natures of whose men were better fitted for them; but what fantastic caprices and unrestrained speculation could do was bravely done through the introduction of any and every invention into the supposed field of observation of the internal sense. A model in this respect has been offered to us by Fortlage, who as extraordinary professor at Jena in 1855 created two thick volumes which he called 'System of Psychology as Empirical Science from the Observation of the Internal Sense.' First he makes it clear what the inner sense is, and attributing to it a series of functions which

διανοητικόν, and μνημονευτικόν. Their business is to apprehend the material delivered by the external senses and to know it consciously (answering to the 'sensus communis' of the Scholastics, the φανταστικόν of Galen), by combination and separation to gain other knowledge from it (cogitatio = διανοητικόν), and to preserve this knowledge and to restore it again to consciousness by recollection (memoria). To these three internal senses special brain-organs were assigned in the front, middle, and back of the head. Above them stood the reason, as essentially of a different nature. This doctrine held sway (comp. e.g. in Melanchthon's Psychology the chap. *De Sensibus Interioribus*), until Descartes, who left the Galenic basis and made a very different distinction, which was later frequently confused with the traditions of an external and an internal sense. According to Descartes, the senses deliver only purely corporeal copies of things in the brain, which are perceived by the soul. This incredibly naïve anthropomorphism, which simply puts a man into a man, is connected with just as naïve an abstraction—that the corporeal pictures of things in the brain are extended; but their perception by the soul is an act of 'thought' (cogitare) in the wider sense, i.e., an extensionless act of an extensionless being. Thus the object of ideation, which it is, properly speaking, that occupies our consciousness, is arbitrarily and irrationally sundered from the act of ideation. But in this way the absolutely non-sensuous and non-spatial thinking which runs through all modern philosophy (the sharpest opposition to this phantom is found in Berkeley) is first made possible, and 'ideas' of the soul are spoken of quite unconcernedly, as though in them the content—and this the only essential thing—was also thought; but as soon as it is a question of maintaining the non-spatiality of the soul, the idea is again conceived as a mere act of ideation, i.e., as something that when separated from the object of the idea is a pure nonentity. Leibniz then gave us the distinction of sensible 'perception' (in Descartes 'perceptio' is the perception of the soul) from 'apperception,' which is the conscious apprehension of the object by the soul; again a distinction which became fused traditionally with the 'internal' and 'external' sense, although Leibniz does not at all concern himself here with the doctrine of the internal sense. But in Wolff, Bilfinger, and others of his chief followers, this doctrine is nowhere expressly treated. Wolff, however, speaks in the 'Rational Psychology' are usually assigned to external sense, then he marks off his field of observation and begins to observe. It would be quite useless to offer a prize to any one who should hunt out a single real observation in the two thick volumes. The whole book deals in general propositions, with a terminology of his own invention, without a single definite phenomenon being described of which Fortlage could tell us when and where he observed it, or how we must proceed in order to observe it too. We are very prettily told how, *e.g.*, in considering a leaf, as soon as we are struck by its form, this form becomes the focus of attention, " of which the necessary consequence is that the scale of forms fusing with the form of the leaf on the law of similarity becomes clear to consciousness."

of an internal and external 'acumen' of sense (§ 269), meaning by this the sharpening of the faculty of sensible perception by an internal or external cause; accordingly a distinction again of quite another kind. Tetens, Phil. Vers. über d. menschl. Natur, 1777, i. S. 45, complains that Wolff does not employ the notion of the internal sense. He himself calls, closely approximating to Locke's 'reflexion' in opposition to sensation, "ideas of the internal sense" those "which we have of ourselves, of our internal changes, of our activities and faculties."

Kant appears to have adopted the 'internal sense' on the same ground on which he allowed to the notions of the traditional psychology and logic so extensive and, in fact, so fatal an influence on his system; namely, that he believed that he had in the old, and in a certain sense verified network of notions, a guarantee for the completeness of the phenomena with which he had to deal. That everywhere not the traditional theory, but the traditional classification was the main point with him, appears in the freedom, partly also in the caution, of his definitions, which everywhere connect themselves

as little as possible with traditional notions, and aim only at an accurate, and never unnecessarily prejudging, delimitation of the matter.

According to Cohen, Kant's Th. d. Erfahr., S. 146 ff., Kant adopts the external sense in order to refute "material idealism" in the very sphere in which it sought its main support, and to deprive the dogma of the soul-substance of its most essential basis. Kant therefore teaches expressly that either no internal sense at all must be assumed, or the subject, which is its object, must, like the objects of the external sense, be *phenomenon*. How far Kant in this (on Cohen's view) was already on the way to a perfectly sound psychology, which transformed the 'faculties' into *processes*, we leave here undetermined. At all events, the immediate effect of the assumption of an 'internal sense' was unfavourable and misleading. Here, too, we must point out that the transcendental deduction of Time which is connected with the doctrine of the 'internal sense' is far from having the same evidence as that of Space, but on the contrary is exposed to the most serious doubts.

We are told that the leaf now "in the space of imagination disappears in the scale of forms," but when, how, or where this has ever occurred, and upon what experience this 'empirical' piece of knowledge is based, remains just as obscure as the mode and manner in which the observer applies the 'inner sense,' and the proofs that he makes use of such a sense, and does not, it may be, crystallize his own crude guesses and inventions at haphazard into a system.

In our opinion it is quite impossible to draw a fixed line between internal and external observation. When the astronomer looks at a star, this is called external observation; but so soon as he recognises at the first glance that it is Mars, he must, according to Fortlage, have used at the same time the internal sense; for the eye sees only a light point; the astronomer sees at once and without reflexion Mars, because he knows him. Has he now used on this account a different mental organ than the man who only sees the star, or the child who only sees the light point, and knows nothing yet even of stars? Fortlage says, "He who by the study of music and listening to the best compositions qualifies himself for a heightened musical appreciation, arms the external by the internal sense, and when afterwards in a piece of music he immediately distinguishes in feeling between faults and beauties, character and superficiality, direct movement from counter-movement, sharp from flat, the distinguishing faculty here is no less one brought about and contributed by the internal sense, than in the case of a foreign tongue, which we only understand when we have learnt it." On our view there lies an extremely interesting problem of the psychology and physiology of the future in inquiring how it is that the painfully acquired connexion between sensations of sound and other brain activities seems later to express its effect quite immediately. So long as we know no method of approaching this problem by following up our own sensations or by some other means, we do well meantime to believe that in all probability in both cases we hear with our ears.

How are we to deal with the cases where the immediate sight of every healthy eye, without any special training, at once effects an elimination, a completing or varying of the mechanically produced picture? Do we see stereoscopically with the internal sense or with the external? Do we fill up those places in the field of vision which coincide with the place of entry of the optic nerve by the internal sense? Do we hear a chord as such with the external sense? But we may go farther and ask, Is it external observation when we touch the nerve terminations in the skin with the point of a pair of compasses, and these are now felt as one point, now as two? Is it self-observation when we turn our attention to an aching corn? When we send a galvanic current through the head and perceive subjective colours or sounds, in which province does this fall. With 'within' and 'without' we can do nothing at all; for I can have no ideas at all outside myself, even if the theory is correct on which I project outwards the objects I perceive. Seeing and thinking are equally internal and equally external. If I wish to think my thoughts again, I call forth those sensations in the vocal organs which we regarded above as the body of thought, as it were. I feel them as externally as any other sensation; and as to the mind, content, meaning of this complex of the subtlest sensations, it is no otherwise than with the æsthetic value of a drawing. It is not to be separated from the lines of the drawing, although it is something different. A similar antithesis between form and matter of sensation reappears, however, constantly in innumerable degrees, without my ever being able to say of a particular class of sensations that here the internal begins and the external ends.

How unconcernedly Fortlage lays down that the field of physiology is man, so far as he is perceived with the external sense, but that of psychology man so far as he is perceived with the internal sense! Most people would call it psychology if we observed the first words of a child in order to draw conclusions as to the development of the mind; physiology, on the other hand, if we prick new-born children with a needle, or tickle them in order to watch the reflex movements in their transition to volition. And yet for both sets of observations we use our ordinary senses, and on Fortlage's principle the internal sense as well, because in both cases what we see and hear requires first to be interpreted. Altogether it is not hard to see that the nature of any and every observation is the same, and that the difference chiefly depends merely on whether an observation is such that it may be also made by others at the same time or later, or whether it evades any such control and confirmation? External observation would never have led to a sure empirical, or even an exact science, unless every observation had been capable of being tested. The elimination of the influences of preconceived views and tendencies is the most important element of exact method, and this element becomes inapplicable just in those observations which are directed towards our own thoughts, feelings, and impulses; even though it be that we have fixed our own thoughts quite impartially by writing or other means, and then examine the sequence of ideas as though they were those of a stranger. Truth to say, however, this kind of self-observation, just because of its comparative trustworthiness, is very little liked, and the boasted system of self-observation seems to be so much liked precisely because of its defects. For even though, as Kant feared, enthusiasm and hallucination are not in its train, yet it will always continue a means of lending to the most fanciful imaginations of metaphysic the appearance of empirical deduction.[44]

[44] It may here be cheerfully conceded that quite recently the observation of phenomena described as 'internal' has made great advances, and that some useful work has been done in this department, not only by

It is with full right, therefore, that modern psychologists have applied to psychology the usual strictly methodical mode of observation, which has done such excellent service in the natural sciences. In this respect Lotze has done admirable service by his 'Medicinische Psychologie,' 1852, though he was not restrained by the title of his book from prefixing to his empirical and critical inquiries a hundred and seventy pages of metaphysic, to which it is owing that medical men have not benefited by the book as they might otherwise have done. Later, the younger Fichte presented himself to physicists and medical men

physiologists, but also by men who are endeavouring to restore an empirical psychology; thus, *e.g.*, by Stumpf in his delicately conducted inquiry into the representation of surface by the sense of sight (Ueber d. psych. Ursp. d. Raumvorst., Leipz. 1873, Kap. i. Much less successful are the inquiries in the second chap. on the 'Representation of Depth'). It is, however, easy to see that the procedure here is absolutely the same as in external observation, and that this kind of 'self-observation,' if we will use the phrase, extends exactly as far as imagination, whose functions are so closely related to those of external perception. Brentano, Psych. v. empir. Standp., i., Leipz. 1874, entirely agrees with our criticism of 'self-observation' in Fortlage's fashion; he maintains, however (S. 41), that I have been led by the confusion in this department to unjustly deny internal 'perception,' *i.e.*, then the 'internal sense'(comp. the previous note). We can never direct our attention immediately to the psychical facts, and, therefore, cannot 'observe' them either, but we may very well 'perceive' them, and this perception may then by the aid of the memory be subjected to a more careful investigation. The objects of 'internal perception' in opposition to external are, according to Brentano, the 'psychical phenomena,' and they are to be distinguished from the physical phenomena by the criterion of "intentional inexistence," *i.e.*, of the reference to something as object (S. 127). Accordingly Brentano reckons among physical phenomena not merely the phenomena which the senses give us, but also the pictures of imagination; psychical, on the other hand, is the idea as act of ideation (S. 103 f.). He thus, indeed, gains, like Descartes (comp. the previous note), a sure distinction between the physical and the psychical, but with the danger of making a mere illusion the foundation of his whole system. The impossibility of separating the act of ideation from its content we have shown in the previous note. But how is it with the emotions? Anger, *e.g.*, is, according to Brentano, a psychical phenomenon, because it refers to an object. But what can we perceive in anger and observe with the aid of memory? Nothing but mere sensuous symptoms, in which again the perception everywhere stands in entire analogy with ordinary external perception. The mental element in anger lies in the mode and manner, in the measure, connexion, and order of these symptoms, not in a separable process, which might be specially perceived.

in his 'Anthropologie' (1856), as it were as a sort of philosophical family doctor and spiritual adviser. Although his book, through its logical weaknesses and pretentious repetition of obsolete errors, has only injured the reputation of philosophy amongst men of science, yet in other circles it has greatly contributed to bring the close connexion of psychology and physiology home to the general consciousness. Nay, in those days happened the miracle that the Epigoni of the Hegelian philosophy partly turned towards a sober, almost scientific, treatment of psychology. George wrote a good little book on the Five Senses; Schaller found himself driven by his struggle against Materialism into a thorough consideration of the physiological element. Later, each of these men published a psychology; and in both of these works the character of the epoch is unmistakable. It deserves all praise that they are fully conscious that in essentials they still stand upon the ground of speculation, although they do so no more than do also the founders of the supposed scientific psychology. We must, on the other hand, always combat pretensions which seem to assume that speculative knowledge is higher and more credible than empirical knowledge, to which it is related simply as a higher to a lower stage. May our readers not take offence at this. It belongs to the central truths of a new epoch of humanity now dawning—not that, with Comte, we should abolish speculation, but certainly that we should once for all assign it its place, that we should know what it can do for knowledge and what not.

Schaller thus expresses himself as to the relation. "Natural science may boast itself as exact knowledge, if it contents itself with discovering the laws of phenomena by observing them and with formulating the quantitative relations which are directly contained in these ascertained laws. Of course every one is at liberty to content himself with this exact knowledge; but then he necessarily resigns also any answering of all the questions with which philosophy has concerned itself from the beginning.[45] Well, then, how variously philosophy has answered the questions with which it has concerned itself is familiar enough. The agreement, however, which prevails, on the other hand, in the natural sciences, proceeds not from those sciences confining themselves to a field where everything is obvious, but from their applying a method whose doctrines, as ingeniously elaborated as they are true to Nature, have only been revealed to mankind after long efforts, and the limits of whose applicability we do not know. The core of all the numerous cautionary measures of this method lies, however, just in the neutralising of the influence of the observer's subjectivity. But it is precisely the subjective nature of the individual man to which speculation owes each of its particular forms. Here, too, we must assume that in the similar organisation of all men, and in the common development of humanity, lies an objective basis for the individual phenomena, much as in architecture or in music similar principles appear amongst different and separated peoples. Whoever now is content under the sway of this mysterious constructive impulse of humanity to build up a temple of notions which is not indeed in serious conflict with the present state of the positive sciences, but is overthrown by every methodically-gained advance, or is razed to the ground and rebuilt in another style by every later builder, may indeed pride himself on a graceful and in itself perfect work of art, but at the same time he also necessarily resigns the hope of advancing by a single step true and permanent knowledge in any department whatsoever. What now each one will choose must remain with himself. As a rule, that will seem to each most desirable which he himself is doing.

To what extent now scientific method can be applied to psychology must be shown by the result. We will premise that it is not merely the borderlands of nervous

[45] Schaller, Psychologie, Weimar, 1860, S. 17.

physiology which admit an exact treatment. However undefined we may leave the boundaries of psychology, at all events we must for the present include in it not only the facts of sentient life, but also the investigation of human action and speech, and generally of all manifestations of life, so far as an inference is possible from them to the nature and character of man. The clearest proof for this is the existence of an Animal Psychology, the materials of which can hardly be very well collected by means of the 'internal sense.' Here, where external observation shows us primarily only movements, gestures, and actions, the interpretation of which is liable to error, we may nevertheless carry out a comparatively very exact procedure, since we can easily subject the animal to experiments and put it into positions which admit of the most accurate observation of each fresh emotion and the repetition or suspension as we will of each stimulus to a psychical activity. Thus is secured that fundamental condition of all exactness; not indeed that error is absolutely avoided, but certainly that it can be rendered harmless by method. An exactly described procedure with an exactly described animal can always be repeated, by which means our interpretation, if it is due to variable bye-conditions, is at once corrected, and at all events thoroughly cleared from the influence of personal preconceptions, which have so great a share in so-called self-observation. If now we have as yet no system of animal psychology, yet we have the beginnings of observations which in accuracy and fruitfulness lead us far beyond the standpoint of Reimarus and Scheitlin. The constant increase in the number of zoological gardens promotes these studies, and however much the free life of the animals in field and forest may differ from their condition in captivity, yet an exact observation based upon this latter condition is not less valuable for the purpose of establishing general propositions. For the problems of Materialism or Idealism the most interesting matter will perhaps be found later, where it has as yet been sought least—in the observation of the lower animals in regard to their sense-perceptions. Indeed, Moleschott has already pointed out that a vorticella with an eye possessing only a cornea must receive different pictures of objects from the spider, which possesses also lenses and corpora vitrea. Much as we missed in our criticism of this passage * a clear conception of the relation of object and subject, yet this observation is certainly important; indeed, it is not improbable that here in a very much wider sense the most remarkable things will be revealed, when exact observations are completed of the sentient activities of creatures organised so differently from ourselves. The effect of the different vibrations which are revealed to us by physics must here be examined quite independently of the question whether they cause particular sense-perceptions in *our* organs or not. If, for example, there should be creatures which smell or taste the light (*i.e.*, perceive it by organs similar to our organs of smell or taste), or which receive visual images through a source of warmth which is dark to us, then the doctrine of the shaping of the sensible world by the subject would receive a new support. On the other hand, should it be shown that through all the manifold forms of the animal world there are probably no sensations essentially different from ours, this would for the present be in favour of Materialism.[46]

* Comp. supra, vol. ii. p. 277.

[46] In this branch, too, since the appearance of our first edition, some very promising beginnings of an insight have been gained. On the one side we have Bert's experiment on the sensations of light in water-fleas, which seems to prove that in these creatures precisely the same rays excite the sensation of light as in man (communicated to the French Acad. 2 Aug. 1869); on the other side the researches of Eimer and Schöbl (Arch. f. mikrosk. Anat. vii. Hft. 3, cit. Naturf. iv. No. 26) on the organs of touch in the snout of the mole and the inner ear of the mouse, where there is such an unusual abundance of apparatus of touch, that we must suppose the kind of sensation as well as the performances of what we call the sensation of touch to be specifically different. Exact experiments are still lacking, as, on the other hand, we still need the physiological and anatomical explanation for the results long known to us of the "bat-sense" (according to Spallanzani's

An important contribution to the foundations of a future psychology lies also beyond doubt in the only very recently systematically instituted experiments on newborn infants. If we wish to understand the mechanism of psychical processes, we must above all seek to observe the first and simplest elements of this mechanism. It is astonishing with what phlegm our good philosophers can conduct an argument on the origin of consciousness, without ever feeling it necessary to go into the nursery and see exactly what takes place there in connexion with this problem. But so long as words patiently allow themselves to be marshalled into a system, and students patiently write down this system, publishers patiently print it, and the public regard the contents of these books as very important, the philosopher does not so easily find any occasion for farther steps. Then at length comes the physiologist,[47] gives new-born infants sugar or quinine to taste, holds a light near them, or makes a noise in their ears, and most accurately describes what movements, muscular contortions, and so on, he has observed. He combines the observations which he has made on prematurely born or mature infants, notes carefully the differences, and compares the results of anatomy and pathology. Finally, he seeks so to arrange his observations as to ascend from simple reflex movements to the sure signs of consciousness, and, in fine, knows a great many things which are quite strange to the philosopher in his solitary study, and yet which are often quite indispensable for the decision of important questions. Even though nothing more resulted from these empirical inquiries than the fact that from pure reflex movement to conscious

experiments). So, too, the hairs moved by the vibrations of sound on the fur body-surface of the crabs (Hensen, St. über d. Gehörorgan d. Decapoden, Leipz. 1863, cit. in Helmholtz, Lehre v. d. Tonempfind., S. 234 f.), as well as the nerve-hairs on the skin of young fishes and naked amphibia (according to F. H. Schulze in Müller's Archiv, 1861, p. 759), must probably produce sensations of quite another quality than ours. Cp. Wundt, Physiol. Psych., S. 342.

[47] Comp. Kussmaul, Unters. über d. Seelenleben d. neugebornen Menschen, Leipz. 1859.

purposeful activity there is the most imperceptible transition, and that the beginnings of the latter reach back into prenatal life, even that, in the light of real science, would be much more than can be learnt from whole volumes of speculative 'Inquiries.'

Another object of recent efforts which bears upon this question is Ethnopsychology (Völkerpsychologie), which, however, has not as yet attained a sufficiently definite form and method to require a discussion, especially as the problems of Materialism are less closely connected with this department. It is, however, noteworthy that linguistics, which is justly regarded as one of the most essential sources of ethnopsychology, has greatly contributed to bring speech into the domain of scientific treatment, and thus to fill up at a new and important point the earlier gulf between the sciences of mind and nature. In this respect, too, is the first half of our century epoch-making. Wilhelm v. Humboldt's famous work on the Kawi Language and Bopp's Sanskrit Grammar and Comparative Grammar appeared in the otherwise so fertile period from 1820 to 1835. After this, linguistic inquiry made wonderful progress in every direction, and Steinthal especially laboured in a long series of important treatises to exhibit clearly the psychological essence of speech, and to do something to prevent the continual confusion of logical thinking with that formation of concepts which goes on hand in hand with speech.

Strikingly unfruitful for psychological problems were for a long time the travels of men of science, and the comparison of their results in anthropological and ethnographical respects. We need only take in hand Prichard's once so famous work on the Natural History of Man to be convinced what a mass of misunderstandings proceeded from the religious prejudices of the reporters, from their pride of race, and from their incapacity to throw themselves into the modes of thought of lower grades of civilisation. Quite recently things have improved. In particular, Bastian's narratives of travel are rich in psychological traits, and his comprehensive works [48] betray a predominant interest for comparative psychology, even though the guiding-points of view oft get lost amid the accumulated material. In Waitz's 'Anthropologie der Naturvölker' we may follow the progress of intelligence from page to page; but the last volume of Waitz's work, written by Gerland, is excellent in this respect. If we now add Lubbock's luminous comparison of the results of palæontology with the condition of modern savages, as well as Tylor's 'Primitive Culture' and 'Early History of Mankind,' we have already such a wealth of facts and combinations that a systematic 'Ethnopsychology,' or a 'pragmatic anthropology' on an entirely new basis, can no longer appear impossible. If we ask, however, for the results which are already most evident, it cannot be denied that in all recent and better observations man, taken in all his various states of civilisation, appears as a natural being, whose whole activity is determined by his organisation. Where earlier, upon a superficial view, we saw only 'savages' or harmless children of nature, we now find the evidences of a history, of an old refined civilisation, and often even the clear traces of decline and retrogression. We see how society, even in people who in other respects are still at a standpoint of childish immaturity, everywhere brings with it quite early peculiar and often bizarre arrangements, which, despite the utmost variety, may yet be developed from some few constantly recurring psychological principles. Despotism, nobility, caste,

---

[48] Der Mensch in d. Geschichte, Leipz. 1830, 3 Bde.; Beitr. z. vergl. Psychol., Berl. 1868; Ethnol. Forschungen, Jena, 1871. Principally in his work 'Das Beständige in d. Menschenrassen,' Berl. 1868, Bastian has indulged in a coarse and exaggerated opposition against Darwinism, which, however, does not affect the value of his leading idea: that the similarities in the mental condition of peoples, and especially in their mythological traditions, are to be explained, not so much by their descent from a common primitive stock, as by the same psychological disposition, which must necessarily lead to the same or similar creations of superstition and story.

superstitions, priestcraft, and fettering ceremonies shoot forth everywhere quite early from the common root of human nature, and in the principles of these widely spread deformities there is often seen the most striking analogy between races which have hardly clothes and huts, and others which possess palaces, proudly built cities, and an abundance of implements and objects of luxury. The state of nature, whose loss was deplored by Rousseau and Schiller, is nowhere visible; rather everything is nature, but a nature as little correspondent to our ideals as the ape-like figure of our hypothetic ancestors to the ideals of Pheidias or Raphael. It seems as though man, while he leaves behind him the limits of brutishness, and as an individual is developed and ennobled by society, in forming a comprehensive ethnopsychology must once more pass through all the perversity and hideousness of apishness, until at length the germs of nobler qualities that lie deep but surely within him—but we have not yet got so far! Even Hellenic civilisation rested upon the rotten basis of slavery, and the noble humanity of the eighteenth century was only the possession of narrowly limited circles, who carefully held themselves aloof from the masses.

Darwin also has contributed magnificent material for the psychological understanding of the human species, and struck out new paths in which plentiful matter may be gained for whole departments of psychology. Here belongs, in particular, his essay on the 'Expression of the Emotions,' often disparaged because of its hardness and one-sidedness. Descartes in his much too little regarded treatise on the emotions had already entered on the way of defining and explaining them by their corporeal symptoms, although on his theory the emotion, as such, can only come about when the soul 'thinks' what it perceives in the brain as a corporeal phenomenon. In more recent times, Domrich in particular has the merit of treating thoroughly the corporeal phenomena by which psychical conditions are accompanied, but his work has been little used by the psychologists.[49] It would necessarily be otherwise, if it were but generally seen in how high a degree the consciousness of our own emotions is only determined and brought about by the sensation of their corporeal reactions. Yet it is, in fact, with them just as it is with the consciousness of our bodily movements; an immediate knowledge of the impulse set up is indeed present, but we only attain to perfect clearness as to the phenomenon through the backward rush of the sensations, which are occasioned by the movement.

But the corporeal symptom attains a quite special importance for the psychical process in the movements of utterance. We need only observe how language in the primary meaning of the expressions for the emotions always keeps to the corporeal symptom, and especially often to the movements of utterance, and we soon see how man has been guided by these symptoms, and how only through them all internal phenomena have received their character and demarcation from other related phenomena. And therefore we can never hope to attain any serious results in the theory of the emotions without the most serious study of their symptoms.

Here again then, we come upon a method in psychology which might be called Materialistic, were it not that this expression includes also a reference to the basis of the whole theory of things, which is here not at all in place. We do better, therefore, to speak of a 'somatic method,' which commends itself as the only one that in most branches of psychology promises success. This method requires that in psychological inquiry we should as far as possible keep to the corporeal processes, which are indissolubly and by law connected with the psychical phenomena. In applying it, however, we are by no means obliged to regard the corporeal processes as the ultimate basis of the psychical element, or even as the only really

---

[49] Die psychische Zustände; ihre organische Vermittelung u. ihre Wirkung in Erzeugung körperlichen Krankheiten, Jena, 1849.

existent, as Materialism does. Just as little, of course, must we allow ourselves to be misled, because of the few departments which are as yet inaccessible to the somatic method, into assuming here psychical events without a physiological basis. We may, that is to say, in the case of the theory of the succession of ideas, *i.e.*, of the influence of already present ideas, or of those newly coming into consciousness, upon the succeeding ones, not only work out the doctrine theoretically, but even support it to a much greater extent than has yet been done upon experiment and observation, without troubling ourselves farther as to its physiological basis. Thus, *e.g.*, the artifice of the teachers of memory, to retain any given succession of words by inserting in thought certain connecting words, may quite well be treated as a valuable psychological experiment, the validity of which, like that of every good experiment, is quite independent of our explanation of it.[50] We may empirically establish a complete theory of mistakes in writing, or, as Drobisch has done, reduce the tendency of a poet to lighter or heavier forms of verse into definite numerical terms,[51] without any regard at all to the brain and nerves. Here it might occur to a critic to maintain either that the independence of the facts from the physiological element must be recognised here, or the procedure is not strictly scientific, because it does not go

---

[50] In my lectures on psychology I have always introduced some experiments of this kind, and have thus convinced myself more and more of their soundness and convincingness, as well as of their didactic value.

[51] Comp. the dissertations in the Berichte d. Königl. Sächs. Ges. d. Wissensch., Phil.-hist. Classe, 1856, 26 Mai, S. 75; 1871, 1 Jul., S. 1. Drobisch in these pioneering inquiries has not merely given a brilliant example of the application of numerical methods to philology, but also supplied the psychologically important proof that in language and poetry there appear regularities of whose production individual authors have no consciousness. What appears subjectively as tact, feeling, taste, is seen objectively as a creative impulse following definite laws. Thus there falls, *inter alia*, an entirely new light upon the numerous metrical 'leges' which have been discovered in the Latin poets since Ritschl's researches on Plautus. Much that, though with some astonishment, has been regarded as conscious rule, now reveals itself as the effect of an unconsciously operating natural law.

back to the presupposed basis of the phenomena. But the alternative is false, because empirically ascertained facts, and even 'empirical laws,' have their own rights, quite independently of their resolution into the bases of phenomena. Otherwise we might with equal justice declare the whole physiology of nerves inadequate, because it has not yet been resolved into the mechanics of atoms, which yet in the last result must underlie every explanation of natural phenomena.

In England, psychology in the time of Dugald Stewart and Thomas Brown was in a fair way to become an empirical science of the succession of ideas (Association-psychology), and in particular the latter follows the principle of association cleverly and keenly through the most various spheres of psychical activity. Since then, psychology has remained a favourite study of the English, and it cannot be denied that the study of their works affords to the statesman, the artist, the teacher, the physician, a much richer abundance of contributions to the knowledge of man, than can our German psychological literature. This psychology is proportionally weaker in the critical sureness of principles and in strict scientific form. In this respect no essential progress has been made since Brown and Stewart. What distinguishes the later works of Spencer, and especially of Bain,[52] is a careful consideration of recent anatomy and physiology, and an energetic attempt to harmonise the association-psychology with our knowledge of the nervous system and its functions. However sound the tendency of these efforts, they are not carried out without venturesome hypotheses and far-reaching structures of theory, which still lack a firm experimental foundation. We have remarked above that with regard to the functions of the brain it may not indeed be the business of exact research, but may very well be that of a preliminary explanation, to

---

[52] Comp. Herbert Spencer, Principles of Psychology, 2d ed., Lond. 1870-72. Alexander Bain, The Senses and the Intellect, 2d ed., Lond. 1864; The Emotions and the Will, 2d ed., Lond. 1865; Mind and Body: the Theories of their Relation, Lond. 1874.

show for once in an elaborate hypothesis how things *might* be connected together: this want is more than amply satisfied by Spencer and Bain, and their works, therefore, constitute in this respect, too, a welcome complement to German literature, however the rigid but somewhat sterile German criticism may batter at the foundations of their theoretical constructions. The distinction between the English and the German procedure in psychology may, in fact, be reduced to this: that the German scholars apply all their powers of mind to attain sure and correct principles, while the Englishmen are chiefly concerned to make out of their principles whatever can be made. This is as true for the association-psychology as such, as for its physiological foundation. Instead of improving the theory of association in its extremely defective foundations and more rigidly defining the method of inquiry, the recent writers give us only broad developments and analyses, while the foundations remain just as they were with their predecessors. A part of this foundation has been recently attacked in Germany from several sides, and particularly the deduction of ideas of space from the principle of association which prevails in England, has been submitted to an entirely just criticism.[53] This criticism, however, hits a point which is indeed of the utmost importance for the theory of knowledge, but for the special foundation of empirical psychology is of subordinate importance. We might drop this explanation of the ideas of space, and the association-psychology would still continue essentially uninjured. Yet there is another point which not only decides the fate of this science, but also proves of the highest importance for the fundamental problems of the relation of body and soul. This is the question whether for the succession of ideas at all there is a thoroughgoing and immanent causality, or not.

---

[53] Dr. Johnson, D. Ableit d. Raumvorst. bei d. englisch. Psychologen d. Gegenwart, in D. Phil. Monatsh., 1 Jan. 1873, S. 43 ff. Dr. Carl Stumpf, Ueber. d. psych. Ursp. d. Raumvorst., Leipz. 1873.

The sense of the pregnant question is easy to understand, if we only look back to Leibniz or Descartes. By an immanent causality we mean one which requires no extraneous connecting link. The ideational condition of a given moment must be explained purely from earlier ideational conditions. In Descartes as well as in Leibniz the ideational content of the soul forms a world complete in itself, separated from the corporeal world. Even those ideas which correspond to a new sensible impression, the mind must develop out of itself. But on what *law* the states of the soul change remains obscure. Descartes as well as Leibniz favour strict mechanism in the corporeal world. This is not applicable to the world of ideas, because here nothing can be weighed and measured; but of what kind now is the bond of causality that here connects the changing states? Descartes has no answer whatever to this question; Leibniz a very ingenious, but still inadequate one. He removes the causality of ideation into the relation of the monad to the universe, into the pre-established harmony. Although, therefore, the monad has "no windows," yet what happens in it is not ruled by an immanent principle, but by its relation to the universe, which is only accessible to speculation, not to observation. In this way any empirical psychology is made impossible, and there can at bottom be no question of laws of association or of any other thoroughgoing laws.

The association-psychology makes, therefore, also, in its exertions to establish a succession of ideas in accordance with law, altogether an exception. The sense-perceptions, in the widest sense of the notion, come from without inwards, without the question being asked how this is possible. They are from the standpoint of the soul as it were creations out of nothing, continually appearing new factors, which very seriously modify the collective condition of the world of ideas, yet which from the moment of their entrance subject themselves to the laws of association. The difficulty involved in this hypothesis was in England easily masked by the traditional Materialism from Hartley and Priestley onwards. Their successors, who declined its consequences, at the same time retained the convenience of its mode of explanation, and did not remember that a new standpoint brings also new problems with it.

Stuart Mill has in his 'Logic'* treated at length the question here raised. He opposes Comte, who decides very positively that in states of mind there are no immanent mental laws, but that they are entirely produced by states of body. Of these there are laws; where there appears a uniformity of succession in the former, it is a merely derivative and not original uniformity, and is, therefore, not the subject of any possible science. In a word, psychology is only conceivable as a branch of physiology.

Against this strictly Materialistic view Mill endeavours to assert the rights of psychology. By giving up at once the whole department of sensible perceptions, he thinks that he can save the autonomy of the science of thought and the emotions. The sense-perceptions he gives up to physiology. Of the remaining psychical phenomena, physiology can as yet explain to us little or nothing; the association-psychology, on the other hand, enables us by means of methodical empiricism to discover a series of laws. Let us keep, then, to these, and leave the question open whether the phenomena of the succession of ideas may perhaps some day be explained as mere products of cerebral activity! Thus the metaphysical question is postponed, and at least a provisional right assured to the association-psychology. The question, however, which goes deeper and demands a critical inquiry, remains unhandled, whether we do not on a closer inspection discover in the association-psychology itself indications that its supposed laws have no absolute validity, because they represent but parts of the consequences of deeper lying physiological laws.

Herbert Spencer favours—thus approaching our own

* Bk. vi. c. 4.

standpoint—a Materialism of the phenomenon, whose relative justification in natural science finds its limitations in the idea of an unknowable absolute. He might, therefore, have quietly adopted Comte's standpoint for the sphere of the knowable; at the same time he maintains that psychology is a totally unique science, independent of all other sciences whatever.[54] He is led to this assertion by the fact that the psychical alone is immediately given to us, while the physical is only presupposed, and may, therefore, in a certain sense be resolved into the psychical. In fact, our ideas of matter and its motions are also only one kind of ideas. But colour and sound, as they are immediately presented to our mind, are, like our emotions, given earlier than the theory of their origin from vibrations and cerebral processes. Accordingly, so much is true that the sphere of psychical phenomena possesses that independence, which Spencer attributes to psychology. But the question is just this, whether the sphere of psychical phenomena may be brought into a causal connexion without reference to the theories of the physical sciences.

Alexander Bain favours a "guarded or qualified Materialism" which preserves the contrast between mind and matter. With him, as with Spencer, the body is the same thing, objectively considered, which subjectively in the immediate consciousness of the individual is soul. But by this idea, which may be traced back to Spinoza, and which Kant also allowed to be a valid hypothesis, Bain is misled into assuming a complete parallelism between mental activity and nervous activity. On his view, every nerve stimulus has a "sensational equivalent."[55] If this were so, then the causal chain on the psychical side must be just as complete as on the physical; but

---

[54] Princ. of Psych., 2d ed., i. p. 140.

[55] Mind and Body, p. 39: "There is a definite change of feeling, a uniform accession of pleasure or of pain, corresponding to an elevation of temperature of 10°, 20°, or 30°. So for each set of circumstances there is a sensational equivalent of alcohol, of odours, of music, of spectacle."

the facts are otherwise. Even the law of Relativity recognised by Bain, according to which we attain a conscious sensation, not so much through the absolute strength of the stimulus, as rather through the fact of a *change* of the state of stimulation,[56] is inconsistent with the sensational equivalent; for it is clear enough that one and the same nervous stimulus may now set up a very lively sensation, and another time none at all. But if by 'sensational equivalent' is meant something that belongs indeed to the inner subjective side of the phenomenon, but at the same time is not sensation properly speaking, we come to the unconscious ideas, of which we shall presently have to speak farther.

But even the strict validity of the law of association must here appear very doubtful. Spencer, indeed, to be quite safe, uses the magic formula, 'all other things equal.' Of course, if all other circumstances are absolutely the same, it seems almost axiomatic that then, *e.g.*, the livelier impression sticks more firmly in the memory; but in this way the force of the principle is reduced almost to nothing. If we say that under like circumstances a faster ship must sooner reach its goal, or a fiercer fire give more heat, we mean by this that the speed of the ship, the heat of the fire, under all circumstances exercise their constant effect, but that it depends upon other circumstances whether a certain external effect, as the attainment of a goal, the warming of a room, is brought about or not. We thus express a principle of great generality and far-reaching import. In the psychological case, however, things are quite different. It is, *e.g.*, not at all improbable that the capacity of recollection is partly conditioned by the absolute strength of the nervous process, or by the lasting organic change which is connected with it, while, on the contrary, the liveliness of the corresponding idea is dependent only on the relative strength of the excitement. So we often have, *e.g.*, in dreams ideas

[56] Ibid., p. 44 ff.

of the most astonishing vividness and clearness, which we can only recall with difficulty and by no means with the original vividness. But there are in a dreaming state only very weak nervous currents, which are the bearers of our ideas. If now we take the condition "all other things being equal" literally, *i.e.*, if we only compare dream-idea with dream-idea, and in general only certain special states of stimulation, the doctrine of the association-psychology may be correct, but it is then obviously of very limited import. In the case of the physical examples just mentioned, the result, the attainment of a goal, the warming of a room, is only a means to make quite clear the constant import of the speed and the warmth. But just this constant validity of the one factor falls away in the psychological example. The greater liveliness of the idea does not supply in all circumstances a like contribution to the end to be gained, but this contribution may in one case be very great, in another absolutely nil. We may, *e.g.*, have had in a dream extremely vivid ideas, which all the same we cannot under any circumstances remember; unless, indeed, we could restore the same dreaming state.

An instance may make this still clearer. Value in political economy undoubtedly arises from a series of physical conditions, amongst which labour plays a prominent part. At the same time, value is not proportional to labour. Other circumstances, as in particular demand, not merely come in from without to determine the result, as, *e.g.*, wind and weather contribute to the swiftness of a ship, but they are necessary in order that there may be value at all. Just so is the collective state of consciousness necessary in order that a stimulus may give rise to sensation at all. Just for this reason, too, there is no law of the 'Persistence of Value,' that would correspond to the physical law of the persistence of force. And just as little does it seem that there can be a law of the 'Persistence of Consciousness.' The whole ideational content may fall from the greatest liveliness down to nil, while in the corresponding brain-functions the law of the persistence of force maintains its validity. But where then remains the possibility of an even somewhat exact association-psychology?

Nevertheless Mill is right in this, that so far as the doctrine of the succession of ideas can really be empirically based, it has pretensions to count as a science, whatever may become of the basis of ideas and their dependence upon the cerebral functions. The methods hitherto applied, however, give very little guarantee against self-delusions. We have some very general propositions, which rest upon a very incomplete induction, and with these the field of psychical phenomena is traversed in extended analyses, in order to see what may be referred to these supposed laws of association. But if, instead of merely analysing the general notions of psychical phenomena, we will but turn to life and try to comprehend the succession of ideas in particular cases, such as present themselves to the alienist, the criminal lawyer, or the schoolmaster, we shall nowhere make a single step forward, without stumbling upon the 'unconscious ideas,' which, quite in accord with the laws of association, strike into the course of our ideas, although they are, strictly speaking, not ideas at all, but only brain-functions of the same kind as those which involve consciousness.[57]

---

[57] Some attempt has recently been made (by Stumpf, Brentano, &c.) to eliminate 'unconscious' or 'latent' ideas out of psychology. When recourse is had for this purpose to Lotze, no great objection can be made, for he expressly assumes that the ideas are connected with brain-functions, which without even exciting consciousness yet participate in the course of our thoughts (Medic. Psych. ss. 409, 410). That Lotze at the same time assigns associations (s. 411), not to physiology, but to a 'metaphysical psychology,' is an inconsistency which on closer consideration must easily disappear. The rest is a question of words. There is, on the other hand, assuredly a material error in Brentano, if he proposes to explain everything by ideas which have been conscious but have been again forgotten. Comp. especially the inadequate way in which Brentano tries to dispose of Maudsley's views as to unconscious intellectual labour (Psych. v. emp. St., S. 138 ff.) Precisely Goethe, whose saying that extraordinary talent is only a slight deviation from ordinary

Besides the doctrine of the succession of ideas, we have now yet another department of empirical psychology which is accessible to strictly methodical inquiry. This is Anthropological Statistics, the core of which so far has been formed by Moral Statistics. We find ourselves here quite strictly in the sphere of what Kant called 'Pragmatic Anthropology;' *i.e.*, we have to do with a science of man as a "freely acting being," obviously, therefore, with the intellectual side of man, although statistics does not trouble itself about the distinction of body and soul. It records human actions and human chances, and by combining these records many an insight may be gained into the machinery not merely of social life, but also of the motives which guide the individual in his actions.

In truth, nearly the whole of statistics can be turned to account in exact anthropology, and it is a mistake to suppose that psychological conclusions can be drawn only from reports as to the number and kind of crimes and trials, the extent of suicides or illegitimate births, or the extent of education, the number of literary productions, and so on. By skilful combinations of the numbers to be compared, it must be just as possible to draw psychological conclusions from the statistics of commerce and navigation, from the traffic reports of the railways, goods and passengers both included, from the average quantities of crops and number of cattle, the results of the subdivision of property and of its aggregation, and innumerable other reports, as from the favourite themes of moral statistics. On the other hand, because the variety of

---

talent, is employed by Brentano against the unconscious labours of genius, has expressed himself so often and so clearly on the unconscious processes from which artistic production proceeds, that we must allow the utmost weight to his testimony. There is nothing in the rarity of great original thinkers, for productive genius is not therefore bound to be rare also. It is found more or less in every artist. A collection of the utterances upon this subject of writers and artists is in J. C. Fischer, Das Bewusstsein, Leipz. 1874 (6 Kap.).

circumstances and motives was not regarded, or because man was regarded too much in the light of an obsolete psychology, results have been often prematurely drawn from the figures of moral statistics. The excellent Quételet has spread many false ideas, especially by the unhappy expression, 'penchant vers le crime,' although with him this term is a tolerably indifferent name for a mathematical idea, in itself irreproachable. Little as a probability arrived at by abstraction can be regarded as an objectively existing quality of an individual thing belonging to the class to which the abstraction was applied, just as little can we expect, by the simple mediation of the calculus of probabilities, to discover a tendency to crime, which, as a real factor in human actions, would have a psychological importance. But the tendency to crime, the inclination to suicide, the propensity to marriage, have been only too often taken literally, and from the remarkable regularity of the figures recurring year by year a fatalism has been deduced, which is at least as strange as Quételet's attempt to save the freedom of the will as well as the reign of law. Quételet, that is to say, allows freewill—of course freewill according to the school-traditions of France and Belgium—its validity within the great sphere of the demonstrated regularity of law as an accidental cause, whose effect, striking in now positively, now negatively, is neutralised by the law of high numbers. It is beyond doubt that there are such individual will-impulses, which now have the effect of adding a unit to the year's budget of volitional acts, now of subtracting one, while the average figure finally balances better than any national budget-calculation. But if now the average will, which approximately represents the great mass of all individual will-impulses, is physically determined by the influences of age, sex, climate, food, kind of labour, &c., should we not conclude then in any other sphere that the individual impulse also is governed by physical conditions? Should we not conclude that it stands related to the average result only as, *e.g.*, the rainfall of the 1st of May, or any other day, is related to the average rainfall of the year? In fact, then, there is not, scholastic prejudices apart, the slightest reason to assume for these individual fluctuations besides the numerous accidental causes which we can trace physically, another special one which preserves the peculiarity that it is restrained to very narrow limits of operation, and yet within these is independent of the general causal connexion of things. This is a wholly superfluous, and, in fact, uselessly disturbing hypothesis, which would occur to no reasonable man, much less then to a man like Quételet, if he had not grown up in the traditionary prejudices of a modernised scholasticism.

As in Germany we have long been accustomed to the idea of a unity of mind and nature, it is natural that our philosophers were not so much affected by this contradiction between the results of statistics and the obsolete doctrine of the freedom of the will. A. Wagner has thought it necessary, in his admirable treatise on the Regularity in apparently Arbitrary Human Actions (Hamburg, 1864), to make it matter of reproach to our philosophers that they have troubled themselves so little with Quételet and his researches; but this reproach is not quite rightly directed. Men like Waitz, Drobisch, Lotze, and many others, amongst whom Wagner may have tried to find some attention to Quételet, are so far beyond this antithesis of freedom and necessity, that it must assuredly be very difficult for them to throw themselves back to a standpoint, from which a serious problem here still presents itself. We may here refer to what we have said in the section on Kant as to the problem of the freedom of the will. Between freedom as form of subjective consciousness and necessity as fact of objective science, there can as little be a contradiction, as between a colour and a sound. The same vibration of a string gives to the eye the picture of an oscillatory motion, to calculation a particular number of vibrations per second, and to the ear a single tone. But this unity and that manifoldness do not contradict each other, and if the ordinary consciousness ascribes to the number of vibrations a higher degree of reality than to the tones, there is no great objection. Interesting and useful as are Quételet's pioneering studies, yet for the more enlightened German philosophers they are not so much interesting for their bearing upon the freedom of the will, as the empirical conditionality and strict causality of all human actions, which Quételet does not even venture completely to affirm, since Kant is treated as certain, and to some extent as a well-known and settled fact. It is also quite right that the importance of freedom is maintained against Materialistic fatalism, especially in the sphere of morals. For here it is not enough to maintain that the consciousness of freedom is a reality, but also that the course of ideas involved with the consciousness of freedom and responsibility has just as essential an importance for our conduct as those ideas in which a temptation, an impulse, a natural stimulus to this or that action, comes immediately into consciousness. When, therefore, Wagner supposes that the explanation of the neglect of moral statistics lies in the repugnance to figures and tables, he is decidedly mistaken. How could we look for such a repugnance in Drobisch, who did not shrink from constructing tables for the hypothetical values of his mathematical psychology, and who, in fact, is not only acquainted with Quételet's inquiries, but thoroughly understands and is able to criticise them? And yet how difficult is such a German philosopher to understand, even for scientifically trained readers, if they have not the different systems and their history in a connected view before them! Thus, *e.g.*, Drobisch says, in a short and excellent criticism of the conclusions of moral statistics: * " In all such facts there are reflected not pure natural laws, to which man must

* Zeitschr. f. ex. Phil., iv. 329.

submit as to destiny, but at the same time the moral conditions of society, which are determined by the mighty influences of family life, of the school, the Church, of legislation, and are, therefore, quite capable of improvement by the will of man." Who, unless he had an accurate knowledge of the Herbartian psychology and metaphysics, would not find in this an apology for the old freedom of the will, such as might be expected from a French professor? And yet the human will, even on the system to which Drobisch has adhered, is only a consequence resulting in the strictest causality from the state of the soul, which, again, in the last result, is only produced by its reciprocal action with other real existences. Since then, in his essay published in 1867 on 'Moral Statistics and the Freedom of the Human Will,' Drobisch has discussed thoroughly, and in a way intelligible to every one, the relation of freedom and natural necessity, and at the same time made some very valuable contributions to the methodology of moral statistics.

Wagner might, in fact, have been led by Buckle, whose brilliant studies have more than once been a stimulus to him, to see that German philosophy in the doctrine of the freedom of the will has for once an advantage which permits it to regard these new studies with equanimity; for Buckle stands, above all, upon Kant, adducing his testimony for the empirical necessity of human actions, and leaving aside the transcendental theory of freedom.*

Although all that Materialism can draw from moral statistics has thus been conceded by Kant, and all the rest has been already rejected,[58] yet, for the practical value

---

* See his note at the end of his first chapter.

[58] How little ethical Materialism is justified in making moral statistics a specifically Materialistic science because of its opposition to the doctrine of Free Will, is shown by the interesting fact that we are indebted for the best treatment of the subject as yet to a strictly Lutheran theologian, who endeavours to support his Christian ethics on this empirical basis; Oettingen, Die Moralstatistik: inductiver Nachweis d. Gesetzmässigkeit sittl. Lebensbewegung im Organismus d. Menschheit: Erlangen, 1868. There is recently a second edition. Of course moral statistics are just as little orthodox and Lutheran as they are Materialistic.

of a Materialistic tendency of the age as against Idealism, it is by no means indifferent whether moral statistics, and, as we would have it, the whole of statistics, is placed in the foreground of anthropological study or not; for moral statistics direct the view outwards upon the really measurable facts of life, while the German philosophy, despite its clearness as to the nullity of the old doctrine of freewill, still constantly likes to direct its view inwards upon the facts of consciousness. Yet it is only by the former method that science can hope gradually to secure achievements of permanent value.

It is true, indeed, that our methods must become much more delicate, and especially our conclusions be more cautious, than they have been with Quételet, and in this respect we may regard moral statistics as one of the nicest touchstones of unprejudiced thinking. Thus, *e.g.*, it is still regarded as an axiom that the number of crimes yearly occurring in a country is to be treated as a measure of its morality. Nothing can be more absurd so soon as we have a notion of morality which rises somewhat above the principle of cunningly avoiding punishment. At least we must begin, if we wish to find a figure proportional to the morality, by dividing the number of punishable actions by the number of opportunities or temptations to punishable actions. It is quite obvious that a certain number of bill-forgeries in a district where bills are much used has not the same significance as the same number in an equally large district where the use of bills is only half as much. But criminal statistics count up only the absolute number of cases, and when they go into comparative figures, they take at most the number of the population as a measure, and not the number of acts or business transactions the abuse of which may lead to crimes. For many kinds of transgressions, moreover, the denominator necessary to fix a correct proportion is not to be had, and yet there is a difference as to their whole moral development between the groups of population that are to be compared, which forbids our supposing that the proportion of crimes to heads of population in the two cases could have the same ethical and psychological significance. As this point has not been sufficiently considered, I may refer here briefly to the important fact of ethical evolution, which I first developed in my lectures on moral statistics at Bonn in the winter of 1857–58, and since then have found constantly confirmed, although I have never found time to publish them. If we compare the condition of a uniformly living pastoral population, such as we might find in several departments in the interior of France, with the condition of a population which is carried away by the industrial, literary, and political play of mind, in which daily life of itself awakes a greater fulness of ideas, demands actions and decisions, excites doubts and stimulates thoughts, and in which, moreover, the alternations of fortune and misfortune are greater for the individual as well as for the community, and extraordinary crises are frequent, we easily see that in the latter population, as is shown by the mere consideration of their faces, their figures, their dresses and customs, there must be found an infinitely greater difference between individuals, and that each single individual is exposed to a much livelier alternation of influences of all kinds. As now, ethically considered, such an evolution develops noble just as much as ignoble qualities, and provokes extraordinary acts of self-sacrifice and disinterested altruism, or of heroic struggles for the general weal, just as much as, on the other hand, it produces the phenomena of avarice, of egoism, and unbounded passions, we may imagine an ethical centre of gravity for the acts of this population from which certain individual acts deviate, now towards the good, now towards the bad side, and again in the direction of some morally indifferent eccentricity. In a population where the process of evolution has not gone so far, all actions will group themselves more closely round the centre of gravity, *i.e.*, eccentric and exceptionally noble acts will be proportionately just as rare as very bad ones. As now the law does not trouble itself with the great mass of actions, and only assigns a limit to egoism and to the passions in certain directions, beyond which prosecution and punishment begin, it is quite natural that a population of a higher stage of evolution with the same ethical centre of gravity has a greater number of immoral actions, partly because, reckoning by heads, more decided individual acts of will occur, but partly, too, because the greater eccentricity of the individuals extends farther from the mean in a good as well as in a bad sense, while only a part of the actions of this latter kind are recorded. As a powerful wave, even when the water is low, more easily foams over the dam than a weak wave when the water is higher, so must it be here too with regard to punishable actions.

A farther discussion of this subject is not suitable here; and we content ourselves with showing how far moral statistics are still removed from penetrating into the heart of psychology. All the more important, however, are the outworks; and we must never forget that if only a vigorous criticism sees that the ground is firm beneath our feet, the most trivial details gain a permanent value, while whole systems of speculation, after they have for a moment shed a dazzling light, fall for ever into the sphere of history.

CHAPTER IV.

THE PHYSIOLOGY OF THE SENSE-ORGANS AND THE WORLD
AS REPRESENTATION.

WE have hitherto seen in every department that it is the scientific, the physical study of phenomena, which is able to throw upon man and his intellectual nature the light of real knowledge, though it may be at first but a few scattered rays. Now we come to the department of human inquiry in which the empirical method has celebrated its highest triumph, and in which, at the same time, it leads us to the very limits of our knowledge, and betrays to us at least so much of the sphere beyond it as to convince us of its existence. This is the physiology of the sense-organs.

While nervous physiology in general at each advance was exhibiting life more and more as a product of mechanical processes, the more exact study of the processes of sensations in their connexion with the nature and mode of operation of the sense-organs leads immediately to show us how, with the same mechanical necessity with which everything else goes on, ideas are produced in us which owe their peculiar nature to our organisation, although they are occasioned by the external world. On the greater or less significance of the consequences of these observations turns the whole question of the thing in itself and the phenomenal world. The physiology of the sense-organs is developed or corrected Kantianism, and Kant's system may, as it were, be regarded as a programme for modern discoveries in this field. One of the most successful inquirers, Helmholtz, has employed the views of Kant as a heuristic principle, and yet in so doing has only followed consciously and consistently the same path by which others too have succeeded in making the mechanism of sensation more intelligible.

Apparently the unveiling of this mechanism is not unfavourable to the theories of the Materialists. The extension of acoustics by the resolution of the vowels into the effect of co-operating over-tones is at the same time a complement of the mechanical principle of explaining nature. The sound, as product of a number of sensations of tone, still remains as an effect of the movements of matter. If we find the hearing of definite musical tones determined by the resonant apparatus of the organ of Corti, or the position of objects of vision in space determined by muscular feeling in the mechanism that moves the eye, it does not seem as if we were leaving this ground. But now comes the stereoscope and resolves the sensations of corporeality in sight into the co-operation of two sensations of flat surfaces. It becomes probable that even the feelings of warmth and pressure in the organ of touch are compound sensations, which are only distinguished by the grouping of the elements of sensation. We learn that the sensation of colours, the ideas of the magnitude and movement of an object, nay, even the appearance of simple straight lines, are not determined invariably by the given object, but that the relation of sensations to one another determines the quality of each individual one; nay, that experience and habit influence not only the interpretation of sense impressions, but even the immediate phenomenon itself. Facts accumulate from all sides, and the inductive conclusion becomes inevitable, that our apparently simplest sensations are not only occasioned by a natural phenomenon which in itself is something quite other than the sensation, but that they are also infinitely compound products; that their quality is by no means merely determined by the external stimulus and the fixed constitution of an organ, but by the constellation of the collective accurrent sensations. We see, in fact, how, if our attention is concentrated, one sensation may be completely supplanted by another disparate sensation.[59]

Let us see now how much of Materialism may be retained.

The ancient Materialism, with its main belief in the sensible world, is done for; even the Materialistic conception of thought which the last century favoured cannot stand. If for each definite sensation a definite fibre in the brain is supposed to vibrate, the relativity and solidarity of sensations and their resolution into unknown elementary effects cannot stand, to say nothing of localising thought. But what may very well stand with the facts is the hypothesis that all these effects of the constellation of simple sensations rest upon mechanical conditions which, when physiology has progressed far enough, we may be able to discover. Sensation, and with it our whole intellectual existence, may still be the incessantly changing result of the co-operation of elementary activities, infinite in number and in the variety of their combinations, which may themselves be localised, somewhat as the pipes of an organ are localised, but not its melodies.

We stride away now right through the consequences of this Materialism by remarking that the same mechanism which thus produces all our sensations produces also our idea of matter. But it has here no warranty for a special degree of objectivity. Matter in general may just as well be merely a product of my organisation—must, in fact, be so—as

---

[59] A special exposition of the points here suggested must be very thorough in order to make the reader in some degree independent of other aids. It is, however, the less necessary, as besides the handbooks of physiology and the larger monographs of Helmholtz, &c., we have also Helmholtz's 'Popular Lectures' (1864 and 1871), besides Wundt's Physiol. Psych., in which all the questions here arising are exhaustively treated. Comp. also Fick, Die Welt als Vorstellung, akad. Vortr., Würzb. 1870; and Preyer, Die fünf Sinne d. Menschen, Leipz. 1870.

colour or as any modification of colour produced by the phenomena of contrast.

Here now we see, too, why it is all but indifferent [60] whether we speak of a mental or physical organisation, and therefore we might so often use the neutral expression; for every physical organisation, even if I can demonstrate it under the microscope or with the knife, is still only my idea, and cannot differ in its nature from what I call mental.

In Kant's days the knowledge of the dependence of our world upon our organs lay generally in the air. The Idealism of Bishop Berkeley had never been got over; but more important and influential was the Idealism of the men of science and the mathematicians. D'Alembert distinctly doubted the possibility of knowing the real objects; Lichtenberg, who loved to controvert Kant, because his nature revolted against even the most completely veiled dogmatism, had understood the one point with which we have here to do, quite independently of Kant, more clearly than any of Kant's own followers. He, who in all his philosophising never forgot that he was a physicist, declares it to be impossible to refute Idealism. To know external objects is a contradiction: it is impossible for man to go outside himself. "When we believe that we see things, we see only ourselves. We can, properly speaking, know nothing of anything in the world except ourselves and the changes that take place in us." "When anything acts upon us, the effect depends not only upon the acting object, but also upon that which is acted upon." [61]

[60] That it is not entirely indifferent, as was said in the first edition, I have been convinced, especially by the way in which recent Kantians persistently speak of the *mental* organisation by which the idea is occasioned, as though this were something separate. It is assuredly, on the contrary, not only more correct in itself, but it also agrees with Kant's view, to see in this "mental" organisation only the transcendental side of the phenomenal physical organisation; the 'Ding an sich des Gehirns,' as Ueberweg used to say. Comp., besides, *supra*, vol. ii. p. 193, note 25.

[61] Lichtenberg's Verm. Schrift. hg. v. Kries, ii. SS. 31, 44.

There is no doubt that Lichtenberg was just the man to exhibit to us the connecting links between these speculative ideas and the ordinary physical theories, but he found for this, as for so much besides, neither time nor inclination. It was only a considerable time after Kant that the first step in this respect was taken in Germany; and clearly as the truth lies here on the one side and error on the other, yet even now imbecile tradition can still transfigure the most trivial error with the glories of empiricism, while a correct observation, which is as simple and significant as the egg of Columbus, is rejected as idle speculation. We refer to the theory of the projection of the object outwards in connexion with the famous problem of Erect Vision.

It was Johannes Müller who first pronounced the true solution of this problem, though without carrying it out in logical completeness, by pointing out that the image of our own body is perceived under entirely the same conditions as the images of external objects.

If men once found it astonishingly difficult to conceive this firm earth upon which we stand, the very type of repose and stability, as in motion, it will be still more difficult for them to recognise in their own body, which is to them the type of all reality, a mere scheme of representation, a product of our optical apparatus, which must just as much be distinguished from the object which occasions it as any other representative image.

The body only an optical image? 'Why we see it,' we can no longer answer, but 'Why we have the immediate sensation of our reality!' 'Away with idle speculations! Who will deny that this is my hand, which I move with my will, and whose sensations are given so immediately to my consciousness?'

These expectorations of natural prejudice might be continued *ad libitum*. The decisive answer is not far to seek. Our sensations, that is to say, must in every case first coalesce with the optical image, whether we concede that the image of the body is not the body itself, or whether we hold fast to the naïve idea of its identity with the object. A man born blind and then couched must first learn the correspondence of his visual and tactual sensations. We only need here an association of ideas, and this must in any case give the same result, whatever we may think of the reality of the body represented in thought.

Müller himself, as we have said, did not attain to perfect clearness, and we shall be led to think that it was the philosophy of nature, with its fantastic interchange of subject and object, of the ego and the external world, that was still in his way. By way of compensation, the correct observation, because of its colossal paradox, was naturally treated as a philosophical fantasy. Nowadays we may frequently hear the opinion that Müller's treatise on the Physiology of Sight (1826) was an immature first production of the famous physiologist, not yet free from the ideas of the philosophy of nature. We will therefore quote the important passage on Erect Vision from the Handbook of Physiology (1840).

"In accordance with the laws of optics, the images are depicted on the retina in an inverted position as regards the objects. . . . The question now arises whether we really see the images, as they are, inverted, or erect as in the object itself. Since the image and the affected parts of the retina mean the same thing, the question physiologically expressed is this: Are the particles of the retina perceived in vision in their natural relation to the body?

"The view which I take of the question, and which I propounded in my work on the Physiology of Vision, is, that even if we do see objects inverted, the only proof we can possibly have of it is that afforded by the study of the laws of optics; and that if everything is seen inverted, the relative position of the objects of course remains unchanged. It is the same thing as the daily inversion of objects consequent on the revolution of the entire earth, which we know only by observing the position of the stars; and yet it is certain that within twenty-four hours, that which was below in relation to the stars comes to be above. Hence it is also that no discordance arises between the sensations of inverted vision and those of touch, which perceives everything in its erect position; for the image of all objects, even of our own limbs, in the retina are equally inverted, and therefore maintain the same relative position. Even the image of our hand while used in touch is seen inverted. The position in which we see objects we call, therefore, the erect position. A mere lateral inversion of our body in a mirror, where the right hand occupies the left of the image, is indeed scarcely remarked; and there is but little discordance between the sensations acquired by touch in regulating our movements by the image in the mirror and those of sight; as, *e.g.*, in tying a knot in the cravat, and so on."

This exposition leaves nothing to be desired in clearness and precision, and we emphasize the fact that in the whole passage there is no trace of that fanciful speculation which distinguishes the Philosophy of Nature. If this view is based upon the Philosophy of Nature, then in this instance its influence is to be praised. It is certainly possible that familiarity with abstract philosophy in this instance, at least, has aided Müller by detaching him from unthinking tradition. But where now are the consequences?

For him who has once recognised the simple truth that Erect Vision is not a problem at all, because the visual image of our body stands in precisely the same circumstances as all other images, there should no longer be any question as to a projection of images outwards. For why should all other images lie in the single image of the body, since the objects of the outer world by no means lie in the real body, which, in fact, in relation to our representation, is also outer world? Of a representation of images instead of the represented retina there can thus be no question. This would be the most paradoxical of hypotheses. How now shall so mythical a phenomenon as the so-called projection contribute to make the external things represented appearing outside the equally merely represented head? To seek here at all for any principle of explanation, one must be at sea as to the whole relation. And Müller, who has so distinctly pronounced the solution of the riddle in his chapter on 'Inverted Vision and Erect Vision,' nevertheless in the next chapter comes back to the theory of projection, and thinks that the idea received in the act of vision "may be conceived as a forward projection of the whole visual field of the retina." Here again then the retina, as conceived and abstracted from images in mirrors and from the appearance of other persons or from anatomical inquiries, is confounded with the actual retina. And Müller could never have relapsed into this confusion, if he had not been entangled in the notions of the Philosophy of Nature as to subject and object. In fact, he says in a previous chapter that the projection outwards of the objects of vision is nothing else than "the discrimination of the objects of vision from the subject, the discrimination of the sensations from the sentient Ego."

Ueberweg has therefore done excellent service not only by bringing once more into view Müller's unjustly neglected remark as to Erect Vision, but also by completely elucidating the relation of the image of the body to the other images of the outer world.* For this purpose Ueberweg employs an interesting illustration. The table of a camera obscura is, like Condillac's statue, endowed with life and consciousness; its pictures are its ideas. It can no more receive an image of itself upon its table than our eye can throw its own image on the retina. The camera might, however, have projecting parts, additions in the nature of members, which should paint themselves on the table and so become an idea. It may mirror other similar constructions; may compare, abstract, and so at length form an

* Henle u. Pfeuffer, Zeitschr. III. Ser., v. 268 ff.

idea of itself. This idea will then take up some place on the table, where the projecting members are usually reflected, or from where these members seem to spring. With admirable clearness Ueberweg has shown that a projection outwards is quite out of the question, just because the images are outside the image, exactly as we must imagine to ourselves the objects setting up sensation as outside our objective body.

A consequence of Ueberweg's conception is that all the space that we perceive is only just the space of our consciousness, while the question meantime remains open whether the retina itself is the sensorium of these visual images, or whether we must seek one further back in the brain.

If we would now suppose for a moment that our sensibility makes no change in things except what we can deduce from the observation of the picture on the retina, there would result, as a probable view of the reality of things, a strange and stupendous idea. Things, including ourselves, are all just inverted as they appear to us, and the whole world which I see lies within my brain. Beyond this the actual things extend in corresponding proportion.

Not in order to free the question from its adventurous aspect (for this has nothing whatever to do with its logical probability), but merely in order to carry the light a step further, we begin by observing that it would be too precipitate to employ the distances of the most distant star as a standard for the measurement of our sensorium. The billions of miles in the calculation of these distances are not a product of our sensibility, but of our calculating reason, and it is only the effect of the association of ideas that the idea of these distances is fused with the sensuous image of the star. To the man born blind who receives his sight by an operation, the objects of visual perception appear oppressively near; the child reaches out for the moon, and even to the adult the figure of the moon or the sun is hardly more distant than the figure of the hand which covers the moon with a threepenny bit. He merely *interprets* this figure differently, and this interpretation reacts of course on the immediate impression of the objects of vision. The whole elaboration of the idea of space based upon vision is a similar process of association, like the fusion of sensations of taste and of feeling with visual images. To make this still clearer we will add another illustration to that of Ueberweg.

In a good diorama the illusion, as regards the perspective of the picture, leaves nothing to be desired. I see before me the Lake of Geneva, and descry the well-known giant summits of the Ufergebirge and the misty heights in the distance with the complete feeling of the distance and grandeur of this magnificent scenery, although I know that I am at 5 Wolf Street in Cologne, where there is in reality no room for such distances. Now the bell sounds in the chapel, and I combine sound and picture into the unity of that solemn and peaceful impression, which I have so frequently enjoyed in nature.

Now let me suppose that the Ego, the consciousness, or some other imaginary being, sits within the skull, and regards the retinal picture, no matter through what medium, as the picture of a diorama with the most splendid perspective, and at the same time in action like the picture of the camera obscura. The being that I imagine is entirely subject to its intuition; beyond this picture it is not capable of any visual perception whatever: it sees nothing of itself, nothing even of the medium through which it sees. But of course this same imaginary being is capable of other impressions; it hears, it feels, and so on. What will happen? The sound will of course very easily fuse with the visual image. If a bell stirs in the picture in some harmony with the corresponding sounds, the association is at once complete. Of itself as hearer and spectator, our supposed being can, of course, thus learn nothing.

We go further. Our being shall also feel, but sensation too shall give him only peripheral ideas; nothing of his own condition and his immediate environment in the brain. Now it shall perceive in its diorama a creature whose movements are in complete harmony with its sensations, whose limbs contract when it feels a pain, and extend themselves when it feels a desire. This creature is quite in the foreground of the scene. Its peculiar, imperfectly cohering parts pass frequently like giant shadows over the whole field of view.

Other creatures show themselves smaller in perspective, very similar, but more perfect and coherent, than the great being in the foreground, with whom the sensations of pain and pleasure are so inseparably connected. Our being combines, abstracts; and as it knows nothing at all of itself beyond its sensations, its sensations are fused also with the great imperfect creature in the foreground of the field of view. By comparison with others, however, this creature is in idea retrospectively supplemented. Now then we have Ego, Body, Outer World, Perspective, everything conformable, regarded from the standpoint of a kind of soul, which through the association of ideas comes to an idea of an Ego without knowing anything whatever of its real self. The idea of the Ego is meanwhile, as it is originally with man, quite inseparable from the idea of the body; and this body is the diorama body, the retinal picture body, fused with the body of the sensations of touch, the sensations of pain and pleasure.

Unless the thread of our argument is kept in view, it might be supposed that we were here suddenly coming round to Lotze's punctual soul; but it must be remembered that we were only constructing a fiction. We personified a phenomenon, and this phenomenon is nothing but the fusion of the sense-perceptions themselves. The intermediate person is superfluous. That an entire spiritual life, in the sense in which we are accustomed to use this term, can be built up from the sensations in their infinite gradation, manifoldness, and complexity, we have already seen. Here it suffices to remark that a unitary connecting point does not seem to us at all necessary in order to allow of the fusion of the functions of all sensoria, in case there are several; if only any connexion is there.

If the individual sensoria in the brain had no connexion, we should have not only a metaphysical riddle before us; but even the mechanical understanding of man as a mere natural creature, as we have pictured him in the chapter on 'Brain and Soul,' would become an impossibility. If, however, a connexion is granted, for which we require no unitary central point nor complete 'images' in the brain, there remains only the metaphysical riddle, how out of the multiplicity of the atomic movements there arises the unity of the psychical image. We hold this riddle, as we have often said, to be insoluble, but so much we can easily see, that it remains equally great, whether we assume a mechanical union of the stimuli into an image in a material centre or not. If we call the act of transition from physical multiplicity to psychical unity a synthesis, then this synthesis remains equally inexplicable, whether it refers to the union of the numerous discrete points of a complete image, or to the mere spatially distributed conditions of the image. The Cartesian and Spinozistic view of the intuition of brain-images by the soul remains, apart from the well-known artifice by which prejudice introduces into man yet another man, every whit as inexplicable as the origin of the psychical image directly from its physical conditions.

Of course if a man stands before a loom, and tries to guess from its mechanism and from the way in which the threads of the chain are stretched the pattern of the tissue, this is more difficult than if he regards the pattern directly on the finished material. As now this perception only takes place through the surface of the material being resolved into a multiplicity of impressions on the particular nerves, and as this resolution is necessary in order to render possible the greatest manifoldness of connexions with other sense impressions in the brain, it cannot help us at all that somewhere in the brain there should be produced again from these individual impressions a physical image of the material; for this must again be resolved back in order to enter into the mechanism of associations. Accordingly, we may just as easily, and more easily, refer the origin of the psychical image of the intuition which becomes conscious in the subject to a direct synthesis of the individual impressions, even if these are dispersed in the brain. How such a synthesis is possible remains a riddle; indeed, we have reason to suppose that the whole assumption of an origin of the unitary psychical image from the numerous individual stimuli is only an inadequate mode of conception with which we have to content ourselves; but so much may be perceived, that in any case such a synthesis is required in order to establish the link between atomic changes and consciousness. But on this very account there is no sense in repeating things over again in the brain, or, to speak more correctly, for the product of the synthesis, for the representation of a thing, to insert a reduced image over again into the represented brain.

Ueberweg indeed found another way out of the difficulty. He was opposed to Atomism, and the continuity of matter appeared to him too as a sufficient link of unity for ideas. He needed no man in man to perceive the brain-images. He attributed 'consciousness' to these images, and thus the ideas were complete. Of course this involved a presupposition to which anatomy will simply not lend itself. He had to suppose somewhere in the brain a 'structureless substance,' in which the ideational images lie imbedded, and by whose power of conduction in all directions they can be placed in connexion with all other sensations. On this postulate the whole thing goes to pieces, though it may also be attacked at many other points. We will, therefore, again not follow Ueberweg, when, true to his principle, he assumes a world of things-in-themselves, which has spatial dimensions, which is completely filled with matter capable of sensation, and the things in which we must conceive as only slightly differing from the things of our ideas. In this, however, we must agree with Ueberweg, much as the metaphysicians may struggle against it, that our ideas, so soon as we understand the word not in the sense of 'actus purus,' have *extension*, for the things as they appear are just precisely our ideas. That they are therefore material cannot, however, be asserted, for only the phenomena are given to us immediately; matter all the same, whether we conceive it atomistically or as a continuum, is a factitious principle to aid us in bringing phenomena into an unbroken connexion of cause and effect.

If now we apply metaphysical criticism to Ueberweg's picture of the world, of course this strange colossal world of things in themselves disappears like a cloud-picture; for if space is only our form of intuition, these things in themselves are and remain absolutely unknowable. As soon, however, as we return to the Materialistic mode of conceiving things outside us, Ueberweg's colossal world returns again with all its rights. But as now no feature of Materialism is so generally spread as the belief in material, self-existent things, and the habit of presupposing them, even though we do not believe in them, the paradoxical theory of Ueberweg acquires besides its metaphysical value a didactic value as well. The metaphysical value is limited to Ueberweg's system; the didactic value serves also for any other system, so far as the hypothesis of a material and self-existing world of things is admitted, at least as a conception assisting us to comprehend phenomena. Here, in any case, the false theory of projection is cut off at the root.

Helmholtz remarks that the controversy as to the explanation of erect vision has only the psychological interest "of showing how difficult it is even for men of considerable scientific capacity to make up their minds really and truly to recognise the subjective element in our sense-perceptions, and to see in them effects of objects instead of unaltered copies (*sit venia verbo*) of objects, which latter notion is altogether contradictory." Helmholtz rejects the theory of Müller and Ueberweg, without impugning its consistency and relative correctness.[62] We need it, of course, no longer when we have once learned to regard phenomena as mere effects of objects (*i.e.*, of the unconscious things-in-themselves) upon our sensibility; but by far the greater number of our present physicists and physiologists not only cannot rise to this standpoint, but remain still deep in the false theory of projection, which has its roots just in the raising of our own body into a thing-in-itself. To cut off this error at the root there is no better means than the Müller-Ueberweg theory, which then indeed is in its turn abolished from the higher standpoint of the critical theory of knowledge.[63]

[62] Hdbuch d. physiol. Optik, § 29, S. 606 f.; 594.

[63] The relative and didactic merit here assigned to the Müller-Ueberweg theory is not affected by the latest turn which Stumpf (Ueber d. psychol. Urspr. d. Raumvorstellung, Leipz. 1873) has attempted to give to the projection theory. Stumpf is wrong in making it appear that my adhesion to Ueberweg's theory is unconditional (S. 190 Anm.), although the difference of the standpoints, which is now more fully exhibited, was still sufficiently indicated in the first edition, and is, moreover, an obvious consequence of my standpoint in the theory of knowledge. As regards Ueberweg, Stumpf begins with the supposition that he has not observed the distinction between "to represent something as existing at a distance" and "to have one's representation at this distance or to represent it as existing at this distance." But Ueberweg must not be so lightly treated, since his philosophy, despite the singularity of the whole, is thoroughly thought out in all its parts. Precisely the question, What, does it mean to represent something as existing at a distance? may be regarded as the starting-point of his psychological constructions; for Ueberweg found that these words have no sense unless the distance itself is also represented in terms of sense. Only the second proposition, therefore, is in his view clear and appropriate; the first rests on the Scholastico-Cartesian illusion of a representation separable from its content. The way, too, in which Stumpf treats Ueberweg's illustration of the table and camera-obscura (S. 191) rests upon an entire misunderstanding. The image of the table embraces, of course, only its external appearance, without that which is pictured upon it, as we perceive a man from the outside into whose brain we cannot see. To identify the image completely with the proper 'self' of the table can

Not less thoroughly than by the elimination of the old theory of projection, the belief in material things is also shaken by an inquiry into the material out of which our senses construct the world of these things. Any one who does not venture with Czolbe to draw the extreme conclusions of belief in the phenomenal world, will nowadays easily admit that colours, sounds, smells, &c., do not belong to things in themselves, but that they are peculiar forms of excitation of our sensibility, which are called forth by corresponding but qualitatively very different phenomena in the outer world. It would lead us too far to recall the innumerable facts that confirm this doctrine; we must only single out a few which throw their light further than the great mass of physical and physiological observations.

First of all, we remark that the main principle of the sentient apparatus, especially of the eye and ear, consists in this, that from the chaos of vibrations and motions of every kind with which we must suppose the media that surround us to be filled, certain forms of a motion repeated in definite numerical relations are singled out, relatively strengthened, and thus made objects of perception, while all other forms of motion pass by without making any impression whatever upon our sensibility. We must begin therefore by declaring not merely that colour, sound, &c., are phenomena of the subject, but also that the motions in the outer world which occasion them by no means play the part which they must have for us as a result of their effect upon the senses.

The tone so high as to be imperceptible and the no longer audible vibration of the air are not in the object separated by such a gulf as lies between audibility and

occur to no one who seriously tries to do justice to Ueberweg's view. Stumpf's ingenious but hazardous deduction that the visual representation must originally have these dimensions we leave unexamined. But when, in order to simplify the problem of the perception of depth, he avoids the notion of 'outside us,' and instead speaks only of ' seeing things at a distance,' this is not to decide as to the core of the problem of projection; for this turns always on the distance of things from our body and of the *represented* things from the *represented* body.

inaudibility. The ultra-violet rays have *for us* an all but imperceptible importance, and all the numerous phenomena in matter, of which we have only indirect knowledge, electricity, magnetism, gravity, the tensions of affinity, cohesion, &c., exert their influence on the relations of matter just as much as the directly perceptible vibrations. If we think of atoms, these can not only not shine, sound, &c., but they have in fact not even the forms of motion corresponding to colours and tones which we perceive. They must rather have other extremely complicated forms of motion, resulting out of innumerable others. Our sense-organs are organs of abstraction; they show us some important effect of a form of motion, which does not even exist in the object itself.

If it is said that abstraction even in thinking leads to the knowledge of truth, we must observe that this is only relatively true, namely, so far as we speak of that knowledge which necessarily results from our organisation, and therefore never contradicts itself. We turn the tables now by explaining here again, on the Materialistic method, the supposed supersensible, thought, by the sensible. If the abstraction which our sense-apparatus brings about with its rods, cones, fibres of Corti, &c., can be shown to be an activity which, by the elimination of the great mass of effects, creates a wholly one-sided picture of the world depending on the structure of our organs, the same, we may conjecture, will be the case with abstraction in thinking.

Recent observation has discovered very interesting relations between the idea and the apparently immediate sense-perception, and sometimes a somewhat fruitless controversy has been carried on as to whether an observed fact was to be explained physiologically or psychologically. An instance is the phenomenon of Stereoscopic Vision. For the main questions with which we have here to deal, it is quite indifferent whether, *e.g.*, the theory of identical positions of the retina in the explanation of the phenomena holds its place or not. To inquirers of a purely physical, if not exactly Materialistic, turn of thought, it is unpleasant to resolve a fact of apparently immediate sense-perception into what seems so vague a thing as an 'idea.' They profess to leave such theories to the philosophers, and try themselves to find a mechanism which necessarily produces the thing. But supposing that they had found this, it would by no means be proved that the thing had nothing to do with the 'idea,' but rather an important step would have been taken towards explaining ideation itself mechanically. Whether this explanation lies somewhat further back or not is for the present indifferent; as also whether the mechanism which has yet to be discovered is innate or developed through experience, and varying again with it. It is uncommonly important, on the other hand, that such fundamental points of sensibility as corporeal vision, the phenomenon of brilliance, the concord and discord of tones, and so on, are resolved into their conditions, and shown to be a product of various circumstances. Thus our previous conception of the corporeal and the sensible must gradually become modified. Meanwhile, it is quite indifferent whether the phenomena of the sense-world are referred to the idea or to the mechanism of the organs, if they are only shown to be products of our organisation in the widest sense of the word. As soon as this is shown, not merely with regard to individual phenomena, but with adequate generality, there results the following series of conclusions :—

1. The sense-world is a product of our organisation.

2. Our visible (bodily) organs are, like all other parts of the phenomenal world, only pictures of an unknown object.

3. The transcendental basis of our organisation remains therefore just as unknown to us as the things which act upon it. We have always before us merely the product of both.

We shall soon reach a further series of conclusions;

but first a few remarks on the connexion between sense-impression and idea.

In stereoscopic vision we left it an open question where the mechanism of the phenomena concerned is to be found. We have, however, a group of highly remarkable phenomena in which the intrusion of an inference, and a fallacious inference, into the visual sensation appears unmistakable. As is well known, the spot where the optic nerve enters the eye is insensitive to light; it forms a blind spot on the retina, of which, however, we are not conscious. Not only does one eye supply what the other eye lacks—otherwise every one-eyed person must perceive the blind spot—but another completion also takes place of an essentially different kind.

A uniformly tinted surface on which we put a spot of any other colour appears without any interruption of the ground-colour, if by a proper adjustment of the axis of the eye we make this spot fall upon the blind spot of the retina. The habit of completing a surface thus presents itself here immediately as a sensation of colour. If the ground-colour is red, then, too, on the blind spot we *see*—if the term is properly understood—red also. This sensation cannot be resolved into the abstract hypothesis that this point is not distinguished from the rest of the surface, nor even into an easily distinguishable imaginary picture, but we *see* as clearly as we are accustomed to see with a spot of the retina pretty far removed from the yellow spot the colour which, if it depended merely on the constitution of our external organ at the place in question, could by no possibility appear.

This experiment has been pursued through many variations. A black line is applied to the white surface, and the middle of it is made to fall on the blind spot. The line appears complete, all the same whether it is perfect or is interrupted at the blind place. The eye makes, as it were, a probable inference; an inference from experience, an imperfect induction. We say the *eye* makes this inference. The expression is intentionally not more definite because we intend briefly to denote by it only that whole group of arrangements and processes from the central organ to the retina, to which is attributed the activity of vision. We regard it as unreliable in point of method to separate in this case inference and sight from one another as two separate acts. We can only do this in abstraction. Unless we give an artificial interpretation to the actual phenomenon, in this case seeing is itself an inferring, and the inference perfects itself in the form of a visual idea, as in other cases it does so in the form of conceptions expressed in language.

That here seeing and inferring are really one is shown by the mere consideration that we simultaneously by the mediation of ideas infer with perfect sureness the opposite of what is given us by the immediate sensible phenomenon. If there belonged to the organ of sight merely the sensation as such, if all inferring took place in a separate organ of thought, we could hardly explain this contradiction between inference and inference, quite apart from the special difficulty of unconscious thinking. This latter difficulty is indeed brought nearer to a general solution if we assume that operations which in their conditions and in their results are identical with inference may be fused into one with simple sensible activity.

How great is, in fact, the unity of inference and seeing in these phenomena is shown by the success of a variation of the experiment, by which, as it were, the eye is made aware of the defectiveness of its premisses. A cross is drawn of different colours, and the point where its two lines intersect, the point of crossing, is made to fall upon the blind spot. Which arm now must the idea complete, since both put in equal claims? It is usually supposed that in this case the colour which makes the liveliest psychical impression asserts itself, or again that there may be an interchange, now the one and now the other arm appearing complete. No doubt, indeed, these phenomena occur, but they are altogether less distinct than in the simple form of the experiment, and on frequent repetition and variation of the experiment vision at this spot finally ceases altogether. We no longer succeed in seeing either the one arm or the other complete. The eye attains, as it were, the consciousness that there is nothing seen at this spot, and corrects its original wrong inference.

I will not omit to observe here that after long occupying myself with these experiments I saw the primitive freshness of the completed colours and forms fall off; the eye seemed, even in the simpler experiments, also to have become distrustful. After suspending the experiments for some time the original sureness in the completion reappeared.

Drobisch* attached great value to Helmholtz's deduction of the sense-perceptions from psychical activities, which involves, he thinks, nothing less than a "refutation of Materialism." But when Helmholtz shows that the perceptions come about as if they were formed by inferences, then the two following principles may be applied:—

1. We have hitherto always found physical conditions for the peculiarities of perception, and therefore we must conjecture that the analogy with inferences also rests upon physical conditions.

2. If there are in the purely sensible sphere, where organic conditions must be assumed for all phenomena, processes which are essentially related with rational inferences, it then becomes much more probable that the latter also rest upon a physical mechanism.

If it were not that the matter has another and a very different side, Materialism would find in the investigations on this subject only a new support. The time when a thought could be regarded as the secretion of a special portion of the brain, or as the vibration of a particular fibre, is of course gone by. Already we must learn to conceive different thoughts as different forms of activity of the same manifoldly co-operating organs. What now could be more welcome to Materialism than the proof that

* Zeitschr. f. exact. Phil., iv. 334 ff.

on occasion of the sense-perceptions in our body there arise *quite unconsciously* processes which in their result entirely correspond with inferences? Does not this bring the highest functions of the reason a considerable step nearer to an at least partially material explanation? If we come to the Materialists with unconscious thinking, they have, on the other hand, not merely the weapon of sound common sense, which finds a contradiction in an unconscious function of the 'soul,' but they may immediately conclude: What is unconscious must be of corporeal nature, since the entire hypothesis of a soul is based only upon consciousness. If the body can without consciousness perform logical operations which we have hitherto attributed only to consciousness, then it can perform the most difficult tasks that the soul has to perform. There is then nothing to prevent us from attributing consciousness as a property to the body.

The only way which leads surely beyond the one-sidedness of Materialism runs right through its consequences. Let it be assumed then that there is in the body a physical mechanism which produces the conclusions of the understanding and the senses, then we stand face to face with the questions: What is the Body? What is Matter? What is the Physical? And modern physiology, just as much as philosophy, must answer that they are all only our ideas; necessary ideas, ideas resulting according to natural laws, but still never the things themselves.

The consistently Materialistic view thus changes round, therefore, into a consistently idealistic view. We cannot suppose that there is a chasm in our being. We must not attribute certain functions of our being to a physical, and others to a spiritual nature; but we are within our rights if we presuppose physical conditions for everything, even for the mechanism of thinking, and do not rest until we have discovered them. We are, however, not less within our rights when we regard not only the outer world as it appears to us, but also the organs with which we conceive it, as mere images of the really existent. The eye, with which we believe we see, is itself only a product of our ideas; and when we find that our visual images are produced by the structure of the eye, we must never forget that the eye too with its arrangements, the optic nerve with the brain and all the structures which we may yet discover there as causes of thought, are only ideas, which indeed form a self-coherent world, yet a world which points to something beyond itself. And with all this we have still to inquire how far it is probable that the phenomenal world is so totally different from the world of things that occasion it, as, for example, Kant supposed when he regarded Space and Time as mere human forms of intuition; or whether we may suppose that at least matter with its motion is objectively existent, and the basis of all other phenomena, however widely these phenomena may vary from the real forms of things. Without the objectivity of space and time we cannot possibly conceive anything like our matter and motion. Accordingly it is the last refuge of Materialism to maintain that order in space and time belongs to the things-in-themselves.

If we leave aside here the moral proof for the reality of the phenomenal world as we find it in Czolbe, none of our Materialists has attempted to supply this proof; on the other hand, we find a noteworthy, but, as we are convinced, an unreliable attempt in Ueberweg's Logic (§§ 38 to 44). Ueberweg justly contests the way in which Kant distinguished space and time as *form* of perception from the matter of perception. He starts, then, from the principle that internal perception can apprehend its objects as they are in themselves with material truth. With admirable clearness he distinguishes the nature of sensation from the nature of things by which it is occasioned. Only the nature of the psychical images in our own consciousness can we know, according to Ueberweg, exactly as it is. As now our internal experience runs its course in time, he regards the reality of time as proved. But order in time presupposes the laws of mathematics, and these presuppose space of three dimensions; and thus the course of the demonstration is completed.

Apart from the fact that the fundamental principle, at least in reference to reproduction, is open to just objections, a decided error seems to me to lie in the transference of the reality of time in us to the reality of time outside us. In us not only has time reality, but space also, without the necessity of the mediation of mathematical laws. Now we must, of course, from the connexion of things in us, necessarily conclude to a corresponding connexion of things outside us; but this connexion need by no means be agreement. As the vibrations of the calculated phenomenal world are related to the colours of the immediately seen world, so too a to us entirely inconceivable arrangement of things might be related to the arrangement in time and space which rules in our perceptions.[64]

Sun, moon, and stars, together with their regular motions, and together with the whole universe, are indeed, according to Ueberweg's own ingenious remark, not images reflected outwards, but elements, portions, as it

[64] Ueberweg has replied to this criticism in the later editions of his 'Logik' and in 'Hist. of Phil.' iii. § 27. As to the reality of time, he observes (comp. § 44 in the 4th ed. of the Logik, hg. v. J. B. Meyer, § 85 Anm.), that it would (in the sense of our criticism) be unjustifiable to transfer time to other things, if it were a mere form of intuition, but that it is a 'psychical reality,' because (as is supposed to be proved in § 40) we necessarily apprehend the mental images immediately presented to us exactly as they are. But 'apprehension' is already a new psychical process, in which the thing apprehended cannot remain unaltered. But the idea of time seems only to appear in such secondary psychical formations. In simple, quite spontaneous intuition, even of objects in motion, as, e.g., passing clouds, a flowing stream, &c., I do not find the least consciousness of time. But if we hold to the simple fact that we represent time to ourselves, as always, therefore the idea of time is really in us, time has in this respect not the least advantage over space, and there is no conclusion by analogy possible to other beings in general, but only, as Kant conceded, to other beings similarly equipped for knowledge to ourselves. Ueberweg's proof for the transcendental reality of space of three dimensions, however, rests entirely on the assertion that a mathematical knowledge of objects would not be possible in the measure in which it is possible for us (e.g., in astronomy), unless the number dimensions of the self-existent world

VOL. III. P

were, of our interior. When Ueberweg says that they are images in our brain, we must not forget that our brain too is only an image, or the abstraction of an image, arising through laws which govern our ideas. It is quite in order that, in order to simplify scientific reflexion, we stop as a rule at this image; but we must never forget that we have thus only a relation between the rest of our ideas and the idea of the brain, but no fixed point beyond this subjective sphere. There is no other way whatever of passing beyond this circle but through conjectures, which must then be subject to the ordinary rules of the logic of probabilities.

Now then we see how great the difference is between an immediately seen object and an object conceived on the theories of physics; we see already in the narrow sphere within which one phenomenon can correct and complement the other, what enormous variations the object undergoes when it passes from one medium with its effects into another; must we not conclude there that the passage of the effects of a thing-in-itself into the medium of our being probably also involves important, perhaps incomparably more important, modifications?

The laws of mathematics cannot make any difference in this.

Let us conceive for an instant, in order to see this, a being which can represent space to itself only in two dimensions. It may be conceived quite on the analogy of Ueberweg's animated camera-table. Would there not be given for this being also a mathematical connexion of phenomena, although it could never apprehend the idea of our stereometry? The relatively real space, *i.e.*, our space agreed with those of the phenomenal world. That even without the fulfilling of this condition some mathematical order of phenomena would be possible, Ueberweg does not at all deny. But in what measure, then, is the world intelligible to us? Astronomy is but a special case, for which, under other conditions, something else might be substituted. For the rest, we have no absolute standard as to what we might demand as regards the intelligibleness of the world, and for this reason alone Ueberweg's standpoint is really based upon a concealed *petitio principii*.

with its three dimensions, as compared with its phenomenal world, would be conceived as 'thing-in-itself.' Then the mathematical connexion between the world that occasions ideas and the phenomenal world of this being would be quite undisturbed, and yet from the projection of surfaces in its consciousness no conclusion can be drawn as to the nature of the things that occasion its ideas. It will easily be seen that in the same way beings are also conceivable with spatial intuitions of more than three dimensions, although we cannot possibly represent anything of the kind to ourselves.[65] It is superfluous to go on accumulating such possibilities; it is enough completely to establish that there are infinite numbers of them, and that the validity of our intuition of space and

---

[65] What is here said as to the conceivableness of ideas of space with more or less than three dimensions is taken unchanged from the 1st ed., and is therefore *earlier* than the well-known 'metamathematical' speculations of Helmholtz and Riemann, which have since made so much sensation. To avoid confusion of views, therefore, it must be here pointed out that the text speaks only of the conceivableness of spatial or quasi-spatial intuitions in less or more than three dimensions; the latter especially with reference to intuitions in more than three dimensions, for which we can find, of course, no analogy of any kind in what we call space. We might therefore disclaim the keen censure which Lotze has recently pronounced in his 'Logik' (Leipz. 1874, S. 217) against the misuse of the notion of space for "logical pranks" with four or five dimensions. It is, however, going too far when Lotze exclaims, "Against all such attempts we must be on our guard; they are grimaces of science which terrify ordinary consciousness by utterly useless paradoxes, and cheat it of its rights in the limitation of concepts." Ordinary consciousness has no such right as against science; least of all with the mathematicians, who have long been accustomed to attain their most beautiful results by the most paradoxical generalisations. Compare negative, incommensurable, imaginary, and complex quantities, broken and negative exponents, &c. The rejection of Dühring, Princ. d. Mechanik, S. 488 f., is also insufficiently based, although it rests on an acute attempt of the author (in the Natürl. Dialektik, Berl. 1865, and first in the noteworthy dissertation 'De Tempore, Spatio, Causalitate atque de Analysis Infinitesimalis Logica,' Berol. 1861) to eliminate the mystical element from mathematics by a sharper apprehension of its conceptions. The 'mystical' element is so much increased in recent mathematics that it is no longer sufficient to criticise particular conceptions. The question must some day be treated as a whole in a philosophy of mathematics, how it is possible that the generalising violation of all the limits of intuition and of real possibility leads precisely to the simplest formulæ, which, when applied to reality, remain absolutely valid What Dühring says, Nat. Dial., S. 162, 163, hardly touches the real problem. On

time therefore for the thing-in-itself appears extremely doubtful. This means, of course, that no Materialism of any kind is any longer maintainable; for even though our inquiry, when directed to sensible intuitions, must with inevitable logic result in showing that for every intellectual excitation there are corresponding phenomena in matter, yet this matter, with everything that is formed from it, is only an abstraction from our representative images. The struggle between Body and Mind is ended in favour of the latter, and only thus is guaranteed the true unity of all existence. For while it always remained an insurmountable difficulty for Materialism to explain how conscious sensation could come about from material motion, yet it is, on the other hand, by no means difficult to conceive that our whole representation of matter and its movements is the result of an organisation of purely intellectual dispositions to sensation.

Accordingly, Helmholtz is entirely right when he resolves the activity of sense into a kind of inference.

We are right, in our turn, when we remark that this does not render the search for a physical mechanism of sensation, as of thought, superfluous or inadmissible.[66]

the other hand, however, it seems precipitate, with Liebmann (cf. esp. his essay in the Phil. Monatsh., vii. 2 Hälfte, 8 H. S. 337 ff., Ueber d. Phänomenalität d. Raumes), to employ these mathematical speculations as positive arguments for the phenomenality of space, since they are as yet nothing more than mathematical developments of the mere conceivability of a general idea of space, which includes, as a special form, our Euklidean space.

[66] Brentano, Psychol., i. 144, observes with reference to what is said above as to the inference of the eye in the phenomena of the blind spot, that it is not quite clear whether I really mean to admit a 'mediative process' similar to conscious inference. The matter seems to me to be pretty clear. It is a question of a subsumption under an inductively gained major proposition. The conscious procedure would say then: As often as I have the partial phenomena $X_1, X_2, X_3, \ldots$ there must be before me a uniform surface. Now the phenomena X_1, X_2, X_3 are given; therefore there is a uniform surface before me. The corresponding physiological process would simply be this, that as a matter of habit (depending upon acquired conductive paths), from the irritation of certain parts of the brain by X_1, X_2, X_3, there results always the idea of surface (i.e., the mechanical conditions leading to a synthesis in the idea of surface). If now the phenomena X_1, X_2, X_3, &c., appear, there follows immediately, if we will, the idea of surface in the con-

At length, however, we see that such a mechanism, like every other represented mechanism, must be itself only a necessarily occurring picture of an unknown state of things.

"Even though we cannot perceive the web of the atomistic world with our bodily senses, yet we think of it under the type of intuitive representation, and construe its phenomena in an intuitive way; for what else is it when we remove the necessarily posited atoms into time and space, and explain to ourselves the relations of the masses by their equilibrium and their various motions?

"As matter generally, so too the atoms constituting it are phenomena, representation; and the question is not less justified in regard to the atoms than with regard to representable matter, what they are besides phenomenon, besides representation, what they are in themselves, what there is dating from all eternity that in them has found expression."

With these words Rokitansky prepares the way for the declaration that it is precisely the atomistic theory which

crete case. That is to say, the 'mediation' lies simply in this, that the special case of the minor proposition comes in contact with the already developed mechanism of the major proposition, whereby the conclusion, the seeing of a surface, results of itself. Any other 'mediation' does not seem to me to take place in any other process of inference, unless we include in the process of inference the search for the middle term, *i.e.*, the major, which is applied in this case. This search for the middle term of course falls away in the case before us. The two premisses are at once brought together by a natural necessity.

As to the reproach, extended also to Helmholtz, Zöllner, &c., that we have not made sure whether the explanation from unconscious inferences is the only possible one, and especially that we should not have omitted an attempt to explain the phenomena by the laws of association, the answer to this is, that the very easy and obvious explanation by associations is not all inconsistent with that by unconscious inference. If, let us say, to keep to the above example, on the phenomena X_1, X_2, X_3, the image of a surface must result by the laws of association, this must already often have been combined with these phenomena, and this is identical with the existence of the inductive major, under which the new special case is subsumed. Nay, the consistent association psychologists explain ordinary conscious inference by association! That more exact research does not care to concern itself with these modes of explanation is very natural, as they are, properly speaking, not explanations at all, but only stopgaps for the needed explanations.

supports an idealistic theory of things; and we may add, that precisely the resolution of psychical activity into brain and nerve mechanism is the surest way to the knowledge that here the horizon of our knowledge closes in, without touching the question what mind is in itself. The senses give us, as Helmholtz says, *effects* of things, not true pictures nor things in themselves. But to the mere effects belong also the senses themselves, together with the brain and the molecular movements which we suppose in it. We must therefore recognise the existence of a transcendental order of things, whether this rests on 'things-in-themselves,' or whether—since even the 'thing-in-itself' is but a last application of our representative thought—it rests on mere relations, which exhibit themselves in various minds as various kinds and stages of the sensible element, without our being able to conceive an adequate appearance of the absolute in a knowing mind.[67]

[67] Comp. Der Selbstständige Werth des Wissens, Wien, 1869, S. 35.

FOURTH SECTION.

ETHICAL MATERIALISM AND RELIGION.

FOURTH SECTION.

ETHICAL MATERIALISM AND RELIGION.

CHAPTER I.

POLITICAL ECONOMY AND DOGMATIC EGOISM.

It might not have been out of place, besides the natural sciences, to submit political economy and the related branches to a close examination; but here we already glide involuntarily over into the sphere of the practical questions, the solution of which forms the result of our critical effort. We examine a science, and we find in its doctrines only the mirror of social conditions; we wish to see where ethical Materialism is nowadays, and we find it developed into a system of dogma unlike anything that Aristippos and Epikuros knew. In place of Pleasure, modern times have put Egoism; and while the philosophical Materialists hesitated in their ethic, there was developed together with political economy a special theory of egoism, which more than any other element of modern times bears on it the stamp of Materialism.

The roots of this phenomenon strike back into the age before Kant and the French Revolution. In Italy, in the Netherlands, in France, the modern spirit of inquiry had long ago subjected commerce, international intercourse, the operation of taxes and imposts, the sources of the prosperity or impoverishment of whole nations, to a theoretical examination; but it was only in England that the doctrines of political economy developed together with the rising flood of industry and world-wide commerce into a kind of science. Adam Smith, who found only moderate approval for his 'Theory of Morals,' won the most extensive reputation by his 'Inquiry into the Wealth of Nations.' Sympathy and Interest were with him the two great springs of human actions. From sympathy he deduced all the virtues of the individual and all the advantages of society; but after he has found Justice also by a somewhat artificial way, he makes it the true foundation of the state and of society. Inclination between the members of society, friendly regard for each other's good, are beautiful things, but they may be lacking without the state being ruined. Justice cannot be spared; with it every community stands and falls. The 'Theory of Morals' allows every individual in the effort after wealth and honour to exert his powers to the utmost in order to surpass his competitors, so long only as he does no injustice; in the doctrine of the 'Wealth of Nations,' the axiom is completely asserted that every one in pursuing his own advantage at the same time furthers the good of all. But the Government has nothing further to do than to maintain all freedom for this struggle of interests.[1]

[1] The two main works of Adam Smith have often been improperly separated, and the 'Theory of Morals' treated as a comparatively unimportant first production, which may be quite left out of account when we come to the 'Wealth of Nations.' That the fundamental idea of both treatises ripened side by side in Smith's mind has been conclusively shown by Buckle (Hist. Civil., c. xx.), and, moreover, Smith himself declares in the preface to one of the later editions of the 'Theory of Morals' that both works sprang from a common plan; that the 'Wealth of Nations,' however, forms merely a fragment of a comprehensive social and political work which was intended to follow the 'Theory of Morals.' At the same time we may doubt, with Lexis (Französ. Ausfuhrprämien, S. 5), whether Adam Smith consciously so employed the method of abstraction as in one world to make man act only from egoism, in the other only from sympathy. Buckle, who tries at some length to establish this view, finds in this procedure an advantage over the induction which starts from the facts. By simplifying the principles, the application of the deductive method is rendered possible, and the fault of one's idleness is supposed to be corrected by starting from dif-

Starting from these principles, he reduced the play of interests, the marketing of Supply and Demand, to rules which even yet have not lost their importance. All the time, this market of interests was not with him the whole of life, but only an important side of it. His successors, however, forgot the other side, and confounded the rules of the market with the rules of life; nay, even with the elementary laws of human nature. This cause indeed contributed to give to political economy a tincture of strict science, by greatly simplifying all the problems of human intercourse. This simplification consists, however, only in this, that men are conceived as purely egoistic, and as beings who can perceive perfectly their separate interests without being hindered by feelings of any other kind.

And, in fact, not the slightest objection could be made to this, if these assumptions had been made openly and expressly for the purpose of giving an exact form to theories

ferent principles, so that the reality would be composed of those influences which, according to the 'Theory of Morals,' result from sympathy, and those which, according to the 'Wealth of Nations,' result from egoism. In answer to this view of Buckle, Lexis briefly points out that human motives cannot be added and subtracted, but that by their very co-operation they become different from what they are in themselves. But in fact, too, Smith has not at all concerned himself with this methodological question. Indeed, even in the 'Theory of Morals' we can everywhere read between the lines that the actions of man are essentially egoistic, and only modified by the effect of sympathy. In the 'Wealth of Nations,' then, Smith deals with a department in which, in his view, the direct effects of sympathy are = nil, and only the indirect effects come into view, i.e., the protection of right by the state. Comp., e.g., the following utterance in the 'Theory of Morals,' Pt. II. sect. 2, chap. ii. :

"In the race for wealth and honours and preferments, he may run as hard as he can, and *strain every nerve and every muscle in order to outstrip all his competitors*. But if he should jostle or throw down any of them, the indulgence of the spectators is entirely at an end." This agrees very well with the notion that in the race of all individuals for wealth, so long only as justice is maintained, the whole at the same time comes nearest to the goal of wealth. The social evils resulting from this competition for wealth Smith did not perceive in their full extent—to which, indeed, his own theory conduced in no small degree—and so far as he knew them he regarded them as immutable. He knew of no form of sympathy which could successfully combat these evils, and therefore, too, he had nothing more to say of sympathy in this section of his social and political work. If we had the whole work, we might perhaps find it to be otherwise in other sections.

of social intercourse, by imagining the simplest possible cases; for it is precisely by abstraction from the entire, manifoldly complicated reality that other sciences too have succeeded in gaining the character of exactness. Only that is exact to us, since we cannot embrace the infinite extent of nature's operations, which we ourselves make exact. All absolute truths are false; relations, on the contrary, may be accurate. And what for the advancement of knowledge is most important; a relative truth, a proposition which is only true on the basis of an arbitrary presupposition, and which deviates from entire reality in a carefully defined sense—just such a proposition is incomparably more capable of permanently advancing our comprehension than a proposition which endeavours at one stroke to come as close as possible to the nature of things, and in doing so carries with it an inevitable and, in their full range, unknown mass of errors.

As geometry, with its simple lines, surfaces, and bodies, helps us forward, although its lines and surfaces do not occur in nature, although the mass of real things is almost always incommensurable; so too abstract political economy may help us forward, although there are in reality no beings who follow exclusively the impulse of a calculating egoism, and follow it with absolute mobility, free from any hindering emotions and influences proceeding from other qualities. Of course abstraction in the egoistic political economy is much more thorough than in any other science, since the opposing influences of indolence and habit, as well as those of sympathy and of the sense of community, are extremely important. Yet abstraction may be boldly ventured, so long as it remains in our consciousness as such. For when we have found how those mobile atoms of a society encouraging egoism, which is hypothetically assumed, must behave on our supposition, we do not merely gain a fiction which is consistent in itself, but also an exact knowledge of one side of human nature, and of an element which in society, and especially in commercial intercourse, plays an extremely important part. We might at least know how man comports himself in so far as the conditions of his activity correspond with the supposition, even although this will never be completely the case.[2]

Materialism in the sphere of political economy consists simply in confounding this abstraction with reality; and this confusion took place under the influence of an enormous predominance of material interests. The English cultivators of political economy started to a large extent from thoroughly practical points of view; 'practical,' not in the old Greek sense, in which vigorous activity from moral and political motives in particular earned this honourable name. The character of those times led men to seek all the true aims of action in the interests of the individual. The 'practical' point of view in political economy is that of a man with whom his own interests are the first thing, and who therefore supposes that it is the same with everybody else. The great interest of these times, however, is no longer, as in antiquity, immediate Enjoyment, but the Accumulation of Capital.

The love of pleasure with which this age is so much reproached is, on a comparative view of the history of civilisation, not nearly so prominent as the passion for work in our industrial chiefs and the compulsion to work

[2] The great mass of our German political economists may be divided, according to their tendency and also their attitude to scientific method, into two classes: those who favour deduction without knowing that it rests on abstraction; and those who avoid abstraction and wish to start from actual facts, but are not able to use the inductive method. Lexis forms a brilliant exception, and in every respect, from the elements of logic to mathematical demonstration, shows himself a master of scientific method. The slight regard which has as yet been shown to his classical work on the 'Französische Ausfuhrprämien,' Bonn, 1870, is one of the clearest tokens of the slight scientific depth of our political economists, as well of the 'Free-trade school' as of the 'Socialists of the Chair.' Lexis regards the whole deductive political economy as a mere preliminary attempt to ascertain our bearings, which must be followed by a real science, essentially based upon statistics. This view perhaps goes too far, but at least the relation of deduction and induction will depend upon the measure in which we attain really valuable inductive investigations.

in the slaves of our industry. Very often, indeed, what seems to be noisy or senseless joy in frivolous amusements is nothing but a result of immoderate, galling, and brutalising labour, since the mind, by perpetual hurrying and scurrying in the service of money-making, loses the capacity for a purer, nobler, and calmly devised enjoyment. Men then involuntarily pursue their recreation also with the feverish haste of acquisition, and pleasure is measured by its cost, and is hurried through as if it were a kind of duty in the days and hours set apart for it. That such a state of things is not healthy, and can hardly exist permanently, seems obvious; but it is not less clear that in the present industrial epoch enormous achievements are accomplished, which at a future time may well serve to make the fruits of a higher culture accessible to the widest circles. What formed the shadow side to the cultured and intellectual enjoyment of Epikuros and Aristippos, the self-sufficient limitation to a narrow circle of friends, or even to one's own person, does not very often appear in our days even amongst wealthy egoists, and a philosophy based upon it would hardly succeed in gaining any general significance. To accumulate the means for enjoyment, and then to devote these means, not to enjoyment, but for the most part to further acquisition, this is the prevailing character of our time. Were all those who have acquired a more than moderate fortune to retire from business life, and henceforth devote their leisure to public affairs, to art and literature, and, in fine, to a cultured enjoyment of life upon moderate means, not only would these persons lead a more beautiful and worthier existence, but there would also be secured an adequate material basis to maintain permanently a nobler culture with all its requirements, and thus to give a higher content to our present epoch than that of classical antiquity. It may be, however, that a larger amount of capital would thus be drawn from business than is drawn as it is by the most irrational luxury; and perhaps this culture could only really profit a small portion of the population. At all events, as it now is, things are sad enough for the great mass of the population. If all the gigantic force of our machines and all the achievements of human hands, so infinitely perfected by the division of labour, were devoted to securing for every one what is necessary to make life tolerable and to find means and leisure for the higher development of the mind, it might perhaps even now be possible, without prejudice to the intellectual task of humanity, to diffuse the blessings of culture over all classes; but so far this has not been the tendency of the age. It is true that forces on forces are created, new machinery continually devised, new means of communication invented; it is true that the capitalists, who have the means at their command, are ceaselessly active in creating, instead of enjoying the fruits of their toil in dignified leisure; but, nevertheless, the constantly increasing activity aims directly at anything rather than the furtherance of the common weal. Where the intellectual capacity of enjoyment is lacking, there are found *wants* which ever increase more rapidly than the means of satisfying them.

It is a favourite principle of the ethical Materialism of our days, that a man is all the happier the more wants he has, if he has at the same time sufficient means for their satisfaction. All antiquity was unanimously of the contrary opinion. Epikuros, no less than Diogenes, sought happiness in freedom from wants, although the former had happiness, the latter freedom from wants, principally in view. In our days, of course, the exacter knowledge of the life of the people, and especially the statistics of mortality, disease, &c., have refuted the old fable of the contented and healthy poor, and the always hypochondriacal and weakly rich. We measure the value of earthly goods by the scale of the tables of mortality, and we find that even the anxieties of crowned heads are not nearly so prejudicial to health as hunger, cold, and ill-ventilated dwellings. On the other hand, however, the sciences have advanced sufficiently to allow of an inference of probabilities which absolutely contradicts this Materialistic principle. The history of civilisation shows us that in the times when princesses slept in walled niches, took long journeys on horseback, and made their breakfast off bacon, bread, and beer, the happiness of these persons did not seem less to their contemporaries than to-day, when they fly through Europe in splendid saloon carriages, and at every point have the products of every zone at their command. The analogies of psycho-physics make it very probable that the feeling of personal happiness is just as relative as the feelings of the senses: it is the *difference* that is perceived; it is the *increase* that is felt, and that is measured by the quantity that previously existed.[3] In fact, no reasonable man will believe that the physical structure of rich Brussels lace can contribute more to the happiness of a person adorned with it than any other ornament which sits comfortably and pleases the eye, though it may be of comparatively no value. And yet the possession of these laces may become a 'want;' the impossibility of getting them may produce the liveliest vexation; their sudden loss may be the cause of tears. It is clear that here the comparison, the struggle for pre-eminence, plays the most essential part; and from this it results at once that at least this one kind of want, the want to surpass others, is capable of increasing *ad infinitum*, without anything being gained for the well-being of any one concerned that is not lost to the others. From this it further irrefragably results that a continuous increase of the productions of wealth and of the means for the production of wealth is conceivable without the enjoyment of any man being essentially heightened, and without the labouring masses being brought a single step nearer to the goal of obtaining what is most necessary for an existence worthy of man. Such an increase of the wants

---

[3] For more on this point see the chapter on Happiness in my book 'Die Arbeiterfrage,' 3 Aufl., S 113-132 and notes.

of all those who can satisfy them, in consequence of the failing sense of community and exorbitant pleonexia, is, in fact, one of the characteristics of our time. The commercial and industrial statistics of most countries show irrefutably that an enormous development of power and wealth is taking place, while the circumstances of the labouring class show no decided advance, and without the haste and greed of acquisition in the propertied classes being in the slightest degree moderated. We live, in fact, not for enjoyment, but for labour and for wants; but amongst these wants that of pleonexia is so overbearing, that all true and lasting progress, all progress that might benefit the mass of the people, is lost, or, as it were, gained only incidentally.

We may now reconcile ourselves to this in itself very unjoyous fact, if we think that sooner or later, in one way or another, an altered tendency will establish itself, while the forces of production remain, for the most part, unaffected. The view might again assert itself, which was the foundation-stone of classical culture, that there is a certain Measure which is most wholesome in all things; and that enjoyment depends not on the *quantity* of satisfied wants and the difficulty of satisfying them, but on the *form* in which they are produced and satisfied, much as physical beauty is determined, not by masses of material, but by the observing of certain mathematical lines. Such a revolution of views would lead from ethical Materialism to Formalism or Idealism; it would be inconceivable without the elimination of our luxuriant pleonexia, and must, moreover, arise from a magnificent revival of the sense of community.

Political economy has so far made little effort to reduce the *distribution of wealth* to correct principles. Rather, in this respect, it took the result arising from the relation of capital and labour as a datum, and merely occupied itself with the question how the greatest possible quantity of wealth is produced. This Materialistic view of the subject harmonises completely with the recognition of Egoism, and with the defence or toleration of pleonexia. It is attempted to show that the progress produced by the restless struggle of Egoism always to some extent improves the position of the most depressed strata of the population, and here is forgotten the importance of that comparison with others which plays so great a part among the rich. In face of the most crying absurdities a sort of pre-established harmony is imagined, thanks to which the most favourable result for the sum of people comes about through every man's recklessly pursuing his own interests. Though this nowadays chiefly happens with the consciousness of being in the wrong which marks all apologists, yet it happened at the time of the first development of political economy with an unmistakable *naïveté*. It was the universal practice in the last century to deduce the good of the whole from the co-operation of all egoistic effects. However easy, too, it was to protest against the exaggerations in Mandeville's notorious 'Fable of the Bees' (1723), yet the principle that even vices contribute to the general good, was to some extent a secret article of enlightenment which, though seldom mentioned, was never forgotten,[4] and in no department is the appearance of truth so great for such a principle as just in that of political economy. The sophisms of Helvetius in the glittering garb of rhetoric are yet easily seen through; and every attempt to explain even the virtues of patriotism, of self-sacrifice for one's neighbour, and of bravery, from the principle of self-love, must be shattered on the fact that the natural understanding, agreeing with scientific criticism, contradicts it. It is otherwise in political economy.

[4] On Mandeville's 'Fable of the Bees,' see the First Book, especially note 75, third section (vol. ii. p. 79). Worthy of mention, moreover, is the strikingly mild and comparatively approving judgment of Mandeville in the 'Theory of Morals,' pt. vii. sec. ii. chap. v., where it is shown that the 'Fable of the Bees' could never have caused so much excitement if it did not contain truths which were only disfigured by exaggeration. Mandeville's chief mistake was in this, that, in agreement with certain popular ascetic notions, he conceived every passion as at once a vice.

Its tendency has been from the first directed to the furtherance of the people's material welfare, and here it seems so natural to assume that the progress of the collective whole is simply the sum of all the progress of the individuals; but the individual—so much the mercantile experience of all times seemed indubitably to show—can only attain to material prosperity by the reckless pursuit of his own interests; let virtue then be exercised in other spheres, so far as our means admit!

If from the first political economy had only been based upon Egoism, in order by temporary abstraction from other motives to obtain a hypothetical and, within the limits of the hypothesis, an exact science as a first step to fuller knowledge, then there could be no question of a blameworthy Materialism in this sphere. Instead of that, the practical maxims of mercantile acquisition in daily life were transferred wholesale to nations. The question of the material advancement of nations was separated from the ethical questions exactly as these have long been separated in life and business intercourse. Regard was had not to the form of the relations of possession, but to the quantity and the commercial value of wealth; and instead of asking how man *would* act if he were only egoistic, it was asked how *does* man act in the sphere in which Egoism alone is decisive. The former question is that of the exact theorist; the latter that of popular practice, which has nowhere striven so zealously to choke true science as in political economy.

The idea that there is a special department of life for pursuing our interests, and again another for the exercise of virtue, is even yet one of the favourite ideas of superficial Liberalism, and in widely spread popular writings, such as Schulze's 'Arbeiterkatechismus,' it is quite openly preached.[5] Indeed, it has been made into a sort of theory

[5] Comp. Capitel zu einem deutschen Arbeiterkat., Leipz. 1863, S. 45 f., the deduction of commercial progress from the self-interest which is explained as "the love which every one has for his own Ego;" further, S. 91 ff., the regulation of "brotherliness" as an economical principle. At S. 93 we find: "Sie (die Brüderlichkeit) beginnt da, wo das Wirth-

of duty, which expresses itself in daily life much oftener than in literature. Any one who omits to pursue a debtor, if necessary, with all the rigour of the law, must either be a rich man, who may indulge himself in that sort of thing, or he incurs the severest blame. This blame is directed not merely against his intelligence, against his weakness of character or superfluous good-heartedness, but precisely against his morality. He is a frivolous, negligent fellow, who does not look properly after his interests; and if he has a wife and children, even though they are not in want of anything, he is an unconscientious paterfamilias. But just in the same way, too, is regarded the man who devotes his energies to the public good to the detriment of his private fortune. He who does this with special success receives, indeed, absolution and general applause, all the same whether his success is due to chance or to his own energy; but so long as this *vox Dei* of the mob and the fatalists has not been pronounced, the ordinary judgment maintains itself. It condemns the poet and artist as well as the scientific inquirer and the politician; and even the religious agitator only meets with recognition if he succeeds in founding a church, or creating a great institution of which he becomes director, or if he rises to ecclesiastical dignities; but never if, without hope of compensation, he sacrifices a position to his convictions.

It is obvious that we are here only characterising the feelings of the great mass of the propertied classes, which, however, through their having been developed into a system of daily life, also exert their influence even upon those who personally are not without nobler impulses. Before, then, we can more precisely determine the value of this dogmatic system of Egoism, it is indispensable to consider the source of natural Egoism and the origin of

---

schaften und der Staat aufhört; nicht der Erwerb, nicht Recht und Pflicht sind ihr Reich, nicht der Zwang ist ihre Macht, sondern die freie Liebe." Comp. on this passage my essay, Mill's Ansichten über die sociale Frage, Duisb. 1866, S. 14 ff.

the counteracting impulses in the light of the principles which we have acquired in the previous sections.

If it is true that our own body is but one of our representative images, like all others; if accordingly our fellow-men, as we see them, are, like all nature about us, in a very definite sense parts of our own being, where does Egoism come from? Obviously, in the first place, from this, that the ideas of pain and pleasure and our impulses and desires, for the most part, are fused with the image of our body and its movements. The body thus becomes the central point of the phenomenal world; a relation which, as we may certainly assume, has also its foundation in the nature of things in themselves.

Without following these indications further, we must first point out that all ideas involving pleasure and the contrary by no means have direct reference to our body. The more refined pleasure of the senses, delight in the beautiful especially, fuses not with the representative image of the body, but with that of the object. Only when I close the eyes with which I have been gazing upon a splendid landscape, do I become conscious of the relation of these objects to my body. What the poet says of absorption in intuition, of abstraction in contemplation, is physiologically and psychologically much more correct than the ordinary projection-theory of so-called scientific observation. Accordingly, the much-abused pleasure of the senses forms in itself a natural counterpoise to absorption in the Ego, and only by means of reflexion can it again afford nourishment to Egoism.

Much more important, however, is moral development through the contemplation of the world of man and occupation with its phenomena and problems. Absorption in this object, as it is likewise presented to us by the senses as part of our own nature, is the natural germ of all that is imperishable and worthy of being preserved. Adam Smith may have had a vague sentiment of this when he based morality upon sympathy; but his conception was much too narrow. At bottom he had in his view only those cases in which we interpret the gestures and movements of our fellow-men through recollections or by imaginations of pain and pleasure, in accordance with what we have felt ourselves. But in this there is a latent reference to egoistic motives which co-operate only secondarily and indirectly, while the silent and continuous transference of our consciousness to the object of this human world of phenomena, forms the true source of moral elevation and eliminates the preponderance of Egoism.

These suggestions will enable every reader to work out for himself, how the same advance of civilisation which in epochs of maturity produces Art and Science, also conduces to the bridling of Egoism, the development of human sympathy, and the predominance of common aims. In a word, there is a natural moral progress.

Buckle in his famous work on the 'History of Civilisation' has employed an inaccurate point of view in order to prove that the actual progress of morality, like that of civilisation generally, rests essentially upon *intellectual* development. If it is shown that certain elementary principles of morality have not essentially changed from the days when the Indian Vedas were composed until now, we may similarly point to the elementary principles of logic, which have likewise remained unchanged. We might indeed maintain that the fundamental laws of knowledge have remained the same from immemorial time, and that the fuller application of them which has been made in modern times is to be ascribed to essentially *moral* grounds. It was, in fact, *moral* qualities which led the ancients to think freely and independently, but to content themselves with a certain amount of knowledge, and to lay more stress on the perfection of the individuality than on one-sided advancement in knowledge. It was the *moral* characteristic of the Middle Ages to form authorities, to obey authorities, and to limit free inquiry by traditional formulas. The self-abnegation and determination with which, at the beginning of the modern epoch, Copernicus, Gilbert and Harvey, Kepler and Vesalius pursued their aims, were moral in their nature. Nay, an analogy may even be established between the moral principles of Christianity and scientific procedure; for nothing is so earnestly desired by the men of science as abnegation of their fantasies and hobbies, deliverance from surrounding opinions, and entire devotion to their object. We may say of the greatest inquirers, that they must die to themselves and to the world in order to lead a new life in communion with the revealing voice of nature. Yet we will not here pursue these ideas further. We have exhibited the companion-piece to the one-sided view of Buckle. In truth, neither is intellectual progress essentially a result of moral progress, nor the converse; but both spring from the same root, absorption in the object, the loving comprehension of the whole phenomenal world and the natural inclination to shape it harmoniously.

But as there is a moral progress, resting upon the fact that the harmony of our picture of the world gradually obtains the preponderance over the wild disorders of impulse and the more violent feelings of pleasure and pain, so too the moral ideals progress, according to which man shapes the world about him. Nothing can be more wrong than for Buckle to deduce the progress of civilisation from the co-operation of a variable—intellectual—element and a stationary—moral—element. If Kant has said that we are no further advanced in moral philosophy than the ancients, he has said much the same thing of logic too; and this observation has little to do with the progress of the moral ideals which affect whole epochs of time. What a world of difference there is between the ancient and the Christian notion of virtue! To repel wrong and suffer wrong, to revere beauty and to despise beauty, to serve society and to flee society, are not merely accidental traits of opposite dispositions with similar moral principles, but are antinomies proceeding from utterly and fundamentally different principles of morality. Christianity altogether was, from the standpoint of the ancient world, distinctly immoral, and would have seemed yet more so, but that the moral ideal of antiquity was already breaking up, when these new and strange principles made their appearance. A similar dissolution of moral ideals and preparation for a new and higher standpoint seems at present to be going on, and this makes it more difficult, and at the same time more important, to mark the position of dogmatic Egoism as it shows itself in political economy and in the principles of social intercourse.

It might appear, for an instant, as though this very dogmatic Egoism were the new ethical principle that is destined to replace the principles of Christianity. The Rationalism of the last century, which merely coquetted with physical Materialism, adopted ethical Materialism. The development of material interests has gone hand in hand with the decline of the old ecclesiastical powers. The development of the natural sciences has operated here destructively, there constructively; but with the building up of material interests went on, step for step, the growth of the theory of political economy, and with this dogmatic Egoism. It might therefore seem as though it were one and the same principle which had acted destructively as regards the traditional forms of Christianity, and positively in reference to the material development of the present age; and as though this at once dissolving and newly creating leaven was the principle of Egoism.

We have already seen above how strongly in political economy appearances favour the higher justification of Egoism, and if without idle sophistry it is impossible to base such virtues as patriotism, self-sacrifice, and so on, upon this principle, it is perhaps quite possible to dispense with these virtues. We must for a moment acquiesce in the idea that the prosecution of selfish interests may in the future become the sole motive of human actions; though Voltaire and Helvetius were decidedly wrong in declaring it to be so already, and in denying any other spring of human action than self-love. And we cannot deny that it is at least not *a priori* inconceivable that such a principle—a very different one from Mandeville's!—may result not from decay, but, on the contrary, from moral and intellectual progress. This is a point that requires the most careful and impartial examination, and can by no means be decided in accordance with a preconceived opinion; and, in order to avoid misunderstanding, we will at once bring into the true light the most paradoxical aspect of the matter. It will easily be conceded that intellectual progress might contribute to make Egoism at once more general and harmless, and even useful; but how could moral progress, and moral progress too in the particular sense which we have just insisted on in speaking of Buckle, assist in making Egoism a general principle, while the whole essence of this progress is to lead us beyond the Ego towards the universal?

The answer to this question brings before us at a stroke the consequences of the most widely spread theory of political economy.

If, that is to say, it is true that the interests of the whole are best served when the least care is intentionally taken for the whole, when individuals most uninterruptedly prosecute their own interests, then the exclusive prosecution of our own interests in practical life will be

1. A result of ripe insight;
2. A virtue, and, indeed, the cardinal virtue.

The repression of those impulses, which would mislead us into self-denying altruism, will become the most essential part of self-conquest, and the form necessary for this self-conquest will be given from looking upon the mechanism of the great whole, whose harmony is disturbed, if we follow those emotions of our heart, which were once praised as noble, unselfish, and magnanimous. Those emotions of sympathy arising from devotion to the object are in turn abolished by the devotion of the spirit to the greater object, to the mechanism animated by harmonious Egoism of the whole world of humanity.

When the question has thus been clearly put, it will also be seen that its decision is not so easy. Who does not call to mind how often he has controlled himself to refuse a beggar, because he knows that alms only feed misery, as oil feeds a flame? Who does not remember the many attempts to make men happy which have ravaged the earth with blood and fire, while in nations where every one cared for himself wealth and prosperity developed themselves? So much must, in fact, be at once admitted that sympathy may lead to wrong, as well as Egoism, and that consideration for the greater whole will forbid many actions that might result from sacrifice for a smaller whole or for individual persons. It might now, of course, be easily objected that such a consideration for the great whole is not Egoism, but the contrary; yet this objection can just as easily be refuted.

If, that is to say, the doctrine of the harmony of separate interests is true; if it is true that the best result for the community is reached if each man cares most uninterruptedly for himself, then it is inevitably true also that it is most profitable for each man to pursue his own interests without wasting or losing time in useless reflexions. The naive egoist is in a state of innocence and does right unconsciously; sympathy is the moral Fall; and the man who must remind himself of the mechanism of the great whole, in order to come back to the same virtue which a crude thinker practises in simplicity, only comes back by a roundabout course necessarily based upon human nature to the point at which the childhood of humanity started. In this way Egoism may have been purified, softened, enlightened; it may have learned more correct means of advancing its own welfare, but its principles, its essence, are what they were in the beginning.

The questions whether dogmatic Egoism teaches the truth, and whether political economy is in the right path in the one-sided development of the doctrine of free trade, are both determined by the question whether the idea of the natural harmony of interests is a mere figment or not; for the extreme free-trade theorists have not hesitated to base their doctrine on the supreme principle of *laissez faire*. But they have set up this principle not merely as a defensive maxim against misgovernment, but as the necessary consequence of the dogma that the sum of all interests is best cared for when each individual cares for himself. If this dogma is once so deeply rooted as to outweigh all opposite considerations, we need no longer wonder that the name 'nation' is described as a mere grammatical notion, and that on the one hand the protection of navigation by ships of war is rejected (Cooper, 1826), while on the other, the bloody conquests of an adventurer are regarded merely as a specially difficult and therefore specially profitable form of labour (Max Wirth).[6] Both views spring from the same source; from the purely atomistic conception of society in which all motives ordinarily called moral drop out and can only be restored again by an inconsistency.

We have already seen that the purely atomistic conception of society, as enabling us to gradually approximate to the truth, has much in its favour, while as a dogma it is false. Here we must now add the remark that the theory of Egoism and of the natural harmony of all interests has, in its practical application, brought about great advances in civilisation. Enlightened Egoism, it cannot be denied, is as much a principle of social order as many other principles that have had their day, and for

---

[6] On Cooper, comp. Roscher, Volkswirthschaft, § 12, Anm. 2. The passage from Max Wirth is in the section on Ground-rent, Nationalök., i. 2, 9.

certain transitional periods perhaps the soundest, without our being therefore obliged to attribute to it a higher significance. The system of Free Trade has given a prodigious impulse to the production of civilised peoples. Speculation, though in the first place pursuing its own interests, has so greatly contributed to provide Europe with the means of communication, to regulate commerce, to give a more solid and real character to business, to keep down the rate of interest, to extend and consolidate credit, to limit usury, to make fraud more uncommon, that no prince, no minister, no philosopher, no philanthropist, actuated by the principle of self-denying activity, of benevolent instruction, of wise legislation, could exert anything like the same influence that has been exercised by the gradual removal of the barriers that opposed themselves to the free activity of the individual in the feudal arrangements of the Middle Ages. Since the existence of poor-rates—the introduction of which was indeed the result of another principle—more benevolent institutions and more thorough-going improvements have sprung from the desire not to let these rates rise too high, than could ever have been formed through sympathy or the active recognition of a higher duty. Nay, we may even conjecture that a five- or six-fold repetition of great and bloody social revolutions, even at intervals of centuries, would at last check the pleonexia of the rich and mighty by fear more effectually than it could ever be done by devotion to common interests and by the principle of love.

First we must remark that the great advances of modern times have not, after all, been brought about by Egoism as such, but by the liberation of efforts for private ends as against the suppression of the Egoism of the majority by the stronger Egoism of the minority. It was not fatherly care which in earlier times held the place now taken by free competition, but privilege, exploitation, the antithesis of Master and Man. The few cases in which the earlier social arrangements allowed the benevolence of noble rulers or the intelligence of eminent patriots to exhibit themselves produced very beautiful results. We need only think of Colbert, with whose successful activity the protectionist Carey, not without reason, connects himself. We must always bear in mind that we know as yet only the opposition of ruling dynastic interests to free private interests, but not a pure opposition between an egoistic principle and a principle of community. But if we go back to the better times of the mediæval and ancient republics, we see then the sense of community living indeed, but in such narrow circles that a comparison with the present is scarcely possible. And yet even so defective a comparison shows that the profound feeling of discontent which marks the present, is not found in any community where every individual holds his Egoism in check from regard to the general interests.

If we try to submit the justification of the doctrine of the harmony of interests to a direct test, we must, in order to simplify the problem, first suppose a republic of individuals of equal capacities and working under the same conditions, all endeavouring with all their might to produce as much wealth as possible. It is obvious that with one part of their might they will hinder each other, while with the other part they will produce wealth for the benefit of the whole. To abolish this mutual hindrance is only conceivable in two ways: either if all acquire only for the whole, or if each single individual has his own separate sphere of acquisition without any competition. As soon as it can occur that two or more individuals strive to secure the same object, or to utilise it for purposes of production, hindrance will arise. If you apply this abstraction to human relations we see the germ of two ideas: that of communism and that of private property.

Men, however, are not such simple beings, and it is conceivable that they are quite incapable of completely carrying out either idea. In a state of community of goods the purely egoistic tendency will be directed to the appropriation of a portion of the goods; in a pure system of private property, on the other hand, to the increasing of one's own possessions by over-reaching others. We assume, further, that in our republic there are some goods held in common as well as goods in private ownership, and that there are certain limits to appropriation and over-reaching which are generally recognised; but in such a way that there are always legitimate means by which the individual can gain an advantage in the enjoyment of the common possessions, as well as increase his private property. The most important of these legitimate means is to consist in this, that he who renders greater services to the community receives too a greater reward.

Now we have the idea of the harmony of interests; it is, that is to say, doubtless conceivable that our beings are so constituted that they develop a maximum of force when they think most exclusively of themselves; and, further, that the laws of our republic are such that no one can secure a great advantage for himself unless he produces a great deal of labour for the community. It might too very well be that the gain of force in consequence of the emancipation of Egoism would be greater than the loss arising out of reciprocal interference, and if this were so then the harmony of interests would be established. Yet it is partly difficult to determine how far these presuppositions are fulfilled in human society, and partly we can easily perceive circumstances which at once upset our calculation. Thus, *e.g.*, the means secured by useful labour are at the same time a source of fresh advantages, which are gained by the fact that the possessor makes others work for him. Although now this again involves a gain to the community, yet it is at the same time the germ of a disease which we shall describe further on. Here we wish to exhibit the one aspect of the matter, that he who is once superior to his fellows can also employ his resources to humour his pleonexia with impunity. The more he advances, the more power he obtains to advance yet further, and not only the resistance of his competitors, but the resistance too of the laws becomes continually weaker. The explanation of this phenomenon lies not only in the law of the increment of capital, but also in an as yet little regarded factor of individual and social development. That is to say, the intellectual power of most men is sufficient to perform much greater tasks than those which, in the present condition of society, must devolve upon them. This observation will be found more fully expounded and established in the second chapter of my book on the 'Arbeiterfrage.' Here let it suffice to point out that most men are perfectly capable, as soon as a favourable start has raised them above the necessity of gaining the necessaries of life by physical labour, of making the labour of many others tributary to themselves by speculation, by inventions, or even by the mere regular and steady direction of a business. The fallacy of the harmony of interests is therefore, too, always connected with the special prominence of a principle which is an almost universal prejudice, the principle that in human life every talent and every faculty finally, though it may be through many obstacles, makes its way to a corresponding position. The exaggerated rationalistic teleology of the last century did a great deal to spread this principle. It is so cryingly opposed to experience that the blindness with which it is maintained could hardly be intelligible,[7] were it not that the self-love of the fortunate, the cultivated, the highly placed, finds as high an enjoyment in the idea of this earthly predestination as ecclesiastical arrogance finds in that of heavenly predestination. In life we see how a specially rapid and brilliant rise from poor circumstances, as a rule, only occurs where the favouring circumstances

---

[7] See this more clearly shown in the chapter on Happiness in my Arbeiterfrage (Labourer-Question).

coincide with rare and exceptional qualities, but how upon the whole the capacity for filling a leading position is always found where the material conditions of such a position exist. As the germs of plants float in the air, and, each after its kind, spring up where they find the conditions of their development, so is it also with the capability of men to utilise favourable circumstances in order to procure much greater advantages. But this principle, together with the law of the increment of capital, upsets the whole theory of the harmony of interests. We may show a hundred times that with the success of speculation and great capitalists the position of everybody else, step by step, improves; but so long as it is true that with every step of this improvement the *difference* in the position of individuals and in the means for further advancement also grows, so long will each step of this movement lead towards a turning-point where the wealth and power of individuals break down all the barriers of law and morals, where the state sinks to a mere unsubstantial form, and a degraded proletariat serves as a football to the passions of the few, until at last everything ends in a social earthquake which swallows up the artificial edifice of one-sided and selfish interests. The times that have preceded this collapse have so often occurred in history, and always with the same character, that we cannot any longer deceive ourselves as to their nature. The state becomes venal. "The hopelessly poor will just as easily hate the law as the over-rich despise it." Sparta perished when the whole land of the country belonged to a hundred families; Rome, when a proletariat of millions stood opposed to a few thousands of proprietors, whose resources were so enormous that Crassus considered no one rich who could not maintain an army at his own expense. "In mediæval Italy also popular freedom was lost through a moneyed oligarchy and a proletariat." "It is characteristic that in Florence the richest banker finally became unlimited despot, and that contemporaneously in Genoa the Bank of St. George in a measure absorbed the state."[8]

So long, therefore, as the interests of man are merely individual, so long as the advancement of general interests is regarded merely as the result of the efforts of individuals to advance themselves, it must always be feared that the interests of those individuals who attain the first advantage will gradually become preponderant beyond measure and crush everything else. The social equilibrium of such a state is, as it were, labile; once disturbed, it must ever become more and more disordered. On the other hand, it may be assumed that in a republic in which each individual should have the interests of the community chiefly before him, a state of stable equilibrium might continue. If this requirement is at present nowhere fulfilled, this is equally true of the requirement of universal Egoism. Both are abstractions; in reality, of course, Egoism is much more powerful than the sense of community, if we consider the mass of individual acts which proceed principally from one or other of these principles; which of the two, however, is for a given time historically more important and more full of consequences, is quite another question. However much the enormous development of material interests seems to form the prevailing character of our time; decidedly as the theory of this development has thrust the principle of Egoism into the foreground of the general consciousness, yet, at the same time too, the need for national unity, for societary co-operation, for the fraternisation of hitherto separated elements, has also increased; and which factor of the seething present is chiefly destined to give its character to the future, we can only conjecture. For the present we maintain that if Egoism should for a time maintain the upper hand, we

Roscher, Political Economy, sec. 204, with the notes. Nowadays it is particularly the influence of the great railway companies which makes itself felt in Switzerland, and still more in the United States, to the prejudice of sound republican government.

should not acquire a new principle to give shape to the world, but merely a decomposition that will go still further. As the theory of the harmony of interests is false, as the principle of Egoism destroys the social equilibrium, and with it the basis of all morality, it can even for political economy possess only a passing importance, the time for which is perhaps even now gone by. The superficiality with which the theory of the harmony of interests is ordinarily preached, may for a time be concealed by the disharmony of these interests themselves, by the secret pleonexia of the favoured classes, as the weaknesses of ecclesiastical dogmas are concealed by the endowment of benefices and convents; but it cannot last. How blindly for the most part political economy sweeps together its arguments for the economical theory of interests, may appear from a single example.

Let us consider a European capital, whose millions awake every morning with the most various wants. Even while the majority still lie in profoundest slumber, all are being zealously provided for. Here rolls a heavy waggon, laden with vegetables, through the suburbs; there fat cattle are driven to the slaughter-house; the baker stands before the glowing oven, and the milkman drives his cart from house to house. Here a horse is being harnessed to a cab to carry unknown persons from place to place; there a tradesman is opening his shop, while he counts already the day's takings, without knowing that he can rely upon a single customer. Gradually the streets wake to life and the bustle of the day begins. What governs this immense activity? 'Interest!' Who takes care that every need is satisfied, that all the hungry and thirsty get in good time their bread, their meat, their milk, their vegetables, their spices, their wine and beer, and all that each one needs and can pay for? 'Only business, interest!' What steward, what chief manager of a warehouse could satisfy these million-fold necessities with such regularity on a predetermined plan? 'Impossible idea!'

By considerations like these it is frequently sought to prove how necessary it is to leave the task of providing for the good of men to the economy of interests. In this at least the following points are overlooked:—

1. The whole consideration is an abstraction, which exhibits only one aspect of the reality. All legitimate wants are by no means satisfied, and, so far as they are satisfied, this is effected in innumerable instances not by the mere maxim of self-interest, but with the aid of sympathy, friendship, gratitude, goodwill, and other motives opposed to Egoism.

2. The whole mechanism of providing for our necessities is the result of infinite cares and sacrifices which disappear when considered from without, but in which the history of generations is concealed. Very many arrangements which now are worked by interest originally sprang from humanity, from desire of knowledge, from sympathy, without these human qualities would never have come into existence, and would pass away in time, unless the same qualities could modify them to suit fresh circumstances, or replace them by other means.

3. The ground of historical experience is just as much favourable to any other principle as to Egoism. Every system, no matter whether it be individualistic or communistic, becomes a utopia if it does not connect itself with the existing state of things; and the assertion of one or the other principle means, in practice, only the direction in which further development is to follow. The question is, not whether the influence of interests in the existing system of providing for our wants is great or small, but whether it is wholesome and opportune to make it comparatively greater or smaller.

In this last point especially culminates the whole import of the question, whether Egoism can be the moral principle of the future. That it will in fact play a great part again, as it has done already, is certain. But, after our exposition, it may be considered as also certain that a further development of individualism would mean not a new impetus, but only the decay of our civilisation. So far as a positive progress is seen in history, we always see the opposite principle in increased activity, while increasing individualism only conduces to the decomposition of forms that have become useless. And therefore for our own time also the true current of progress will lie in the direction of the feeling of community. There is, in fact, a natural—we might almost call it a physical—basis for the gradual supplanting of Egoism by joy in the harmony and order of the phenomenal world, and especially by the common interests of mankind. What Adam Smith meant by 'Sympathy,' Feuerbach by his doctrine of 'Love,' Comte by the principle of 'Altruism,'—these are all merely particular manifestations of the preponderance, arising as civilisation advances, of the objective ideas which form part of our nature over the image of an Ego endowed with pain and pleasure. Just as with the settled ordering of our course of life, the alternation of pleasure and pain loses its vivacity, and the desires are subdued; as, on the other hand, our knowledge of the external world and our understanding of others increases, so this preponderance must come about, and must exercise its natural effects. Even a writer so strongly inclined to scepticism as J. S. Mill makes this conception, coming very near to Comte, the basis of his ethical system, and only overlooks in his 'Utilitarianism' the ideal, formal element which underlies this effort after harmony in the moral world, as much as it does the aspirations of art. And, in fact, we have seen this progress from savagery to human morality already take place so often, and amidst the most various circumstances with such essential uniformity, that the mere inductive inference to the natural necessity of the whole phenomenon is not without value; but when we have discovered in our own sensibility the explanation of this process, we can no longer doubt the existence of the motive principle, though we may indeed doubt, of course, whether, at any given time and amongst a given people or group of nations, it is stronger than other also very powerful forces, which either in themselves or through their peculiar combination might give an altogether opposite result.

That the progress of mankind is not continuous, every page of history teaches us; nay, it is still possible to doubt whether there exists upon the whole such a progress as we see unfold itself at some particular point and then again disappear. Although to me it seems unmistakable in our present epoch that, besides the rising and falling of civilisation which we see so clearly in history, there is at the same time a continuous advance, the effects of which are only veiled by this fluctuation, yet this idea is not so certain as is that of progress at a particular point; and we find able thinkers, versed in nature and history, like Volger, who deny this progress. But even supposing that it was absolutely certain in the section of history which we are contemplating, yet this could only be a larger wave, as it were the flood-wave, which always rises while the hills and valleys of the breakers roll themselves away, but which at last also reaches its maximum and always falls back with the same play of restless surge. We cannot therefore aid ourselves here by an article of faith or a generally accepted truth, and we must examine more closely the causes which may bring about the relapse of civilisation from public spirit to Egoism.

We find, in fact, that the most important causes for the decline of the old seats of civilisation have long been known to historians. The most simply operating cause is that civilisation is, for the most part, confined to narrow circles, which after a time have their isolation broken in upon, and are swallowed up by wider circles standing on a lower level. Here we always find, too, that the superior portion of human society, whether it be an individual state or a privileged class, only partially controls Egoism within its narrow circle, while externally the opposition is accentuated, as between Hellenes and barbarians, masters and slaves. The community in whose favour individualism disappears shuts itself off from the outside with all the indications of Egoism, and so invites its own destruction by the imperfect carrying out of the very principles to which, within its own limits, it owes its higher moral culture. A second cause has been already referred to, namely, that within the society which, as a whole, is in a state of progress there are formed distinctions, which gradually become greater, while the points of contact disappear, mutual relations decrease, and thus the chief source of binding sympathy is lost. Privileged classes are thus developed within the originally homogeneous body; but even these attain no proper coherence; and as the accumulation of wealth leads to hitherto unknown luxuries, there arises a new and refined Egoism which is worse than the former. So it was in ancient Rome in the age of *latifundia*, when agriculture was supplanted by the pleasure-grounds of the rich, and half-provinces belonged to single individuals.

This state of things is originally intended by nobody, not even by the stronger and richer classes, so long as the differences are moderate. It arises under the influence of *law*, which originally has the opposite object of maintaining equality and equity, and, on the principle of private property, of securing to every one his own. It arises, moreover, under the unhampered development of social relations, which can only come about with the restraining of brutal Egoism. Even without elevating Egoism into a principle, in all times order has been first brought into society by the institution of property and its regular devolution, so far as it has not rested upon the traditions of force, on the antithesis of master and man, which we here leave out of account. But these very institutions—Property, Law, Inheritance, &c.—which spring from the softening of manners and bring about the prosperity of peoples, at the same time protect the rank evil of inequality of wealth, which, after it has reached a certain height, becomes stronger than any counter influence and inevitably brings about the nation's ruin. This process is repeated in the most various forms. A morally feebler nation succumbs to slighter degrees of the evil; a stronger, or we might say a more advantageously constructed nation, may, like modern England, support an uncommon degree of the evil without destruction.

In a quite uncivilised state such an inequality of wealth, as appears amongst nations approaching their fall, cannot possibly occur. When there is booty to be divided, the stronger takes for himself the largest share; the weaker must perhaps suffer the grossest injustice; but his general condition, even though he fall into slavery, cannot easily be so different from that of the powerful, as is the condition of the poor from that of the rich in the increasing development of industrialism.

This inequality, we repeat, is not originally intended; otherwise the people must, in their earliest youth, have consciously favoured dogmatic Egoism. But their feeling was then very different. 'Privatus illis census erat brevis, Commune magnum,' says Horace of the ancient Romans; and seldom has the contrast between epochs of lively public feeling and of extravagant self-seeking been so sharp and truly exhibited as by this poet. And yet it was those ancient Romans who created the foundations of those legal codes which Europe still admires and employs. If, therefore, the protection of law and the consecration of property allow tares to grow up together with the wheat, there must be circumstances which produce this result against the will of legislators,—circumstances which either were originally not contemplated, or which perhaps cannot be at all avoided. If we reflect that a lawful and orderly state of things can indeed only arise through the awakening of sympathy and public spirit and the slackening of the cruder egoistic impulses, but that Egoism in such a community, as was, for example, ancient Rome, still plays a very considerable part, and is only, as it were, reduced to certain limits, within which it is recognised as legitimate, then we are led to ask why, in like manner, were not limits set up to the excessive inequality of wealth, in order to maintain the healthy equilibrium between Egoism and public spirit? We find, then, that precisely in ancient Rome the noblest and best of her citizens vainly attempted the solution of this problem. It is, moreover, quite natural that those amongst the propertied class who are not exactly distinguished for their perspicuity or their unselfishness—without, for all that, being dogmatic egoists—are inclined to see in all attempts at such a limitation of acquisition merely an attack upon property, and that the shaking of the foundations of society appears to them in an exaggerated light, because their interests are too closely connected with the existing state of things. If it had been possible to exhibit to the Roman optimates of the age of the agrarian struggles the history of the succeeding centuries as in a mirror, and to demonstrate to them the causal connexion between decline and the accumulation of riches, perhaps Tiberius and Caius Gracchus would not have had to pay for their higher insight with their blood and good fame.

It is not quite superfluous to point out that it would be a mere petitio principii to maintain the limitation of acquisition to be wrong. The very point at issue is what is right. The primitive right—a right which all nature recognises—is the right of the stronger, the right of might. Only after a higher right has been recognised, does this become unright; but only then so long as the higher right actually renders higher services to society. If the constitutive principle of right becomes lost, then the right of the stronger always revives, and in a purely moral aspect one form of it is not better than another. Whether I wring my fellow-man's neck because I am the stronger, or whether by my superior knowledge of business and law I lay a trap for him and cause him to groan in misery, while I 'lawfully' appropriate the profit of his labour, makes very little difference. The very misuse of the mere might of capital on the one side against hunger on the other is a new right of force, even though it be only directed to make the man who has nothing ever more dependent. What legislation has not originally foreseen is the possibility of making such a use of the command of capital and knowledge of law as, in its disastrous effects, surpasses even the old right of force. This possibility lies partly in the capacity already mentioned of every propertied person for the exploitation of hired labour, but partly in certain relations between the law of population and the accumulation of capital, which were discovered by the political economy of last century, but which even yet, despite the great services which Mill, in particular, has rendered in the elucidation of this point, are not completely understood in their nature and operation. In my work, 'Mill's Ansichten über die Sociale Frage und die angebliche Umwälzung der Social-Wissenschaft durch Carey,' I have endeavoured to do something for the critical solution of these questions, and I will here confine myself to the application of the results, so far as they can serve our purpose.[9]

In the last century several leading men, amongst them Benjamin Franklin, took up the observation that the natural increase of mankind, like that of animals and plants, if it were unhindered, must very soon more than fill the earth.[10] This incontrovertible and obvious but, until then, unregarded truth must, at that time, have forced itself upon any observing mind, that compared the rapid growth of population in North America with the

---

[9] The main question here is to show that a *rent* accrues to the presence of an object from the labour of others, the most important species of which is *ground-rent*. The conception of ground-rent as a 'priority-rent' is further developed and more clearly established in the two later editions of my Arbeiterfrage, cap. 6; 3 Aufl. S. 297-322.

[10] Franklin, Observations Concerning the Increase of Mankind, 1757, Comp. Mohl, Gesch. u. Lit. d. Staatswissensch. iii. 476. On other forerunners of Malthus, ib.; besides Roscher, Volkswirthsch. § 242, A. 15; and Marx, Das Kapital, 1te Aufl. S. 603, A. 76.

condition of European countries. It was found that the increase of population depends not upon the fertility of marriages, but upon the quantity of food produced. This simple conception, which Malthus rendered famous, but also provided with erroneous additions, which we here leave out of view, has since, by the perfection of statistics, been shown to be indubitable.

Almost simultaneously there appeared another doctrine, erroneous indeed in its original form, the doctrine of Rent. It was supposed that the owners of the soil derive from its inexhaustible forces, besides the interest of their capital and the reward of their labour, yet another profit, which results from the monopoly of the use of these natural forces. Later, it was shown that this is only so far true as the quantity of ground is limited, or in consequence of certain circumstances—dread of emigration, lack of capital for the working of fertile bottom-lands, want of liberty, &c.—which must be regarded as limited. Thus there occurs in a relative sense the same state of things that must exist absolutely, if the whole cultivable surface of the earth had become private property. Although, therefore, the doctrine of rent has only a relative validity, yet for each country there is a certain point at which it becomes to a certain degree applicable.

Finally, it has been found that the amount of the wages which is paid by an employer provided with capital to those who, having no land or other property, must maintain themselves solely by their labour, is, like all other prices, determined by supply and demand. In so far, therefore, as the supply exceeds the demand, the wages of labour must sink to a minimum. It is very natural that just here the theory of Egoism should approximate very closely to reality, as we have to deal with a succession of small differences; and the employer who regards his own interests from the standpoint of existing legal rights, has himself, to begin with, only a vague idea of the results of this relation.

In less civilised times the population is continually being decimated partly by unfavourable climate, together with want of food, partly by feuds and wars, with the barbarous treatment of the conquered; the accumulation of capital cannot go on uninterruptedly, and upon superfluity of labour follows want, upon want of soil the possibility of acquiring extensive territories by slight exertion. So soon, however, as the worst passions are subdued, and common feeling and legislation have begun their work, there begins also, like the tares that grow up amidst the corn, the operation of the circumstances just referred to.

The population increases, soil for tillage begins to fail; rent rises, wages fall; the difference between the positions of the proprietors and the tenants, the tenants and the hired labourers, becomes even greater. Now the flourishing state of industry offers the labourer higher wages; but soon so many arms come streaming in that here the same process is repeated. The only factor which now checks the growth of the population is poverty, and the only salvation from extreme poverty is the taking of work at any price. The fortunate employer finds immeasurable riches pouring in upon him; the workman receives nothing but his miserable existence. So much happens quite apart from dogmatic Egoism.

Now the misery of the proletariat shocks sympathising hearts; but the way from this state of things back to the old simplicity of morals is impossible. Very gradually the propertied classes have become accustomed to the rich and manifold enjoyment of refined luxuries. Art and science have developed themselves. The slave labour of the proletariat provides many capable minds with leisure and means for researches, inventions, and creations. It seems a duty to preserve these higher possessions of humanity, and men easily console themselves with the thought, that some day they may become the common property of all; meanwhile the rapid growth of wealth admits many to these enjoyments, whose mind within is all uncultured. Others degenerate morally, no longer retaining any care, or any sympathy for anything that lies beyond the circle of their pleasures. The more active forms of sympathy with suffering disappear simply through the monotonous enjoyment of the more fortunate. These begin to regard themselves as peculiar beings. Their servants are as mere machines to them; the unhappy are regarded as inevitable accessories; they have no longer any feeling for their fate. With the tearing away of moral bonds dies out the shame which before held them back from too unrestrained enjoyments. Their intellectual form is choked by luxurious living; the proletariat alone remains rude, oppressed, but fresh in mind.

In such a condition was the ancient world when Christianity and the migration of the peoples put an end to its magnificence. It had become ripe for its destruction.

CHAPTER II.

CHRISTIANITY AND ENLIGHTENMENT.

THE present state of things has been frequently compared with that of the ancient world before its dissolution, and it cannot be denied that significant analogies present themselves. We have the immoderate growth of riches, we have the proletariat, we have the decay of morals and religion; the present forms of government all have their existence threatened, and the belief in a coming general and mighty revolution is widely spread and deeply rooted. At the same time, however, our age possesses powerful remedies; and unless the storms of the crisis of transition surpass all our ideas, it is not probable that humanity must begin once more its intellectual efforts from the beginning, as in the times of the Merovingians. And one of the most important remedies lies, beyond doubt, in those very ideas of Christianity, whose moral effects are just as often undervalued as they are exaggerated.

It is true that civil society very early concluded its separate peace with the principles of the New Testament. It was with business and social intercourse as with high politics and even with the Church. "All Christians," says Mill in his admirable book 'On Liberty,' "believe that the blessed are the poor and humble, and those who are ill-used by the world; that it is easier for a camel to pass through the eye of a needle than for a rich man to enter the kingdom of heaven; that they should judge not, lest they be judged; that they should swear not at all;

... that they should take no thought for the morrow; that, if they would be perfect, they should sell all that they have and give it to the poor. They are not insincere when they say that they believe these things. They do believe them, as people believe what they have always heard lauded and never discussed. But in the sense of that living belief which regulates conduct, they believe these doctrines just up to the point to which it is usual to act upon them. ... The doctrines have no hold on ordinary believers — are not a power in their minds. They have an habitual respect for the sound of them, but no feeling which spreads from the words to the things signified, and forces the mind to take them in, and make them conform to the formula."

And yet it could not happen without leaving some traces upon mankind that, through centuries, just *these* formulas were repeated, *these* sayings recognised, *these* ideas again and again recalled. In all ages there have been many more impressionable souls; and it is hardly an accident that it is just the Christian countries in which at length—even though it was after eighteen hundred years, even though it was only when the decay of ecclesiastical forms and dogmas had begun—that a regular system of poor-relief began, and in which the idea was developed that the misery of the masses is a disgrace to humanity, and that everything must be done to get rid of it for good. We must not allow ourselves to be misled by the fact that in the palmy days of ecclesiastical domination poverty was, as it were, artificially encouraged in order to provide for ceremonial almsgiving; that the peoples have sighed so heavily under no yoke as under that of the priests; we must not be dazzled by the remark that the professedly pious only too easily make terms with morality, and that it is often the freethinkers, nay even the enemies of the existing churches, who have devoted all their thoughts and deeds to oppressed humanity, while the servants of the Church sit at the tables of the rich and preach subjection to the poor. If we admit that the morality of the New Testament has exercised a profound effect upon the peoples of the Christian world, it is by no means therefore to be assumed that this effect must be chiefly seen amongst the persons who, in our own days, most occupy themselves with repeating the words of the doctrines. We have seen, with Mill, how slight the immediate effect of these words upon the individual usually is; and especially upon those very persons who have been familiar with these sounds from their youth up, and have been wont to connect certain solemn feelings with them, without ever reflecting upon their full meaning, or feeling a breath of the force which originally dwelt in them. We will not here institute a psychological inquiry, whether it is perhaps more probable that traditional ideas exert a greater effect where their mere continuance is interrupted by doubt, by partial opposition, by the appearance of new and strange trains of thought; all we want to establish is that just because these words everywhere resound throughout the Christian world and are transmitted from generation to generation, their real meaning and their kindling power may at least as well take hold of a mind that presents a new soil to them, in which they may germinate, as of a mind that is wholly given up to the old associations of ideas. On the whole, therefore, it is very probable that the energetic, even revolutionary, efforts of this century to transform the form of society in favour of the downtrodden masses, are very intimately connected with the New Testament ideas, although the champions of these efforts feel themselves bound in other respects to oppose what is nowadays called Christianity. History affords us a voucher for this connexion in the fusion of religious and communistic ideas in the extreme left of the reformation movement of the sixteenth century. Unfortunately the purer forms of these efforts are still not sufficiently enough appreciated, and the isolated caricatures which have been handed down to us in crude colours, are torn away from their background of a powerful and wide-spread idea. Even highly cultured men of the Catholic party could not then remain inaccessible to these ideas. Sir Thomas More wrote his 'Utopia,' a work of communistic tendency, not merely as a jest, but with the intention of influencing his contemporaries, even though only by a picture of, literally speaking, an impossible state of things. The 'Utopia' was, with him, a means of spreading thoughts which one could hardly dare to present in any other form, and which were, in fact, far in advance of their age. Thus he represented the idea of religious toleration, which in our time has found universal acceptance. His friend and the sharer of his views, L. Vives, protested indeed in a mildly written treatise against the communistic violence of the Peasant War; but he was also one of the first to declare openly that the care of the poor should not be left to casual charity, but that it must be recognised among Christians as a duty to provide adequately and regularly for the poor by definite civil institutions.[11] Not long afterwards it was decided, first of all in England, to establish a system of civil poor-relief; and this very institution, which, since the French Revolution, like civil marriage, civil baptism, and similar institutions, seemed rather to form an antithesis to ecclesiastical institutions, has demonstrably sprung from Christian principles. Such metamorphoses of an idea are not uncommon in the history of civilisation; and without exactly resolving everything with Hegel into its opposite, it must be admitted that the operation of a great thought very frequently assumes an almost diametrically opposite tendency through a fresh combination with other elements of the age. Very striking, too, is the relationship between Comte's moral principles and those of Christianity; a religious impulse is unmistakable in Comte, and most of the phenomena of French

[11] Comp. my article 'Vives' in the Encykl. d. ges. Erzieh.- u. Unterrichtswesens, 9 Bd. 737-814, esp. 761 f.

and English Communism have common features. Most deserving of attention is the venerable Owen, who devoted his riches to the poor, and was denounced by the luxurious and arrogant professors of religion because he denied that existing Christianity could bring relief to the masses in their misery. It is indeed only too natural that in times of overweening egoism, when traditional religion has come to terms with material interests, such natures, seized by a breath of the old spiritual life of religion, break with the existing forms. It is therefore not impossible that amongst the analogies between our time and the decline of the ancient world there may reappear also that creative and combining element which then produced from the ruins of the old order the community of a new faith. Yet here we stumble on the assertion that the power of religion is over, since the natural sciences have destroyed dogma, and the social sciences have shown us how to order the life of the people more satisfactorily than the principles of religion ever could. Well, we have seen that at least the social sciences have not as yet produced any such effect. They succeed indeed in showing us that a powerful and ambitious ecclesiasticism always serves to hamper a people economically, intellectually, and morally; that enlightenment and education, as a rule, go hand in hand with a decrease of the clergy in relative numbers and influence; that the diminution of crime corresponds with the diminution of superstition, which is inseparably connected with the worship of the letter. We know that belief and unbelief make no discoverable difference in the conduct of men upon the whole, and so far as it is externally observable in obvious actions. The believer, like the unbeliever, behaves morally or immorally, and even criminally, from causes, the connexion of which with his principles is only seldom apparent, and even then appears to be rather an incidental effect of the association of ideas. It is merely the mode and manner of the psychical process that are different; the one man succumbs to a temptation of Satan, or follows, while retaining his senses otherwise, a supposed higher inspiration; the other sins with cold frivolity or in the intoxication of passion. We are very unjustly accustomed to dispose of pious criminals by simply regarding them as hypocrites; the cases in which religion is assumed merely as a cloak are nowadays rare; while, on the other hand, the most disgraceful acts are very frequently combined with really deep religious emotions; of course emotions just as subject to the weaknesses which we have characterised above in the words of Mill, as those of the irreproachable pious. It may, too, be true that continual occupation with religious feelings often leads to moral enervation; but this is assuredly not always the case, and belief seems often to act wonderfully in hardening the strength of character. How otherwise could we explain the figures of Luther or Cromwell? Scientifically speaking, nothing is ascertained as to the moral effects of belief and unbelief in themselves; for the greater moral barbarism of districts which are enslaved to belief in the letter may be an indirect result, which proves nothing as to the main point. It is just in such districts that emancipation from religion is most often found united with moral degeneracy, while in more enlightened districts the most abandoned are rather the believers. Statistics show us indeed that, *cæteris paribus*, in Germany Protestant districts exhibit more fraud, Catholic districts more violence. But all these facts allow of no inferences as to internal morality; for the more numerous cases of fraud, rightly regarded, arise from the larger amount of business, and the acts of violence spring not from belief in the Immaculate Conception, but from a want of education, which is primarily connected with the external presence of the ecclesiastical régime and the poverty which is its result. How difficult it is altogether to draw conclusions from moral statistics we have already seen, and we refrain therefore here from a special criticism of some interesting points, since the final result in reference to the question immediately before is, at all events, only negative. So much is certain, that the parsons' doctrine of the moral depravity of all infidels is not confirmed by experience, and that just as little can moral injury be shown to result from belief. But if we survey the whole course of history, it seems to me to be scarcely doubtful that we may in great part attribute to the quiet but continual operation of Christian ideas, not merely our moral, but even our intellectual progress; and yet that these ideas can only develop their full activity by bursting asunder the ecclesiastical and dogmatic form in which they have been enclosed, as the seed of a tree in its hard shell.

The wrong side of this beneficial influence of Christianity is to be sought just in those doctrines and institutions, through which a permanent and unconditional dominion of dogmas and of the Church was to establish itself over men's hearts. Above all, it is the doctrine which early forced its way into the circle of Christian dogmas, of the universal damnation of all mankind and of the eternal tortures of hell, which, by the depressing of men's minds and the raising of priestly arrogance, has brought unutterable evils upon modern nations. The right of the Church to bind and to loose became the corner-stone of the hierarchy, and the hierarchy in all its forms and gradations became the curse of modern nations. But even when it was apparently broken up, the love of power remained the most prominent characteristic of the clergy as a special class, and with only too much success the plentiful resources of religious ideas and ecclesiastical traditions were employed to produce an enslavement of the mind, that must end in insensibility to any immediate action of great ideas. Thus historical Christianity produced an enormous gulf between the small flock of elect and really free minds and of the debased and down-trodden masses. It is the same phenomenon in the spiritual sphere which Industrialism has produced in the material sphere, and here, as there, this break in the national life is the great mother-evil of our days.

The ethical characteristics of a religion consist not so much in its moral doctrines themselves as in the form in which it seeks to establish them. The ethics of Materialism remain indifferent with regard to the form in which its doctrines establish themselves; they hold to the matter, to the content of the individual element, not to the way in which the doctrines shape themselves into a whole of a definite ethical character. This is most conspicuous in the Interest-morality, which, when most favourably regarded, is a casuistic system that teaches us to set permanent interests above fleeting ones, and great interests above small ones. The often-attempted deduction of all the virtues from self-love remains, therefore, not merely sophistical, but also cold and tedious. But the morality, also, which results from the principles of natural altruism not only harmonises, as we have already shown, very well with physical Materialism, but it even bears itself a Materialistic character, so long as the ideal is wanting according to which man endeavours to order his relations to his fellow-men, and generally to establish harmony in his phenomenal world. So long as morality merely insists that we should yield to feelings of sympathy, and counsels us to care and to work for our fellow-men, so long it still bears an essentially Materialistic character, however much it may counsel self-sacrifice instead of enjoyment; only when a principle is set up as the central point of all our efforts do we get a formalistic tendency. Thus in Kant, whose ethics materially very nearly coincide with those of Comte and Mill, but, nevertheless, are very sharply distinguished from any other utilitarian doctrine by the fact that the moral law, with its serious and inexorable reference to the harmony of the whole of which we are parts, is regarded as given *a priori*. As to the truth of this doctrine, it will be in much the same case as the truth of the doctrine of the Categories. The deduction of the principle is incomplete, the principle itself capable of improvement; but the germ of this consideration for the whole must be given in our organisation prior to all experience, because otherwise the beginning of ethical experience would be altogether inconceivable. The principle of ethics is *a priori* not indeed as a ready-made, developed conscience, but as an arrangement in our original disposition, the nature and operation of which, like the nature of our body, we can only gradually and *a posteriori* learn partially to know. This knowledge, however, is by no means hindered by the fact that a definite principle is expressed, which only contains one aspect of the truth. It must here, at least theoretically, be admitted, as is admitted in physical inquiry, that the idea is just as important for progress as experience. But in so far now as we are concerned not to *know* the most correct moral philosophy, but to be *moved* to good and noble actions, the idea, which even in the sphere of knowledge appeared as the real spring amidst the wheelwork of experience, attains a heightened significance. But of course the question may be renewed here, whether the guiding idea does not often guide us astray ? and especially with regard to religious systems it may be asked, whether it is not better simply to resign myself to the ennobling influence of natural sympathy, and so slowly, but surely, to advance, than to listen to prophet-voices, which already but too often have led to the most hideous fanaticism ?

Originally religions are by no means intended to serve the purpose of morality. The offspring of the fear of violent natural phenomena, of fantasy, and barbaric inclinations and conceptions, the religions amongst uncivilised people are a source of horrors and crudities, which could hardly arise from the mere conflict of interests even in its crudest form. How much of such disfiguring elements still adheres to religion, even amongst civilised peoples, may appear from the judgment of

Epikuros and Lucretius, since we, dazzled by the sublime aspects of the ancient mythology, find it difficult to think ourselves into the religious system of the ancients. And yet the mere belief in supersensuous, powerfully ruling beings, must of itself afford an important starting-point for the natural development of ethical ideas. The antithesis of the whole of human society as opposed to the individual is not easy for the savage to apprehend, but thought of an avenging being *outside* humanity might very well act as an early substitute for this; and, in fact, we find the Deity as an avenger of human misdeeds even amongst people whose ideas are still very crude, and whose religious observances are in part abominable. With the advance of civilisation the ideas of the gods advance also, and we see how deities who originally only personified a terrible or beneficent natural force gradually receive a more decided ethical significance. Thus in the classical period of ancient Hellas we can discover at once the traces of the old natural import of the gods by the side of their ethical import, and side by side with both was the degeneracy of the cruel popular superstition which played a much greater part in the religious practices of daily life than we should be led to suppose by the magnificent traditions of Hellenic poesy and sculpture. Thus can religion simultaneously conduce to ethical progress and sanctify horrors, while in correspondence with a people's character it develops in peculiar forms the varied creations of an ideal world.

In the creations of human thought is repeated the primeval problem of the relation of the whole to its parts. Materialism will never be able to refrain from analysing even the spiritual creations of religion into their elements, as it resolves the corporeal world into atoms. Fantasy, fear, and fallacy in its view make up religion, which is a product of these separate influences, and if it assigns to it an ethical influence, it will explain this as a transference of natural morality to supernatural ideas. When we see how often religion exerts an astonishing power over mankind for good or evil, how in medieval times it drives thousands of children to a crusade, and in our own days makes the Mormons flee amidst battle and privations to the wilderness of the Salt Lake; how Mohammedanism, with the swiftness of a blazing flame, remoulds nations and agitates whole continents; how the Reformation founds an epoch in history; this is all in its view but a specially efficient combination of these factors of sensibility, passionateness, and error, or imperfect knowledge. We, on the contrary, shall remember that, as in external things, so too here the value and the essence of the object does not lie in the bare fact that these and those factors co-operate, but in the *form* which this co-operation takes, and that this form—for us, practically considered, the most important point—is only recognisable in the peculiar *whole*, and not in the abstracted factors. What led Aristotle to give precedency to Form over Matter and to the Whole over its Parts was his profoundly practical nature, his ethical sense; and though in exact science we must always oppose him, and ever and ever again must explain the whole by the parts, the form, so far as we can, by the matter, yet we know very well since Kant that the whole necessity of this procedure is only a reflex of the organisation of our analytically inclined understanding, that this process is a *processus in infinitum*, which never completely reaches its goal, though, on the other hand, it must never shrink back from any problem presented to it. We know that there always exists the same great contradiction between the complete and peculiar nature of a whole and the approximate explanation of it from its parts. We know that in this contradiction is reflected the nature of our organisation, which only gives us things whole, complete, and rounded in the way of poesy; partially, approximately, but with relative accuracy in the way of knowledge. All great misconceptions, all historically important errors, spring indeed from the confusion of these two modes of conception: either we bring the results of poesy, the commandments of an inner voice, the revelations of a religion as absolute truths into conflict with the truths of knowledge, or we allow them no place at all in the consciousness of the people. True, indeed, all the results of poesy and revelation purport to our consciousness to be absolute, immediate, since the conditions from which these products of conception proceed do not come with consciousness; it is also true, on the other hand, that all poesy and revelation are simply false, so soon as we test their material contents by the standard of exact knowledge; but this Absolute has a value only as an image, as a symbol of that other Absolute, which we cannot know at all, and these errors or intentional deviations from reality only do harm when they are treated as material knowledge. Religion has, therefore, in times which united a certain degree of culture and piety always been inseparable from *art*, while it is a sign of decline or of stagnation when its doctrines are confounded with sober *knowledge*. There the true value of ideas lies in the form, as it were in the style of the architecture of our ideas, and in the impression of this architecture of ideas on the soul; here, on the contrary, all ideas should, as well individually as in their connexion, be materially correct.

But religion must at any price contain truth! It must originate, if not from human knowledge, yet from a higher insight, a science of the essence of things, which is revealed to men by the Deity. We have already sufficiently declared that we cannot in any way admit either a co-ordination or a subordination of religious knowledge as compared with the results of methodical science, and we are disposed to assume that this principle, together with the classification of religion with art and metaphysic, will at no very distant time be generally conceded; nay, it appears to us as though this circumstance is even by the most decided believers recognised, or at least suspected, very much more widely than is commonly supposed. The great mass of the professors of all religions may indeed still be in a state of mind like that in which children listen to fairy-tales. The full masculine sense for reality and verifiable accuracy is simply yet undeveloped. Only with its appearance does the credibility of those stories disappear, because another standard of verity is applied; but the sense for poesy remains true to the genuine man through all the stages of life.

The ancients regarded the poet as an inspired seer, who, full of his subject, was quite carried away, and in spirit raised above vulgar reality. Should not the same possession by an idea have its justification in religion too? And if then there are souls which are so sunk in these emotions that, as compared with them, the vulgar reality of things sinks into the background, how otherwise shall we characterise the vividness, the persistency, the activity of their spiritual experiences than by the word "truth"? Of course the word here has then but a figurative sense, but the sense of a figure which is more highly prized by men than the reality, which receives its whole worth only from the light which the rays of this figure shed upon it. In the case of the nominal Christian, you can by the aid of logic clear from his mind the notions which his memory may have retained from the age when he learnt his catechism, but you cannot argue away to the believer the value of his inner life. And even though you prove to him a hundred times that it is all but subjective sensations, he lets you go your way with subject and object, and mocks your simple efforts to overturn by the breath of a mortal man the walls of Sion, whose towering battlements he sees lighted by the radiance of the Lamb and the everlasting glory of God. The masses, poor in logic as in faith, hold the might of prophetic conviction as just as much a criterion of truth as the proof of a sum; and as language is the possession of the people, we must, therefore, in the meantime, admit the double use of the word "truth."

But talk not to me here of "bookkeeping by double entry!" This idea, doubly objectionable, has in the first place a false name, invented by a professor who had probably never seen a mercantile book, and who, at all events, meant something very different from what the *tertium comparationis* expresses; but next it belongs in truth to that twilight world of childish tales that we just now described. It corresponds to the standpoint of people who, as a result of acquired scientific activity, have got so far as to be able to distinguish true and false with method and conscience within their special subject, but who cannot yet carry the genuine criterion of truth into other spheres, and in these, therefore, meanwhile, admit as true what best agrees with their vague feelings. The philosopher may allow the second signification of the word "truth," but can never forget that it is a *figurative* one. He may indeed warn us from a blind zeal against the "truths" of religion, if he is convinced that their ideal content still retains a value for our people, and that this value suffers more by an inconsiderate attack upon forms than is gained on the other hand by enlightenment. He cannot, however, go further, and he can never allow that doctrines which in their nature are variable with the changing character of different times should be imported into any book in which account is kept of the lasting treasures of human knowledge. In the relations of science we have *fragments* of truth, which are continually multiplying, but continually remain fragments; in the ideas of philosophy and religion we have a figure of the truth, which presents it to us as a whole, but still always remains a figure, varying in its form with the standpoint of our apprehension.

But how then does it stand with rational religion? Have not the Rationalists, or Kant, or the Free Congregations of our own day, succeeded in establishing a religion, which teaches pure truth in the strictest sense of the word, which is purified from all the dross of superstition, or, as Kant says, from the stupidity of superstition, and the delirium of enthusiasm, only satisfies the ethical end of religion?

The answer to this is, if we understand truth in the ordinary, not figurative sense of the word, a very decided No; there is no rational religion without dogmas, which are incapable of proof. If, however, we regard reason, with Kant, as the faculty of ideas, and simply substitute ethical verification for proof, then everything that is ethically verified is equally justified. Kant's minimum of God, Freedom and Immortality, may indeed be dispensed with; the Free Congregations have already thrown it overboard, and the principles which they retain may also be dispensed with.

All these doctrines may in principle be dispensed with, in so far that it cannot be shown from the universal characteristics of man, or from some other reason, that a society without these doctrines must necessarily fall into immorality. But if we take the case of a particular community, *e.g.*, that of the Germans in the present epoch, it is quite possible that the ethically most valuable combination of conceptions demands very many more ideas than Kant was willing to base his rational religion upon. This is, to speak plainly, a matter of taste; only that, of course, it is not the subjective taste of an individual that is the real determinant, but the whole state of culture in a nation, the dominant forms of the association of ideas, and a certain fundamental disposition of mind, which is the result of innumerable factors.

The Rationalists of last century shared in the general tendency of the culture of their age towards intellectual aristocracy. Even though, as a rule, they cared more earnestly for the weal of the people than the orthodox, yet they started from the needs and aspirations of the educated classes. Amongst these an entirely new religion could still be held possible, because they were not yet sufficiently convinced that after the elimination of all that is doubted by the critical understanding *nothing whatever is left*. From Kant, at all events, they might have learnt this, but he, with his purely ethical basis of religion, was understood by too few, and thus even in this century the idea could return of a religion purified from all error. Uhlich very admirably describes in a pamphlet penetrated by the noblest feeling for the truth—'Antwort auf einen offenen Brief,' 1860—how the transition from Rationalistic ecclesiasticism to complete severance from Protestantism led the founder of the Free Congregations a great step farther. "We had been of opinion that if we only got rid of all in our Church against which reason and conscience in us had long protested, what was left would satisfy us both in doctrine and form, and would be for us the true and beatific religion. But we gradually learned that if to think for one's self in religion is once recognised as a right and exercised as a duty, we must then keenly examine all traditional ideas, even those that never offended us before, to see whether or not they rest on the basis of eternal truth." But what now is this basis of eternal truth upon which the religion of the Free Congregations is supposed to rest? It is no other than science itself, especially the natural sciences. Uhlich calls religion the "science of sciences;" he rejects all dogmas that rest only upon probability or conjecture, as, *e.g.*, the hypothesis of a conscious world-soul; he explains truth as "the reflexion of reality, of the real world with its things and forces, laws and processes, in the soul of man." What lies beyond the limits of scientific inquiry cannot belong either to religion. At the same time, religion, in an ethical regard, is with him "the recognition of the relation of mankind to an eternal order, or, if we prefer it, to a sacred power to which it has to submit itself." The "one thing needful" is the building up of a kingdom of the true, the good, and the beautiful. The basis of the whole doctrine must, therefore, of course, lie in the point of union of the ethical and intellectual part, in the principle by which strictly scientific knowledge attains to moral influence. But this principle is the unity of the true, the good, and the beautiful. With the attainment of truth, it results from this principle that a fuller and higher humanity is also attained, and conversely, and both united lead to the utmost beauty, to the purest joy and blessedness. Here, then, we have, in the full sense of the word, a *dogma* which not only is not proved, but which, in fact, when logically tested, is *not true*, but which, if held as an *idea*, may, indeed, like any other religious idea, edify mankind and raise him above the limits of sense. Truth, in the sense of reality, not only does not coincide with Beauty, but stands, in fact, in distinct opposition to it. All beauty is poesy, even that which is the immediate object of the senses; for even the most primitive sense-activity, as we have shown in the previous Section, includes a contribution from our mind. The artist *sees* his subject even in immediate observation as more beautiful than the less susceptible layman, and the realists in painting are only distinguished from the idealists by this, that they take up more of the qualities of reality into their work, and allow the pure ground-idea of the object to appear crossed by the ideas of its circumstances; but if they did not idealise at all, they would be no longer artists. The eye of love poetises, the longing of the heart poetises; melancholy remembrance and joyful meeting, all passions and activities of the senses poetise; and if we could entirely abolish this poesy, it is a question whether anything would be left to make life worth living. So, then, Uhlich's whole view of nature also—an indispensable part of his religion—is nothing more than a poem. "It is my true and real feeling," says Uhlich, "when I bow down and gaze at a flower, that the Deity looks at me from it, and sends towards me a sweet perfume." Very well; but then, too, it is the true and real feeling of the believer when, in prayer, he feels and knows the presence of his God, that he is heard. We may contest the external source of the feeling, but never the feeling itself. But if, in nature, I linger over the contemplation of the beautiful and comparatively perfect in order to edify myself, then I make nature itself my idea of the good and beautiful. "I overlook the withered spot in the calix of the flower and the ravages of the caterpillar on the leaves, and if a flower grows in my garden that smells unpleasantly, I do not use it in order to pray a little to the Devil also, but I tear it up and fling it to another part of nature, which can still less serve me for edifying contemplation.

It depends upon me, whether perfection or imperfection seems to preponderate in nature, whether I carry into it my idea of beauty and then receive it back a thousand-fold, or whether I am met everywhere by the traces of corruption, of spoliation, and of the struggle of extermination. And if then I conceive the succession of life and death, of swelling abundance and sudden decline, I find myself at the point of origin of Dionysos-worship, and with a glance at the contrast between the highest ideal and all living things, I feel at once the need for a redeemer.

This suggestion is not, of course, meant to show that edification, in the sense of the Free Congregations, is to be absolutely rejected, but only that, as compared with other forms of edification, it cannot lay claim to the privilege of unconditional truth. It is a question of more or less of truth and poesy, and the fact that this is not recognised by the founders of the Free Congregations places their religious conception intellectually behind Kant and Fichte, while, however, it lends it a character of naïveté which is otherwise only to be found in orthodoxy.

It has indeed been observed from the philosophical side, that in the advance of knowledge we must take as a basis for the religion of the future such a point as would admit of our still really and unaffectedly believing as the Free

CHRISTIANITY AND ENLIGHTENMENT.

Congregations do, and in which the difference between the result of critical thought and religious feeling would completely disappear for us, even though it should arise again for later times. But what else is this than to support religious belief upon a metaphysical belief? If now the latter cannot exist unless through poesy, why should not religion itself exist through poesy without any need for metaphysical mediation? But if speculation can help to bring about that the religious ideas of the future shall not be too much determined by the subjective leanings of a few too powerful characters—which was certainly the case at the period of the Reformation —if it can help to bring it about that these ideas shall be taken right from the centre of all our culture, and not merely be gathered from the surface of ecclesiastical polemics, then their labour will be welcome; only that it will be quite impossible for us to exercise a child-like faith with regard to them.

A champion of the advanced Reform theology, the spiritual and eloquent Pastor Lang, in his 'Versuch einer christlichen Dogmatik,'[12] has combated our stand-

[12] Comp. Lang, Versuch einer christlichen Dogmatik, allen denkenden Christen dargeboten, 2te Aufl. Berl. 1868, S. 3-6. The objection there raised, that from my standpoint it is "quite indifferent" whether the philosopher "as a religious man" kneels before Mary or the personal God, is disposed of by pointing out that we assume a necessary course of development in the ideas of humanity. Not any given poetical idea can serve our purpose, but only that which is adapted to our time and to the character of our culture. That Lang comes back also to the 'bookkeeping by double entry,' is only explained by the onesidedness with which he tries to conceive everything, even against the most express declarations, from the standpoint of knowledge. Thus, too, he could arrive at the proposition: "If there is in the world so absurd a dualism between knowing and believing, then there is no scientific knowledge of the world." Why not, if science keeps exclusively to knowledge? It is only the incarnate theologian who persists in thinking that the articles of his creed must also be taken into account. "A dualistic world is not an object of knowledge; only a world of a single principle can be known." But science knows nothing of a dualistic world, for to it all life in its idea rests only upon psychological processes, which, though they may be infinitely subtle and deeply hidden, yet follow in fine the same natural laws as all other psychical facts. So far the demand for monism is entirely justified. But if it is also proposed to remove the dualism of

point with the assertion that religions always fall, "if they are no longer believed," while works of poesy, if they are æsthetically satisfying, retain their value. Nearly the same thing might be said of metaphysical speculation, which has also, till now, maintained pretensions to unconditional truth, and whose disciples have formed a circle of believers. And yet even the most important systems have scarcely ever found an unconditional follower; and where this has been the case, as with Herbart's school, it testifies to a certain poverty and hardness in the whole circle of ideas. How many strictly orthodox Kantians have there been? Amongst the great minds that have mainly gained the system its renown, and that have been the most important bearers of its influence, scarcely a single one. Has not Hegel's system exercised an influence far beyond the circle of believers, and only borne its best fruits where it was handled with perfect freedom? What shall we say, moreover, of Plato, whose speculative imaginings still, after thousands of years, to-day exercise their mighty influence, while, even from his first successors onwards, no one has ever believed that his deductions are so strictly valid as they claim to be?

And then as to religions! Did not even in ancient days the Stoics for hundreds of years treat the popular superstition as the imaginative clothing of ethical ideas, and thus did more for the propagation of religious life than all the priesthoods? Jupiter, according to Lang, had to give place to Jehovah, Olympus to the Christian heaven, because the sensuous theology of polytheism ceased to meet the requirements of advancing knowledge, because a higher truth was recognised in the perfected

thought and poesy, feeling and willing, perception and creation, this is just as foolish as if for the sake of the unity of knowledge we should propose to abolish the antithesis of day and night. Thus, then, the antithesis of ideal and reality must remain; but scientific knowledge has only to do with the latter. It establishes unity by recognising that the ideal world is at the same time a psychological fact.

monotheism of Christianity. But had knowledge in the imperial age of Rome so much increased since the age of Sokrates and Protagoras? Were the masses ever more superstitious, the great ever more eager for miracles, the philosophers ever more mystical, than in the age of the spread of Christianity? And when, then, did that religion of Jupiter and the combined Olympus, that was then doomed to fall, ever exist? It struggled simultaneously and hand in hand with the commencing enlightenment painfully through against the old comminution of the national faith into thousands of local cults. The right of speculation to develop and shape religion might not indeed be announced in the market-place, but it existed, and the whole flowering time of Hellenic culture shows us poets and philosophers occupied in the development of religious doctrines and conceptions. In the local cult, indeed, absolute faith was demanded; but what else was this faith than the pious submission of the soul to the sacred story of one's own native city; what else could it be in an age when faith changed from town to town, from village to village, and when every educated man made it a strict rule to tolerate and to respect each faith in its own home? And was it, then, in the age of the spread of Christianity really the most enlightened minds, the philosophic thinkers, who first yielded to the new faith? Or do knowledge and reflexion play the chief part in the history of the conversion of eminent personages? Had the mass of the people really lost faith in the old gods, when they saw themselves compelled to adopt the new religion? History exhibits to us quite another process than that of a growing enlightenment: universal social decomposition, conflict and distress in all strata of society, world-weariness and unspeakable longing for a salvation which should not be of this world, are the true sources of the great revolution. Mere enlightenment might very well have attached itself to Jupiter and Olympus; they would have found it much easier to deal with them than our theological reformers of to-day with their attempt to transform Christianity into a pure religion of reason.

"Why," asks Lang, "is it that in the Reformation the Catholic heaven with its saints fell and gave way to a far more colourless, much more unpoetical heaven?" The answer is again found in an advance of knowledge. But why is it, we ask, on the other hand, that this Catholic heaven amongst such enlightened nations as the French and Italians did *not* fall? Did Germany carry out the Reformation because it was ahead of all other nations in scientific knowledge, or has it in course of time been able to surpass the other nations in knowledge, because it had, from quite other reasons, broken down the ban of the hierarchy and of absolute unity of faith? When, finally, it is asked why the Protestant world is more and more turning away from orthodoxy, and when the answer is found in the influence of scientific discoveries, we must remark, on the other hand, that these discoveries come into the sharpest conflict just with what the reforming theologians propose to retain from the inventory of Christianity, while they are much more indifferent as regards other doctrines, as, *e.g.*, that of the vicarious sacrifice of the Son of God. It is a narrow strip of land surrounded by the waves, upon which the reformed theology tries to maintain itself against the waves of invading Materialism, and nowhere is speculative imagination more necessary than just here, if a few dogmas must still be maintained. Lang himself, immediately after the criticism he directs against us, claims the fatherhood of God for his religious needs. But his God is nothing but "the ground of all existence, eternally complete within itself, and exempt from all the changes of the processes of the universe." He works no miracles, he has no human sympathies, he does not trouble himself in detail with the weal or woe of his creatures, he nowhere interferes with the course of natural laws; his existence rests merely upon this, that, in opposition to

Materialism, there is postulated, besides the mere totality of all that exists, also a special ground of it, and then from this ground of all existence is made a 'father.' Why? Because the soul cannot but imagine to itself a being that loves us personally, and that stretches out its strong arms to us when we are in need. Can we ask a stronger testimony of the imaginative element in religion?

Homer did not always maintain his value, but he regained it when a generation arose that knew how to prize him, and the gods of Greece came to life again with him. When Schiller said of them, "Ah! that which gains immortal life in song, to mortal life must perish!" he knew very well that it is the essential element, the spiritual core of the Greek theology, which has exercised its influence upon us, as it did upon Sokrates and Plato.

CHAPTER III.

THEORETICAL MATERIALISM IN ITS RELATION TO ETHICAL MATERIALISM AND TO RELIGION.

THE Materialism of antiquity was, in its ripest form, directed immediately and openly against religion, the complete annihilation of which Lucretius considered to be the most important business of man. The Materialism of the last centuries frequently betrays the same tendency, but it only rarely shows itself openly, and, when it does so, is usually directed rather against Christianity than against religion as such. The thought of a gradual purification of popular belief from all superstitious elements has taken such deep root, that most of the adversaries of superstition involuntarily exhibit this tendency, even where their proper principle goes much further. Since Voltaire pursued the Church and the Church's creed with implacable hate, although anxious to retain belief in God, the shock of the storm has ever been directed, above all, against orthodoxy, against the literalism of traditional dogmas; while the foundation of all belief, the feeling of dependence upon super-terrestrial powers, is but seldom attacked, and is often expressly recognised. The philosophical modifications and interpretations, the artifices of translation and transference, which succeed in educing out of the 'ground of all existence' a loving Father, play a great part in the development of young clerics, a somewhat smaller one in the maintenance of a certain connexion between the popular faith and the ideas of the educated, and hardly any at all in the attacks made upon religion by Materialists and other apostles of unbelief. The way in which scientific theology reconciles itself with dogmas is often strikingly ignored; the freer middle stand-points, the spiritualised conception of ecclesiastical traditions, are overlooked, and Christianity is pitilessly made responsible for all the crudities of the vulgar creed, and all the excrescences of extreme opinions. But for all this, a 'Christianity purified from all superstition,' a 'pure theology,' or even a 'religion without dogmas,' is very frequently admitted as an indispensable element in the life of humanity.

The effects of this kind of polemic are easily seen. The great mass of more or less enlightened theologians do not feel themselves at all hit by these attacks, and look down with disdain upon the 'want of science' in such opponents. Believers are hurt by the mockery against what to them is sacred, and turn away from all criticism, even in cases where, but for such attacks, they might themselves, perhaps, have been disposed to exercise it. The only conquests are of minds that are hesitating and have long been strangers to belief, who are impressed by the confidence of the new apostles; while all those are strengthened and still more embittered against believers, who already belonged to the party[1] of Materialism and of radical enlightenment. The result is an exacerbation of the oppositions that distract the life of our people, an aggravation of the difficulty of the peaceful solution of the problem of the future.

Very different must be the effect of a polemic which should seriously and decidedly dispute the very continuance of religion. Our own age, it is true, still offers material enough for the Lucretian 'Tantum religio potuit suadere malorum,' and it would be well worth while for once to examine more closely the relation between the fruits of the tree and its roots. If able and pious theologians, like Richard Rothe,[13] can entertain the thought that the Church must gradually be absorbed in the State, it would be well for the freethinkers, on their side too, to subject to a strict criticism the dualism of political life and of religious community, instead of blindly transferring the old forms into an entirely different content. We have recently seen a fraction amongst the 'Free Congregations,' not only throwing overboard every remnant of the old articles of faith, but even finding a special sign of progress in the rejecting of the solemn and ceremonial performance of certain acts which have reference to the relation of the individual to the religious community. 'Baptism,' for example, which hitherto has been combined with a solemn exhortation to the parents as to the training up of the child, and with a recommendation of the child to the goodwill of all the members of the congregation, was given up, because it contained an unnecessary interference of the clergyman, and, therefore, a remnant of priestly authority. Ronge, Baltzer, and other former leaders of the movement, who adhere to definite although very general doctrines, and correspondingly simple forms of worship, are frequently treated by men of this school as arrogant priests, and are almost ranked with the infallible Pope.[14] At the same time, congregations continue to be formed, preachers are appointed, and edification is found, as far as it may be found, in the monotonous repetition of negation. Frequently, indeed, the limit between congregation and association becomes vague, partly, it is true, through the fault of the state, which still opposes great hindrances to the freedom of associations, while it allows the formation of religious communities with an infinitesimal minimum of religion. Sometimes men have appeared as preachers in such con-

---

[13] Comp. Stille Stunden, Aphorismen aus Richard Rothes handschriftl. Nachlass, Wittenberg, 1872, S. 273 ff., 319 ff.

[14] Comp. the essay Die neue Bilderstürmerei, in the paper Neue religiöse Reform, Darmstadt, 1874, Nos. 29-31, by Johannes Ronge.

gregations who scarcely conceal their repugnance to any and every form of religion. If, however, we consider their writings, we find them holding by preference to the uttermost extremes of orthodoxy and pietism, and only exhibiting their radicalism in audacious raillery and satire, while it never occurs to them to submit the justification of religion itself to a thoroughgoing criticism of principles which shall also embrace free standpoints. For the ideal side of religious life we find amongst these people simply no sense, and the rejection of everything that cannot be shown to the common understanding to be true is regarded as a matter of course.[15]

The same one-sided predominance of the rational principle betrays itself in the attempt of a decided 'Naturalist' to form a religious community of 'Cogitants;' yet here there appears a new element, which may be shortly described as a decided protest against ethical Materialism. The Cogitant community of Dr. Löwenthal is intended to be a 'union of social and humanitarian cultus,' a society which, on the one hand, makes thinking and knowledge themselves the objects of cultus, but, on the other hand, is based on the cultivation of human dignity and human affection.[16] Dr. Edward Reich lays still greater stress on cultus and ceremonies, a writer who in a series of works has advocated the Materialistic theory, and who at the same time in a special treatise has sketched the plan of a 'Church of Humanity.' Reich proposes to provide, moreover, for the needs of the soul and the poetical feeling in man, and, accordingly, is not sparing of festivals and festal hymns, of choirs, and imposing processions. Symbolical acts, elaborate church decorations, vows, and consecrations lend the religion of "everlasting light" a

---

[15] Comp. inter alia, Dr. Friedr. Mook, Das Leben Jesu, für das Volk bearbeitet, Zürich, 1873.

[16] Comp. the first numbers of the periodical published by Löwenthal in 1865, Der Cogitant, Flugblätter für Freunde naturalistischer Weltanschauung. The editor, Dr. Löwenthal, is author of the book, which has gone through several editions : System u. Gesch. d. Naturalismus, Leipzig, 1862.

pomp that cannot be paralleled in existing religions; drums, trumpets, and cymbals unite with organs and carillons to give a higher impulse to the religious feelings of the crowd of worshippers.[17]

It is Comte who has carried furthest the idea of this worship of humanity, and on his system religion would assume a much larger place in the life of individuals and nations than ever before. Two whole hours in the day are dedicated only to prayer, which consists in an effusion of feeling, with which we call up within us the ideas of reverence, of love, and of dependence under the figures of mother, wife, and daughter. Public worship demands four-and-twenty festivals in the year, and has nine sacraments at its disposal. But the most remarkable feature, besides a hundred oddities of a harmless kind, is the decided predilection for a hierarchical guidance of the people.[18] In the case of Reich, too, we have a hierarchically organised priesthood, and the religion of the Cogitants has, at least, its 'Cultus-magister,' who is clothed with a certain official authority.

Here, then, is taken up a factor of the 'outlived' Christian religion, which is unquestionably one of the most doubtful and dangerous of them all—Organised Priesthood and Official Authority. We may very seriously ask ourselves whether our decision must not be quite otherwise, if we had the choice, either to retain certain untenable dogmas and mystical and obscure articles of faith, and in exchange to be able to break up the hierarchy, or, while attaining complete rationalism as to dogmas, to submit again to the fetters of the hierarchy?

Are not the psychological laws which make every hierarchy, every priesthood, that is elevated above the people, ambitious of power, and that awake in it jealousy of the maintenance of its authority, immutably based in human nature and independent of the content of the creed?

[17] Reich, Die Kirche d. Menschheit, Neuwied, 1873.
[18] Comp. Mill, Auguste Comte and Positivism, London, 1865, p. 140 ff.

In fact, we find this inevitable effect not only in the great typical forms of the Tibetan, the Mediæval Christian, and the old Egyptian hierarchies, but, as is shown by recent ethnographical inquiries, even amongst the smallest religious groups of the most remote peoples, among the most degenerate negro races, and on the smallest islands of the Pacific.

If we would suppose that complete enlightenment in the sphere of theory would afford protection against this phenomenon, yet it must first be shown whence a power is to come that would supply so strong a counterpoise to the involuntary and insidious lust of power. It can hardly be inferred from purely theoretical considerations, and whatever may be said of the purifying power of truth, yet it has nowhere proved itself to be equal to this task. The Reformers, too, believed that they had comprehended all truth and got rid of all error; and what ambition, intolerance, and persecution did not all the same manifest themselves among the Lutheran clergy, until they were subdued and held in check by the preponderance of the modern state! If, perhaps, it is supposed that the ecclesiastical dogmas of absolute enlightenment would no longer afford matter for great and embittered controversies and heresies, let us only consider for a moment the scanty scientific doctrines which Ronge holds to be important and irrefragable enough to be adopted into his religious handbook for the instruction of the young.[19] Here we find very many assertions that have partly been recognised as erroneous, partly been rendered very doubtful by the advance of science. Such errors are, indeed, constantly forcing their way into our schools or being spread by popular scientific literature, and they often maintain their ground with astonishing tenacity. Views as to the

[19] Religionsbuch für den Unterricht der Jugend, 1 Thl. Die Gesetze der Natur sind Gesetze Gottes und in Harmonie mit den Gesetzen der Sittlichkeit, oder die natürliche und sittliche Weltordnung Gottes als freies Vorbild unserer Lebensordnung. Frankfurt a. M., 1863. (With black wrapper. Why?)

existence of a central sun, as to the self-complete system of the Milky Way, which repeats itself in the nebular masses, as to the habitability of the majority of the planets by "rational creatures like men," as to the comets as transitional forms in the formation of planets, and many such views long float in this way in the opinions of men, without very much harm being done. But if such propositions receive a religious consecration, and if, finally, such a religion is maintained and cultivated by a priesthood jealous of its authority, they must become much more fatally rooted, and it becomes quite impossible to see whether pure natural science could exist at all for any length of time. What conflicts might arise through the first appearance of great principles such as that of Darwinism! Even as it is, it produces conflicts; but how harmlessly they run their course compared with religious controversies of any kind, and how much more harmlessly still would they be carried on if it were not that, even as it is, references to religion bring with them a certain bitterness.

When the state at last determines, agreeably to its natural function, to introduce instruction in natural science into all primary schools, a great and beneficial advance will have been attained. The chasm between the modes of thought of the people and those of the educated will be lessened, the independence of each individual citizen, the capacity to resist delusions and superstitions of every kind, will be increased, and the relation of science to religion must gradually take the same shape as that in which it now exists amongst the educated, without any conflict of views being provoked. The more unconcernedly and positively, without any polemical *arrière-pensée*, such instruction is imparted, the more favourably must the process of accommodation between the old and the new views be brought about. But a Church or a religious community of any kind whatever cannot possibly deal with the matter so harmlessly and unconcernedly. It will give to doctrines a consecration and a weight which they do not require, and the more deeply it impresses details, all the more will it modify the spirit of the whole.

For the propagation of theoretical insight and enlightenment we do not want any emotional fervour at all. It is not even beneficial; for it is in the utmost calm of quiet and methodical inquiry that correct knowledge is most quickly and most easily found. Just as little does the truth require a great international association; it forms one itself, and breaks down all social and geographical limits.

It is otherwise with morality, with the purification of the desires, and with the direction of the impulses towards the general good. But even here mere moral teaching will hardly be likely to produce a frame of mind to which trumpet-peals and hymns are appropriate. All religion, like all poetry, connects itself with human joys and sorrows, with fear, longing, and hope; and though it is often mentioned, to the disparagement of religion, that it has sprung from fear and covetousness, yet we may set off against this, that for that very reason religion is fitted to purify and to ennoble fear and covetousness. Whether, however, the natural incidents of human life, birth and death, marriages and misfortunes, suffice for this, is very doubtful. If the object of the emotions is to be transferred from the present to a distance, and our impulses to be thus directed from the finite to the infinite, then mythus asserts its rights. A material which on the one hand is genuinely human, while on the other it stirs our hearts by pointing to the divine and the eternal, forms the basis with which the ethical tendency of religion is indissolubly connected. The tragedy of the suffering Son of God has therefore perhaps, from the mysteries of the ancient Greeks down to the offshoots of Christianity in Protestantism, been a more essential constituent of the truly religious life than all other traditions and dogmas. But such a material cannot be made. It must grow. If we need it no longer, then it becomes very questionable whether we need religion at all any longer.

A certain cultus of humanity has already been set on foot, but fortunately it contains no germ of an ecclesiastical system with fixed forms and a separate priestly caste. Festivals in memory of great men, of the foundation of important centres of culture, of the establishment of benevolent institutions and associations, great national and international assemblages for the cultivation of science and art or for the advocacy of important principles, are much healthier beginnings of an age of humanity than the arbitrarily composed calendar of saints of Comte and the festivals of 'Harmony' of 'Great Men,' &c., which Reich proposes to substitute for Christian festivals. But though even here we can recognise a beginning cultus of humanity, yet this has nothing of the essence of religion in it. We have already mentioned the absence of the exclusive priestly order; but in its inner aspect, too, the spirit of these new preparations for the elevation of the heart and the union of forces in the struggle for the high aims of humanity is utterly different from everything that we are accustomed to call religion. In great men we celebrate not dæmonic beings on whose favour we feel ourselves dependent, but splendid flowers and fruits from a tree of which we ourselves, too, are part. Even the undoubted dependence of our thoughts and feelings on the forms which have been expressed by the great minds of the past is not conceived in the sense of religious submission, but as a joyous recognition of the sources of life from which we draw, and which are ever and ever bubbling forth and promising to pour forth constantly new and fresh life.[20]

[20] Stuart Mill, in his just published Essays on Religion (Lond. 1874), calls the sentiments which we entertain for the good of the human race and the moral elevation by the thought of great men or our dead friends a real religion. At the same time he declares the essence of religion

Thus it appears that Theoretical Materialism not only proceeds most consistently, but also aims at the comparatively most favourable result for the spiritual future of mankind, when it rejects religion altogether, and leaves the charge of morality and humanity partly to the state, but partly also to private efforts. A great part of the functions which now fall to the Church will then devolve upon the School; but care must be taken that this does not become an exclusive institution, directing mankind, and as it were entering upon the vacated inheritance of the Church. This would only produce a new priestdom. Only as an organ of the state, and as the free undertaking of self-conscious social circles, can the School attain a development which secures the progress of true culture and genuine morality, without bringing with it the dangers of hierarchical authority and the ambition of a scheming corporation.

But now we must further ask whether the last consequence of Theoretical Materialism must not carry us still further, and, with the rejection of all ethical aims in the state, tend towards a social atomism, in which each individual social atom would simply follow its own interests?

In answering this question, we must not, on the one hand, be led away by the mere analogy of Atomism with extreme Individualism, nor, on the other hand, would it be sufficient to point to the protest made by Materialists against this consequence. The analogy, quite apart from its inadequacy as a principle, would not lead us far, for the Materialist recognises the things which are formed from the atoms, and which in virtue of their form react as a whole upon the motion of the parts. Why should he

to be the strong and earnest direction of the emotions and desires towards an ideal object, recognised as of the highest excellence, and as rightfully paramount over all selfish objects of desire. Measured by this standard, all Schiller's dramas and two-thirds of his lyrics are religious poetry. Nay, even poetry itself, conceived at its true value, becomes identical with religion, while it must be ranged under a wider conception.

not also recognise social formations, which, as a whole, determine the course of particular individuals? The protest of the Materialists, however, cannot decide this question, just because it is a question not of persons but of principles. Though there may be Materialists who make their peace with existing religions, or would like to establish a new religion, while others wish to destroy the basis of all religions by means of Materialism, it might be just as possible for all our present Materialists to protest against Ethical Materialism, while a later school should adopt it as a necessary and correct consequence. Historically Ethical Materialism has been developed amongst the money-making classes; Theoretical Materialism amongst men of science. The former has gone excellently with ecclesiastical orthodoxy, the latter has almost always worked in favour of enlightenment. At the same time, there might exist a deeper connexion, which should make both phenomena, as the result of the same condition of civilisation, proceed from essentially the same sources. Rising at first apart, they would only gradually reveal their internal connexion, and end by a complete union.

The protest of the Materialists is, of course, quite justified against the view which by Materialism understands only the ' pursuit of sensual pleasures.' The unrestraint of sensual appetite is chiefly a matter of temperament and education, and is in principle, though not in practice, irreconcilable with any philosophical standpoint. Even though the individual sensual pleasure, as with Aristippos or Lamettrie, is raised to a principle, *self-control* still remains a requirement of philosophy, if only in order to assure the permanence of the capacity for enjoyment; and conversely, even when the principles of a philosophy are extremely ascetic, sensual appetite frequently enough asserts itself in its disciples, either in open violation of their own principles or in the tortuous labyrinths of self-delusion.

We have seen in the First Chapter of this Section that the love of pleasure cannot be regarded as a conspicuous feature of our age; much rather is it the most inconsiderate regard for self-interest, especially in the sphere of money-making. The principle of exclusive regard for self-interest, which we have found to be the essence of Ethical Materialism, is indeed not seldom found in combination with Theoretical Materialism; thus, *e.g.*, in Büchner, in the first edition of 'Force and Matter;' much more frequently, of course, amongst those Materialists who write no books.[21]

What decides the question of a connexion is, however, neither the historical view nor the collection of voices from the present, but an inquiry whether an ethical principle may be naturally established according to the views of Theoretical Materialism, and conversely whether Theoretical Materialism can still be harmonised with a given ethical principle. We have already found that from a rigidly Materialistic view of things by no means only the principle of Egoism may be deduced, but also the great counterpoise to it — Sympathy. Both principles, without any influence of transcendental ideas or superstitious assumptions, may simply be deduced from the sensuous nature of man, and he who favours them may still be, in the full extent of the word, a Materialist. Kant's moral principle must, however, at least be brought down from the height of its *a priori* validity, and be established on a purely psychological basis, if it is to be harmonised with Materialism; and conversely no one who is convinced of the apriority of this moral law can remain at the point of Theoretical Materialism. The question as to the origin of the moral law will always lead him beyond the limits of experience, and he cannot possibly regard a picture of the world which rests simply upon experience as complete and as absolutely correct.

[21] Kraft u. Stoff, Frankfurt, 1855, S. 256 f.

But even sympathy is not the same thing to the Materialist as to the Idealist. Büchner says in one place that sympathy is at bottom only a "refined egoism," and this may, in fact, be very well admitted, at least for his Materialistic conception of it.[22] Then sympathy naturally begins in the narrowest circles of common interests, e.g., in the family, and it is consistent with the grossest egoism towards all beyond this circle. The Idealist, on the contrary, is at a bound in the universal. The bond which links him to his friend is only the nearest link in an infinite chain, embracing all creatures, 'From the rude Mongol,' as Schiller says, 'to the starry Greek, Who the fine link between the mortal made, And Heaven's last Seraph.' The natural feelings which awake in narrower circles are forthwith referred to a universal cause and connected with an idea which claims unconditional validity. The image of an ideal perfection springs up in the soul, and the contemplation of this ideal becomes a guiding star in all his acts. Theoretical Materialism cannot, without inconsistency, rise to this standpoint, because to it this starting from the whole and from a general principle existing before all experience, is an error. The Materialist cannot follow Schiller's words: 'Take courage, then, in erring and in dreaming;' for the exact correspondence of his picture of the world with the results of understanding and sensibility is his highest law.

Capable, therefore, as Materialism may be of deducing from its principles all the virtues necessary to the existence of society, yet here too the psychological law will assert itself, that in the application of our principles the first starting-points always attain a certain preponderance, because they are oftenest repeated, and most deeply impress themselves on the mind. The spread of the Materialistic theory of things will on this ground also necessarily favour the continuance of Ethical Materialism, just as conversely

---

[22] Die Stellung d. Menschen in d. Natur, Leipz. 1870, S. cxliii f.

the worshippers of egoism as a moral principle gradually see themselves drawn to Materialism, even though they have originally held quite other theoretical views.

In fact, we can hardly fail to recognise already that the philosophy of those circles which seek above all things to make money, and which favour a practical egoism, more and more incline to Materialism; while the theoretical Materialists are fond of attacking those features of Christianity which form so sharp an opposition to the spirit of modern industrial acquisition. Amongst the attacks which have quite recently been directed not only against the mythical traditions of Christianity, but also against its morality, that is not the least prominent which characterises Christianity as a religion of the envy and hatred of the poor against the rich.

All these reciprocal relations and connexions will become still clearer to us, as we proceed to consider the theories of things held by two men, who are distinguished by consistency and clearness of thought as well as by philosophical training, and who only in their riper years decidedly leaned to a Materialistic theory of things. We shall at the same time be presenting what may be a welcome complement to our History of Materialism, since at least one of the two systems has quite recently created a great sensation, while the other is here first given to the light from the stillness of a correspondence: we refer to the systems of Friedrich Ueberweg, and David Friedrich Strauss.

Materialism is with Ueberweg, as with Strauss, only the last result of a long development. This may appear surprising, as Materialism represents naturally the first and crudest form of philosophy, from which it is easy to pass on to Sensationalism and to Idealism, while no other self-consistent standpoint can, by the mere widening of the sphere of experience or by logical elaboration, be resolved into Materialism. Nor, in fact, was this the course of the development, although we shall see that Darwinism exercised upon both men a considerable, and perhaps decisive, influence. On the contrary, Ueberweg as well as Strauss at the beginning of his speculation found himself through tradition and the course of his studies upon sloping ground; they had thought themselves into a theory of things which was neither objectively tenable nor agreeable to their subjective disposition and inclination. Their advance from one stage to the other was, therefore, essentially a process of decomposition and a final rest on the apparently firm ground of Materialism.

Ueberweg was from the first as it were predestined to Materialism by the decided aversion to Kant [23] which guided him from the outset in the working out of his own views. As a disciple of Beneke, who started from the English philosophy, and regarded psychology as the fundamental science, Ueberweg, even while a student, represented, as against his master, a naturalistic aspect of this psychology. But he stood, at the same time, under the powerful influence of the Aristotelian Trendelenburg, and thus, in fact, it was essentially elements of the Aristotelian philosophy that separated him from Materialism, and the gradual overcoming of which determined this transformation of his way of thinking. We may distinguish three stages in this movement: the first, in which the teleological principle still has its full force with him; the second, in which it is in conflict with his naturalism; and lastly, the third, in which it was completely broken down.

How far Ueberweg at the first stage was still removed from Materialism may be shown by the following brief sketch, which Dr. Lasson, an intimate friend and indus-

[23] Comp. my memoir: 'Friedrich Ueberweg, Von F. A. Lange, Berl. 1871,' (repr. from the Altpreus. Monatss., Bd. viii. S. 487-522). The letter there mentioned from Ueberweg to Prof. Dilthey (S. 37), with special reference to Ueberweg's relation to Kant, was, in fact, addressed not to Dilthey, but to Dr. Hermann Cohen, the author of 'Kant's Th. der Erfahrung.' This letter was sent by Cohen to Prof. Dilthey, by the latter to Ueberweg's publisher, Dr. Toeche, and by the latter sent to me, without envelope or any particulars, among other materials.

trious correspondent of our philosopher,[24] gives of Ueberweg's conception of Metaphysic, at the time he was writing his Logic (1855): "It ought to contain a rational Ontology, Theology, and Cosmology. The introduction should consist of a Phenomenology, with reference to Logic. Ontology considers the empirically given forms, starting from the most abstract, and tests their reality and import. It is divided into the theory of Being in general (Time, Space, Force, and Substance, corresponding to Perception); of Being-for-self (Individual, Species, Essence, and Phenomenon, corresponding to Intuition and Idea); and of Being-together (Relation, Causality, Purpose, corresponding to Judgment, Inference, System). Then Theology (general rational Theology) considers on the basis of these ontological expositions the proofs for the Existence of God, and also the Nature of God. Cosmology seeks to explain the world and its forms from the Nature of God and the Purpose of Creation. The world is considered as the Revelation of God, as the representation in time and space of the eternal and indivisible perfection of God."[25]

One would gain, of course, from these constructions, which almost remind us of Hegel, a very imperfect notion of Ueberweg's views at that time. The Materialistic trait in his philosophy, which is entirely concealed in this survey of Metaphysic, was at that very time very considerably developed in the plan of his Psychology, which he would have liked to take in hand immediately after the Logic. I made Ueberweg's acquaintance in the autumn of 1855, and in my almost daily discussions with him heard a good deal of this Psychology, but

[24] I may take the opportunity to make a slight correction in my Memoir. On p. 16, instead of the 'Herbartian Lazarus,' Dr. Lasson should be written. Ueberweg frequently called him 'Lazarus' in his letters, as Dr. Lasson before his conversion to Christianity was called Lazarussohn.

[25] Lasson, Zum Andenken an Friedr. Ueberweg, Berl. 1871, S. 20 (reprinted from Bergmann's Philos. Monatsh., Bd. vii., H. 7).

nothing of the Metaphysic. Whether even then he had already begun to waver in his metaphysical and theological views I cannot say. At all events, the wavering followed very soon after, while, on the other hand, he remained undeviatingly firm to his fundamental views on Psychology.

This Psychology is a very paradoxical one, though it rests upon a substantial series of inferences, which we will here reproduce as briefly as possible.

The things of the world that appear to us are our ideas. They are extended; therefore our ideas are extended. The ideas are in the soul, therefore the soul too is extended, and, moreover, the extended soul is also material, in accordance with the notion of matter as an extended substance. We cannot have ideas outside the soul; therefore our soul reaches as far, and farther, as the entire sum of all the things that we perceive, including sun, moon, and stars. It is now very probable, in accordance with strong analogies, that these worlds are not produced in the soul without external causes, and that the occasioning causes (Ueberweg's 'Things-in-themselves') are not indeed the same as the phenomena, but at least very similar to them. The image of the camera obscura leads to the previously described hypothesis of a comparatively gigantic and perhaps inverted world, which mirrors itself in the corresponding world-pictures of individuals. If the soul, as a 'thing-in-itself,' is material, it must be supposed that things in themselves are so generally. We have then a material body with a material brain, and in some small portion of this brain lies the space in which our ideas are formed, and which, therefore, as a simple, structureless substance, embraces the world of our phenomenal things.[26]

We have already mentioned how Ueberweg believed that he could demonstrate with mathematical rigour that

[26] Comp. supra, p. 210; and my memoir of Ueberweg, S. 12 ff.

the world of things in themselves must be in space, and, like our phenomenal world, must have three dimensions. It still remains to exhibit his views of matter and its relation to consciousness.

Ueberweg did not admit atoms, but a continuous filling of space by matter, and he attributed to this matter in all its parts the capacity to be moved by mechanical forces, and then to attain 'internal states,' which are produced by the mechanical movements, but can also react upon them. The internal states of our brain-matter are our ideas; those of lower organisms and of inorganic matter he conceived to be in a similar relation to our consciousness, as Leibniz may have conceived the 'ideation' of the lower monads related to that of the higher; only that with him the dreamy, or even less than dreamy, ideation of inorganic matter was not, as with Leibniz, an imperfect representation of the universe, but it was something simple and elementary; bare sensation, or a weak analogon of sensation, from which with a more perfect organisation of matter there were formed also the more perfect psychical products.

Here now the point can be sharply indicated at which Ueberweg's views at that time separate from Materialism. If we suppose that the 'internal states' of matter are absolutely dependent upon external movement, then we have a decided Materialism, equal or even superior to the atomistic theory. It is not necessary to give up all reaction of the internal states upon the motion of matter, but the reaction must result according to the mechanical equivalents of the previous effects; in other words, the law of the persistence of force must be applied to organisms as well as to the inorganic world; the movement of all bodies must, with the intercalation of internal states, result just the same as if there were no internal states. But this view was at this time certainly not Ueberweg's view. He assumed that the law of the persistence of force is interrupted by psychical processes.[27]

What forced him to this assumption was, above all, his adhesion to the Aristotelian teleology. As soon as Ueberweg gave this up, his system must necessarily pass into Materialism. So long, that is to say, as there arise in organisms out of their idea forces which determine their form, this form cannot be exclusively a product of the physical and chemical forces. In human thought, moreover, the succession of ideas is entirely freed from the physiological basis. The thoughts are, indeed, in a certain sense properties of the brain-matter, but they follow purely logical laws, and can produce a final result, which is quite incapable of being explained by the mechanical conditions of molecular change. This hypothesis, too, is in so far teleological, as in Aristotle the end is at the same time the guiding thought to which all the other logical elements must be subservient. If man is to fulfil his destiny, the thought of his rational life-purpose must attain the mastery without any reference to matter.

Upon teleology he based also his assumption of a God consciously ruling the world; but it was just here, too, that he first began to waver. In the anonymously pub-

---

[27] Again, in a letter of 9th January 1863, Ueberweg tries to show that we have mere mechanism only when the internal states of matter remain unaltered and exert no influence on the direction of the motion. This, however, in the case of psychical processes, seems to him very improbable. Yet he will not dispute the 'scientific justification' of a hypothesis that seeks to explain all movements only in accordance with the law of the persistence of force, and therefore on purely mechanical principles. It is, in fact, time that this hypothesis should be proposed, and he who should carry it out in the best possible way would gain a permanent place in the history of psychology. Prof. Dilthey unjustly supposes in his essay, Zum Andenken an Friedr. Ueberweg (Pr. Jahrb., Bd. xxviii.), the following proposition to be Ueberweg's view: "And in fact it is at every point the same real fact which appears in a twofold shape, as a psychical fact and as a fact of motion." This view Ueberweg frequently distinguishes from his own as the *Spinozistic* view, on which the internal states are indeed excited by external motion and exert influence upon its direction, but are not identical with it.

lished 'Sendschreiben des Philalethes,' his primary effort is to save the mere *possibility* of the existence of God against the argument derived from the form of the universe; only in the second place does he try from teleology to establish its reality. The objection referred to might perhaps, to many people, have had but little weight, but for Ueberweg himself it was almost crushing. The analogy with the internal states of the animal world, and especially of man, must of necessity lead him to assume also for divine thought an analogous concentration of the elements of consciousness distributed in the universe, and for this he needed, just as Du Bois-Reymond demands, a world-brain and nervous system. The weaknesses, too, of the teleological system were not unknown to him, although he still steadfastly defended it. Thus he wrote to me in a letter of the 18th November 1860 as follows :—"I know very well that the purely subjective meaning of the notion of finality is often maintained; but even this is very doubtful. Whoever stands in this point on the side of Spinoza must show how the phenomena of organic life, which we can most conveniently explain by the aid of this notion, are at all conceivable without it. 'Causality,' at least, is commonly taken objectively; but the mere accumulation of atoms alone will certainly not help us out of the difficulty. Hegel's 'immanent finality,' 'creative idea,' however, holds an uncertain mean between atomism and theology, and points to something beyond itself. Kant's theory is inseparable from the general theory of Kantianism, which, as a whole, as it is presented in the three 'Criticks,' is not tenable, and with Fichte becomes only more wild. I am almost in the same strait in which Herbart found himself: on the one hand, the hypothesis is necessary; on the other, either impracticable (according to Herbart's metaphysic), or at least scarcely practicable (from Fechner's standpoint and mine). Help me out of this strait and I will be grateful to you; but for this it is not enough to prove to me to be improbable what I myself recognise to be in itself little probable, but you must open to me some other prospect which may appear to me to be even slightly plausible. I know of none."

In reference to the existence of God he writes in the same letter: "Do not suppose, however, that my only object, or even my principal object, has been to save a personal God, as it were, at any price. As to forms of worship, there is no doubt amongst intelligent people that they must contain much that is anthropomorphic, and that, therefore, has only poetical validity. But if anthropomorphism is to have a religious justification, then something must have reality that is anthropomorphically presented; and it is an important question for the philosopher and for all religious communities based upon philosophy, what it is that poetic representation thus embellishes. The unity of the universe? But in what form has this objective existence? Of the human mind? What is the relation of the universal to the individual mind? &c., &c." Farther on he observes that he had been more concerned (in the 'Sendschreiben des Philalethes') for the discussion itself than for its result. He wished, at the same time, to show to those who wish to be liberal, but who have a horror of 'Atheists,' that indeed irrefragable considerations make the assumption of a God plausible, but also that difficulties mountain-high pile themselves up against it, and therefore that room must be allowed for a free discussion.

This second stage of Ueberweg's development, that of hesitation between Materialism and teleology, I have made the basis of my account of his philosophy in the Memoir published at Berlin in 1871. I did not consider myself justified by the few traces occurring also in my correspondence with him of a decision in favour of Materialism to proclaim this as the last result of his philosophy; especially as the Ueberweg portrayed by me was as it were the official Ueberweg, the author of the so widely appreciated and admirable text-books, the many-sided, keenly criticising, and yet everywhere so tolerant thinker. Soon after the appearance of my little biography I received several letters from Dr. Czolbe, the well-known Materialist, who was Ueberweg's most intimate friend in Königsberg, and who till the last daily associated and philosophised with him. Czolbe disputes in these letters that Ueberweg had retained any weakness for the Aristotelian teleology; he disputes that Hartmann's 'Philosophy of the Unconscious' excited any sympathy in him, and maintains that Ueberweg had become a decided Darwinian. Then he goes on in a letter of the 17th August 1871: "He was in every way distinctly an Atheist and Materialist, though in his official position as professor he regarded it as his chief duty to impart to students the knowledge of the history of Philosophy and skill in Logic. He belongs essentially to your History of Materialism, and is to me a brilliant illustration of the absurdity of the opinion held by certain theologians and philosophers, that ignorance, stupidity, and vulgarity are the basis of Materialism. It would meet with Ueberweg's complete approval that you should number him among the Materialists."[28]

The voucher for this consists of four letters of Ueberweg to Czolbe,[29] who was then staying in Leipzig, dated the 4th January, 17th and 21st February, and 16th March 1869. In the letter of the 4th January Ueberweg writes, *i.a.*: "What happens in our brain would not, in my view, be possible, unless the same process, which here appears most powerfully or in the greatest concentration, in a like way, only in a much slighter degree, took place

[28] It is hardly necessary to say that I judge Ueberweg's character in this respect just as Czolbe does. I am convinced that if Ueberweg had foreseen his death (he hoped, according to Czolbe, to recover down to the last moment), he would have had no rest until his essential views in their full connexion had been written down for publication.

[29] These letters, with some others, were given to me by Czolbe to be made the fullest use of, and therefore have remained among my papers after Czolbe's death.

quite universally. A pair of mice and a meal-tub—you know that I have often used this illustration. If well fed, these creatures multiply, and with them sensations and feelings; the few of which the first pair were capable cannot simply have been diluted, for then their descendants must feel less strongly; therefore the sensations and feelings must be present in the meal, even though feebly and weakly, not concentrated as in the brain: the brain acts like a distilling apparatus. But if the sensations and feelings in the creatures' brain are excitable by means of vibrations, we cannot see how they could have acquired this property unless it belonged to them from the beginning, that is, in some slight degree already existed in the meal-form (that is, while they were still meal or in the meal)." Farther on in the same letter: "In a certain sense, you say with justice, I entirely give up matter. My view is just as much on the one hand 'crassly Materialistic' as it is on the other exclusively Spiritualistic. Everything that we call Matter consists of sensations and feelings (only not as the Berkeleians will have it, merely of our own), and is in this sense psychical; this psychical, however, is extended, therefore 'material,' for matter is, according to its definition, 'extended substance.'"

The three remaining letters contain Ueberweg's Cosmogony, which is distinguished by the addition of a peculiar feature to the views of Kant and Laplace. Ueberweg, that is to say, endeavours (starting from an expression of Kant's) to deduce as necessary that two neighbouring planets or entire solar systems, or even larger cosmical units, must in course of time necessarily come into collision. The result will always be the same: ignition and distribution of matter through space, upon which the play of forces makes a new world-formation follow. Life, on the gradual cooling of the planets, disappears, but the collision sooner or later restores the heat, and there is no reason why life, though we do not know how, should not reproduce itself from precisely the same causes from which it has been produced with us. The initial state of Kant and Laplace is therefore only relatively an initial state. It presupposes the collision of earlier worlds, and will infinitely often recur, as we have no reason to doubt the infinity of matter and space.

With this theory, as ingenious as it is capable of defence, Ueberweg went on to connect a further view, upon which he laid great stress, and which presupposes Darwinism. Through the successive collisions of worlds, according to Ueberweg, ever greater heavenly bodies must be formed; and if life is developed upon them, the struggle for existence must also assume ever greater dimensions, and thus ever more perfect forms must be produced.

If we combine these new features with the basis of Ueberweg's philosophy as above described, there results a consistent and self-contained Materialistic system. Whether it may in another sense be called at the same time 'spiritualistic,' may be doubted; for true spiritualism always excludes the strictly mechanical connexion of cause and effect in the universe. Ueberweg, too, very seldom dwells on this side of his philosophy, while in his letters he frequently, and by preference, describes himself as a Materialist. The idea that really consistent Materialism might be established on the basis of his theory, pleased him at a time when he had not fully decided on this change of attitude. Thus he quotes in a letter to me from Königsberg, on the 14th December 1862, the following epigram against Czolbe from the 'Walhalla deutscher Materialisten' (Münster, 1861):—

"Völlig ist Deine Vernunft noch immer zum Ziel nicht gekommen,
  Da die unendliche Welt nicht Dir den Schädel erfüllt."

"Fully is thy Understanding not yet arrived at perfection,
  Since this Infinite World cannot yet fill up thy skull."

On this he makes the following remark: "Had the poet known my treatise 'Zur Theorie der Richtung des Sehens,' perhaps he would have felt called upon to compose a distich against me, since, in fact, I draw that very consequence. I should like to know whether he would then have kept the title 'Materialism is unworkable;' I should agree with him if he wrote, 'Materialism does not work' (with Czolbe and the rest)."

That we must credit Ueberweg with the conception of a comprehensive and original Materialistic system can thus not be doubted. At the same time, we may doubt whether Czolbe is justified in categorically describing Ueberweg as 'Atheist and Materialist.' To begin with, we must ask whether, if Ueberweg had lived longer, he would not have surmounted this standpoint also, and again given a fresh turn to his definitive system. As it appears to me, he had never fully made up his mind; and even in his last letters there is betrayed a certain inclination, if more time and leisure permitted, to revise once more whole important sections of his theory of things. As regards Atheism, Czolbe, despite his intimate friendship with Ueberweg, is here scarcely a quite competent witness. As Czolbe himself was, with all his Materialism, zealous for the Papacy, there were in this sphere few points of contact between him and Ueberweg; accordingly there are in Ueberweg's letters to Czolbe no traces of a discussion of the religious question. Ueberweg's Materialism still does not entirely exclude the hypothesis of a world-soul, and he does not require more, in order to attain to the worship of a God, than the existence of a being fitted to be transformed into a God in an anthropomorphic conception of it.

If now we put generally this question of the Ethical consequences of Ueberweg's theory of things, it may first be pointed out that in his political views he was essentially conservative. Of course, he did not favour the poisonous plague of reactionism which maintained itself so long in Germany as 'conservative;' but he went with the great stream of moderate liberalism, though with decided personal predilection for monarchical institutions, and for the correctest possible solution of every problem on the basis of existing legal relations. This principle led him even to be a defender of legitimism, which seemed to him, as it were, to take the place of logic in politics. The right of ideas, as opposed to antiquated traditions, and, therefore, the right of revolution, he could not as a philosopher reject, but he wished to see it limited to the rarest and most undoubted cases of intrinsic necessity. The changes brought by the year 1866 caused him no uneasiness, as indeed he was, on the whole, uncommonly content with the course of events in Germany since 1358.

On the social question, he confessed, in the absence of special studies of his own, to an "instinctive sympathy with Schultze-Delitzsch." My books, written in quite a different sense, he read with attention; agreed with many ideas, especially in the purely theoretical discussions, but in all practical consequences returned as much as possible to the defence of the existing state of things.[30]

All the more radical was Ueberweg with regard to religious traditions. Even at the beginning of the second period of his philosophical development, he was occupied with the idea whether it was not his duty to join the Free Congregations; and he was only restrained by the reflexion, that he was fitted only for the professorial career, and that this exclusiveness of his natural disposition justified him in maintaining his position so far as he could do so without open insincerity.[31] Against positive Christianity he expressed himself all the more keenly in his letters, as he was oppressed by the consciousness that in his lectures and books he did not indeed say anything untrue, but also could not say the whole truth. In an unusually excited letter to me of the 29th December 1862, he says, amongst other things, that in order to secure

---

[30] Ueberweg set down his impressions on reading my 'Arbeiterfrage'—the first, still very defective, edition—in a letter of February 12, 1865.

[31] Ueberweg's letters to me of 18th November 1860 and 28th December 1861.

the recognition of the Reformation a bloody struggle of thirty years and more was necessary. He did not believe that communities resting upon a Materialistic theory would find recognition and security "until fanatical Materialists should have sprung up, ready, like the old Puritans, to set their lives at stake, and with joy to shoot down with grapeshot Catholic and Protestant Christians, as well as the old Rationalists, for thirty years long, if need be. Only afterwards, when the victory, the bloody victory is won, only then will it be a joyous and beautiful task again to make way for the principles of kindness and humanity. A purely religious war will not come, any more than the wars of Constantine and the Thirty Years' war were so; but I am quite convinced that, in no very distant future, the religious element and the antagonistic theories of the world will be very intimately complicated with political antagonisms and wars." [32]

Three years later, at a time when the theory of things of his third period had doubtless become fixed with Ueberweg, he wrote (in a letter to me of 31st December 1865) as to the religious question, for which he was more concerned than for the social question, as follows:—"A religion whose system of dogma shall contain nothing scientifically false I hold indeed (1) as possible, (2) as a necessity. But, my dear friend, 'in the name of God,' do not treat this proposition as equivalent to the other proposition, that religion must pass into science. Science and poesy must appear side by side in a pure religion, clearly separated and yet intimately united. This separation and this co-operation must take the place of the original unity, which becomes intolerable, and leads to the horrible dilemma of narrowness or of servile hypocrisy, according as the scientific consciousness of the age has got beyond it. . . . I do not hold it to be essential to

---

[32] I cannot even now abandon the psychological explanation of this excited letter which I have attempted at S. 22 of my Memoir. At the same time I must, on the other hand, now attribute greater importance to his hard judgment of Christianity than as that of a momentary discontent.

religion that we should continue in a state of childishness. No other 'dogmatics,' no other 'catechism,' than natural and historical science, conveyed comprehensively so as to direct the attention to the whole, to the order of the universe, and thus to complete the education of the school. But this teaching belongs as little to the pulpit as ecclesiastical dogmatics, as such, to Christian pulpits; the doctrine forms only the theoretical basis for the sermon, only the point of connexion for song and organ, or, if you will, pictures and ceremonies also. But with the clearest separation there must also exist an intimate relation." From the new theory he tries to show further there must also result a new religious Art.

Here, then, we have still the prospect of a worship quite analogous to that of Christianity. This evolution theory is somewhat differently put in a letter of the 28th April 1869. Here Ueberweg observes that the three functions, knowledge, feeling, and willing, only become more definitely separated with the progress of culture, and then appear Science, Art, and Morality, the Theoretical, the Æsthetic, and the Ethical, side by side. "Originally there exists a germinal interfusion (or, to speak in Schelling's language, an 'indifference') of them, and this primitive interfusion is essentially also the stage of religion. . . . The resolution of what is united in religion into these three forms (not the mere apprehension of religious ideas as æsthetic creations) would be the progress which is needed, agreeably to Goethe's saying—

> "Wer Wissenschaft und Kunst besitzt
> Der hat Religion;
> Wer diese beiden nicht besitzt
> Der habe Religion!"

> "He who Science has and Art,
> He has Religion too;
> Let him who in These has no part
> Make his Religion do!"

Here we may, in fact, ask whether Ueberweg, with regard

to religion, has not completely attained to the same standpoint as Strauss, whose views we shall presently consider.

An unmistakable difficulty of this evolution theory is that the theoretical, æsthetical, and ethical elements, which are supposed to develop from the 'germinal interfusion,' at the same time undergo a qualitative change, and become almost the opposite of what was contained in the religious germ. As to the theoretical element, it is quite needless to say anything more; but even the æsthetical and ethical requirements, which Ueberweg makes of the religion of the future, deviate very widely from Christian principles. I often tried to show that Christianity, in the first place, has still powerful roots in the life of the people, and in the next place is in some of its main features from psychological and social grounds quite irreplaceable. The man of philosophic culture who would really help the people forward must also remain in intimate union with them, and be capable of understanding how their hearts beat. But for this a religious and philosophical mediation is necessary, such as Kant and Hegel prepared; an art of translating religious forms into philosophical ideas. If this is genuine, then the emotional facts of worship must be essentially the same with the philosopher as with the believer. For the philosopher, therefore, to leave the Church is not only not a duty, but, on the contrary, he must be strongly urged not to do so, because thus an element in its nature tending to encourage progress would be withdrawn from the life of the people, and the masses would be helplessly abandoned to the spiritual domination of blind fanatics.

This 'isomorphism' of the emotional processes in the philosopher and naïve believer, Ueberweg would only admit as very slightly justified; no doubt, principally because he rejected in principle the emotional processes demanded by Christianity. As regards the æsthetical side of religious life, we were, of course, agreed that the religion of the future must be essentially a religion of reconciliation and of joy, with a pronounced tendency towards the perfection of this present life, which Christianity gives up. As a result of this principle, Ueberweg rejected all the Christian poetry of pain and sorrow, together with all the heart-stirring melodies that belong to it, and with the sublime architecture of the Middle Ages, which was so dear to me. He reproached me with wishing to build the new Temple of Humanity in the old Gothic style; he wanted a new and cheerful order of architecture. I pointed out that, after all, we could not do away with social misery and the woes of individuals; that a deep meaning lies in the guilt of all, even the most righteous, and that an inconsiderate appeal to the will of the individual involves deep untruth and injustice. Accordingly I demanded, besides the gay temple of the religion of the future, at least my Gothic chapel for troubled souls, and in the national worship certain festivals, when even the happy should learn to plunge down into the depths of misery, and find himself with the unhappy, and even with the wicked, in a common need of salvation. In a word, if in our present Christianity sorrow and tribulation form the rule, cheerfulness and the joy of victory the exception, I would indeed invert this relation, but not ignore the dark shadow which, after all, rests upon our life.

I still remember very distinctly that one day I was saying that we must take over our best church hymns into the new worship, as the Psalms had been adopted into Christian worship. Ueberweg asked me what hymn I would propose to take from the Protestant hymn-book; and in full consciousness of our difference, I answered immediately, "O bleeding Head, so wounded!" Ueberweg turned away, and gave up any hope of agreeing with me as to the religious poetry of the Church of the future.

Almost as absolutely opposed was Ueberweg to the Christian ethics. He recognised, indeed, the principle of love, and was ready to assign to it a permanent value; but love as *grace* must be all the more stoutly combated. It is characteristic that my book on the 'Arbeiterfrage' was the occasion of a sharp expression of his views on this matter (in a letter of 12th February 1865). He expects important social improvements, not from the carrying out, but, on the contrary, from the transformation, of Christian principles. "The rich man and poor Lazarus, giving to the poor, earthly resignation and the vengeance beyond the grave which the God who loves the poor wreaks on the privileged ones by the everlasting torments of hell, these are the fundamental ideas of the founder of the kingdom of Messiah, and Zacchæus knew very well what Jesus liked when he promised him to give away the half of his possessions. This is ethical dualism in the most decided shape. Mammon is unjust, as is his nature: not to serve Mammon, to look for alms from God and man, that is right; and if wicked men are too hard-hearted to give (or if they expect you to work rather than beg), there is no idea of a positive dignity of labour, but then misery is to be endured and forgotten in the opium-intoxication of ideas of the blessedness of the Messiah's kingdom, or of a life beyond this. Paul was too cultivated and too much accustomed to labour to have such crude ideas as Jesus of labour and mendicity, but with him the pitiable begging principle of Christianity struck inwards, where its effects were almost more mischievous; the *grace* of God took the place of self-conscious ethical action, the principle of revelation that of the labour of inquiry. For the first subjugation of barbarians the intellectual opium-intoxication might be useful; now its results are crippling and depressing." In the same sense he expressed himself in a letter of 29th June 1869, with reference to the criticism of the Christian morality in Valliss's [33] 'Doctrine of Human

---

[33] Die Lehre von den Menschenpflichten in ihrem Verhältniss zur christlichen Sittenlehre. Aus den hinterlassenen Papieren eines Philosophen herausgegeben von Rud. Valliss: Winterthur, 1868. .

Duties:' "When the writer points to the defects of the Christian ethics, especially to the depreciation of labour (in the widest sense of the term), as compared with the favour shown to moral show-pieces, such as 'Love of our enemies' (coupled with the condemnation of opponents and of those who are the objects of envy to eternal torments in hell), to the sacrifice of independence and personal dignity in favour of servile subjection to the master, who is stamped as the Messiah, as the only-begotten Son of God, he has my full sympathy."

From this it will be obvious that Ueberweg put ethics as a science on a purely naturalistic and anthropological basis. The brief outlines of a system of ethics which Rudolph Reicke published from Ueberweg's papers (Königsberg, 1872), so far, however, approximate to the systems which rest on the assumption of an *a priori* principle of morality, inasmuch as Ueberweg bases his ethics on the *differences of value* between the various psychical functions. He divides them into two principal classes. "The difference between that which is useful and hurtful is shown by pleasure and pain; the difference between higher and lower functions by feelings of self-respect and shame." But if there is such an original feeling of the difference between lower and higher functions, then there is a natural conscience, and the inquiry will suggest itself, whether a connexion cannot be shown between the subjective basis of this conscience and an objective principle.

While Ueberweg was snatched away by death from amidst his labours and projects, David Friedrich Strauss had the good fortune to live out his life. By his own testimony in his last book he has also spoken the last word that he had to say to the world. But this last word is an adhesion to a Materialistic view of the world. He remarks, indeed, appealing to Schopenhauer and the author of the 'History of Materialism,' that Materialism and Idealism pass into each other, and at bottom form only a common opposition to Dualism; but it is impossible to treat this relation as though it were indifferent from which point we start, or as though Materialism and Idealism were interchangeable at will. In truth, Materialism is but the first, the most obvious, but also the lowest stage in our philosophy; once passed over into Idealism, as a speculative system it entirely loses its validity. The Idealist can, and must in fact, in natural science everywhere apply the same conceptions and methods as the Materialist; but what to the latter is definitive truth is to the Idealist only the necessary result of our organisation. Nor is it enough merely to admit this. As soon as the idea comes to the front that this result of our organisation is the only thing about which we need concern ourselves, the standpoint still remains essentially Materialistic, unless we choose to invent a special name for this position, which, as is well known, is that recently taken up by Büchner. Genuine Idealism will always set up beside the phenomenal world also an ideal world, and will concede to it, even when it is regarded as a product of the brain, all those rights which follow from its relations to the needs of our intellectual life. It will therefore, too, always love to refer to those points in which is seen the impossibility of a Materialistic explanation of the whole essentiality of things. In Strauss we do not find either the positive or the critical principle of Idealism anywhere suggested, and the very way in which he speaks of Du Bois-Reymond's limits of knowledge shows clearly how decided is his Materialistic position.[34] With striking acuteness Strauss singles out all those points which show that Du Bois-Reymond, in thinking of the 'limits' of the knowledge of nature, cannot be proposing to throw a doubt on what is its very essence, namely, the consistent mechanical conception of the universe, or to allow antiquated dogmas to take up

[34] Comp. Postscript to the new ed. of D. Alte u. d. Neue Glaube, Bonn, 1873, S. 22 f., E.T., ii. 241.

their abode behind these limits. The true core, however, of the problem of the theory of knowledge Strauss discusses almost without understanding it, and as though it were matter of indifference. The absolute gulf between the motion of cerebral atoms and sensation is with Strauss, to say nothing of his doubting it, no reason for giving up his case; as soon, at least, as the causal connexion between the two sets of phenomena is made probable.[35] But this is precisely the standpoint of Materialism, which postpones the insoluble problem and holds fast to the closed circle of the causal law, in order from here to open its polemic against religion.

As with Ueberweg the collapse of his Aristotelian teleology, so with Strauss the deliverance from the fetters of the Hegelian philosophy, must almost necessarily lead to Materialism; for no modern philosophy had so thoroughly concealed the salient point of philosophical criticism and overgrown it with its fantastic notions, as Hegel had done with his doctrine of the identity of thought and existence. The whole mind of a true Hegelian was, as it were, schooled and exercised to pass over unsuspectingly the point where Materialism and Idealism separate. In Strauss this direction, or at least the beginning of it, set in soon after his great theological labours; it might, however, be difficult, and will be one of the functions of his biographer, which we may not here attempt, to exhibit this process in all its stadia.[36] His Materialistic testament, the treatise 'Der Alte und der Neue Glaube,' Leipzig, 1872, has all the appearance of a fruit ripened through many years, and there can be no question of any inclination of the writer to go on beyond this standpoint again.

[35] L.c., S. 28 f., E.T., p. 247: "Whether the master's assertion is really destined to be final, time, after all, only can decide; happily I can accept it meanwhile without therefore giving up my case for lost." Yet this is a matter with which the authority of no master has anything to do, and on which the judgment of every man who understands the question is equally valid.

[36] Meantime we have some points of support in Zeller's admirable book, 'David Friedrich Strauss in s. Leben u. s. Schriften geschildert,' Bonn, 1874. That this does not pretend to be a complete biography is set forth by the author himself, S. iv.

The little book, which made so great a sensation and called up so many antagonists, contains all that we need for our purpose. It is a result of his theological tendency that two chapters are prefixed in which the writer seeks to answer the pregnant questions, Are we still Christians? and, Have we still a Religion? Then follows the chapter, What is our Conception of the Universe? in which the author first makes his Materialistic confession of faith. The last chapter, What is our Rule of Life? leads us into the sphere of ethics, and gives us abundant opportunity to learn the writer's views on the state and society. We deal first with the two latter chapters, and will afterwards take a glance at the contents of the earlier ones.

The answer to the question, What is our Conception of the World? is a masterpiece as a concise and lively sketch of a complete cosmology. Without much polemic or unnecessary digression, Strauss allows his system to direct itself through the natural order of the exposition. Beginning from sense-impressions, he comes with swift but sure steps to our conception of the universe, whose infinity he expressly asserts. In his cosmogony he rests almost entirely upon Kant, having careful regard to the present state of the natural sciences. Like Ueberweg, he supposes that the original dispersion of matter must be regarded merely as the result of the collapse of earlier planetary systems. But while Ueberweg infers from this process, in connexion with Darwinism, a progress of the world to ever greater perfection, Strauss rather lays stress upon the eternity and essential uniformity of the infinite whole. In the universe, in its absolute sense, there are planetary systems continually cooling and perishing, and just as continually other systems forming themselves anew from the collapse. Life is eternal. If it disappears here, it is beginning there, and again at other points is in the full vigour of its strength. This everlasting process can, as Kant believed, as little have had a beginning as it can have an end; and thus vanishes, too, any ground for assuming a Creator.

In the able discussion of the question of the inhabitability of other heavenly bodies which there follows, the limits, according to the conditions of nature known to us, should perhaps be drawn somewhat more strictly; but here too there are no serious objections to be taken. Keeping closely to the views now prevailing among specialists, Strauss briefly describes the epochs of the formation of the world, in order to dwell at greater length on the question of the origin and development of organic creatures, including man. Here Strauss everywhere follows the views of Darwin and the leading German Darwinians, and almost everywhere, where he had to choose between different ways, strikes with sure tact the most probable and natural. The whole section gives us the impression of a serious and appreciative study of these questions, of which only the final result of a careful and comprehensive examination is presented in an easy and agreeable form to the reader. Nowhere, therefore, do the polemics of his numerous opponents make a weaker impression than when they strive to convict Strauss of all kinds of scientific errors, and especially to represent his Darwinism as an unreflecting acceptance of scientific dogmas. Theological and philosophical opponents drag together out of the controversies of men of science material of the most doubtful kind in order to demolish Strauss with it, while every accurate student of this province easily gains the conviction that Strauss was quite familiar with these objections, but that, properly appreciating his object and the space that he could devote to these things, he saw no reason to mention and refute them.

Although, therefore, in details Strauss is almost everywhere right as against his opponents, yet it is only *correct Materialism* that he expounds, and all the weaknesses and inadequacies of this theory of things affect him in the same way as they affect modern Materialism generally. We shall find some examples of this farther on, and turn now to his ethical and political views.

Here we have quite another picture. Strauss moves on

the ground of scientific studies and penetrating reflexion only so far as he is concerned to obtain a general Naturalistic foundation of ethic, and even here hardly one definite principle is rigidly carried out. As soon, however, as he comes to political and social arrangements, we find a strong predominance of subjective impressions and views with little deep foundation.

Quite consistently Strauss begins by deducing the fundamental virtues from sociality and the needs of an ordered social life, and then adds the principle of sympathy. This seems to him, however, not sufficiently to explain the sphere of morality, and he springs from the Naturalistic principles to an Idealistic principle: in moral action man directs himself by the idea of species. How man comes to the idea of his species, how, further, he attains to a conception of the 'destiny' of humanity, is not examined; the succeeding expositions aim rather to develop objectively what man is and in what he finds his destiny. From this our duties are then deduced.

It is not worth while to follow this deduction in detail, but the results are of interest. Strauss shows himself everywhere more conservative than Ueberweg, and while the latter at least shows that he appreciates divergent views, Strauss is in this field as peremptory and dogmatic as he is short-sighted and superficial. It requires all the narrowness of German Philistine life of olden days to explain in some measure how a man of such acuteness could remain entangled in these views.

Strauss directs his sharpest attack against Socialism, and this with him, as with Ueberweg, is closely connected with his high appreciation of modern Industrialism, and with his severe condemnation of the hostility to labour shown in Christianity. Also Strauss mentions with sharp censure the hell-torments which befall the rich man, and the commandment to the wealthy young man to sell his goods and give the produce to the poor. "Christianity, in common with Buddhism, teaches a thorough cult of poverty and mendicity. The mendicant monks of the Middle Ages, as well as the still flourishing mendicancy at Rome, are genuinely Christian institutions, which have only been restricted in Protestant countries by a culture proceeding from quite another source." Strauss adopts Buckle's eulogy of wealth, industrial activity, and the love of money, and adds the following remark: "It does not therefore follow that the love of acquisition should not, like every other impulse, be kept within reasonable bounds and subordinated to higher aims; but in the teaching of Jesus it is ignored from the very first, and its effectiveness in promoting culture and humanitarian tendencies is misunderstood, Christianity in this respect manifesting itself as a principle directly antagonistic to civilization. It only prolongs its existence among the enlightened and commercial nations of our time by the emendations which a cultivated but profane reason has made in it, this being at the same time so magnanimous as to impute them not to itself but to Christianity, to the spirit of which they are, on the contrary, entirely opposed."[37]

It need hardly be said that Strauss also rejects the principle of self-mortification, the fanatical asceticism, the contempt of the world, and other characteristic features of Christianity. His ethic, so far as we can gather it from his restless polemic against everything Christian, rests entirely on the idea that it is the destiny of man to order himself suitably in this world by labour and social order, and to strive by means of art and science to ennoble his existence, and to attain to more delicate intellectual enjoyments. The question, Are we still Christians? he answers then quite unreservedly, No; the question, however, Have we still religion? with a conditional Yes. It depends, that is to say, upon whether our feeling of dependence as regards the universe and its laws is to be regarded as religion or not. A cult we shall no longer build upon this feeling, but it still has a moral effect, and

[37] D. Alte u. d. Neue Glaube, 2 Aufl., S. 63, 64; E.T., i. 71-73.

is connected with a certain piety. We feel ourselves hurt if this piety is contemned, as it is, for instance, by Schopenhauer's pessimism. The individual cannot lift himself above the universe; the universe, so full of law, and life, and reason, is our highest idea; and every genuine philosophy is therefore necessarily optimistic.[38]

Of the religious worship of the Free Communities Strauss judges unfavourably; they proceed consistently enough indeed in giving up dogmatic tradition, and taking their stand on the ground of natural science and history, but this is no basis for a religious society. "I have attended several services of the Free Communities, and found them terribly dry and unedifying. I quite thirsted for an allusion to the Biblical legend or the Christian calendar, in order to get at least something for the heart and imagination, but the cordial was not forthcoming. No; this is not the way either. After the edifice of the Church has been demolished, to go and give a homily on the bare, pitifully levelled site, is dismal to a degree that makes one shudder." Strauss himself, then, would not enter into a 'Church of Reason' if the state should liberally endow it with all the rights of the old Church. He and his fellows can do without any Church. They edify themselves by keeping their minds open for all the higher interests of humanity, above all, for national life. They seek to sustain their national feeling by historical studies, and at the same time to increase their knowledge of nature; "and finally, in the writings of our great poets, in the performances of the works of our great musicians, we find a stimulus for the intellect and heart, for humour and imagination, which leaves nothing to be desired. 'Thus then we live, so find our happiness.'"

And we can do so. Our means allow it; for the 'we'

---

[38] L. c., S. 141-147, E.T., i. 161-168. It is worth while to remark here the shocking fallacy by which Strauss tries to refute pessimism (S. 145): If the world is bad, then the thought of the pessimist is bad also; if this is bad, then it follows that the world is good!

in whose name Strauss speaks are, according to his own enumeration, "not exclusively scholars or artists, but civil servants and military men, business men and landed proprietors." The people are only very lightly to be relied on. He has, moreover, our national poets, if for a time he cannot go to concerts. Lessing's 'Nathan' and Goethe's 'Hermann and Dorothea' also contain 'saving truths,' are, moreover, easier to understand than the Bible, which not even many theologians understand. Of the 'saving truths' which the people through tradition, from father to son, read into the Bible, and of the understanding of them which people suppose that they have, nothing further is said. They are errors, and therefore without justification for their existence; even though in these very traditional ideas there lies the highest value that the Bible can have for the woe-begone heart of the poor and feeble. When the schools waste less time over Jewish history, then our great poets will have a better chance of being generally understood. But from whence, in our present excellent political state, the impulse is to come for so eventful a change, is not discussed. Nor is it, in fact, necessary; for the proper consequence of this whole standpoint is at bottom this: the people may remain where they happen to be, thanks to the sacred laws of the universe, if only 'we,' the cultured and propertied, can at last free ourselves from the burden of appearing and being called Christians, though we are no longer so.

A detailed criticism of this standpoint [39] will hardly be necessary after what has been already said; besides, our next and final chapter will once more clearly exhibit our

---

[39] It may here be just mentioned in passing that even the Straussian minimum of religion still has its unproved dogmas and its principles which on ethical grounds go beyond reality. Unproved and unprovable especially is the infinity of the world. Optimism, moreover, is a pious error, for this, as well as its opposite, Pessimism, is only a product of human ideology. The world of reality is in itself neither good nor bad.

attitude towards these questions. It is, however, no mere accident that two so highly gifted and noble men, and yet two such entirely different natures as Strauss and Ueberweg, combine with their Materialism the justification of modern Industrialism, and that for the religion of the wretched and oppressed they substitute a religion of the privileged aristocracy, which refuses all churchly community with the great masses. A current of Materialism runs through our modern civilisation, which carries away with it every one who has not somewhere found "firmer anchorage." Philosophers and economists, statesmen and business men, agree in praising the present and its achievements. With the praise of the present is combined the cult of actuality. The ideal has no quotation on our exchanges; what cannot scientifically and historically show its legitimacy is condemned to perish, even though a thousand joys and refreshments for the people depend upon it, for which we no longer care.

In his 'Postscript as Preface,' Strauss points out that by his combination of Materialism with conservative political principles he had lost the favour of all parties. In this he forgot only his own army, the 'we' in whose name he speaks. After reading this passage in his postscript, I laid the book down a moment, and turned over the leaves of an illustrated paper that happened to lie upon the table. My first glance fell on the caricature of a 'Communist;' my second on a picture of Feuerbach's study, with a biographical sketch of Feuerbach, which knew no end to his praises. The editors of these papers know very well what the public likes, and it seems very much as if their public is very decidedly related to the society in whose name Strauss has spoken his confession.

But the Socialists also favour Materialism. This is by no means inconsistent with the remark that we have made. Socialists and worshippers of existing social conditions agree in this, that they ·reject the reference of religion to the future, and find the happiness of humanity in this present life. Besides, the leaders of the Socialists, who give the cue in this respect, are for the most part men of education, who, at all events in Germany, have been trained in Feuerbach's ideas. The great mass of their followers are tolerably indifferent in this respect. Driven by the consciousness of their necessities, they throw themselves into the arms of him who promises them a decided improvement, or even a decided struggle and prospect of revenge, whether in other respects he favours Papal infallibility or Atheism. For many years Socialism has learnt to hate the Church as the partner of the State; but as soon as serious difference occurs between the Church and the State, a portion of the Socialists—very imprudently but very naturally—begin to coquette with the Church. Revolution is with the extreme leaders of this party their only aim, and it is in the nature of circumstances that only extreme leaders are possible, because only extreme tendencies move the masses. Should Socialism ever attain this immediate but purely negative aim, and then, amidst general confusion, have to give shape to its ideas, the cool sway of abstract understanding will hardly maintain its predominance. If it comes to the dissolution of our present civilisation, it will hardly be that any existing Church, and still less Materialism, will succeed to the inheritance, but from some unsuspected corner will emerge some utter absurdity, like the Book of Mormon or Spiritualism, with which the justified ideas of the epoch will fuse themselves, to found a new centre of universal thought, to last perhaps for thousands of years.

There is but one means to meet the alternative of this revolution or of a dim stagnation; but this means does not consist, as Strauss thinks, in the cannon which are to be directed against Socialists and Democrats, but solely and entirely in the timely surmounting of Materialism, and in the healing of the breach in our popular life which is produced by the separation of the educated from the people and its spiritual needs. *Ideas* and *sacrifices* may yet save our civilisation, and transform the path that leads through desolating revolution into a path of beneficent reforms.

CHAPTER IV.

THE STANDPOINT OF THE IDEAL.

MATERIALISM is the first, the lowest, but also comparatively the firmest stage in philosophy. Starting immediately from natural knowledge, it becomes a system by looking beyond the limits of this knowledge. The necessity that rules in the sphere of the natural sciences lends to the system which is most immediately based upon them a considerable degree of the uniformity and certainty of its separate parts. A reflexion of this certainty and necessity falls also upon the system as such, but this reflexion is deceptive. Precisely what makes Materialism a system, the fundamental hypothesis which elevates the particular branches of natural knowledge by a common bond into a whole, is not only its most uncertain part, but is, in fact, untenable before a deeper-going criticism. But exactly the same relation is repeated in the particular sciences upon which Materialism is based, and therefore, too, in all the separate parts of the system. The certainty of these parts is, rightly considered, nothing but the certainty of the facts of the science, and this is always greatest for the immediately given particular. The unity which makes the facts into a science and the sciences into a system is a product of free synthesis, and springs therefore from the same source as the creation of the ideal. While, however, this deals quite freely with the materials, synthesis in the province of science has only the freedom of its origin from the speculative mind of man. It is, on the other hand, tied to the task of establishing the utmost possible harmony between the necessary factors of knowledge, which are independent of our will. As the artisan, in the case of an invention, is tied to its purpose, while at the same time the idea of it springs freely from his mind, so every true scientific induction is at once the accomplishment of a given task and a product of the speculative mind.

Materialism more than any other system keeps to reality, *i.e.*, to the sum total of the necessary phenomena given to us by the compulsion of sense. But a reality such as man imagines to himself, and as he yearns after when this imagination is dispelled, an existence absolutely fixed and independent of us while it is yet known by us—such a reality does not exist and cannot exist, because the synthetic creative factor of our knowledge extends, in fact, into the very first sense-impressions and even into the elements of logic.[40] The world is not only *idea*, but also our *idea*; a product of the organisation of the *species* in the universal and necessary characteristics of all experience; of the *individual* in the synthesis that deals freely with the object. We may also say that the reality is the phenomenon for the species, while the delusive appearance, on the contrary, is a phenomenon for the individual, which only becomes an error by reality, *i.e.*, existence for the species, being ascribed to it.

But the task of producing harmony among phenomena and of linking the manifold that is given to us into unity belongs not merely to the synthetic factors of experience,

[40] That to the principle $A = A$ strictly understood reality nowhere corresponds, A. Spir has recently energetically insisted on and made it the basis of a philosophical system of his own. All the difficulties involved in this fact may, however, be much more easily disposed of in another way. The principle $A = A$ is indeed the basis of all knowledge, yet is not itself knowledge, but an act of the mind, an act of primitive synthesis by which there is posited as the necessary starting-point of all thinking an equality or a persistence which are found in nature only relatively and approximately, but never absolutely and completely. The principle $A = A$ accordingly indicates at the very threshold of logic the relativity and ideality of all our knowledge.

but also to those of speculation. Here, however, the connecting organisation of the species leaves us in the lurch: the individual speculates in his own fashion, and the product of this speculation acquires importance for the species, or rather for the nation and contemporaries, only in so far as the individual creating it is endowed with rich and normal talents and is typical in his modes of thought, while by his intellectual energy he is called to be a leader.

The conceptional poesy of speculation is, however, not even so completely free; it still strives, like empirical research, after a unitary exhibition of data in their connexion, but it lacks the guiding compulsion of the principles of experience. Only in poesy, in the narrower sense of the word, in poetry, is the ground of reality consciously abandoned. In speculation form has the preponderance over matter; in poetry it is completely dominant. The poet creates in the free play of his spirit a world to his own liking, in order to impress more vividly upon the easily manageable material a form which has its own intrinsic value and its importance independently of the problems of knowledge.

From the lowest stages of synthesis, in which the individual still appears completely bound by the characteristics of the species, up to its creative dominance in poetry, the essence of this act is always directed to the production of unity, of harmony, of perfect form. The same principle which rules absolutely in the sphere of the beautiful, in art and poetry, appears in the sphere of conduct as the true ethical norm which underlies all the other principles of morality, and in the sphere of knowledge as the shaping, form-giving factor in our picture of the world.

Although, therefore, the very picture of the world which the senses give us is involuntarily formed upon the ideal within us, yet the whole world of reality, as compared with the free creations of art, appears inharmonious and full of perversities. Here lies the source of all Optimism and

Pessimism. Without comparison we should not be able to form a judgment as to the quality of the world. But when from some elevated point we regard a landscape our whole nature is attuned to ascribe to it beauty and perfection. We must first destroy the powerful unity of this picture by analysis, in order to remember that in those huts, peacefully resting on the mountain slope, there dwell careworn men; that behind that little sheltered window perhaps some sufferer is enduring the most terrible torments; that beneath the murmuring summits of the distant forest birds of prey are rending their quivering prey; that in the silvery waves of the river a thousand tiny creatures, scarcely born to life, are finding a cruel death. To our sweeping glance the withered branches of the trees, the blighted cornfields, the sun-scorched meadows, are only shadows in a picture which delights our eye and cheers our heart.

Thus the world appears to the optimistic philosopher. He praises the harmony which he himself has introduced into it. As compared with him, the Pessimist a thousand times is right; and yet there could be no Pessimism at all without the natural ideal of the world which we carry within us. It is only contrast with this that makes reality bad.

The more freely synthesis exerts its function, the more æsthetic becomes the image of the world, the more ethical is its reaction upon our activity in the world. Not only poetry, but speculation too, however it may appear to be directed to knowledge only, has essentially æsthetic, and, through the attractive force of the beautiful, also ethical intent. In this sense we might indeed say, with Strauss, that every genuine philosophy is necessarily optimistic. But philosophy is more than mere imaginative speculation; it embraces also logic, criticism, the theory of knowledge.

We may call those functions of the senses and of the combining intelligence, which produce reality in us, individually low as compared with the lofty flight of the spirit in freely creative art; but as a whole, and in their combination, they may not be subordinated to any other mental activity. Little as our reality may be a reality after our own hearts, it is nevertheless the firm basis of our whole intellectual existence. The individual grows up from the soil of the species, and general and necessary knowledge forms the only safe basis for the elevation of the individual to an æsthetic apprehension of the world. If this basis is disregarded, speculation too can no longer be typical, no longer be full of significance; it loses itself in fantasies, in subjective caprice and puerile frivolity. But, above all, is the most genuine possible conception of reality the whole basis of daily life, the necessary condition of human intercourse. The community of the species in knowledge is at the same time the law of all interchange of ideas. But it is even more than this: it is also the only way to the mastery of nature and its forces.

However much the modifying influence of the psychical synthesis reaches down to our most elementary ideas of things, of an object, yet we have the conviction that something lies at the bottom of these ideas and of the world arising from them that does not spring from ourselves. This conviction rests essentially upon the fact that we discover between things not merely a *connexion*, which might indeed be just the plan upon which we have conceived them, but also a *co-operation*, which goes on irrespective of our thought, and which acts upon us ourselves and subjects us to its laws. This strange element, this 'non-ego,' of course only becomes again 'object' for our thought by being conceived by each individual in the universal and necessary forms of knowledge of the species; yet it does not therefore consist merely of these forms of knowledge. We have before us in the laws of nature not merely laws of our knowledge, but also evidences of *something else*, of a power that now compels us and now is dominated by us. In our commerce with this power we are exclusively dependent upon experience and upon reality, and no speculation has ever found the means of penetrating by the magic of pure thought into the world of things.

The method, however, which leads equally to the knowledge and to the mastery of nature, demands nothing less than a continual disintegration of the synthetical forms under which the world appears to us, so as to eliminate every subjective element. Withal indeed the new knowledge that better harmonised with the facts could in its turn only attain to form and stability by means of synthesis; but science found itself driven to simpler and ever simpler views, until at last it had to halt at the principles of the mechanical theory of the world.

Every falsification of reality attacks the bases of our spiritual existence. As opposed to metaphysical imaginations, which make pretensions to penetrate into the essence of nature and to determine from pure notions what only experience can teach us, Materialism as a counterpoise is therefore a real benefit. Moreover, all philosophemes which tend to regard reality alone must necessarily gravitate towards Materialism. On the other hand, Materialism lacks relations to the highest functions of the free human spirit. It is, apart from its theoretical inadequacy, unstimulating, barren for science and art, indifferent or inclined to egoism in the relations of man to man. It can hardly close the circle of its system without borrowing from Idealism.

If we observe how Strauss decks out his universe that he may be able to adore it, the thought presents itself that in truth he is not so very far removed from Deism. It seems almost a matter of taste whether we adore the masculine 'God,' the feminine 'Nature,' or the neuter 'All.' The sentiments are the same, and even the mode in which we conceive the object of these sentiments offers no essential difference. In theory, indeed, 'God' is no longer personal; and in the rapt elevation of the soul even the 'All' is treated as a person.

Natural science cannot lead to this. All natural science is analytical and clings to the particular. The particular discovery delights us; method compels our admiration, and by the continual succession of discoveries our glance is perhaps conducted to an infinite perspective of ever more perfect insight. Yet with this we are already quitting the ground of strict science. For the universe, as mere natural science enables us to comprehend it, we can as little feel enthusiasm as for an 'Iliad' spelt out letter by letter. But if we embrace the whole as a unity, then in the act of synthesis we bring our own nature into the object, just as we shape the landscape that we gaze at into harmony, however much disharmony in particulars may be concealed by it. All comprehension follows æsthetic principles, and every step towards the whole is a step towards the Ideal.

Pessimism, which likewise clings to the whole, is a product of reflexion. The thousand contrarieties of life, the cold cruelty of nature, the pains and imperfections of all creatures, are collected in their individual features, and the sum of these observations is contrasted with the ideal picture of Optimism as a terrible indictment of the universe. A complete picture of the universe, however, is not reached in this way. Only the Optimist picture of the world is destroyed, and this involves a great service, if Optimism is inclined to become dogmatic and to pass itself as the representative of truth and reality. All those beautiful ideas of the individual disharmony which is resolved into the harmony of the great whole, of higher, divine contemplation of the world, in which all riddles are solved and all difficulties disappear, are successfully destroyed by Pessimism; but this destruction affects the dogma only, not the ideal. It cannot do away with the fact that our mind is so constituted as ever anew to produce within itself a harmonious picture of the world; that here as everywhere it places its ideal beside and above the reality, and recreates itself from the struggles and necessities of life by rising in thought to a world of all perfections.

This ideal effort of the human spirit acquires now fresh strength through the knowledge, that our reality also is no absolute reality, but appearance; for the individual conclusive and corrective of his casual combinations, in the species a necessary product of its disposition in co-operation with unknown factors. These unknown factors we conceive to ourselves as things which exist independently of us, and which, therefore, would possess that absolute reality which we have just declared to be impossible. But the impossibility remains; for even in the notion of the thing, that stands out as a unity from the infinite coherency of existence, there lies that subjective factor which, as a constituent part of our human reality, is quite in place, but beyond it only helps to fill up, on the analogy of our reality, the gap for that which is absolutely inconceivable, but which must at the same time be assumed.

Kant has abandoned metaphysical inquiry into the true bases of all existence because of the impossibility of a certain result, and has limited the task of metaphysic to the discovery of all *a priori* given elements of experience. It is, however, questionable whether this new task is not equally impracticable; and it is no less questionable whether man, on the strength of the natural impulse to metaphysic which Kant himself maintains, will not continually make fresh efforts to break through the barriers of experience, and to build up into empty air brilliant systems of a supposed knowledge of the absolute nature of things. The sophisms by which this is possible are indeed inexhaustible; and while sophisms cunningly elude the position of criticism, a splendid ignorance easily breaks through all barriers with a still more brilliant success.

One thing is certain, that man needs to supplement reality by an ideal world of his own creation, and that the highest and noblest functions of his mind co-operate in such creations. But must this act of intellectual freedom always keep on assuming the deceptive form of a demonstrative science ? In that case Materialism, too, will always reappear, and will destroy the bolder speculations with an attempt to satisfy the instinct of the reason towards unity by a minimum of exaltation above the real and demonstrable.

We may not doubt of another solution of the problem, especially in Germany, since we have in the philosophical poems of Schiller a performance which unites with the noblest vigour of thought the highest elevation above reality, and which lends to the ideal an overpowering force by removing it openly and unhesitatingly into the realm of fantasy. This must not be taken to mean that all speculation must also assume the form of poetry. Schiller's philosophical poems are more than mere products of the speculative instinct. They are emanations of a truly religious elevation of the soul to the pure and troubled sources of all that man has ever worshipped as divine and supermundane. May Metaphysic ever continue its efforts towards the solution of its insoluble problem! The more it continues theoretical, and tries to compete in certainty with sciences of reality, all the less will it succeed in obtaining general importance. The more, on the other hand, it brings the world of existence into connexion with the world of values, and tries to raise itself by its apprehension of phenomena to an ethical influence, the more will it make form predominate over matter, and, without doing violence to the facts, will erect in the architecture of its ideas a temple of worship to the eternal and divine. Free poetry, however, may entirely leave the ground of reality and make use of myth in order to lend words to the unutterable.

Here then we stand too before an entirely satisfactory solution of the question as to the immediate and more distant future of religion. There are only two ways which can permanently call for serious consideration, after it has been shown that mere Rationalism loses itself in the sands of superficiality, without ever freeing itself from untenable dogmas. The one way is the complete suppression and abolition of all religions, and the transference of their functions to the State, Science, and Art; the other is to penetrate to the core of religion, and to overcome all fanaticism and superstition by conscious elevation above reality and definitive renunciation of the falsification of reality by mythus, which, of course, can render no service to knowledge.

The first of these ways involves the danger of spiritual impoverishment; the second has to deal with the great question whether, at this very time, the core of religion is not undergoing a change which makes it difficult to apprehend it with certainty. But the second difficulty is the lesser one, because the very principle of the spiritualisation of religion must facilitate and lend a more harmonious form to every transition rendered necessary by the intellectual requirements of a progressive age.

There is the additional difficulty, whether the abolition of all religion, however desirable it may appear to many well-meaning and thinking men, is at all possible. No reasonable man will entertain the notion of a sudden or even violent step. He will rather descry in this principle primarily a maxim for the attitude of the more highly cultured, somewhat in the sense of Strauss, whose residuum of religion is here little concerned. But next an effort will be made to employ the State and the School in order gradually to withdraw the ground from under religion in the life of the people, and systematically to prepare the way for its disappearance. If we suppose such a course of proceeding, it would be very doubtful whether it would not necessarily produce, in spite of scholastic enlightenment, a popular reaction in favour of a thoroughly fanatical and narrow-minded conception of religion, or whether ever fresh, perhaps wild, but at the same time vigorous, shoots would not spring up from the roots that had been left behind. Man seeks the truth of reality and hails the extension of his knowledge so long as he feels himself free. But let him be chained down to what can be attained by the senses and the understanding, and he will revolt, and will give expression to the freedom of his imagination and his spirit, perhaps, in still cruder forms than those which have been successfully destroyed.

So long as men sought the core of religion in certain doctrines on God, the Human Soul, the Creation and its Order, it was inevitable that every criticism which began by separating upon logical principles the chaff from the wheat must end in complete negation. The sifting process went on till nothing was left.

If, on the other hand, we descry the core of religion in the elevation of our souls above the real and in the creation of a home of the spirit, then the purest forms may produce essentially the same psychical processes as the charcoal-burner's creed of the uncultured masses, and all the philosophical refinement of ideas will never bring us to zero. An unrivalled model of this is the way in which Schiller, in his 'Realm of Shadows,' has generalised the Christian doctrine of redemption into the idea of an æsthetical redemption. The elevation of the soul in faith here becomes the flight into the idea-land of beauty, where all labour finds its rest, every struggle and every want their peace and their reconciliation. But the heart which is terrified by the awful power of the law which no mortal can resist, opens itself to the divine will, which it recognises as the true essence of its own will, and thus finds itself reconciled with Deity. If these moments of elevation are but fleeting, yet they work with freeing and purifying effect upon the soul, and in the distance appears the perfection which no one can any more deprive us of, figured under the image of Herakles mounting to the skies.

This poem is a product of a time and a sphere of culture which were certainly not inclined to concede too much to what was specifically Christian; the poet of the

'Gods of Greece' does not conceal himself; everything here is in a sense pagan; and yet Schiller here stands nearer to the traditional life of Christian faith than the rationalising dogmatism which arbitrarily maintains the notion of God, and abandons the doctrine of redemption as irrational.

Let us accustom ourselves, then, to attribute a higher worth than hitherto to the principle of the creative idea in itself, and apart from any correspondence with historical and scientific knowledge, but also without any falsification of them; let us accustom ourselves to regard the world of ideas, as figurative representation of the entire truth, as just as indispensable to all human progress as the knowledge of the understanding, by resolving the greater or less import of every idea into ethical and æsthetic principles. This advice will indeed appear to many an old or even new believer, as if we were to draw the ground from beneath his feet and ask him to remain standing as though nothing had happened; but the question is, what is the ground of ideas, whether it is their ordering into the whole of the world of ideas on ethical considerations, or the relation of the conceptions in which the idea finds expression to empirical reality? When the revolution of the earth was demonstrated, every Philistine believed that he must fall unless this dangerous doctrine were refuted, much as nowadays many a man fears that he will become a barber's block, if Vogt can prove to him that he has no soul. If religion is worth anything, and if its lasting worth lies in its ethical, and not in its logical content, this must, of course, have been so earlier also, however much we might like to regard literal belief also as indispensable.

If this state of affairs had not been clearly present in the consciousness of the wise, and at least dimly in the consciousness of the people also, how could the poet and the sculptor in Greece and Rome have ventured to shape the course of the living myth and to give new forms to the ideal of deity? Even Catholicism, rigid as it appears, handled dogma at bottom only as a powerful clamp to hold together in its unity the gigantic fabric of the Church, while the poet in legend, the philosopher in the profound and daring speculations of Scholasticism, dealt as they pleased with the material of religion. Never indeed, never since the beginning of the world, has a religious dogma been held by people who could rise above the standpoint of the rudest superstition as true in the same manner as a piece of sensible knowledge, a result of calculation or of a simple inference of the understanding, even though perhaps never down to the latest times has there prevailed entire clearness as to the relation of these 'eternal truths' to the invariable functions of the senses and the understanding. We can always with the most orthodox zealots, discover in their sayings and writings the point where they obviously pass into symbol, and reproduce the plastic representation of a subjective development of the religious idea, with the same expressions and the same emphasis, with which they can so sensuously and concretely exhibit the relatively objective doctrines, that are admitted by a wide community, and are regarded by individuals as inexpugnable. If these truths of the universal doctrine of the Church are prized as 'higher,' and put above all other knowledge, even that of the multiplication-table, yet there is always present at least a suspicion that this superiority does not rest upon greater *certainty*, but upon a greater *value*, against which neither logic, nor touch of the hand, nor sight of the eye, can avail, because for it the idea, as form and essence of the constitution of the soul, may be a more powerful object of longing, than the most real matter. But even where the greater certainty, the higher sureness and trustworthiness of religious truths are vaunted in express terms, these are only the periphrastic expressions or confusions of an exalted mind for the stronger impulse of the heart towards the living source of edification, of strengthening, of fresh life, which flows down from the divine world of ideas, as compared with the sober knowledge which enriches the understanding with small change, for which we happen to have no employment. Carried away to the height of this spiritual condition, Luther, though he himself, by the destructive force of his conviction, threw down an edifice that had stood a thousand years, rises to the point of cursing the reason that opposes itself to what he with all the might of his glowing spirit has conceived as the idea of a new epoch. Hence, too, the value which really pious minds have always given to inward *experience* as an evidence of faith. Many of these believers, who owe their peace of soul to a fervent wrestling in prayer, and hold spiritual communion with Christ as with a person, know theoretically very well that the same emotional processes are found also with the same success and with the same authenticity in connexion with entirely different articles of faith, nay, among the adherents of entirely foreign religions. The opposition to these and the equivocal character of an evidence which equally well supports contradictory ideas, they do not as a rule realise, since it is rather the common opposition of every belief against unbelief that stirs their minds. Does it not here become manifest that the essence of the thing lies in the form of the spiritual process, and not in the logical and historical content of the particular views and doctrines? These may well be connected with the form of the process, as are in the corporeal world chemical composition and crystalline form; but who is there to demonstrate to us this connexion, and what phenomena of isomorphism shall we only here find exhibited?

This predominance of the form in belief betrays itself also in the remarkable trait that the believers in varying and even mutually hostile confessions, show more agreement with each other, betray more sympathy with their most eager opponents, than with those who appear indifferent in matters of religious controversy. The most peculiar phenomenon of religious formalism, however, lies in the *philosophy of religion*, as it has shaped itself in Germany, especially since Kant. This philosophy is a formal translation of religious into metaphysical doctrines. A man, who was so far removed from the charcoal-burner faith in regard to unhistorical traditions and scientific impossibilities as the Materialists could ever be, Schleiermacher, brought about, by dwelling on the ethical and ideal content of religion, a real torrent of religious revival. The mighty Fichte announced the dawn of a new historical epoch by the outpouring of the Holy Spirit upon all flesh. The Spirit, of which it is prophesied in the New Testament that it shall lead the disciples of Christ into all truth, is no other than the Spirit of Science, which has revealed itself in our days. It teaches us in revealed knowledge the absolute unity of human existence with the divine, which was first preached to the world by Christ in a parable. The revelation of the kingdom of God is the essence of Christianity, and this kingdom is the kingdom of liberty, which is won by the absorption of our own will into the will of God— death and resurrection. All doctrines of the resurrection of the dead in the physical sense are only misunderstandings of the doctrine of the kingdom of heaven, which is in truth the principle of a new constitution of the world. Fichte was entirely in earnest with his requirement of a transformation of the human race by the principle of humanity itself in its ideal perfection as opposed to the absorption of the individual in self-will. Thus the most radical philosopher of Germany is at the same time the man whose feelings and thoughts form the profoundest contrast to the interest-maxims of political economy and to the whole dogmatic theory of Egoism. It is not, therefore, without significance that Fichte was the first in Germany to raise the Social Question, which would, indeed, never exist if self-interest were the only spring of human actions, if the, abstractly considered, perfectly correct rules of political economy, as the only ruling laws of nature, everlastingly and invariably guided the machinery of human toils and struggles, without the higher idea ever asserting itself, for which the noblest of mankind have for thousands of years suffered and wrestled.

"No, abandon us not, sacred palladium of mankind! comforting thought, that from our every labour and our every suffering there results for our brother-men a new perfection and a new delight; that we labour for them and do not labour in vain; that on the spot where we now exhaust ourselves and are trodden underfoot, and—what is worse than this—grossly err and fail, there will in the future flourish a race that may always do what it wills, because it will will nothing but what is good; while we from loftier regions rejoice over our descendants, and find developed in their virtues each germ that we implanted in them, and know them for our own. Arouse us, prospect of this time, to the sense of our dignity, and show it to us at least in our disposition, though our present state is at variance with it. Shed boldness and high enthusiasm upon our undertakings, and if we are crushed beneath them, while we are sustained by this thought, 'I have done my duty,' let us be invigorated by this other thought, 'No seed that I have sowed is lost in the moral world; in the day of ingathering I shall see its fruits and weave me from them immortal garlands.'"[41]

The poetical fervour with which Fichte wrote these words had seized him not on occasion of a vague religious contemplation, but in regard to Kant and—the French Revolution. So intimately fused with him were life and teaching; and while the word of life was perverted by the hirelings of the Church to the service of death, of ignorance, of the prince of this world, there arose in him the spirit of the breaker of all chains, and

[41] (J. G. Fichte's) Beitrag zur Berichtigung der Urtheile des Publikums über die französische Revolution, 1793, 1 B., 1 Kap.

loudly confessed that the fall of society in France had at least brought forth something better than the despotic governments whose aim is the degradation of mankind.

It is remarkable how, on a closer inquiry, the views and efforts of men often group themselves very differently from the common notion of them. It is a trivial saying that extremes meet; but it is far from being always true. Never, never will the decided free-thinker feel any sympathy with rigid ecclesiasticism and the dead worship of the letter; but he may feel much with the prophetic enthusiasm of a pious soul, in which the word has become flesh, and which bears witness of the spirit that has taken possession of it. Never will the enlightened dogmatist of Egoism feel sympathy with the quiet souls who in their humble closets seek upon their knees a kingdom that is not of this world; but he may well feel it with the rich rector who can valiantly defend his creed, maintain his dignity, and prudently manage his property, and who drinks with him in champagne, if he sits near him at some luxurious christening dinner, or at the festive inauguration of a new railway.

Because it is the form of spiritual life that determines the inmost character of the man, so too their attitude to those who differ from them is a genuine touchstone of minds, whether they be of the truth or not. He must be a bad disciple of Christ, in the strictest sense of the religious, who cannot conceive that when the Lord appears in the clouds to judge the quick and the dead, He may place an Atheist like Fichte on His right hand, while thousands go to His left who cry, with the righteous, 'Lord, Lord!' He must be a bad friend of truth and justice who despises a man like A. H. Franke as an enthusiast, or treats the prayer of a Luther as idle self-delusion. In fact, so far as religion in its inmost essence forms an antithesis to Ethical Materialism, it will always retain friends amongst the freest and most enlightened minds, and the only question is whether in religion itself the principle of Ethical Materialism, of 'secularisation,' as theologians call it, is not gaining such ascendancy that our better consciousness must tear itself free of all its previous forms and strike out new paths. In this point, in the relation of existing religions to the collective aims of our present civilisation, lies the true secret of their modifications and their persistence, and all attacks of the critical understanding, however justified and irresistible they may be, are yet not so much the cause as rather only the symptoms of their decay, or of a great fermentation in the whole spiritual life of their adherents. Hence it is, also, that even the conservative tendency which religious philosophy took with Hegel, accompanied by very similar modifications to those of Fichte, has borne no lasting fruits, either for the Church or for Philosophy. It can no longer be permitted that knowledge of the unveiled truth should be reserved for the philosophers alone, while the masses are forced back into the solemn twilight of the old symbols. As in politics the doctrine of the reasonableness of the actual state of things has done unholy service to the cause of Absolutism, so Philosophy contributed, chiefly through Hegel and Schleiermacher, to promote a tendency which, deserted by the naïve innocence of the old mysticism, attempted to save religion by a negation of negation. What protected the dogmas of religion against the teeth of criticism in the ages when the cathedrals grew up, or when the mighty melodies of worship arose, was not the anti-criticism of ingenious apologists, but the reverent awe with which the soul received the mysteries, and the holy fear with which the believer shrunk from approaching in his inmost soul the border where truth and poesy separate. This holy fear is not the *consequence* of the fallacies which lead to the belief in the supernatural, but rather their *cause*, and perhaps this relation of cause and effect runs back to the earliest ages of undeveloped civilisation and undeveloped religions. Why, even Epikuros, besides fear, regarded the sublime dream-images of the gods as amongst the sources of religion !

What will become of the 'verities' of religion when all piety has disappeared, and when a generation grows up that has never known the deep emotions of religious life, or that has grown weary of them and has turned away from them? Every young fool triumphs over its mysteries, and looks down with self-complacent disdain on those who can still believe this silly stuff. So long as religion stands in its full strength, it is not always its most paradoxical principles that are the first to be doubted. Theological critics exert themselves by the application of the greatest acuteness and the most extensive erudition to correct tradition in some point or other far enough removed from the core of faith; men of science find reason to refer some particular miracle to a physically intelligible phenomenon. At such points the process of boring is continued, and when all the arts of attack and defence have been exhausted, as a rule the nimbus of venerableness and inviolability that enwrapped religious tradition is gone also. Only then do we come to the much simpler questions: How God's omnipotence and goodness are compatible with the evil in the world; why the religions of other peoples are not just as good as our own; why there are not still miracles, and those very palpable ones; how God can be angry; why the servants of God are so malicious and vindictive, and so on. When ecclesiastical tradition has at length lost the special credit which it claims, and when the Bible is regarded with the same eyes as any other book, we can hardly conceive any degree of intelligence so low as not to see clearly that three times one cannot make one, that a virgin cannot bear a child, and that a man cannot, body and all, soar up into the blue sky. If now some little scientific knowledge is added, such as is current in every primary school, there is no end to the absurdity over which a scoffer can make merry, without in any degree possessing any special intelligence or any thorough education. If now, withal, men of keen understanding and solid education still hold fast to religion, because they have led from childhood up a rich emotional life, and cling to the old, familiar soil with a thousand roots of imagination, of the heart, and of recollection of beautiful and consecrated hours, we have then before us a contrast that shows us plainly enough where are the sources from which flows the stream of religious life.

So long, of course, as religion is cultivated in close ecclesiastical communities by priests who present themselves before the people as privileged dispensers of the divine mysteries, so long the standpoint of the ideal in religion will never be able to assert itself clearly. And, indeed, ideology only too easily becomes the prey of the poison of letter-worship, The symbol involuntarily and gradually becomes a rigid dogma, as the image of the saint becomes an idol, and the natural contradiction between poetry and reason easily degenerates in the religious sphere into antipathy to the absolutely True, Useful, and Practical, which in our age seem to limit on every side the space in which a free soul may use its wings. We know the mischief that has been wrought in many a nobly disposed mind by the transition from crude ideology to romantic perversity, and finally into angry pessimism. No one can take it ill of the friends of truth and progress, if they feel distrust of everything that opposes itself to the ruling tendency of the age towards prose, especially if a tincture of clericalism is visible. For if in the age of the Liberation Wars Romanticism seemed to fulfil its higher purpose, it is obvious, on the other hand, that the tendency of the age towards inventions, discoveries, political and social improvements, has now to perform enormous tasks which may perchance decide the future of humanity, and it cannot be doubted that the utmost sobriety of serious labour, the full unadulterated feeling for truth of a critical conscience, are needed to accomplish these tasks worthily and successfully. When then the day of harvest comes, the glance of genius will again be there also, which from the atoms creates a whole without knowing how it has been done.

Meanwhile the old forms of religion have by no means entirely outlived themselves, and it will hardly ever come to be with their ideal content as with a squeezed lemon, until new forms of Ethical Idealism appear. Things do not go on so simply and unmixedly in the interchange of earthly opinions and aspirations. The worship of Apollo and Jupiter had not yet lost all significance as Christianity broke in, and Catholicism still held a rich treasure of life and spirit within it when Luther began to strike about him. So even to-day again a new religious community might, by the power of its ideas and the charm of its social principles, conquer a world by storm, while still many a stock of the old planting remains in full vitality and bears its fruit; but mere negation recoils where ends the province of the obsolete and dead, that has become its prey. Whether even out of the old confessions such a stream of new life might proceed, or whether conversely a religionless community could kindle a fire of such devouring force, we do not know. One thing, however, is certain; if the New is to come into existence and the Old is to disappear, two great things must combine— a world-kindling ethical idea and a social influence which is powerful enough to lift the depressed masses a great step forward. Sober reason, artificial systems, cannot do this. The victory over disintegrating egoism and the deadly chilliness of the heart will only be won by a great ideal, which appears amidst the wondering peoples as a "stranger from another world," and by demanding the impossible unhinges the reality.

So long as this victory is not won, so long as no new social bond makes the poor and miserable feel that he is a man among men, we must not be so precipitate in combating belief, lest haply child and bath be poured away together. Let knowledge be spread, let truth be proclaimed in every street and in every tongue, let come of it what may; but let the battle for emancipation, deliberate and mortal battle, be directed against the points where the menacing of liberty, the hindering of truth and justice have their roots—against the secular and civil institutions by which ecclesiastical societies secure a corrupting influence, and against the enslaving power of a perfidious hierarchy that systematically undermines the freedom of the peoples. If these institutions are removed, if the terrorism of the hierarchy is broken, then the extremest opinions may move side by side without fanatical encroachments, and without the steady progress of insight being hindered. It is true that this progress will destroy superstitious fears, a work which is indeed in great part already accomplished even amongst the lowest classes of the people. If religion falls together with the superstitious fears, so let it fall; if it does not fall, then its ideal content will have maintained itself, and it may then continue to be maintained in this form until time produces something new. It is not then matter of any regret if the content of religion is regarded by most believers, and even by a part of the clergy, as literally true; for that utterly dead and meaningless belief in the letter, whose effect is even more pernicious, is hardly possible any longer where all compulsion disappears.

If the clergyman, as a result of the associations of ideas which dominate him, *cannot* represent the ideal element of life which he represents otherwise than in attributing to it vulgar reality and in taking everything as historical that should only be regarded as symbolical, this must be conceded to him without hesitation, supposing that he does his duty in the more important regard. If the hierarchy is entirely deprived of all worldly power, not excepting even the rights of a civil corporation, and if the formation of a state within a state is resisted in every form, the most dangerous weapon of spiritual tyranny is broken. Moreover, there must be maintained, not merely unconditional freedom of teaching for strict science as well as for its popularisation, but also free scope for public criticism of all wrongs and abuses. That it is the right and duty of the State, so far as it continues to support existing religious communities with its power and resources, to require from their clergy a certain standard of scientific culture is obvious; and we must guard against neglecting these duties, and losing ourselves in the labyrinth of a so-called separation of Church and State. There is only a clear and good sense in the separation of state and faith. Every ecclesiastical organisation of a community of believers is already a state within the state, and may at any moment easily encroach upon the secular province. There may be circumstances in the conditions of civilisation by which such a power may be justified, and may, in fact, be destined to shatter a rotten and outlived form of government; as a rule, however, and especially in our present age, which is more and more assigning to the State the civilising functions that were formerly left to the Church, the political organisation of the latter must simply be to the State a matter of distrust and the most serious anxiety. Only with the dissolution of the political Church is an unconditional freedom of creed possible. At the same time, so long as the Church, with all its ambitious aspirations, still represents also Ethical Idealism among the people, it cannot be the function of the State to aim at the dissolution of its dogmatic system. Fichte, indeed, demanded that the spiritual teacher to whom it falls to mediate between the people and the men of scientific culture, should actually form his religious system in the school of the philosopher. Theology he proposed, unless she solemnly renounced her 'pretension to be a mystery,' to banish entirely from the universities; but if she renounced it, then the practical part of theology must be separated from the scientific part, and the latter be completely resolved into general scientific education.[42] This in itself justifiable requirement is at present still less practicable than when Fichte expressed it. The task of mediation between the people and the better educated, even when it is attempted with all earnestness, is only to be performed by observing the psychological conditions, and that means only gradually and in long periods. But even the imparting of a sufficiently deep philosophical culture to the clergy cannot be effected by a mere organisation of studies. Meanwhile the cultivation of the ideal amongst the people must not be interrupted. It is, of course, to be wished that every clergyman should at least be enlightened as to the limits of the validity of the ideal; but if, because of narrowness of mind and lack of suitable means of instruction, this cannot be without weakening the force which is destined to spread ideas, then it is, on the whole, better for the present to sacrifice enlightenment rather than force.

The case of the Materialistic man of science, on the other side, is entirely analogous. Without doubt, the success of his beneficent and self-sacrificing researches essentially depends upon his devotion to the branch of human activity which he has chosen. There cannot be the slightest doubt that only methodically strict empiricism leads him to the goal, that keen and unprejudiced contemplation of the sensible world and unhesitating consistency in his conclusions are indispensable to him; finally, that Materialistic hypotheses always offer him the greatest prospect of fresh discoveries. If his mind is deep and comprehensive enough to combine with this ordered activity the recognition of the ideal, without introducing confusion, obscurity, or sterile timidity into the sphere of his researches, he then assuredly reaches a higher

---

[42] Deducirter Plan einer zu Berlin zu errichtenden höhern Lehranstalt; geschrieben im J. 1807: Stuttg. u. Tüb. 1817, S. 59 ff.

standard of genuine and complete humanity. But if this cannot be hoped for, it is in most cases far better in these departments to have crass Materialists than phantasts and muddled weaklings. As much of the ideal as is indispensably necessary—and more than the great mass of men ever attain—is already involved in the mere devotion to a great principle and to an important subject. Those Materialists who really accomplish something in their science will, for the most part, have little inclination to play the missionary of negation; and even if they do, they do less harm to mankind than the apostles of confusion.

If, however, both extremes, even in their one-sidedness, are really justifiable, then, too, it must be possible for them to live together in society at least tolerably, if not comfortably, so soon as the last traces of fanaticism are eradicated from our legislation. Whether, of course, this will ever come to pass, is quite another question. It is with the religious revolution just as it is with the social revolution which is before us. It would be very desirable to live through the period of transition in peace, but it is more probable that it will be stormy.

Thus the Materialistic controversy of our days stands before us as a serious sign of the time. To-day again, as in the period before Kant and before the French Revolution, there underlies the spread of Materialism a general enfeeblement of philosophical effort, a retrogression of ideas. In such times the perishable material to which our forefathers gave the stamp of the sublime and divine, as they could comprehend them, is devoured by the flames of criticism, like the organic body, which, when the vital spark dies out, becomes subject to the more general action of chemical forces, and has its earlier form destroyed. But, as in the circuit of nature from the decay of lower materials new life struggles into being and higher phenomena appear where the old have disappeared, so we may expect that a new impulse of ideas will advance humanity another stage.

Meanwhile the dissolving forces act only as they must. They obey the inexorable categorical imperative of thought, the conscience of the understanding, which is awakened so soon as in the creation of the transcendental the Letter becomes conspicuous because the Spirit leaves it in search of newer forms. But one thing only can finally bring humanity to an ever-during peace—the recognition of the imperishable nature of all poesy in Art, Religion, and Philosophy, and the permanent reconciliation, on the basis of this recognition, of the controversy between investigation and imagination. Then, also, will be found a changeful harmony of the True, the Good, and the Beautiful, instead of that dead unity to which our Free Congregations are at present clinging, when they make empirical truth their only basis. Whether the future will again build lofty cathedrals or will content itself with light and cheerful halls, whether organ-peal and the sound of bells will with fresh force thunder through the land, or whether gymnastic and music in the Greek sense will be elevated to the centre of the training of a new epoch—in no case will the past be entirely lost, and in no case will the obsolete reappear unaltered. In a certain sense the ideas of religion, too, are imperishable. Who will refute a Mass of Palestrina, or who will convict Raphael's Madonna of error? The 'Gloria in Excelsis' remains a universal power, and will ring through the centuries so long as our nerves can quiver under the awe of the sublime. And those simple fundamental ideas of the redemption of the individual man by the surrendering of his own will to the will that guides the whole; those images of death and resurrection which express the highest and most thrilling emotions that stir the human breast, when no prose is capable of uttering in cold words the fulness of the heart; those doctrines, finally, which bid us to share our bread with the hungry and to announce the glad tidings to the poor—they will not for ever disappear, in order to make way for a society which has attained its goal when it owes a better police system to its understanding, and to its ingenuity the satisfaction of ever-fresh wants by ever-fresh inventions. Often already has an epoch of Materialism been but the stillness before the storm, which was to burst forth from unknown gulfs and to give a new shape to the world. We lay aside the pen of criticism at a moment when the Social Question stirs all Europe, a question on whose wide domain all the revolutionary elements of science, of religion, and of politics seem to have found the battlefield for a great and decisive contest. Whether this battle remains a bloodless conflict of minds, or whether, like an earthquake, it throws down the ruins of a past epoch with thunder into the dust and buries millions beneath the wreck, certain it is that the new epoch will not conquer unless it be under the banner of a great idea, which sweeps away egoism and sets human perfection in human fellowship as a new aim in the place of restless toil, which looks only to the personal gain. It would indeed mitigate the impending conflict if insight into the nature of human development and historical processes were more generally to take possession of the leading minds ; and we must not resign the hope that in a distant future the greatest transformations will be accomplished without humanity being stained by fire and blood. It were indeed the fairest guerdon of exhausted intellectual labour if it might even now contribute, while averting fearful sacrifices, to prepare a smooth path for the inevitable, and to save the treasures of culture uninjured for the new epoch; but the prospect of this is slight, and we cannot hide from ourselves that the blind passion of parties is on the increase, and that the reckless struggle of interests is becoming less and less amenable to the influences of theoretical inquiries. Yet our efforts will never be wholly in vain. The truth, though late, yet comes soon enough; for mankind will not die just yet. Fortunate natures hit the right moment; but never has the thoughtful observer the right to be silent because he knows that for the present there are but few who will listen to him.

PREFACE TO THE SECOND BOOK

[*AS POSTSCRIPT*].

———

THE appearance of the Second Book, and especially of its second half, has been long delayed by the aggravation of a serious illness, which leaves me little strength to devote to work. This has also made it impossible for me to include in my discussions certain important works which have recently appeared, and which are closely connected with my subject. In particular, I regret this with regard to Tyndall's Address on Religion and Science, and the three Essays on Religion of Stuart Mill.

Tyndall's address is, as it were, the official announcement of a new era for England, which plays so important a part in the History of Materialism. The old hollow truce between natural science and theology, which Huxley, and recently Darwin, had seriously shaken, is now broken, and men of science demand their right to follow out in all directions, undisturbed by any subsisting traditions, the consequences of their theory of the world. The continuance of religion is indeed secured by the Spencerian philosophy, but it will henceforth no more be considered a matter of indifference with what dogmas and what demands upon our credulity religious feelings find expression. And thus commences a struggle, such as earlier took place in Germany, which can only find a peaceful termination by the removal of religion into the sphere of the ideal.

It was to me extremely remarkable how near in his Essay on Theism, the last great work of his life, Stuart Mill approached to the view which is also established as the result of our History of Materialism. The inexorable empiricist, the champion of the utilitarian philosophy, the man who, in so many earlier works, appeared to recognise only the rational principle, here makes the confession that the narrow and inadequate life of man needs greatly to be exalted to loftier hopes of our destiny, and that it seems wise to let imagination shape these hopes, so long as it does not come into conflict with obvious facts. As the cheerfulness of soul which every one appreciates rests upon the inclination to linger in thought upon the lighter side of the present and the future, and this means an involuntary idealisation of life, so we are to think more favourably of the government of the universe and of our future condition after death than the very slender probability would permit: nay, this ideal character of Christ is represented not only as a principal feature of Christianity, but as something that even the unbeliever can appropriate. How far is it from this to our ideal standpoint! The slight, rapidly disappearing probability that the dreams of our imagination can be realised is at best a weak tie between Religion and Science, and at bottom only a weakness in the whole system, for it is opposed by a greatly preponderating probability the other way, and in the sphere of reality the morality of thought demands from us that we shall not cling to vague possibilities, but shall always prefer the greater probability. If the principle is once conceded that we should create for ourselves in imagination a fairer and more perfect world than the world of reality, then we shall be compelled to allow validity to Mythus as Mythus. But it is more important that we shall rise to the recognition that it is the same necessity, the same transcendental root of our human nature, which supplies us through the senses with the idea of the world of reality, and which leads us in the highest function of nature and creative synthesis to fashion a world of the ideal in which to take refuge from the limitation of the senses, and in which to find again the true Home of our Spirit.

A. LANGE.

MARBURG, 2d *January* 1875.

INDEX.

Abraham, iii. 16
Adam, iii. 16, 107
Adams, John Couch, iii. 9
Adhémar, iii. 92
Ænesidemus, i. 176
Æschylos, i. 6
Agassiz, iii. 88
Albertus Magnus, i. 209; ii. 356
Alcuin, i. 188
Alexander of Aphrodisias, i. 94, 221, 224
Alexander the Great, i. 51, 83, 99, 100, 118
Alkibiades, i. 61
Alsted, ii. 356
Amerbach, i. 228
Ammann, ii. 62, 68
Ampère, A. M., ii. 365, 370, 379
Anaxagoras, i. 6, 9, 20, 53, 64, 65, 135; ii. 355
Anaximander, i. 8, 9, 114
Anaximenes, i. 9
Andokides, i. 7
Antipater, i. 100
Apelt, ii. 155
Apollonius of Tyana, i. 170
Aquinas. See Thomas Aquinas
Archimedes, i. 114
Archytas, i. 120
Argens, Marquis d', ii. 77, 137
Aristarchus of Samos, i. 118, 120, 278
Aristarchos of Samothrace, i. 114, 232
Aristippos, i. 44, 45, 50, 51, 102, 103, 128; ii. 54; iii. 233, 238, 302
Aristodemos, i. 61
Aristophanes, i. 7, 40, 48, 63
Aristotle, i. 5, 7, 8, 9, 15, 17, 18, 20, 24, 25, 26, 27, 28, 29, 30, 33, 41, 45, 48, 53, 54, 56, 59, 60, 64, 68, 69, 76, 78, 80–92, 93, 94, 95, 96, 99, 108, 112, 118, 124, 138, 140, 158, 167, 177, 178, 179, 187–195, 198–203, 205, 210, 212, 213, 217, 222, 223, 226–229, 254, 257, 277, 278, 282, 303, 322; ii. 33, 41, 157, 250, 265, 277; iii. 33, 169, 279
Aristoxenos, i. 93, 94
Arnobius, ii. 62
Arnold, ii. 142
Arnoldt, Emil, ii. 154, 202
Augustus Cæsar, i. 131
Augustine, St., i. 262, 263; iii. 15
Averroes, i. 94, 175, 177, 178, 226; ii. 45
Avicenna, i. 178, 208
Avogadro, ii. 359, 360, 375

Bacon, Francis, i. 11, 15, 20, 22, 115, 213, 216, 228, 235, 236, 237, 239, 240, 241, 242, 244, 253, 254, 275, 276, 277, 286, 294, 296, 317; ii. 3, 12, 34, 50, 287, 304, 343, 344
Bacon, Roger, ii. 3
Baer, iii. 102
Baier, Johann Jakob, ii. 135
Baier, Johann Wilhelm, ii. 135
Bain, Alexander, iii. 186, 187, 190, 191
Baldæus, ii. 36
Baltzer, iii. 294
Barach, i. 209
Barchusen, ii. 356
Bardili, i. 221
Bartholmèss, i. 233
Basil the Great, i. 186
Bastian, iii. 18, 182
Batalin, iii. 73
Bauer, Bruno, ii. 284
Baumann, i. 288; ii. 31, 125, 132
Baumann (Maupertuis), Dr., ii. 31
Baumgarten, i. 197
Baur, i. 62, 170
Bayle, P., i. 217; ii. 9, 10, 11, 17, 34, 38, 47, 88, 127

Beattie, ii. 8, 206
Becker, K. F., i. 212
Becker, J. C., ii. 188
Beier, ii. 135
Bekker, Balthasar, ii. 35
Bell, Sir Charles, i. 119
Bellarmine, Cardinal, i. 279
Beneke, ii. 247; iii. 306
Bennet, iii. 48, 49
Bentley, i. 315; ii. 210
Bergmann, ii. 148
Berkeley, Bishop of Cloyne, i. 38, 109; ii. 50, 112, 129, 157, 158, 159, 164, 275, 327; iii. 205
Bernays, i. 143
Bernhardy, i. 129
Bernier, i. 266, 267
Bernouilli, Daniel, ii. 374
Bernouilli, Johann, i. 313
Bert, Paul, iii. 179
Berzelius, ii. 360
Biedermann, ii. 126, 143
Bilfinger, ii. 134; iii. 170
Blaigny, ii. 39
Blanqui, Auguste, i. 151
Blass, i. 7
Blumenbach, iii. 87, 106
Boccaccio, i. 217
Boerhaave, ii. 55, 56, 78, 356
Böhmer, H., ii. 244
Bonaparte family, i. 272
Boniface, ii. 28
Bonitz, i. 188
Bonnet, Charles, iii. 16
Bopp, Franz, iii. 181
Borelli, i. 310
Börne, ii. 257
Boscovich, ii. 364
Boucher de Perthes, iii. 89, 95
Bourgeois, the Abbé, iii. 90
Bouriguon, Antoinette, iii. 169
Boyle, Robert, i. 125, 255, 299-305, 309, 317; ii. 3, 8, 12, 33, 146, 351, 353, 356, 363, 364, 374
Brandis, i. 18, 39
Brehm, iii. 136
Brentano, iii. 168, 175, 193, 228
Brewster, i. 306
Brown, Thomas, iii. 186
Browne, Sir Thomas, i. 317
Bruck, Von, ii. 262
Brunet, ii. 36
Brutus, i. 128
Bucher, iii. 38
Büchner, Dr. Louis, i. 41, 261; ii. 240, 265-276, 281, 298, 302, 306, 307, 351, 366, 368, 370, 388; iii. 26, 85, 119-121, 303, 304, 324
Büchner, Louise, ii. 270
Buckingham, i. 294
Buckle, i. 9, 248, 261, 294, 298, 299, 301, 317; ii. 11; iii. 234, 235, 246, 247, 329
Buffon, ii. 6, 52, 93, 356; iii. 87

CABANIS, ii. 63, 93, 242, 243
Cæsar, Julius, ii. 67
Cagliostro, i. 170
Caligula, i. 167
Camper, iii. 87
Cardan, i. 225
Carey, i. 161; iii. 253
Carrière, i. 221, 233, 234
Cartouche, ii. 14
Carus, iii. 134, 135, 167
Cassius, i. 128
Castle, iii. 115, 116
Cato, i. 127
Cauchy, ii. 365, 368, 369, 370
Cavendish, Lord, i. 271, 277
Celsus, i. 176
Charles the Great, i. 163, 189
Charles II. of England, i. 273, 294; ii. 293, 294, 302, 317
Charron, i. 260; ii. 9
Christ. See Jesus
Christine, the Grand Duchess, i. 234
Chrysippos, i. 103, 111, 127
Cicero, i. 8, 24, 127, 128, 129, 232, 326; ii. 42, 98
Clarke, i. 301; ii. 8, 14, 16, 116, 117
Clausius, ii. 374, 384; iii. 11
Clavius, i. 269
Clement VII. (Pope), i. 231
Cohen, Hermann, ii. 154, 173, 178, 190, 202, 216, 217, 219; iii. 171, 306
Colbert, iii. 253
Coleridge, i. viii.
Colingwood, J. F., ii. 265
Colland, iii. 96
Columbus, Christopher, i. 118, 124, 138
Combe, iii. 121
Combette, iii. 116
Comenius, ii. 41
Comte, Auguste, ii. 154, 220, 235, 247, 248, 255, 256, 335; iii. 170, 190, 260, 272, 276, 296, 300
Condillac, i. 38; ii. 50, 51, 52, 53, 63; iii. 209

Condorcet, i. 210, 213
Constantine, iii. 318
Constantine the Monk, i. 181
Contzen, i. 163, 164
Cooper, iii. 251
Copernicus, i. 81, 92, 115, 118, 137, 138, 229, 230, 231, 232, 237, 263, 264, 277, 278, 307, 313; ii. 156, 158, 237, 335, 344; iii. 247
Corneille, ii. 69
Cornelius, iii. 164
Cotes, i. 316
Cotta, Bernard, iii. 118
Cousin, Victor, i. 247, 253
Cowper, ii. 74
Crassus, iii. 256
Cremonini, i. 220; ii. 164
Cromwell, Oliver, i. 272; iii. 274
Cudworth, ii. 43
Cunningham, ii. 23
Curtius, i. 6
Cus, Nicholas de, i. 231
Cuvier, George, i. 83; iii. 87, 88, 99, 105. 130
Czolbe, Henri, ii. 214, 215, 218, 246, 284–294, 298, 322; iii. 7, 12, 217, 224, 313, 315, 316

D'ALEMBERT, ii. 16, 27, 31, 32, 52, 92, 157; iii. 205
Dædalos, i. 29
Dalton, i. 255; ii. 354, 355, 357–359, 363
Damm, ii. 145
Dante, i. 177, 182
Daremberg, i. 181, 182
Darwin, Charles, i. 32, 35; ii. 132, 239, 292; iii. 26, 27, 30–32, 35, 44, 45, 49, 51–53, 58, 65, 89, 93, 102, 103, 108, 183, 327, 363
Delaunay, the Abbé, iii. 89
Delbœuf, ii. 180
Demokritos, i. 3, 13, 14, 15, 16, 17, 18, 20, 22, 23, 24, 25, 27–32, 35, 38, 39, 41, 42, 45, 46, 56, 59, 81, 93, 95, 99, 104, 105, 111, 115, 120, 123–125, 132, 140, 141, 142, 167, 201, 236, 254, 255, 269, 287, 289, 304, 316; ii. 28, 33, 47, 157, 226, 240, 389
Demosthenes, i. 50, 99
Descartes, i. 12, 29, 98, 125, 201, 216, 228, 235, 236, 241, 242, 243–248, 253, 260–262, 263, 268, 269, 276, 280, 304, 305, 309, 310, 312, 313, 314, 317; ii. 9, 10, 15, 16, 34, 59, 60, 65, 67, 76, 111, 126, VOL. III.

157, 311, 316, 325, 352, 353, 354, 363; iii. 130, 170, 183, 188
Deslandes, ii. 90
Desnoyers, iii. 89
Dewar, ii. 198
Diagoras of Melos, i. 6, 7
Dikæarchos, i. 93, 94; ii. 45
Diderot, ii. 9, 23–26, 27, 28, 31, 32, 52, 71, 72, 90, 92, 95, 108, 109, 121, 122, 235; iii. 78
Dilthey, iii. 306, 310
Diogenes, i. 50; iii. 239
Diogenes of Apollonia, i. 4, 7, 13, 28, 96
Diogenes Laertius, i. 130, 150
Dionysius of Syracuse, i. 50
Dohrn, ii. 148
Domrich, iii. 183
Dove, ii. 259
Draper, J. W., i. 167, 179, 181
Drobisch, iii. 185, 196, 198, 222
Droz, ii. 75; iii. 111
Dryden, i. 295
Du Bois-Reymond, ii. 13, 16, 131, 308–325, 378, 381; iii. 74, 156, 311, 324
Dühring, i. 302, 310; ii. 376; iii. 227
Dulong, ii. 360

EHRENBERG, ii. 259; iii. 18
Ekphantos, i. 232
Eimer, iii. 179
Empedokles, i. 8, 20, 30, 33–36, 130, 135, 136; ii. 102, 226, 356; iii. 32, 36
Enke, iii. 10
Epicuros, i. 7, 15, 17, 24, 25, 26, 31–34, 35, 39, 40, 45, 94, 98, 99, 100–113, 128, 129–132, 150, 151, 152, 154, 165, 167, 174, 176, 201, 253, 254, 256–258, 263, 265, 266, 283, 291, 296, 304, 306, 316; ii. 9, 47, 96, 101, 113, 123, 124, 158, 212, 243, 288, 352; iii. 3, 98, 233, 238, 239, 278, 352
Erasistratos, i. 115
Erasmus, i. 216; ii. 34
Eratosthenes, i. 120
Erdmann, ii. 124
Esquirol, ii. 259
Ettmüller, Michael, ii. 48
Eucken, i. 81, 83, 88
Euklid, i. 114, 117; ii. 171, 178, 179, 180
Euripides, i. 7, 50
Eve, iii. 107

2 A

INDEX.

Fabricius, J. Alb., ii. 145
Famintzin, iii, 73
Faraday, ii. 3, 365, 385; iii. 163
Fechner, G. Th., i. 255; ii. 198, 364-368, 388, 394, 395, 396; iii. 24, 25, 43, 44, 47, 70, 153, 311
Fermat, i. 248; ii. 16
Ferrier, iii. 145, 150
Feuerbach, ii. 246-256, 275, 276, 277, 284, 286, 335, 345; iii. 260, 332, 333
Feuerlein, ii. 144
Fichte, J. H., i. 54, 236; iii. 191, 226, 238, 242; iii. 175, 286, 311, 349-351, 352, 357, 358
Fichte, son, ii. 347
Fick, iii. 204
Filhol, iii. 94
Fischer, J. C., iii. 194
Fischer, Kuno, i. 237, 276, 280; ii. 51, 125, 154, 190, 191, 212
Flourens, ii. 259; iii. 116, 130, 132, 133, 134, 138
Fontenelle, ii. 16
Forster, ii. 141
Fortlage, i. 202; iii. 170, 173, 174
Fraas, iii. 90, 91, 94
Franck, Ad., i. 231, 237, 235
Frank, iii. 73
Franke, iii. 351
Franklin, Benjamin, iii. 265
Frantzen, ii. 137
Fredegisus, i. 188
Frederick the Great, i. 293; ii. 53, 54, 77, 89-91
Frederick II., Emperor of Germany, i. 182, 183, 217
Frei, i. 15, 39, 41, 43
Fresnel, ii. 363
Fries, ii. 155

Galen, of Pergamos, i. 119-121, 176, 224, 237; iii. 169
Galilei, i. 27, 114, 138, 216, 220, 231, 237, 248, 264, 278, 309, 310
Gall, iii. 113, 114, 122, 163
Garrigou, iii. 94
Gassendi, i. 125, 128, 201, 216, 217, 225, 235, 245, 253-269, 278, 286, 290, 291, 304, 327; ii. 3, 9, 29, 90, 101, 352, 356, 363, 364, 374
Gassner, i. 170
Gauss, ii. 385, 396
Gay, ii. 5
Gay-Lussac, ii. 359, 365
Gegenbaur, iii. 41

Genthe, i. 182; ii. 36
Geoffroy, St. F., ii. 357
Geoffroy de St. Hilaire, iii. 87
George, iii. 176
Gerhard, i. 6, 180
Gerland, iii. 72, 182
Gesenius, ii. 137
Gervinus, ii. 144, 257
Gesner, J. M., ii. 144, 145
Gessner, Konrad, i. 228, 229; ii. 144, 145
Gessner, Jacob, i. 229
Gibbon, i. 162, 164, 170
Gilbert, W., i. 237; iii. 163, 247
Giordano Bruno, i. 231, 232, 234, 235, 259
Gleim, ii. 145
Gliddon, iii. 106
Gmelin, i. 299, 303
Goethe, Wolfgang von, i. 33; ii. 28, 96, 108, 142, 148-150, 218, 236, 244; iii. 38, 61, 87, 88, 193, 319, 331
Goltz, iii. 127
Gorgias, i. 39, 59
Gracchus, Tiberius, and Caius, iii. 264
Grösse, ii. 135
Grassmann, ii. 187
Grimm, Baron, ii. 90, 93, 102, 109, 121
Grote, G., i. 40, 41
Grutzmacher, i. 222
Gutenberg, iii. 132
Gutzkow, ii. 246, 260

Hæckel, Ernest, iii. 19, 20, 23, 24, 42, 55, 56, 59, 60, 62, 63, 64, 108
Hagedorn, ii. 145
Hagenbach, i. 314, 315
Haller, Albrecht von, ii. 64, 137, 138, 218; iii. 169
Halley, i. 315
Hamilton, Sir William, i. 210
Hammer, i. 183, 184, 185
Hankel, ii. 184, 187
Hannibal, i. 126
Hansemann, ii. 258
Hartley, David, ii. 4-9; iii. 189
Hartmann, Ed. von, i. viii., 329; iii. 71-73, 75, 77, 78, 313
Harvey, i. 237, 246, 278; iii. 247
Häser, i. 181
Hauréau, i. 219
Hegel, i. 30, 40, 57, 82, 93, 236, 279; ii. 49, 50, 53, 196, 226,

236, 237-240, 246, 247, 252, 254, 257, 260, 265, 275, 276, 284, 300, 301, 303, 346; iii. 80, 272, 288, 307, 311, 320, 325, 352
Heim, iii. 102
Heine, Heinrich, ii. 245, 257
Heinroth, ii. 259
Heliogabalus, i. 167
Helmholtz, Hermann, ii. 75, 188, 307, 321, 336, 385, 391, 392, 393; iii. 3, 4, 8, 10, 11, 22, 24, 155, 180, 204, 215, 216, 222, 227-230
Helmont, Van, iii. 14
Helvetius, ii. 51, 52, 84, 87, 93, 114; iii. 242, 249
Hengstenberg, ii. 260
Henle, iii. 209
Hennings, ii. 129, 140; iii. 16
Hensen, iii. 180
Herakleides, i. 232
Herakleitos, i. 8, 16, 19, 39, 74, 77, 135; ii. 226, 265
Herbart, i. 194, 321; ii. 189, 196, 300; iii. 163-167, 288, 311
Herbert of Cherbury, ii. 36
Herder, ii. 22, 141, 244
Hermann, i. 6, 15; iii. 144, 145, 155
Hermolaus Barbarus, ii. 41
Herodotus, i. 15, 83
Herophilos, i. 115
Herschel, i. 237; ii. 170
Hertwig, iii. 132
Hesiod, i. 99
Hettner, i. 294, 295, 310, 320, 325; ii. 4, 7, 10, 11, 13, 14, 17, 19, 20, 24, 35, 51, 82
Hiketas, i. 232
Hildebrand, ii. 62
Hipparchos, i. 114, 120; iii. 7
Hippias, i. 39
Hippokrates, i. 40, 93, 224
Hitzig, iii. 145, 149, 150, 153
Hobbes, Thomas, i. 38, 211, 213, 214, 216, 225, 235, 236, 254, 256, 257, 269-290, 291, 292, 296, 297, 298, 299, 300, 301, 304, 309, 311, 317, 318; ii. 3, 6, 9, 10, 12, 18, 19, 21, 28, 29, 34, 36, 38, 50, 51, 84, 90, 104, 115, 143, 146, 148, 248, 304, 305, 353, 354, 363
Hocheisel, ii. 38
Hofmann, ii. 372
Hofmeister, iii. 73
Holbach, Baron, ii. 25, 26, 50, 51, 80, 87, 90, 94-123, 129, 134, 148, 158, 256, 355

Hölderlin, ii. 284
Hollman, ii. 139
Homer, i. 85, 115, 224
Hooke, i. 314, 315
Horace, i. 128, 165, 166; iii. 263
Horwicz, iii. 126
Howen, i. 258
Huizinga, iii. 18
Humboldt, Alexander von, ii. 236, 239, 258
Humboldt, Wilhelm von, i. 83, 121, 179, 180, 184, 185, 186, 229-231, 232; ii. 210, 236; iii. 181
Hume, David, ii. 8, 50, 159, 162, 170, 204-211, 212, 215, 235, 304, 313, 324
Huschke, iii. 134
Huxley, i. vii., 3, 19, 20, 353
Huyghens, i. 309, 310, 312, 327; ii. 376
Hypatia, i. 120

Ideler, ii. 223
Isaac, iii. 16

Jacobi, ii. 139, 148
Jäger, iii. 102
Janet, Paul, ii. 248
Jean de Brescain, i. 218
Jerusalem, ii. 8
Jesus, i. 182, 222; iii. 322, 364
Jobert de Lamballes, ii. 60; iii. 127
John, i. 306
Johnson, Ed., ii. 294; iii. 187
Joly, iii. 14
Joshua, i. 305
Julian, Emperor, i. 62, 170; ii. 289
Jurain, the Abbé, ii. 6
Justi, ii. 143, 145
Juvenal, i. 165, 166

Kant, i. 12, 19, 28, 30, 42, 54, 55, 98, 194, 196, 197, 236, 247, 262, 292, 311, 316, 322; ii. 5, 17, 18, 19, 23, 29, 50, 83, 93, 114, 116, 133, 136, 137, 153-170, 174, 178, 179, 180, 181, 183-205, 209-212, 215, 216, 217-234, 236-240, 244, 247, 249, 250, 251, 265, 266, 267, 275, 277, 282-284, 286, 287, 305, 322, 324, 369, 379, 386, 393; iii. 3, 4, 9, 23, 69, 70, 86, 96, 108, 118, 165, 168, 169, 171, 190, 194, 196, 197, 198, 205, 224, 233, 247, 279, 282-284, 286, 306, 314, 315, 320, 326, 342, 349, 359
Kekulé, ii. 363, 373

Keller, Dr. Ferdinand, iii. 100
Kepler, i. 115, 138, 216, 230, 231, 237, 278, 308; ii. 32, 155; iii. 247
King, ii. 5
Kirchmann, i. 202, 203, 276; ii. 322
Klein, Dr. H., ii. 383; iii. 89
Klopstock, ii. 146, 237
Knight, iii. 73
Knutzen, Martin, ii. 136
Knuzen, Matthias, ii. 35
Koelliker, Albert, iii. 52-54, 56
Köhler, ii. 144
Kolbe, ii. 372; iii. 56
Kopp, i. 299; ii. 352, 355, 356
Kortholt, ii. 36, 37
Kriegk, i. 172
Kroenig, ii. 374
Kussmaul, iii. 180

LACHMANN, i. 133, 143
Lagrange, ii. 95, 102
Lamarck, i. 35; iii. 46
La Mettrie, i. 38, 147, 241, 243, 246, 291, 292; ii. 9, 14, 25, 26, 29, 49-92, 93, 110, 116, 121, 138, 139, 240, 270; iii. 87
La Mothe le Vayer, ii. 9, 10, 34
Lang, Pastor, iii. 287, 290
Lange, F. A., i. ix.-xiv.
Lange, Dr. J. P., i. ix.
Langsdorf, iii. 77
Langwieser, ii. 313, 314, 317, 325
Laplace, ii. 16, 72, 132, 155, 268, 308, 309, 310, 314, 317, 319; iii. 4, 7, 9, 77, 314, 315
Lartet, iii. 90
Lasaulx, E. de, i. 170, 171
Lassalle, i. xi.
Lasson, iii. 306, 307
Lau, T. L., ii. 35
Laube, ii. 246
Launoy, i. 269
Lavater, ii. 141
Lavoisier, ii. 334, 335
Law, ii. 5
Lecky, i. 163, 164, 168-171, 180
Legendre, ii. 181, 182
Leibniz, i. 12, 98, 194, 236, 242, 307, 313, 322, 326; ii. 6, 14, 15, 29, 59, 65, 67, 111, 112, 124-134, 141, 145, 147, 157, 179, 180, 196, 275, 305; iii. 165, 170, 188, 309
Leo X., Pope, i. 223
Leon, i. 63
Leonardo da Vinci, i. 217, 237
Lerminier, i. 248

Le Sage, i. 314; ii. 374
Less, iii. 169
Lessing, ii. 11, 22, 126, 139, 140, 146; iii. 331
Leukippos, i. 20, 269, 316
Leuret, ii. 259
Lewes, i. 10, 15, 40, 44, 61, 64, 67, 72, 73
Lexis, iii. 234, 235, 237
Lichtenberg, i. 232, 262; ii. 126, 141, 147; iii. 205, 206
Liebig, i. 161, 180, 236, 237, 301; ii. 258, 297, 298, 329-331, 342-344, 361
Liebmann, ii. 154, 195; iii. 228
Linné, ii. 52; iii. 42
Litaudus, i. 269
Littré, ii. 248
Littrow, i. 306, 313
Locke, i. 38, 76, 211, 213, 236, 288, 301, 318-325; ii. 5, 14, 15, 17, 18, 19-22, 30, 34, 39, 50, 51, 61, 64, 132, 133, 158, 160, 286, 304; iii. 119
Loewenthal, iii. 295
Longet, ii. 259; iii. 116, 117, 133
Lotze, ii. 285, 347; iii. 175, 196, 212, 227
Louis XIV., i. 293; ii. 10, 11
Lowndes, i. 319
Lubbock, Sir John, iii. 92, 96, 98, 182
Lucian, i. 170
Lucretius, i. 24, 25, 27, 34, 105, 126, 128, 255, 266, 267, 283; ii. 29, 83, 101, 115, 123, 374; iii. 278, 292, 293
Luther, i. 227, 248; ii. 334; iii. 274, 348, 355
Luzak, Elie, ii. 77
Lyell, Sir Charles, ii. 329; iii. 45, 89, 92, 97
Lysias, i. 7

MACAULAY, i. 237, 293, 294, 298
Macchiavelli, i. 222, 223
Mach, ii. 388
Mæcenas, i. 131
Magendie, ii. 259
Mahaffy, ii. 163, 205, 223
Malebranche, ii. 57, 67, 111
Malthus, iii. 265, 266
Mandeville, i. 295; ii. 22, 23, 79, 80; iii. 242, 249
Manetho, i. 114
Marbach, i. 8
Marcus Aurelius, i. 163

Mariotte, i. 301, 302; ii. 375
Marius, i. 128
Martin, i. 231
Marx, i. 295, 319, 320; ii. 23; iii. 265
Maudsley, iii. 193
Maupertuis, ii. 16, 25, 31, 52, 137
Maxwell, ii. 382, 383, 384, 385
Mayer, ii. 307, 392; iii. 8, 9, 10
Maywald, i. 218, 219
M'Kendrick, ii. 198
Meier, G. F., i. 6; ii. 136; iii. 16
Meiklejohn, ii. 184
Meiners, i. 181, 182
Melanchthon, Philip, i. 227, 231, 238; ii. 34, 42, 45, 46, 62; iii. 170
Memmius, i. 129, 130
Mendelssohn, ii. 137
Mersenne, i. 225, 248, 256, 273, 278, 280
Meyer, Jürgen Bona, ii. 136, 154, 190; iii. 225
Meyer, Lothair, ii. 360, 372, 387
Meynert, iii. 139, 140
Mill, John Stuart, i. xi., 210, 211, 214, 237; ii. 170-178, 182-187, 193, 213-215, 235, 321; iii. 189, 193, 260, 265, 269, 271, 274, 276, 300, 363, 364
Mitscherlich, ii. 361
Mohammed, i. 182, 184, 222
Mohl, Hugo von, ii. 303, 332; iii. 265
Mohl, Von, ii. 346
Moigno, the Abbé, ii. 365
Moleschott, i. 41, 292; ii. 60, 241, 259, 264, 271, 272, 273, 275, 277-281, 286, 377, 378, 381; iii. 26, 127, 179
Molesworth, i. 274, 275
Mommsen, i. 166
Montaigne, i. 245, 260; ii. 9, 34, 88
Montesquieu, ii. 52
Mook, iii. 295
More, Sir Thomas, i. 323; iii. 272
Morhof, i. 317; ii. 144
Mortillet, iii. 90
Moscati, iii. 86
Moses, i. 174, 182, 222, 233, 284
Mosheim, ii. 37
Mozart, iii. 61
Mullach, i. 15, 16, 17, 20, 22, 23, 26, 27
Müller, Johannes, ii. 259; iii. 114, 130-132, 206-209, 216
Mundt, ii. 246, 260
Munro, i. 130, 140
Musset, iii. 14

Nadir Schah, ii. 14
Naegeli, iii. 52, 54
Naigeon, ii. 50, 95
Naudäus, Gabriel, i. 245, 258
Naumann, i. 255; ii. 374
Nausiphanes, i. 99
Nees von Esenbeck, ii. 346
Nero, i. 131, 167
Neumann, C., ii. 396
Neumann, F. E., ii. 385
Newton, i. 125, 138, 201, 255, 267, 269, 296, 299, 301, 303, 306-317, 327, 329; ii. 3, 8, 12, 14, 15, 16, 26, 146, 155, 156, 304, 337, 345, 353, 355, 356, 363, 375, 383, 384, 396; iii. 3
Nicolaus of Autricuria, i. 225, 226
Niebuhr, ii. 210, 236
Nietzsche, L 62
Noah, iii. 27, 115
Nothnagel, iii. 145, 146, 149
Nott, iii. 106

Occam, i. 210, 211, 213, 214; ii. 3
Oersted, ii. 215; iii. 163
Oettingen, iii. 198
Oken, i. 35; ii. 237, 346; iii. 20
Origen, i. 170
Osiander, i. 230
Oswald, ii. 8, 206
Owen, ii. 77; iii. 273
Oxenford, i. 280

Paetus, Thrasea, i. 131
Palestrina, iii. 360
Palleske, ii. 28
Paracelsus, i. 239, 240; ii. 33; iii. 14
Parmenides, i. 19
Pascal, Blaise, i. 245, 248, 259, 302; ii. 10, 16
Pasteur, iii. 14, 18, 23
Paul III., Pope, i. 230
Peirescius, i. 258
Peisse, Louis, ii. 242, 312
Pemberton, i. 309
Perikles, i. 46, 48, 49, 167
Petit, ii. 360
Petrarca, i. 217, 226
Petronius, i. 165; ii. 67
Petty, i. 320
Pfeffer, iii. 73
Pfeuffer, iii. 209
Pflüger, iii. 19, 126, 127
Pheidias, i. 40, 46
Philippos the actor, L 29
Philolaos, i. 278

Picard, i. 310
Piderit, iii. 125
Pinel, ii. 113
Pistorius, ii. 6
Plato, i. 5, 17, 18, 40, 41, 43, 44, 45, 48, 50, 52, 53, 54, 56, 57, 59, 60, 63, 68, 69, 71, 72, 73, 74–81, 83, 88, 89, 93, 94, 95, 96, 109, 115, 117, 120, 122, 123, 124, 190, 222, 260, 277, 278; ii. 158, 231, 233, 337; iii. 288, 291
Plantus, iii. 185
Pliny the Elder, i. 118, 120, 121, 224
Pliny the Younger, i. 171
Plotinus, i. 167, 175; iii. 78
Pluche, ii. 65, 66
Plücker, iii. 163
Plutarch, i. 232
Poggendorf, ii. 374
Poisson, iii. 78
Politiano, Angelo, i. 216
Polyænos, i. 120
Polybios, i. 114
Pomponatius, Petrus, i. 220, 221–225
Porphyry, i. 175, 187, 190
Pouchet, Felix, iii. 14, 18, 50
Poussin, ii. 54
Prantl, i. 187, 188, 189, 209, 210, 214, 217, 225
Preyer, iii. 61, 204
Price, Richard, ii. 7
Prichard, iii. 106, 181
Priestley, i. 327; ii. 4, 7, 8, 9, 101, 206; iii. 189
Prillieux, iii. 73
Prodikos, i. 39, 56
Pröhle, i. 145
Protagoras, i. 6, 39–49, 54, 56, 59, 68, 75, 99, 109, 110, 287; ii. 157, 159, 276
Ptolemy, i. 118, 119, 120, 121
Puteanus, Eryceus, of Louvain, i. 258
Pythagoras, i. 33, 73, 109, 117, 120, 122, 124, 260, 278; ii. 158

QUERARD, ii. 57, 75
Quételet, ii. 259; iii. 194–199

RADENHAUSEN, iii. 32, 36
Radicke, ii. 348, 350
Rames, iii. 94
Ramus, Petrus, i. 269; ii. 33
Raphael, iii. 183, 360
Raumer, ii. 144
Raymund, i. 245

Redtenbacher, ii. 368–370, 380
Reich, Edward, iii. 295, 296, 300
Reichel, i. 95, 97, 150, 168
Reichenbach, ii. 345
Reicke, iii. 323
Reid, ii. 8, 206
Reimann, ii. 36, 137
Reimarus, H. S., ii. 137, 140
Reimarus, J. A., iii. 178
Reinhold, ii. 194
Renan, Ernest, i. 175, 177, 178, 182, 218, 219, 220
Rhäticus, i. 230
Richardson, ii. 24
Richter, ii. 345, 358
Riemann, ii. 188; iii. 227
Ritschl, iii. 185
Ritter, i. 18, 130; ii. 236
Robinet, J. B., ii. 25, 29–31, 60
Rogerius, ii. 36
Rokitansky, iii. 229
Ronge, iii. 294, 297
Rönne, ii. 247
Rorarius, Hieronymus, i. 245, 258; ii. 134
Röschel, ii. 38
Roscher, i. 162, 163; iii. 257
Rose, ii. 3, 259
Rosenkranz, ii. 23, 24, 27, 31, 52, 95, 109
Ross, Alexander, ii. 36
Rothe, Richard, iii. 294
Rousseau, i. 110, 282; ii. 17, 52, 70; iii. 183
Roux, iii. 106, 107
Ruge, ii. 261

SACHS, iii. 73
Sanctorius, ii. 344
Sauppe, ii. 144
Scaliger, i. 114
Schaaffhausen, iii. 93
Schaller, i. 240, 254, 280; ii. 255; iii. 176
Scheitlin, ii. 135; iii. 136, 178
Schelling, i. 35, 236; ii. 29, 236, 237, 238, 256, 257, 275, 284, 303, 365; iii. 80, 319
Schiller, i. 10, 80; ii. 22, 27, 28, 81, 89, 142, 146, 147, 203, 232, 233, 235, 236, 238, 239, 242, 245, 257; iii. 102, 183, 291, 301, 304, 343, 345, 346
Schilling, ii. 124, 203, 212
Schleiden, ii. 155, 221, 229
Schleiermacher, i. 177, 188; ii. 8; iii. 352

INDEX.

Schlosser, i. 172; ii. 51
Schmerling, Dr., iii. 89
Schmidt, Oscar, iii. 52, 72, 108
Schöbl, iii. 179
Schömann, i. 6, 7
Schönbein, ii. 362
Schoner, i. 230
Schopenhauer, ii. 154, 256, 266, 267, 323; iii. 43, 323, 330
Schramm, H., i. 314
Schultze, Max, iii. 20
Schultze-Delitzsch, iii. 317
Schulze, F. H., iii. 180, 243
Schuppe, i. 188
Schwann, iii. 16, 17, 18
Scotus, Duns, i. 208
Scotus Erigena, i. 189, 191
Seguin, ii. 365
Seneca, i. 128, 131, 224; ii. 67, 83
Sennert, ii. 33
Seydel, iii. 154, 156
Sextus Empiricus, i. 176
Shaftesbury, i. 318, 319, 324, 325; ii. 19, 20-24, 27, 28, 146, 147
Shakespeare, i. 295
Sharp, ii. 75
Siebold, iii. 41
Sigwart, ii. 185
Sime, ii. 140
Simonides, i. 224
Sklarek, iii. 19
Smith, Adam, i. 295; iii. 234, 235, 260
Snell, i. 248, 315; iii. 109
Sokrates, i. 5, 17, 39, 40, 41, 43, 44, 45, 48, 53, 54, 55, 57, 60, 61, 62, 63, 64, 65, 66, 67, 70, 71, 72, 74, 76, 79, 80, 83, 84, 93, 94, 95; ii. 23, 24; iii. 289, 291
Sömmering, i. 119
Sophie Charlotte, Queen of Prussia, i. 326; ii. 127
Sophokles, i. 3
Spalding, ii. 6
Spallanzani, iii. 179
Spencer, Herbert, iii. 186, 187, 189-191, 363
Spicker, ii. 22
Spiller, ii. 322, 323
Spinoza, i. 12, 236, 242, 301, 323, 326; ii. 35, 36, 39, 55, 147, 148, 157, 226, 265, 304; iii. 32, 190, 311
Spieren, Von, ii. 6
Spir, iii. 336
Spurzheim, iii. 114, 115, 121
Stadler, iii. 69

Stahl, ii. 242, 334
Steenstrup, iii. 36
Steffens, ii. 346
Stephani, i. 6
Stephen, Leslie, i. 330
Stewart, Dugald, ii. 170, 171; iii. 186
Stilpo, i. 6
Stirner, ii. 255, 256
Stokes, ii. 385
Stosch, ii. 35
Strato of Lampsakos, i. 93, 94, 203; ii. 39, 45, 58
Strauss, David Friedrich, ii. 13, 19, 246, 260, 284, 289, 290; iii. 305, 306, 320, 323-334
Stricker, iii. 139
Stuarts, the, i. 272
Stumpf, iii. 187, 193, 216, 217
Sturm, ii. 144
Suetonius, i. 171
Sulla, i. 128
Swift, ii. 79
Sydenham, i. 318; ii. 78
Syrbius, ii. 37

Tacitus, i. 171
Tait, iii. 22
Tappert, ii. 144
Tardy, iii. 90
Tempier, Bishop Etienne, i. 208
Tertullian, i. 290
Tetens, iii. 171
Teuffel, i. 62, 130
Thales, i. 4, 8, 9, 114
Themistius, ii. 45
Theon, i. 120
Theophrastus, i. 6, 27
Thomas Aquinas, St., i. 205, 221, 322
Thomasius, Chr., ii. 145
Thomasius, Jenkin, ii. 135
Thomson, Sir W., ii. 385; iii. 21, 22
Thukydides, i. 272
Tiberius, i. 131, 171; iii. 264
Toeche, iii. 306
Toland, John, i. 324-330; ii. 90, 99, 100, 127, 273
Tomaschek, ii. 239
Toqueville, de, ii. 12
Torricelli, ii. 66
Tralles, ii. 137, 139
Trembley, ii. 72
Trendelenburg, i. 81, 188, 196, 211; ii. 154, 202, 212, 300; iii. 306
Tycho Brahe, i. 263; ii. 226
Tylor, Ed., ii. 186; iii. 182

Tyndall, i. vii.; iii. 10, 363
Twesten, Carl, ii. 154

UEBERWEG, i. x. 9, 35, 85, 94, 108, 109, 170, 176, 187, 188, 192, 196, 205, 212, 237, 266, 313, 314, 322; ii. 32, 180-182, 247, 349; iii. 5, 209-211, 214-216, 224-226, 305-310-326, 328, 332
Uhlich, iii. 285
Uz, ii. 145

VAHLEN, i. 226
Valerius Maximus, i. 15.
Valla, Laurentius, i. 216, 226
Valliss, iii. 322
Vanini, i. 225
Vaucanson, ii. 75, 230; iii. 111
Vesalius, iii. 247
Vierordt, ii. 349
Villonius i. 269
Virchow, ii. 285; iii. 38, 39, 146
Virgil, i. 129, 131
Vives, Luis, i. 217, 228, 237, 260; ii. 33; iii. 272
Vogt, Carl, ii. 259, 264, 284, 286, 298, 312; iii. 14, 16, 18, 26, 28, 39, 41, 85, 88, 96, 118, 346
Voit, ii. 350
Volger, iii. 261
Volney, ii. 80, 85, 87
Voltaire, i. 13, 174, 254, 267, 294, 296, 311, 327; ii. 11, 12-19, 23, 25, 30, 38, 39, 51, 52, 61, 88, 98, 103-106, 143; iii. 249, 292

WACHLER, i. 181
Wagner, And., iii. 28, 30, 31, 106, 196, 197
Wagner, R., ii. 264, 285
Waitz, iii. 72, 106, 166, 182, 196
Wallace, iii. 48, 100
Weber, E. H., ii. 259
Weber, W., ii. 371, 384
Weihrich, ii. 355, 360, 372, 373, iii. 56

Weinkauff, ii. 36
Welcher, i. 6
Weller, ii. 37
Wernekke, i. 232
Westphal, ii. 38
Whewell, i. 11, 27, 114, 248, 306, 309, 310, 313, 314, 315, 317; ii. 170, 171, 172, 173, 174
Widmanustadt, i. 231
Wigand, iii. 34
Winckelmann, ii. 143, 144, 145, 146, 210
Winckler, ii. 37, 136
Wirth, Max, iii. 251
Wittstein, iii. 164
Wolf, F. A., ii. 144
Wolff, C., i. 197, 201; ii. 67, 133, 134, 136, 138, 145, 157, 196; iii. 170, 171
Wolff, P., ii. 47, 48
Worsae, iii. 90
Wren, Sir Christopher, i. 314
Wundt, iii. 127, 129, 144, 153, 154, 180, 204

XENOCRATES, i. 99
Xenophanes, i. 33, 36
Xenophon, i. 41, 60, 63
Xerxes, i. 15

YOUNG, ii. 363

ZEDLITZ, ii. 266
Zeller, i. 5, 7, 8, 10, 13, 15, 18, 24, 28, 30, 36, 39, 60, 72, 73, 94, 95, 97, 109, 110, 130, 150, 152, 168; ii. 33, 35, 50, 124, 125, 126, 239; iii. 325
Zeno, i. 98, 103
Zimmermann, ii. 54, 57, 139, 179, 181-183, 190
Zöllner, ii. 325, 326, 328, 388, 396; iii. 9, 10, 21, 22, 23, 24, 43, 44
Zopyros, i. 60

THE END.

www.ingramcontent.com/pod-product-compliance
Lightning Source LLC
Chambersburg PA
CBHW030347230426
43664CB00007BB/561